Left Behind in the Race to the Top

Realities of School Reform

Left Behind in the Race to the Top

Realities of School Reform

edited by

Julie Gorlewski
State University of New York–New Paltz

Brad Porfilio
Lewis University

INFORMATION AGE PUBLISHING, INC.
Charlotte, NC • www.infoagepub.com

Library of Congress Cataloging-in-Publication Data

A CIP record for this book is available from the Library of Congress
http://www.loc.gov

ISBN: 978-1-62396-328-6 (Paperback)
        978-1-62396-329-3 (Hardcover)
        978-1-62396-330-9 (ebook)

CONTENTS

PART I

TESTING ... TESTING

PART II

PRIVATIZATION AND MILITARIZATION: REDEFINING SCHOOLS

PART III

ALIENATION: DISPLACING STUDENTS AND TEACHERS

PART IV

RESISTANCE: OPTING OUT AND HOPE FOR CHANGE

ACKNOWLEDGMENTS

Thanks are due to the many contributors, including but not limited to the chapter authors, to this text. To begin, we are grateful to Rachel Mattson, who suggested this book and then mandated that it take precedence over any other publication projects. Rachel, you were right! Thanks, also, to Adrienne Long, whose fact-checking and editing expertise were well exercised in this volume. Most of all, we wish to express our admiration and respect for all the educators and students who work every day to support the ideals of democracy in a context that, in many ways, endeavors to oppose this work. To them, we hope this book offers two messages: First, the realities of contemporary neoliberal reforms are harmful to teaching, learning, and social justice. Second, you are not alone and solidarity is our best hope.

FOREWORD

Just looking at the table of contents is rather overwhelming. Under the name of School Reform everything—well almost—that I've tried to change in our public system is being reinforced in its name. Impersonalization, large class sizes, scripted and dumbed down teaching, standardized testing, and control removed far from the scene of action—out of reach of parent, child or teacher. That's the new prescription, at least for children in the lower classes, children of poor black and Latino families, and maybe low-income whites too. Might it even spread upwards? This book reminds us: that shouldn't and needn't happen.

In the 1980s, the country as a whole made a swing to the right politically. I used to marvel at how odd it was that in my special arena of public urban schooling we were marching hand in hand – right to left—toward a more and more progressive system. I thought we had won the battle between Thorndike and Dewey, and testing as we knew it was on its way out, to be followed by serious high standard assessment approaches that really got to the intellectual, social and moral roots of schooling for democracy.

I was dead wrong.

The shift was swift, and had probably been well-rehearsed.

The trouble with schooling, the new experts proclaimed, was that it rested on the unreliable, lazy, incompetent judgment of public employees—school teachers and principals and central office bureaucrats, and elected school boards—and state legislators. The Constitution had it wrong—schools were too precious to be placed in the hands of locals. We needed the expertise of almost any professional except educators—of business people, economists, and military leaders above all.

Schools, as had been proclaimed in the infamous 1983 report, A Nation at Risk, (how had I forgotten it) might as well have been in the hands of our rivals and enemies—the global forces with whom our corporations had to contend for the future of our national survival, much less as the greatest nation on earth. We were in a CRISIS—something had to be done, and fast. It took a while for this to sink in—time I spent happily trying to find another kind of solution.

Every aspect of American life would be improved if…The new line was, if students, teachers and districts were held to account—or else, "off with their heads". How? By testing them—often—and demanding ever-rising scores so that within a decade or two everyone would be on a level plain in math and English literacy. According to the No Child Left Behind Act of 2001, the deadline set was 2014, with penalties built in for those who lagged behind the pace needed for 100% success in 14 years (NCLB). As the 14th year approached, "waivers" from NCLB were offered to states (none had succeeded) that agreed to other draconian measures—such as accepting a national "curriculum" (called CORE Standards), a system of evaluating employees based on student test scores, of closing many failing schools and finally, of increasing the accessibility of charter schools or other forms of choice.

I'm often skeptical about the democratic heart of our Constitution—based on the limitations of its originators—but they certainly had this one right. A single Best Definition of being well-educated would be a strong nail in the coffin of democracy. It's the one virtue about the free market place that I truly believe in—the importance of a diversity of sources of wealth, competing interests when it comes to where power rests.

That also requires competing interests over whose ideas are right, whose have the official stamp of approval. It's one thing to take a test about driving a car—although biases will slip in. Ditto even to most civil service exams. But not for an exam that defines *who is well-educated.* Leave that to the States. What we need the Feds for is making sure that no child has less than equal access to that of the most wealthy child—at least in so far as the state has the power to even the playing field. And while otherwise states may have biases that find their way into law or regulation (what's needed to get a diploma, to be a licensed teacher, etc.) at least they would have to "compete" with other states over the "products" they produced (students, future citizens). Many states, maybe most, turned this over to locals—small districts. In 1931 there were about 15,000 such districts. Today there are fewer than 15,000 covering probably twice as many school children—or more. But the regulators are afraid that democracy won't work at that level—we should limit what is possible to one federal district, with one set of criteria.

If you don't like it—you can always choose a private school, and that too should be made easier via charters and vouchers covering the cost of schools that are not accountable to the public.

The best definitions, it's argued, are those that do not rely on fallible human judgment, interpretation or individual opinions, but rely rather on The Facts, The Evidence, The Data. Standardized tests, they argue, are the best tool for this, plus just a few others thrown in—attendance data, graduation data, and drop-out-data. The latter three are—some of us know—unbelievably unreliable. Add so are standardized tests—now and forever. It's like polling data; the measurement error regarding reliability alone makes them useless for any precise and significant stakes. Furthermore, there is no instrument on earth that more closely aligns with class and race than standardized tests—including so-called aptitude and IQ tests which, in turn, align with all achievement tests.

If we don't want to have the world shift its balance of power, increase equality, et al—we have designed a wonderful tool and a lot of rhetoric to disguise it.

I've spent the past 50 years exploring how we might get around it—if we ever truly chose to do so. It was a decision of accident that became a passion, and a joy. From Prekindergarten through high school, my colleagues and I had a chance to rearrange not just the chairs on the ship, but the whole design of the ship itself, perhaps even of the idea of ship'iness.

We didn't reinvent the wheel. We just borrowed from the ideas the wisest and richest people had discovered worked for their kids—only now for all kids. I tried to reproduce in a different setting the underlying respect and expectations of the schools my brother and I attended. The keys were respect and expectations.

Unlike President Obama or Secretary Duncan, I couldn't see why we had a better shot at succeeding if we developed schools that abandoned everything we had sought for our own! So I looked at the Lab School and Washington D.C. Quaker Friends School as models. They were relatively small (compared to the big schools in the cities where they were located), had much smaller class sizes (maybe half the size), had classrooms filled with interesting materials and books, and everywhere I looked I saw young and old working together. They took plenty of field-trips. Their parents were spoken of with great respect and deferred to when necessary. They were provided with the best health care, and both body and mind, which—in the old Greek tradition—were seen as critical to growing up right. They rarely if ever took standardized tests, but rather experienced many times in which vocal and written exposition was required—as a demonstration of their competence. They had libraries and time to spend with trained librarians who understood the world of childhood and book-hood.

They learned to cook, make stuff in shop classes, paint, sing in the chorus, play musical instruments and produce great drama and poetry.

The Central Park East schools and their many offspring in NYC and elsewhere did their best to meet all these inputs on a budget very close to what everyone else had. It was insufficient, but... We came close. "Inputs" is a passé word now—the new reformers only want to hear about "outputs" (scores, et al). We figured if we were right, one would lead to the other. So we tested our beliefs by following the kids themselves: the real hard data.

We were right; and many others learned the same. Yes, it was harder work than we expected, and our outcomes, unsurprisingly, didn't quite match those of kids who had all that and much much more, not to mention a network of powerful allies on the outside world. It would be easier to break the odds for the kids we served if we had the $40,000 dollars per student per year that my old private school spends.

But, maybe it could be done—and we could have normal lives too—for somewhere around a half that amount, coupled with the same respect for our work that the best progressive independent schools offer their staff. And democracy doesn't have to be thrown out the window for us to achieve that. If we want it badly enough there are plenty of models—if, happily, never a single one—that are compatible with our shared goals of creating an adult citizenry accountable and responsible for nourishing, preserving and expanding a high standard democracy.

You are about to read a wonderful collection by wonderful people that provide closer details on how this happened and suggestions for how we can get back on track.

—**Deborah Meier**

INTRODUCTION

Public education today is under attack. Students, teachers, administrators, and community members are experiencing the effects of policies that have increased standardization of learning and privatization of the public sphere. What does this mean? The assault on education is multifaceted, nuanced, complex, and very well funded. Many of those who are affected by the forces that seek to dismantle and disinvest in public education feel powerless and desperate but have difficulty mounting a clear defense that does not seem . . . well, defensive. Explanations come across as making excuses, and professional educators who attempt to expose the forces aligned against them are accused of caring more about adults than about children. When parents, teachers, administrators, teacher educators, and scholars describe the negative effects of current reforms on children, these interested, knowledgeable adults are accused of protecting the status quo. Nothing could be further from the truth.

Furthermore, it is essential to situate current reforms internationally: the Global Education Reform Movement (GERM). Historian and education scholar Diane Ravitch draws on Sahlberg to explain:

> In his excellent book *Finnish Lessons*, Pasi Sahlberg [2011] explains the nature of the Global Education Reform Movement (GERM). GERM adores testing, accountability, competition, and choice. GERM squeezes all joy out of learning. GERM treats educators as interchangeable parts with no wisdom. GERM relies on market mechanisms, which are totally inappropriate in education.

Contemporary educational reforms involve numerous promoters and related personnel. Some reformers truly hope to improve schools in order

Left Behind in the Race to the Top, pages xv–xxvi
Copyright © 2013 by Information Age Publishing
All rights of reproduction in any form reserved.

to benefit students. Others aim to profit from private schemes designed to capture public funds for corporate or individual gain. These divisions can be difficult to discern.

True educational reform is incremental; it involves careful deliberation and investment in communities—not just schools. As Jean Anyon notes, "[T]rying to fix an urban school without fixing the neighborhood in which it is embedded is like trying to clean the air on one side of a screen door" (1997, p. 170). Meaningful reform does not reduce learning to numbers, nor does it relentlessly rank learners, teachers, schools, and even nations on the basis of standardized test scores. Finally, genuine reform involves a commitment to continuous improvement—not a series of quick fixes and turnarounds.

Resistance to the negative effects is made more difficult by the discrepancy of resources: "reformers" are well funded and organized, while resistors (those of us who believe that a vibrant, dynamic system of public education is essential for democracy) are dispersed, under/unfunded, and must find energy for the endeavors *in addition to* everyday work. Reformers also enjoy the advantages of access to multimedia outlets that, perhaps unwittingly, reinforce the messages that deify reformers and vilify educators and young people—especially young people who live in poverty.

In this book, we intend to support public education, an endeavor that is essential to democracy, by revealing and explaining some of the forces aligned attacking it. In a broad sense, what we are pushing back against is a globalized movement that has the overarching aim of privatizing public entities to increase corporate profit. This is accomplished through a variety of measures, including starving public entities of financial support and then declaring them as failures. Because the biggest obstacle to this endeavor is solidarity, reformers aim to destroy the possibility of solidarity.

These conditions make it difficult for educators and citizens to gather the information they need to mount meaningful resistance, especially since mainstream media tends to be uncritically supportive of neoliberal reforms. The Orwellian language of reforms is adopted and promoted through news outlets, politicians, and film; thus, arguments *against* these reforms must bubble up through social media and alternative outlets. By providing a coherent, comprehensive description of contemporary initiatives and analyzing their effects on students, teachers, administrators, and teacher education, this book allows readers to strengthen their resolve to save public education and, therefore, rescue democracy.

ORGANIZATION OF THE BOOK

In this first chapter of the volume, which introduces the section *Testing... Testing*, "The Mistake Policymakers Make About Teaching," Larry

Cuban argues convincingly that the dominant educational policymakers in the U.S. have made an egregious error by confusing "teacher quality with teaching quality." Time and time again, in dominant media outlets, they continually "accentuated personal traits far more than the organizational and social context in which teachers teach daily." In contrast to this shallow way of charactering educators and teaching, the author taps Gary Fenstermacher and Virginia Richardson's (2005) analysis of quality teaching in order to make evident what are key components of "good teaching" and how this form of teaching impacts "successful" student learning. He believes if teachers uphold this view of good teaching, the teaching profession will have more power to invoke successful learning in U.S. schools.

In the next chapter, "'Pay No Attention to the Man Behind the Curtain!': False Pretenses and the Humbug of High-Stakes Testing," Wayne Au pulls back the covers to reveal "high-stakes tests as anything but objective, fair, and accurate." The author begins the chapter by providing a critical historical examination of how the high-stakes standardized movement has come to dominate life in K–12 school as well as frame educational debates in the U.S. Next, Au documents additional historical process behind the current testing mania. For instance, he lays bare that today's high-stakes movement has its "origins I.Q. testing and eugenics—the belief that intelligence is genetic and that certain races or ethnic groups are biologically inferior to whites." Third, the author shows standardized testing is a form of technology that has been controlled by the dominant elite. The elite garners public support for high-stakes examinations by perpetuating the idea students succeed on the exams purely by their own efforts and intelligence. Au concludes the chapter by pinpointing the "non-objective measures of standardized testing." For instance, some of the factors that impact students' performance on examination can range from:

> whether or not a child ate breakfast on test day, if a window was open and a distracting dog was barking outside during the test, whether or not a child got into an argument with parents or peers on the way to school, which other students happened to be in attendance while taking the test, whomever happened to be administering the test, etc., accounts for 50–80% of any gains or losses on a given student's standardized test score. (Kane & Staiger, 2002)

In the third chapter of this volume, "APPR, Solution or Problem?: A Critical Examination of Education Law §3012-c," Emily A. Daniels provides a critical examination of why policymakers in New York state recently amended Education Law §3012-c. She begins the chapter by showing why educators and concerned citizens must be "very suspicious of educational laws that originate in legislative bodies—far from the hands (and worlds) of educators," as she unveils how the No Child Left Behind, which was generated by U.S. federal lawmakers in 2001, has had a deleterious impact on students of color, educators, and urban communities. Next, she situates the construction of the New York Law with the "historical contexts of educational reforms in connection to (several) philosophical standpoints." Third, Daniels details how the Education Law §3012-c mirrors past the historical standpoints of "measurement, 'effectiveness,' numerical evaluation, and performance." The author concludes the chapter by exploring her own personal narrative with the Annual Professional Performance Review (APPR), which was created under New York state law. She details how APPR is supported by corporate interests because it gives them the ability to profit off of students and educators, rather than giving support to teachers and families to help students learn.

In the fourth chapter, "Cost-Benefit Analyses of Human Capital: Are Value-Added Measures Valid?," Fred Floss sheds light on whether value added models (VAMs), which are based upon applying economic principles to social endeavors and policy initiatives, ought to be used for "evaluating teaching and learning in public schools." The author begins the chapter by providing a brief explanation of the models and how they are aligned to evaluate student learning in public schools. Next, the author argues that the models are problematic for those who are concerned about whether there are quality teachers in every classroom because the models do not account for teacher quality. He also notes that policymakers have used the argument that VAMs should be used to rank educators. This gives them the power to implement several pernicious policy recommendations, including "firing the bottom 10% of low-performing teachers, closing schools, and shuttering teacher education program that graduate low-ranking teachers." Foss concludes the chapter by detailing why more and more policymakers are pushing for VAMs as the central evaluation method in K–12 schools. He states:

> Part of the answer may be that with the push for accountability, the appearance of scientific accuracy makes VAMs an easy sell with the public. VAMs also offer a relatively straightforward turnkey implementation process that can be purchased from a university or testing company. VAMs look like a simple solution with very little downside, since the statistical arguments are so complex and the discussions on assumptions are so easy to hide.

In the next chapter, "The National Council on Teacher Quality: Judges with an Agenda," Anthony Cody illustrates why certain organizations, including the NCTQ (National Council on Teacher Quality), are bent on displacing schools of education from preparing future teachers to educate our next generation. He opens the chapter by documenting that the nonprofit organizations that are advocating standardized measures to gauge teacher effectiveness and student learning are ideologically aligned with similar organizations that are now attempting to be the chief evaluators of future teachers. Many organizations, including the Fordham Institute and NCTQ, support market policies to improve education as well as embrace "test scores to create a means of measuring, rewarding and punishing all aspects of the educational system, including schools of education." Next, Cody outlines how NCTQ's specific vision for preparing educators is linked to promoting dutiful, compliant schoolteachers who will not challenge educational mandates dedicated to marginalize students, supporting corporate interests or supporting nonprofit organizations, such as NCTQ. The author concludes the chapter by revealing why schools of education are susceptible to having think thank organization scrutinize their work as well as how concerned citizens can engage reflective critique of the "war of ideas regarding what we should value in our schools."

The second section of the volume, *Privatization and Militarization: Redefining Schools*, explores how education in the U.S. is being influenced by private and military forces. In the sixth chapter of the volume, "The New Market Bureaucracy in U.S. Public Schooling," Kenneth J. Saltman captures how corporate-inspired education reform since the early 1990s only has "failed at the central aim of bureaucracy reduction" as well as "smuggles into schooling an entirely new, largely unstudied kind of privatized bureaucracy with high social costs." The first part of chapter details how today's corporate forces are new and different from the "positivism in the era of the hidden curriculum and reproduction under Fordism." Next, Saltman pinpoints how today's corporate formations are embedded in numerous corporate reforms:

> Standardized testing is at the center of No Child Left Behind and its Blueprint for reauthorization, Race to the Top, the push for Value Added Assessment, the creation of database tracking projects to longitudinally measure teacher "performance" on students' standardized tests, the linkage of teacher evaluation and pay to such standardized test based measures, the imposition of "urban portfolio districts," legislative moves to stifle the power of teachers unions, the unbridled entry of corporate managers into school reform bypassing professional educators and educational scholarship, and the use of corporate media to frame educational problems and solutions.

Third, the author explains "how the new market bureaucracy is involved in producing a new kind of privatized, two-tiered educational system that rejects the egalitarian aspirations of the Civil Rights movement and the Great Society." Saltman concludes the chapter by reminding us that as "long as the framing of educational quality remains trapped within the current frame of allegedly neutral and allegedly objective quantifiable 'student achievement,' public education stands to be dismantled."

In the next chapter, "Missing the Mark: Neoliberalism and the Unwarranted Rise of Charter Schools," Richard Mora and Mary Christianakis "discuss the expansion of charter schools, particularly of for-profit schools, and examine their impact on public schooling." The authors begin the chapter by illuminating how school choice discourse is linked to the rise of neoliberal logics controlling educational policies and practices in U.S. schools for the past decade. Next, they lend a critical examination of how Arne Duncan ushered in neoliberal practices in Chicago schools and how these reforms impacted urban educators, students, and the wider community, while concomitantly suggesting why RTTP (Race to the Top) educational incentives promulgated by the Obama administration are dedicated to opening more charter schools in the U.S. Mora and Christianakis conclude the chapter by exposing "the failed promises of charter schools and the conflicts of interest that keep them alive."

In the eighth chapter of the volume, "Gates of Hell: Abandon All Hope, Ye Who Enter Here," Susan Ohanian unveils the corrosive impact the Gates Foundation is having on the U.S. education system. The Foundation "combines money with the fear, real and imagined, of local reprisals to keep educators silent." First, the author shows how Gates remade his image on the world stage in 1998. Prior to 1998, Gates was viewed as "the bully, the socially inept predator, the despotic potentate, the guy with 'the emotional make-up of a petulant 10-year-old,' 'egomaniacal and dangerous,' or even the 'nerd king.' Now, he is characterized by positive shibboleths in the press such as 'Philanthropist,' 'creator of the country's largest charitable foundation,' 'the world's richest man.'" Next, she documents the form of educational reform promoted by Gates. Gates supports a corporate educational systems that promotes "excellent teachers (by student standardized test scores), put more kids in their classes, get rid of the less excellent, and the reduction in staff enables districts to save money." Third, the author demonstrates how Gates is working behind the scenes to control educational policy formation in the US. For instance, most U.S. citizens do not know that "the Bill and Melinda Gates Foundation financed the Common Core State (sic) Standards," or that "the U. S. Department of Education serves as an echo chamber for Bill and Melinda Gates Foundation education policy." Ohanian concludes the chapter by calling on critical educators and scholars to continue to inform the public on how the corporate world shapes educational reform, as most teachers do not recognize "the real stakes" having elite men like Gates controlling the educative process.

In the next chapter, "The Secretary and the Software: On the Need for Integrating Software Analysis Into Educational Spaces," Thomas Liam Lynch interrogates the grand social myth that educational technology is generated to merely "improve teaching and learning." First, Lynch highlights how corporate giants are pushing for the adoption of technology to in schools. It is not necessarily being done to improve teaching and learning, but rather to increase their coffers. Next, the author shows that corporations are gaining entry into schools by incorrectly lulling the public that the "use of learning technologies" in schools will improve the U.S.'s failing economy. Next, he shows specifically that corporate giants are promoting technology use in schools in ways that will not necessary enhance student learning. For instance, under President Obama's RTTP program, technology is required to measure "student and teacher performance on high-stakes examinations." However, "in order for this kind of information to be captured, the very social and complex actions that comprise teaching and learning must be distilled into discrete tidbits that can be neatly housed in databases." Third, Lynch lends information to help us critical evaluate the educative value of software being employed in schools. He concludes the chapter by providing educators an additional insight so as to leverage computing software "to deepen teaching and learning," rather than merely promoting corporate interest through computing use in K–12 schools.

In the tenth chapter of the volume, "The Era of Recruitment: The Militarization of Everything," William Reynolds captures how the new public military pedagogy is impacting "our society, the lives of our youth, and all of us." The author opens the chapter by documenting how the U.S. government has supported the new public military pedagogy by spending more and more money "on military agendas, wars and recruitment as well as by providing a brief history of our progress toward a militarized society." Next, he provides a "discussion of the ways in which this militarized society leads to increasingly militarized schools." Third, Reynolds outlines "several ways in which schools and universities are now military friendly and sites for recruitment of youth from elementary schools to colleges." Finally, the author makes important "connections made between the entertainment industry and the military." For instance, he documents how "the Army, Navy, Air Force and Marines have become commodified."

> They have become logos. First, anyone can purchase name brand clothing with the various military logos. It is possible to buy Under Armour performance wear with the logo of the various armed services emblazoned across the front of the shirt or the shorts. You can lift weights, run, and cycle wearing the logo of your favorite branch of the armed services. Run as a Marine, even if you are not one. But logo t-shirts and performance wear are only a small part of the commodities available for purchase and consequently advertising for the military.

Articles in the third section of this book have been placed under the heading *Alienation: Displacing Students and Teachers*. Chapter 11, written by Joshua Garrison, is entitled "Teacher and Student Labor in the Twenty-First Century Schools." There, he poses this essential question: For whom does the worker labor, and for what reasons? Garrison argues that, increasingly, external agencies are imposing social, political, and economic demands on school workers—demands that have little to do with student learning and even less to do with inner well-being, or the cultivation of creative capacities. In doing so, he explores (from a Marxist perspective) the concept of a "commodity" by focusing on the Seventh Circuit's 2007 *Mayer v. Monroe* decision. He writes: "The commodity that teachers exchange for a wage is the ability and willingness to speak a curriculum that prioritizes capital while, simultaneously, omitting 'opinions' or 'idiosyncrasies' (*Mayer v. Monroe*) that challenge or bring into question the school's overriding aim." That aim, he contends, is to train productive workers and, not, as articulated in Mayer v. Monroe, to offer personal opinions and perspectives. Teachers' speech, therefore, "effectively becomes the property of elected officials." The same holds true for students. For whom do they labor? Quoting Brosio (2003), Garrison writes: "test scores and letter grades allow(s) for the stratification to continue along a historical head-hand divide. The capitalist class-stratification system needs criteria in order to assign various people to specific places on the ladder." The author points out that, increasingly, student achievement is used to determine teacher merit and effectiveness. Finally, Garrison points to the rapid rise in "for profit" educational institutions that exacerbate the sense of alienation as teachers and students find themselves working not for themselves but for corporate shareholders.

Chapter 12, entitled "Soldiers or Students? JROTC, the Military Presence in Schools, and Educating for a Permanent War," Shannon McManimon, Brian Lozenski, and Zachary Casey explore the interrelationships between and among the Junior Reserve Officer Training Corps (JROTC), America's public schools, the culture of militarism, and school reform. The authors trace the history of JROTC by providing the reader with a chronological review of the organization's evolution. JROTC (dating back to 1916) has primarily targeted "at risk" students, which, the authors note, is code for students of color or students from low-income families. McManimon, Lozenski, and Casey provide an analysis of the curricular ideology of the JROTC by viewing it through the lens of "official knowledge" as posited by Apple (2000). By reviewing portions of a JROTC Cadet Handbook, the authors contend that ideologies of strict obedience, heterosexuality, a decontextualized concept of "citizenship," and unquestioning nationalism dominate over social history and critical thinking. The chapter also outlines concerns about the type of cultural capital embodied in the JROTC program as well as its own brand of alienation. The authors conclude with a section equating JROTC with what they call a "neoliberal education" designed to support a "permanent war."

Sue Books and Rian de Villiers offer a sobering report on the effects of neoliberalism on the teaching profession in Chapter 13, entitled "A Neoliberal Assault on Public Education as We Know It." The authors lay out a series of factors (the erosion of teachers' union collective bargaining rights, undocumented claims of teacher shortages, chronic underfunding of urban and rural schools in the United States, underpayment of teachers in other countries) which, taken together, have resulted in the unprecedented recruitment of international teachers to work in U.S. schools. In addition to outlining the number of H-1B and J-1 visas issued to foreign primary and secondary teachers from 2004 through 2011, Books and de Villers note the concerns raised by the American Federation of Teachers, the National Education Association, and the Association of International Educators during that same period. Each group decried the lack of federal data on this trend. It is now estimated that between 14,000 and 20,000 foreign teachers are currently working in this country. Lured to the U.S. by recruiters who promised master's degrees, housing assistance and eventual citizenship, international teachers found that, "[b]y and large . . . these promises were never kept." The vast majority of international teachers end up returning to their homeland. In some cases, recruiting agencies extorted international teachers' wages. All of this is made possible, say the authors, by assertions that there is a teacher "shortage" in the United States. In fact, the opposite is true, as school districts nationwide have "cut 278,000 teaching jobs between September 2008 and September 2011." Books and de Villers argue that "[t]he international teacher-recruitment industry needs to be more transparent and regulated more diligently."

Chapter 14, "The Cult of Personality v. Expertise in the Education Debate" is the work of P.L. Thomas, who argues that national figures such as Arne Duncan, Bill Gates, Michelle Rhee, and Sal Khan are, essentially, "bullies" who use their power (gained through wealth, notoriety, or political connections) to promote and drive their vision of education reform. Thomas attacks these reformers for their lack of both credentials and credibility. To fight these top-down reform efforts, Thomas makes a case for teachers to be "political" but not "partisan," and he differentiates the two terms. The author also provides the reader with various perspectives on the concept of accountability, viewing it within the context of *license* (which he sees as "above accountability" and "cancerous to both democracy and freedom—and often [coming] in the wake of privilege"), *compulsion* (consisting of the mandates of authority and the need for compliance), and *autonomy* (freedom that comes with consequences). Thomas asserts that personalities like Duncan, Rhee, and Gates embrace only the first two concepts of accountability (license and compulsion), thereby exhibiting "accountability without autonomy" which, he writes, is "tyranny." In terms of institutions which operate in a tyrannical manner, the author cites the National Council on Teacher Quality (NCTQ)—aided and abetted by the popular media which report uncritically on the findings of neoliberal think tanks.

In Chapter 15, Eve Tuck provides an analysis of the uses and misuses of the General Education Development credential. "The GED as a Cover for

School Pushout" begins with an overview of the impact of the federal No Child Left Behind legislation and how it has evolved into the current Race to the Top (RTTP) initiative. Tuck points out that RTTP is based on neoliberal assumptions relative to competition, charter schools, and the power of the private sector. In this chapter, the author focuses on the overuse of the GED. By applying methods similar to her *Gateways and Get-aways Project,* Tuck worked with youth co-researchers to study the role of the GED credential within the current framework of RTTP. The chapter is filled with direct statements from administrators, teachers and students who confirm the use of the GED as a mechanism for pushing "at risk" students out of school so that they will not jeopardize the school's standardized test scores and, as a result, the school's overall rating. Other consequences of RTTP, as revealed in Tuck's study, include increased students suspensions, limited student access to untested subjects, excessive test prep activities, and higher incidences of cheating by teachers and other school personnel. Tuck concludes her chapter with a listing of seven "key conditions" of school pushout.

In Chapter 16, "See Something, Say Something," author Barbara Madeloni writes, "Daily, I make choices that either confirm or deny my values and beliefs. I face these choices with two competing fears. One is that I will lose my job. The other is that I will lose my soul." With these words, Madeloni begins her chronicle of struggle, both personally and professionally, with what is potentially the new national assessment for student teachers—the Teacher Performance Assessment (TPA). Madeloni cites a range of serious concerns relative to this assessment, not the least of which is its connection to Pearson, Inc. (a for-profit company and the largest assessment corporation in North America), its evaluation out-sourcing to "anonymous scorers," its "dangerous pretense of objectivity" and, perhaps most critically, "the standardization of teacher assessment." The author sees the implementation of TPA as nothing less than the complete privatization of teacher education. Madeloni's institution, the University of Massachusetts Amherst, had agreed to pilot the TPA, and this is when Madeloni's resistance took shape. Citing coercive language by UMASS Amherst administrators to student teachers, the lack of informed consent in their field testing research, and the utter disregard for the privacy of children, Madeloni elaborates on the actions taken by her students to maintain their privacy, nurture their budding professionalism, and underscore their identity as students who are in a continual process of learning and growing. These actions were done at great risk to the author's position at her institution with consequences that continue to this day.

Scott Harding and Seth Kershner outline the dimensions of the Counter-Recruitment Movement (CR) in Chapter 17, "Students Against Militarism: Youth Organizing in the Counter-Recruitment Movement." CR represents an effort to oppose militarism in U.S. public schools by providing alternative information to students about career options outside the military, and by addressing broader issues such as economic injustice due, in part, to a culture of militarism. Harding and Kershner cite the 2002 NCLB legislation which, among other things, grants U.S. military personnel almost unlimited access to students in public schools. "Recruiters' presence in schools," notes Harding and Kershner, "goes beyond providing information to students who express an interest in armed forces...recruiters are urged to immerse themselves in high school activities—by volunteering to chaperone dances, proctoring tests, coaching sports, and through other means—in order to achieve 'school ownership'." The chapter focuses on CR activities in Chicago ("the most militarized public school system in the nation"), New York (where the NYCLU reported that class time is used by recruiters), and Oakland (where the efforts of activist groups like Better Alternatives for Youth are bearing fruit). Harding and Kershner concludes with a call for more assistance—from individuals to progressive organizations—in supporting the CR movement in its efforts to minimize the culture of militarism in our society and in our schools.

In Chapter 18, Doug Selwyn and Bob Howard offer readers a glimpse into their experiences fighting against the deleterious effects of the high-stakes standardized Washington Assessment of Student Learning (WASL) test. The WASL, the product of reform movements in the state of Washington in the 1990s, tested students at the end of grades 4, 7, and 10. In the case of grade 10, students had to pass the WASL in order to graduate despite their GPAs, teacher recommendations, school activities, or scores on other examinations (such as the SAT). Selwyn, who taught elementary level classes during the initial administrations of the WASL, noted that the generally poor (based on the Federal Free and Reduced Lunch guidelines) and English Language Learner populations struggled with virtually all aspects of the test, including its lengthy reading passages, multiple days of administration, and unrealistic writing mandates. Resistance at the building level eventually blossomed into an array of activities on the part of Selwyn, Howard, and an associate, which led to statewide Initiative 780 which, if passed, would require "any candidate running for any local or statewide office in Washington to take the same high-stakes test required of all tenth-grade students and to post their scores in the voter's pamphlet and on the Secretary of State's website." Selwyn and Howard outline the process to get I-780 on the ballot and their responses to the publicity that the initiative created.

Chapter 19 provides a parent's perspective on the effects on high-stakes testing on children, teachers, and schools. In this chapter, Dora Taylor shares the experiences of her daughter, whose perceptions about school and learning were deeply affected by a "test-prep" culture. In addition, Taylor discusses her work as a teacher of introductory architecture to students in grades 3 through 12. Taylor asserts that widespread implementation of standardized assessments is, itself, untested territory. She states, "Until we know without any doubt that there is a fair and reliable way to measure student performance and growth, these tests should not be used to control the fate of our public schools." Taylor concludes by presenting information about the growing resistance to standardized assessment, information that suggests that possibilities exist for positive change, beginning at the grassroots level.

In Chapter 20 ("Teaching Young Children Social Justice Basics: The Public. Equality and the Common Good"), Ann Berlak details her efforts to teach social justice to elementary level students in Oakland, California. She writes: "Each lesson I taught... provided additional evidence... that elementary school-age children have already begun to take for granted some of the basics of *in*justice, including competition, individualism, hierarchy, obedience to authority, consumerism, and the primacy of private property." Berlak was inspired by the various "occupy" activities that sprang up nationwide in 2012, as well as the efforts to unseat the governor of Wisconsin for his anti-labor agenda. Her chapter provides a listing of fourth- and fifth-grade classroom activities that explored topics such as unemployment, a living wage, taxation, and the concept of meritocracy. Additional classes focused on the meaning of the word "public" in relation to what the students saw as essential characteristics of their community. Berlak also developed activities to help student grasp the disparities in wealth in the United States, empathize with the homeless, and understand the nature in inequity. The author employed literature and student poetry to help student understand the plight of the underemployed. She concludes by pointing out that "the neoliberal climate of... hostility to the creation of a truly democratic... society" continues to negate the efforts of teachers who wish to teach social justice to elementary students.

REFERENCES

Anyon, J. (*1997*) *Ghetto schooling: A political economy of urban educational reform.* New York: Teachers College Press.

Apple, M. W. (2000). *Official knowledge: Democratic education in a conservative age.* New York, NY: Routledge.

Brosio, R. (2003). High-stakes tests: Reasons to strive for a better Marx. *Journal for Critical Education Policy Studies, 2.* Retrived from http://www.jceps.com/print.php?articleID=17

Fenstermacher, G., & Richardson, V. (2005). On making determinations of quality in teaching. *Teachers College Record, 107,* 186–213.

Ravitch, D. (2012). How GERM spreads. [Web log post]. Retrieved from http://dianeravitch.net/2012/10/25/how-germ-spreads/

Sahlberg, P. (2011). *Finnish lessons: What can the world learn from educational change in Finland?* New York, NY: Teachers College Press.

PART I

TESTING . . . TESTING

CHAPTER 1

THE MISTAKE POLICYMAKERS MAKE ABOUT TEACHING

Larry Cuban
Stanford University

This chapter was written by Larry Cuban, a former high school social studies teacher (14 years), district superintendent (seven years in Arlington, VA), and professor emeritus of education at Stanford University, where he has taught for more than 20 years. His latest book is *Inside the Black Box of Classroom Practice: Change Without Reform in American Education.* This chapter first appeared as a post on the author's blog.

As a result of inhabiting a different world than teachers, policymakers make a consequential error. They and a cadre of influentials confuse teacher quality with teaching quality; that is, the personal traits of teachers—dedicated, caring, gregarious, intellectually curious—produce student learning rather than the classroom and school settings.

Both are important, of course, but policymakers and their influential camp followers have accentuated personal traits far more than the organizational and social context in which teachers teach daily. So if students score low on tests, then who the teachers are, their personal traits, credentials,

Left Behind in the Race to the Top, pages 3–5
Copyright © 2013 by Information Age Publishing

and attitudes come under close scrutiny, rather than the age-graded school, neighborhood demography, workplace conditions, and resources that support teaching. The person overshadows the place (Kennedy, 2010).

In attributing far more weight to individual teacher traits rather than seriously considering the situation in which teachers teach, policymakers and civic and business leaders end up having a cramped view of teaching quality.

Quality teaching is complex because an essential distinction is masked: the difference between "good" teaching and "successful" teaching. Both "good" and " successful" teaching are necessary to reach the threshold of quality instruction and student learning. To lead us through the thicket of complexity, I lean on Gary Fenstermacher and Virginia Richardson's (2005) analysis of quality teaching.

"Good" teaching is about the how and what of teaching. For example, the task of getting a child to understand the theory of evolution (or the Declaration of Independence or prime numbers) in a considerate and age-appropriate way consistent with best practices in the field is "good" teaching.

"Successful" teaching, however, is about what the child learns. For example, getting the same child to write three paragraphs filled with relevant details and present-day examples that demonstrate understanding of the theory of evolution or the Declaration of Independence is "successful" teaching. Ditto for a student able to show that she knows prime numbers by completing Eratosthenes Sieve. "Good" and "successful" teaching, then, are not the same, nor does one necessarily lead to the other.

Does that last sentence mean that good teaching may not automatically lead to successful teaching? Yes, one does not necessarily produce the other. How can that be?

Fenstermacher and Richardson point out that learning, like teaching, can also be distinguished between "good" and "successful." The above examples of student proficiency on the theory of evolution, the Declaration of Independence, and prime numbers demonstrate successful learning.

Good learning, however, requires other factors to be in place. Good learning occurs when the student is willing to learn and puts forth effort, the student's family, peers, and community support learning, the student has the place, time, and resources to learn, and, finally, good teaching.

In short, good teaching is one of four necessary components to good learning. In making this mistake, policymakers unintentionally snooker the public by squishing together good teaching and successful learning. In doing so, policymakers erase three critical factors that are equally important in getting students to learn: the student's own effort, support of family and peers, and the opportunity to learn in school.

"No excuses" reformers (see above) glide over these other factors critical to learning. Current hoopla over paying teachers for their performance based on student test scores is an expression of this conflation of good teaching with successful learning and the ultimate deceiving of parents, voters, and students that good teaching naturally leads to successful learning.

Not only does this policymaker error about quality classroom instruction confuse the personal traits of the teacher with teaching, it also nurtures a heroic view of school improvement where superstars (e.g., Geoffrey Canada in "Waiting for Superman," Jaime Escalante of "Stand and Deliver," Erin Gruwell of "Freedom Writers") labor day in and day out to get their students to ace AP calculus tests and become accomplished writers and achieve in Harlem schools.

Neither doctors, lawyers, soldiers, nor nuclear physicists can depend upon superstars among them to get their important work done every day. Nor should all teachers have to be heroic. Policymakers attributing quality far more to individual traits in teachers than to the context in which they teach leads to squishing good teaching with successful learning doing even further collateral damage to the profession by setting up the expectation that only heroes need apply.

By stripping away from good learning essential factors of students' motivation, the contexts in which they live, and the opportunities they have to learn in school—federal, state, and district policymakers inadvertently twist the links between teaching and learning into a simpleminded formula, thereby miseducating the public they serve while encouraging a generation of idealistic newcomers to become classroom heroes who end up deserting schools in wholesale numbers within a few years because they come to understand that good teaching does not lead automatically to successful learning.

Fenstermacher and Richardson help us parse "quality teaching" into distinctions between good and successful teaching and learning while revealing clearly the error that policymakers have made and continue to do so.

REFERENCES

Kennedy, M. (2010). Attribution error and the quest for teacher quality. *Educational Researcher, 39*(8), 591–598.
Fenstermacher, G., & Richardson, V. (2005). On making determinations of quality in teaching. *Teachers College Record, 107*, 186–213.

CHAPTER 2

"PAY NO ATTENTION TO THE MAN BEHIND THE CURTAIN!"

False Pretenses and the Humbug of High-Stakes Testing

Wayne Au
University of Washington–Bothell

The Wizard of Oz: Do you presume to criticize the great OZ, you un-
grateful creatures? . . . The great OZ has spoken. . . . Pay
no attention to that man behind the curtain! The great
OZ has spoken!
Dorothy: Who are you?
The Wizard of Oz: I am the great and powerful wizard of Oz.
Dorothy: You are? I don't believe you.
The Wizard of Oz: I'm afraid it is true. There is no other wizard except me.
The Scarecrow: You humbug!
The Wizard of Oz: Yes. It is exactly so. I am a humbug."

—From *The Wizard of Oz,* 1939

Left Behind in the Race to the Top, pages 7–22
Copyright © 2013 by Information Age Publishing
All rights of reproduction in any form reserved.

The above dialogue comes from the classic, 1939 film version of *The Wizard of Oz*. At this point in the story, after trembling in fear at being in the presence of what they thought was the ALL-POWERFUL WIZARD, Dorothy's dog, Toto, jumps to the ground, pulls back a curtain, and exposes the Wizard for what he really is: a regular person hiding behind a veil of power. Once the truth is revealed, the Wizard is suddenly not so powerful after all, in large part because Dorothy and her fellow travelers realize there is no reason to cede power to him in the first place. Much like the Wizard of Oz, the power of high-stakes, standardized testing has become ubiquitous in public education in the United States. Within the mainstream media, among politicians and business leaders, in the halls of billionaire philanthropies, and within public discourse, these tests are assumed to be objective, fair, and accurate measures of learning, teaching, and educational achievement. And they are driving education "reform" in the United States.

In this chapter I want to channel Toto by pulling back the curtain to expose high-stakes tests as anything but objective, fair, and accurate—in the process channel the Scarecrow by calling them out as the "humbug!" that they really are. Here I challenge the presumed goodness and objectivity of high-stakes, standardized testing. First I provide a brief overview of the rise of modern-day high-stakes testing as the central tool of "accountability" in education reform. I then turn to the origins of such testing within the IQ testing and the racist eugenics movement in the United States. I follow by discussing how high-stakes standardized testing acts as a fundament to corporate views of schools as sites of capitalist production, including ways the tests objectify students and justify stratification vis-à-vis the ideology of meritocracy. I then argue that high-stakes standardized testing ultimately commodifies students, teachers, learning, and teaching, thus negating the complexity of their human qualities and contexts. Finally, I extend this argument to discuss how we also see the test scores themselves as disembodied commodities, objectively existing apart from subjectivity or error. In turn I provide evidence that modern-day high-stakes standardized testing is instead rife with problems and is in fact quite far from being the objective measurements of teaching or learning that proponents claim.

A BRIEF HISTORY OF MODERN-DAY HIGH-STAKES, STANDARDIZED TESTING

The modern high-stakes standardized testing movement can effectively be traced back to the publication of *A Nation At Risk* (National Commission on Excellence in Education, 1983). This Reagan-era report sounded an alarm within public education in the U.S., despite the reality that much of the report's data was found to be manufactured (Berliner & Biddle, 1995).

Within one year of the report's publication, 54 state-level commissions on education were created. Within three years of publication, 26 states raised graduation requirements and 35 states instituted comprehensive education reforms that revolved around testing and increased course loads for students (Kornhaber & Orfield, 2001). By 1994, 43 states implemented statewide assessments for K–5, and by the year 2000, every U.S. state except Iowa administered a state-mandated test (Jones, Jones, & Hargrove, 2003). The march toward high-stakes, standardized testing continued through then Vice President George H. Bush's campaign for the presidency and, as President, G. H. Bush carried this agenda forward into his Summit on Education. President Bill Clinton and Vice President Al Gore subsequently committed themselves to following through on the goals established by Bush's America 2000 plan, including the pursuit of a national examination system in the United States. Within the first week of taking office in 2001, President G. W. Bush pushed for federal Title I funding to be tied to student test scores (Kornhaber & Orfield, 2001).

In 2002, with the support of both parties, the U.S. government passed the No Child Left Behind Act (NCLB) into law (U.S. Department of Education, 2002). As a policy, NCLB relied upon high-stakes testing as the central mechanism for school reform, mandating that all students be tested in grades 3–8 and once in high school, in reading and math, with future provisions that students be tested at least once at the elementary, middle, and high school levels in science. If schools do not show consistent improvement on these tests in subgroups related to race, economic class, special education, and English language proficiency, among others, they face sanctions such as a loss of federal funding, with the ultimate policy goal of all students reaching 100% proficiency by 2014 (Karp, 2006). Thus, NCLB can be seen as part of a 30-year ascendant trajectory of high-stakes, standardized testing as *the* policy tool for enforcing educational reform in the United States—a tool now fully embraced by Democrats and Republicans alike and regardless of the election of President Obama (Au, 2009).

THE RACIST ROOTS OF STANDARDIZED TESTING IN THE UNITED STATES

While the modern history of high-stakes, standardized testing is fairly well known, less well known is that, fundamentally, standardized testing in the United States has as its origins IQ testing and eugenics—the belief that intelligence is genetic and that certain races or ethnic groups are biologically inferior to whites (Selden, 1999). Psychologist Alfred Binet first developed the IQ test in France in 1904 to assess whether young children had mild developmental disabilities. His work established the "Binet Scale" of intelligence based on a measurement of a child's level of intellectual development in comparison to their chronological age. By dividing the first (mental age) by the second (chronological age), the idea of "intelligence quotient," or IQ was born (Gould, 1996). It is important to note that Binet's use of testing was very specific in that it was to be used on young children, was not connected to any sense of hereditary or innate intelligence, was considered to be a general empirical tool for making general decisions (as opposed to being a precise measurement for precise decisions), was never intended to be used to measure children who were developing "normally," and was used with the intent of signaling that a child may need more help in his or her intellectual development (Gould, 1996).

However, cognitive psychologists in the United States like Henry Goddard, Lewis Terman, and Robert Yerkes took up Binet's testing and measurement of IQ, distorting the original use of the tests and their underlying presumptions about humans and human ability. Through the work of these psychologists, IQ became conceived of as hereditary and fixed, laying the groundwork for testing to be used to sort and rank different people by race, ethnicity, gender, and class according to supposedly inborn, biologically innate intelligence (Gould, 1996). In the United States, Yerkes played a particularly important role in this process. In 1917, as a psychologist and Army Colonel in charge of the mental testing of 1.75 million recruits during World War I, Yerkes worked with Goddard, Terman, and others to develop and administer the Alpha and Beta Army tests. These tests were used to sort incoming soldiers and to determine their "mental fitness." Yerkes drew several dubious conclusions using this incredibly large pool of test data. The first was that, according to his interpretation of the Army test results, the average White adult in the United States had an average mental age of thirteen. The second conclusion Yerkes arrived at was that the intelligence of European immigrants could be judged according to their country of origin: The darker peoples of eastern and southern Europe were less intelligent than their fairer-skinned, western and northern European counterparts. Yerkes' third conclusion was that African Americans were the least intelligent of all peoples. Not surprisingly, these findings were used by eugenicists of the time to rally around the idea that average American intelligence was declining due to the unregulated breeding of the poor and stupid, as well as the idea that race mixing was spreading the supposedly inferior intelligence of African Americans and immigrants (Giordano, 2005).

Standardized IQ testing soon found its way into the institution of education. As Tyack (1974) explains, "Intelligence testing . . . provided the technology for classifying children. Nature–nurture controversies might pepper the scientific periodicals and magazines of the intelligentsia, but schoolmen found IQ tests invaluable means of channeling children" (p. 180). Horace Mann, as secretary of the Massachusetts Board of Education in 1845, oversaw some of the first standardized testing of children in public schools. For Mann, these tests promised the development of a more efficient, standardized, and accountable way of assessing student learning (Chapman, 1988; Sacks, 1999). The trend of developing tests to measure efficiency in schools continued to grow into the early 1900s, and by 1911 the National Education Association had appointed the "Committee on Tests and Standards of Efficiency in Schools and School Systems" and by 1913 several handwriting and arithmetic tests had been created and were being used in some schools (Callahan, 1964).

A Stanford University professor of psychology, Terman, under the sponsorship of the National Academy of Sciences, played a key role in adapting the above-mentioned army tests into the National Intelligence Tests for schoolchildren in 1919. By 1920, over 400,000 copies of these tests had been sold nationwide. Terman and others also created the Stanford Achievement Test in 1922, and by late 1925, he reported sales of this test to be near 1.5 million copies. A 1925 survey of 215 cities found that 64% of these cities used intelligence tests to classify and sort elementary students, 56% used the tests to classify and sort junior high school students, and 41% did the same for high school students (Chapman, 1988). By 1932, 112 of 150 large city school systems in the United States had begun to use intelligence testing to place students into ability groups, and colleges had also begun to use these tests to justify admissions as well (Haney, 1984). Thus, the sorting function of standardized tests and their explicit justification for social hierarchies matched perfectly with the rise of scientific management and "social efficiency" in education.

SCIENTIFICALLY MANAGED EDUCATION

In the early 1900s, educational leaders became enamored with the application of Frederick Taylor's concepts of scientific management in factory production to systems of education. For Taylor, efficient production relied upon the factory managers' ability to gather all the information possible about the work which they oversaw, systematically analyze it according to "scientific" methods, figure out the most efficient ways for workers to complete individual tasks, and then tell the worker exactly how to produce their products in an ordered manner. Scientific management also became the backbone for what has been termed the "social efficiency movement." This movement, with the "science" offered by Taylorism, promoted the idea that social and governmental waste could be identified and cut, and that social order would spring from carefully studied systems of "scientific" planning (Kliebard, 2004).

Historically, no single person exemplified the social efficiency movement more than John Franklin Bobbitt. Bobbitt was first brought to the University of Chicago's Department of Education as a lecturer in 1909. By 1910 he was promoted to the position of Instructor of School Administration, and by 1912 Bobbitt published his first article, "The Elimination of Waste in Education" (Bobbitt, 1912). Bobbitt's vision of the social efficiency in education embodies a constellation of concepts that reflect Taylor's vision of scientific management in industry. According to Bobbitt (1920/2002), efficiency in education is built upon the predetermination of objectives that fundamentally drive the entire process of education. In Bobbitt's (1913) model, the objectives for students are based on their predicted future social and economic lives "according to their social and vocational destiny" (p. 26). Essentially, Bobbitt mapped the industrial metaphor on to schools in a very simple and neat way. Students are the "raw materials" to be shaped into finished products according to their future social positions. Teachers are the workers who employ the most efficient methods to get students to meet the predetermined standards and objectives. Administrators are the managers who determine and dictate to teachers the most efficient methods in the production process. The school is the factory assembly line where this process takes place.

The logics of social efficiency and scientific management embody a means-ends rationality that assumes that "it is a *technical* matter to decide such issues as instructional method and content, a matter best reserved for people with technical expertise about the methods and content optimally suited for particular objective" (Posner, 1988, p. 80, original emphasis). The means-ends rationality of socially efficient, scientifically managed education maintained and justified socioeconomic hierarchies. With an unapologetic eye towards social engineering, socially efficient education would only teach learners information that they would use in their future roles in life. Thus, as Sacks (1999) explains, standardized testing, with its penchant for sorting human populations, went hand in hand with the social efficiency movement: "Ideology... under the guises of... managerial and social efficiency, drove these grand social experiments in the testing of army recruits, schoolchildren, and people aspiring to a college education. Testing became an early tool to try to weed out the intellectually weak from the cognitively strong" (p. 73).

The push to measure intelligence and compare different people is part and parcel with the social efficiency movement generally, and in education particularly. Echoing Bobbitt's calls for efficiency, schools needed a way to sort and rank their students according to their supposedly innate, native intelligence, thus preparing them for their "proper" future social roles. That poor people, African Americans, and darker southern and eastern Europeans were determined to have less intelligence just proved to these researchers that the tests were accurately measuring where each group fit within existing social and economic hierarchies (Selden, 1999). Standardized testing, with its very root in intelligence testing and the eugenics movement, simply offered both the technology and the ideological justification to sort groups of people along race, class, and socioeconomic hierarchies (Au, 2009).

The SAT and Embedded Inequality

The SAT college entrance exam is another good example of just how deeply inequalities can be embedded within high-stakes standardized testing. The SAT was developed by Princeton University professor and noted eugenicist, Carl Brigham (Sacks, 1999). Using the same World War I Army test data as Yerkes, Brigham arrived at similar racist, nativist, and classist conclusions as his colleagues. After leaving a position as an Army psychologist, Brigham returned to Princeton to work in the admissions office, where he continued his work on testing and intelligence by developing an exam that would sort through the young men applying for entrance into the elite halls of Princeton. To do so, Brigham created the "Scholastic Aptitude Test." This test was the first mass-based college entrance exam. Today it is simply known as the SAT (Sacks, 1999).

In addition to its origins amongst eugenicists, a contemporary study of SAT questions finds significant racial bias buried deep within the modern-day structure of the test construction itself. Kidder and Rosner (2002–2003) performed a study of over 300,000 SAT test takers, analyzing test questions from four SATs given between 1988 and 1989. As Rosner (2003) explains, they found that the SAT test question selection process is systematically built around a process of a self-reproducing racism:

> Each individual SAT question ETS chooses is required to parallel outcomes of the test overall. So, if high-scoring test takers—who are more likely to be white—tend to answer the question correctly in [experimental] pretesting, it's a worthy SAT question; if not, it's thrown out. Race and ethnicity are not considered explicitly, but racially disparate scores drive question selection, which in turn reproduces racially disparate test results in an internally reinforcing cycle. (p. 24)

Couched in the language of statistical reliability and validity, the supposedly race-neutral process of test question selection ultimately structures very race-biased results into test questions themselves (Kidder & Rosner, 2002–2003). Based on his study, Rosner (2003) hypothesizes that "every SAT in the past ten years has favored whites over blacks.... Skewed test question selection certainly contributes to the large test score disparities between blacks and whites" (p. 24).

The encoding of racial bias in the very structure and definition of what makes a "valid" SAT question speaks to how deeply the race implications of high-stakes standardized testing extend into contemporary institutions and society. In the end, the issue is all about how "objective" validity and reliability of test items are determined, and within such determination, we can still see the legacies of IQ testing and eugenics at play (Au, 2009).

STANDARDIZED TESTING AS TECHNOLOGY AND IDEOLOGY

It is important to recognize, however, that the technology of standardized testing, beyond its role in IQ and eugenics, proved to be a pivotal technology for efficiently comparing and sorting populations—a technology that also supported the myth of the individual merit (meritocracy) in the United States.

Standardization, Objectivity, and Objectification

Standardized test results are seen as valid based on the assumption that they can provide a fair and objective comparison of individuals and groups in different settings. This assumption, for instance, is what allows policymakers to assert that student X in Massachusetts has met a tested standard, but that student Y in California has not (and therefore conclude that student X is a "better" student with a "better" teacher). The validity of such comparisons is only possible because of the assumed objectivity of the test itself. In order for such comparisons to be made, however, standardized tests have to ignore certain amounts of individual variability or difference, and thus establish a common measurement. This is what enables test proponents and policymakers to claim they are accurately comparing student A to student B, school C to school D, district E to district F, state G to state H, and country I to country J. In this way, standardization, in order to maintain a guise of objectivity, must assume that local, individual conditions and local, individual factors make no difference in either student performance or test-based measurement. Indeed, the assumed validity of objective measurement provided by standardized tests rests upon this denial of individual differences: The tests are considered objective because they supposedly measure all individuals equally and without the influence of any outside circumstances. Thus when students (and teachers, schools, districts, states, and countries) are measured by standardized testing and compared to other students, they are decontextualized in order to make such comparisons possible.

In her study of the impact of high-stakes testing policies in Chicago schools, Lipman (2004) explains this process:

> Students, as well as teachers, with all their varied talents and challenges, were reduced to a test score. And schools, as well as their communities, in all their complexity—their failings, inadequacies, strong points, superb and weak teachers, ethical commitments to collective uplift, their energy, demoralization, courage, potential, and setbacks—were blended, homogenized, and reduced to a stanine score. (p. 172)

In the process of the quantification of student knowledge and understanding, students themselves are necessarily quantified as a number. This quantification lies at the heart of the measurement itself, which turns real people and real social conditions into oversimplified and comparable numbers and categories. As De Lissovoy and McLaren (2003) observe:

> The key principle at work in the use of standardized tests, which is also what allows them to serve as the mechanism for accountability initiatives, is the reduction of learning and knowledge to a number, i.e., a score. Once this takes place, scores can be compared, statistically analysed and variously manipulated.... In reducing learning to a test score, policy makers seek to make the knowledge of disparate individuals commensurable. (p. 133)

Individuality is omitted, and student variability is disregarded and reduced "to one or two characteristics common to the larger universe of objects" (McNeil, 2005, p. 103). Standardized tests thus, by definition, literally "objectify" students by reducing them to numerical objects for comparison. By reducing students to numbers, standardized testing creates the capacity to view students as things, as comparable quantities apart from their human qualities. In this way high-stakes, standardized tests do not accurately measure the complexities of student learning and the act of teaching.

Within systems of standardized testing, then, the value of students (or most workers in the educational production chain—teachers, administrators, and even parents) is therefore not to be found in their humanity. Rather, students' value is found in their test scores—reified, objectified, commodified, one-dimensional, and highly abstracted versions of the human beings in a classroom or school community. Lost in this vision of students-as-commodities are the social relations that exist "behind" these test scores. Hence, students' lives, home cultures, histories, educational differences, and socioeconomic conditions mean nothing within the logics of high-stakes standardized testing. Consequently, in distancing test scores from the realities of students' lives and school conditions, systems of high-stakes testing effectively mask the existence of social relations and structural in-equalities exploitation that persist in their lives, resulting in what some have called the "new eugenics" (Baker, 2002).

Standardized Testing and the Ideology of Meritocracy

Perhaps ironically, the masking of social conditions and human relations behind a façade of objectivity has been one of the ways high-stakes test-ing has been constructed as a tool to end educational inequality. As Sacks (1999) explains, many believe that "standardized testing, rendered with complete objectivity and couched in terms of an empirical 'science,' would be the death knell to the insidious influences of class privilege perpetuated by the blueness of one's blood" (p. 264).

Due to the assumed fair and objective measurement of individuals, stan-dardized tests seemingly hold the promise that every individual who takes a test gets a fair and equal shot at educational, social, and economic suc-cess. Problems like institutionalized racism and class privilege are thus sup-posedly ameliorated through testing. This characterization of standardized testing as a means of challenging inequality is rooted in the ideal that the United States operates as a meritocracy: That is to say, regardless of social position, economic class, gender, or culture (or any other form of differ-ence), we all have equal chances at becoming "successful" based purely on individual merit and hard work—which by extension also means that any failure is simply our own individual fault (Lemann, 1999; Sacks, 1999). Thus, the ideology of meritocracy masks structural inequalities under the guise of "naturally" occurring aptitude among individuals (Bisseret, 1979). Vis-à-vis the ideology of meritocracy, the low achievement on standardized tests (and in education generally) of working class people and non-White populations can then be simply attributed to the failure of individual stu-dents or individual groups (or cultures), and not attributed to existing structural inequalities (see, e.g., Rushton & Jensen, 2005).

However, the idea of individuals freely competing in the realm of educa-tion has not been borne out by the realty of standardized testing. Clearly, the historical outcomes of early standardized tests reflected race-, ethnic-, gender-, and class-based differences and provided supporting evidence for the racist eugenics movement (Selden, 1999), and our modern-day test score achievement gaps produce roughly the same results, albeit 100 years later (Au, 2009). Further, there is a mountain of evidence that demonstrates how nonschool factors such as food insecurity, inadequate health care, and environmental pollutants, among others, have an overwhelming effect on educational achievement (Berliner, 2009).

What many mainstream proponents of testing do not understand is that, much like our current system of economics, systems of accountability built upon high-stakes standardized testing cannot function—for both technical and ideological reasons—if everyone is a "winner." Ideologically, if everyone passed the tests as they are currently constructed, there simply would be no way to justify elite status or any form of disparity of education performance at all: Every kid could qualify for the most elite colleges and jobs, thereby rendering the very hierarchy of elitism obsolete. While this might sound good to many (myself included), there is a long history of elite groups' resisting educational reforms that challenge their elite status (see, e.g., Au, 2005; Oakes, Welner, Yonezawa, & Allen, 1998), such that it is more than unlikely real educational equality could be reached.

The technical reason why systems of accountability built upon high-stakes standardized testing cannot function if everyone is a "winner" is that the statistical logic of such tests requires some students to fail (Popham, 2001). Put differently, if everyone passed a standardized test (or in the language of NCLB, if all students achieved 100% proficiency), the results of that test would immediately be called into question on technical grounds (e.g., there is something wrong with the test itself), on ethical-political grounds (e.g., someone must have cheated), or on both (Au & Gourd, in press). Not to mention that 100% passing on a standardized test is a statistic impossibility that no country or system anywhere has ever accomplished (Linn, 2003). This point is particularly important when it comes to the discourse of race and class issues surrounding current education reform and the hyper-reliance on high-stakes testing to achieve racial and economic equality. One of the great ironies about this discourse is that "closing the achievement gap" does not mean having everyone succeed on the tests. Rather, "closing the achievement gap" really means having proportional rates of failure and success amongst different groups. If we "close the achievement gap," we are simply making sure that equal numbers of rich kids and poor kids pass and fail, equal numbers of White kids and Black kids pass and fail, and equal numbers of native English speakers and English language learners pass and fail, and so on (Au & Gourd, in press). Such evenly distributed failure is a far cry from all kids having equal success in schools and life.

The Non-Objective Measures of Standardized Testing

[O]nce it is recognized that . . . "objectivity" is rather contingency and bias, then it follows that the success and failure that the tests pretend to report are actually manufactured by the instruments themselves.

—De Lissovoy & McLaren, 2003, p. 135

More than just students and learning, however, are turned into com-modities within systems of high-stakes standardized testing. The test scores themselves are commodified as well: Because of their assumed objectivity, tests and the scores they produce tend to be perceived as perfect "things" apart from the processes and social relations that go into their production, and apart from any possible error in measurement. Thus, in mainstream discourse, the scores produced by such tests are crystallized into neat, tidy perfection, with no defect and no reason to doubt their accuracy. When we look closely at both the numbers and the tests, however, we can see how this commodification and presumed perfection are far from reality. For instance, a U.S. Department of Education's National Center for Education Statistics report found a statistical error rate of 35% when using one-year's worth of test data to measure a teacher's effectiveness, and an error rate of 25% when using data from three years (Schochet & Chiang, 2010). Other research has found that one-time, randomly occurring factors like whether or not a child ate breakfast on test day, if a window was open and a distract-ing dog was barking outside during the test, whether or not a child got into an argument with parents or peers on the way to school, which other students happened to be in attendance while taking the test, whoever hap-pened to be administering the test, and the like, account for 50–80% of any gains or losses on a given student's standardized test score (Kane & Staiger, 2002). While there are other significant technical problems with the objec-tive accuracy of standardized testing (see, e.g., Au, 2010–2011; Rothstein et al., 2010), these two research examples highlight just how problematic the use of these tests are when used to make high-stakes decisions regarding the performance of students, teachers, and schools: They simply are not as accurate as we might assume.

The lack of objectivity, accuracy, and perfection also shows up in the scoring of the tests themselves. As Farley (2009b), a former employee of 15 years in the testing industry, reflects:

> [T]he test-scoring industry cheats.... It cheats on qualification tests to make sure there is enough personnel to meet deadlines/get tests scored; it cheats on reliability scores to give off the appearance of standardization even when that doesn't exist; it cheats on validity scores and calibration scores and any-thing else that might be needed.... Statistical tomfoolery and corporate chi-canery were the hallmark of my test-scoring career, and while I'm not proud of that, it is a fact. Remember, I was never in the testing business for any rea-son other than to earn a pay check, just like many of the testing companies are in it solely to make a buck. (n.p.)

Farley's experience working in the testing industry was not an anoma-ly, unfortunately, and the lack of objectivity is perhaps most clear when it comes to the grading of standardized writing tests specifically. Like Farley,

DiMaggio (2010) worked as a writing test grader for several years and explains what it is like to be a paid temp worker for Pearson:

> In test-scoring centers, dozens of scorers sit in rows, staring at computer screens where students' papers appear (after the papers have undergone some mysterious scanning process). I imagine that most students think their papers are being graded as if they are the most important thing in the world. Yet every day, each scorer is expected to read hundreds of papers. So for all the months of preparation and the dozens of hours of class time spent writing practice essays, a student's writing probably will be processed and scored in about a minute.
>
> Scoring is particularly rushed when scorers are paid by piece-rate, as is the case when you are scoring from home, where a growing part of the industry's work is done. At 30 to 70 cents per paper, depending on the test, the incentive, especially for a home worker, is to score as quickly as possible in order to earn any money. (n.p.)

Perhaps even worse, DiMaggio explains how he and other scorers were told to change their scores in order to create results consistent with the previous year's tests:

> Usually, within a day or two, when the scores we are giving are inevitably too low (as we attempt to follow the standards laid out in training), we are told to start giving higher scores, or, in the enigmatic language of scoring directors, to "learn to see more papers as a 4." For some mysterious reason, unbeknownst to test scorers, the scores we are giving are supposed to closely match those given in previous years. So if 40 percent of papers received 3s the previous year (on a scale of 1 to 6), then a similar percentage should receive 3s this year. (n.p.)

Similar stories have been chronicled in detail by Farley (2009a) and have been reported at Salon.com, the *New York Times,* and the *Minneapolis City Pages.* These stories and the myriad technical issues highlight the nonobjectivity of high-stakes standardized test scores. They are much further from perfect measurements than many assume.

CONCLUSION: PULLING BACK THE CURTAIN AND EXPOSING THE WIZARD

Just as Toto pulled back the curtain to expose the Wizard of Oz, in this chapter I sought to challenge the very validity and objectivity of high-stakes standardized testing. Not only are the tests rife with technical and ideological problems, they seem to do now what they have done since their origins in the racist and classist eugenics movement of 100 years ago: serve as a sorting mechanism along racial, ethnic, cultural, linguistic, and class lines, and serve to mask systemic inequality through the propagation of the myth of meritocracy and individual achievement. Indeed, such consistency of results and use over a century should raise serious questions about what testing actually measures.

The evidence and arguments I have presented in this chapter are not secret, but test proponents either remain naïve, choose to ignore them, or at some fundamental level believe in biologically based intelligence. It has become clear to me, however, that in the current policy discourse surrounding education "reform," reality and evidence rarely matter. Rather, ideology and politics trump all. This means that, as politicians from both sides of the aisle, business leaders, billionaire philanthropists, and policy wonks continue to shove testing down the throats of students, teachers, parents, administrators, schools, and communities, we need to pay attention to the man behind the curtain, be like the Scarecrow in the *Wizard of Oz,* and call out high-stakes, standardized testing for what it is—a "humbug" that should not be used to drive education policy in the United States (or anywhere). The tests are only powerful if we cede that power willingly.

REFERENCES

Au, W. (2005). Power, identity, and the third rail. In P. C. Miller (Ed.), *Narratives from the classroom: an introduction to teaching* (pp. 65–85). Thousand Oaks, CA: Sage.

Au, W. (2009). *Unequal by design: High-stakes testing and the standardization of inequality.* New York, NY: Routledge.

Au, W. (2010–2011). Neither fair nor accurate: Research based reasons why high-stakes tests should not be used to evaluate teachers. *Rethinking Schools, 25*(2), 34–38.

Au, W., & Gourd, K. (in press). Asinine assessment: Why high-stakes testing is bad for everyone, including English teachers. *English Journal.*

Baker, B. (2002). The hunt for disability: The new eugenics and the normalization of school children. *Teachers College Record, 104,* 663–703.

Berliner, D. C. (2009). *Poverty and potential: Out-of-school factors and school success.* Boulder, CO & Tempe, AZ: Education and the Public Interest Center & Educational Policy Research Unit. Retrieved from http://epicpolicy.org/publication/poverty-and-potential

Berliner, D. C., & Biddle, B. J. (1995). *The manufactured crisis: Myths, fraud, and the attack on America's public schools.* Reading, MA: Addison-Wesley.

Bisseret, N. (1979). *Education, class language and ideology.* Boston, MA: Routledge & Kegan Paul.

Bobbitt, J. F. (1912). The elimination of waste in education. *The Elementary School Teacher, 12*(6), 259–271.

Bobbitt, J. F. (1913). *The supervision of city schools: The twelfth yearbook of the National Society for the Study of Education.* New York, NY: Teachers College Press.

Bobbitt, J. F. (2002). The objectives of secondary education. In J. R. Gress (Ed.), *Curriculum: frameworks, criticism, and theory* (pp. 135–144). Richmond, CA: McCutchan. (Original work published 1920)

Callahan, R. E. (1964). *Education and the cult of efficiency: A study of the social forces that have shaped the administration of the public schools* (First Phoenix ed.). Chicago, IL: University of Chicago Press.

Chapman, P. D. (1988). *Schools as sorters: Lewis M. Terman, applied psychology, and the intelligence testing movement, 1890–1930.* New York, NY: New York University Press.

De Lissovoy, N., & McLaren, P. (2003). Educational "accountability" and the violence of capital: A Marxian reading. *Journal of Educational Policy, 18*(2), 131–143.

DiMaggio, D. (2010). The lonliness of the long-distance test scorer. *Monthly Review, 62*(7). Retrieved from http://monthlyreview.org/2010/12/01/the-loneliness-of-the-long-distance-test-scorer

Farley, T. (2009a). *Making the grades: My misadventures in the standardized testing industry.* San Francisco, CA: Berrett-Koehler Publishers.

Farley, T. (2009b, December 18). My misadventures in the standardized testing industry. *Washington Post.* Retrieved from http://voices.washingtonpost.com/answer-sheet/standardized-tests/-gerald-martineaupost-today-my.html

Giordano, G. (2005). *How testing came to dominate American schools: The history of educational assessment.* New York, NY: Peter Lang.

Gould, S. J. (1996). *The mismeasure of man* (Rev. and expanded. ed.). New York, NY: Norton.

Haney, W. (1984). Testing reasoning and reasoning about testing. *Review of Educational Research, 54*(4), 597-654.

Jones, G. M., Jones, B. D., & Hargrove, T. Y. (2003). *The unintended consequences of high-stakes testing.* New York, NY: Rowman & Littlefield Publishers, Inc.

Kane, T. J., & Staiger, D. O. (2002). Volatility in school test scores: Implications for test-based accountability systems. In D. Ravitch (Ed.), *Brookings papers on education policy 2002* (1st ed., pp. 235–284). Washington, DC: The Brookings Institution.

Karp, S. (2006). Leaving public education behind: The Bush agenda in American education. *Our Schools/Our Selves, 15*(3), 181–196.

Kidder, W. C., & Rosner, J. (2002–2003). How the SAT creates "built-in headwinds": An educational and legal analysis of disparate impact. *Santa Clara Law Review, 43*, 131–212.

Kliebard, H. M. (2004). *The struggle for the American curriculum, 1893–1958* (3rd ed.). New York, NY: RoutledgeFalmer.

Kornhaber, M. L., & Orfield, G. (2001). High-stakes testing policies: Examining their assumptions and consequences. In G. Orfield & M. L. Kornhaber (Eds.), *Raising standards or raising barriers?: Inequality and high-stakes testing in public education* (pp. 1–18). New York, NY: Century Foundation Press.

Lemann, N. (1999). *The big test: The secret history of the American meritocracy.* New York, NY: Farrar, Straus, and Giroux.

Linn, R. L. (2003, July). *Accountability, responsibility and reasonable expectations.* Center for the Study of Evaluation, National Center for Research on Evaluation,

Standards, and Student Testing, Graduate School of Education & Information Studies, University of California, Los Angeles. Retrieved from http://www.cse.ucla.edu/products/reports_set.htm

Lipman, P. (2004). *High stakes education: Inequality, globalization, and urban school reform.* New York, NY: RoutledgeFalmer.

McNeil, L. M. (2005). Faking equity: High-stakes testing and the education of Latino youth. In A. Valenzuela (Ed.), *Leaving children behind: How 'Texas-style' accountability fails Latino youth* (pp. 57–112). Albany, NY: State University of New York.

National Commission on Excellence in Education. (1983). *A nation at risk: The imperative for educational reform.* Washington DC: United States Department of Education.

Oakes, J., Welner, K., Yonezawa, S., & Allen, R. L. (1998). Norms and politics of equity-minded change: Researching the "zone of mediation." In M. Fullan (Ed.), *International handbook of educational change* (pp. 953–975). Norwell, MA: Kluer Academic Publishers.

Popham, W. J. (2001). *The truth about testing: An educator's call to action.* Alexandria, VA: Association for Supervision and Curriculum Development (ASCD).

Posner, G. J. (1988). Models of curriculum planning. In L. E. Beyer & M. W. Apple (Eds.), *The curriculum: Problems, politics, and possibilities* (pp. 77–97). Albany, NY: State University of New York Press.

Rosner, J. (2003). On white preferences. *The Nation, 276*(14), 24.

Rothstein, R., Ladd, H. F., Ravitch, D., Baker, E. L., Barton, P. E., Darling-Hammond, L., Haertel, E.,…Shepard, L. A. (2010). *Problems with the use of student test scores to evaluate teachers.* Economic Policy Institute. Retrieved from http://www.epi.org/publication/bp278/

Rushton, P. J., & Jensen, A. R. (2005). Thirty years of research on race differences in cognitive ability. *Psychology, Public Policy, and Law, 11*(2), 234–294.

Sacks, P. (1999). *Standardized minds: The high price of America's testing culture and what we can do to change it.* Cambridge, MA: Perseus Books.

Schochet, P. Z., & Chiang, H. S. (2010). *Error rates in measuring teacher and school performance based on test score gains.* Washington DC: U.S. Department of Education, Institute of Educational Sciences, National Center for Educational Evaluation and Regional Assistance. Retrieved from http://ies.ed.gov/ncee/pubs/20104004/pdf/20104004.pdf

Selden, S. (1999). *Inheriting shame: The story of eugenics and racism in America.* New York, NY: Teachers College Press.

Tyack, D. (1974). *The one best system: A history of American Urban Education.* Cambridge, MA: Harvard University Press.

U.S. Department of Education. (2002). *No child left behind: A desktop reference.* Washington, DC: Author.

CHAPTER 3

APPR, SOLUTION OR PROBLEM?

A Critical Examination of Education Law §3012-c

Emily A. Daniels
State University of New York–Plattsburgh

> The New York State Board of Regents has committed to the transformation of the preparation, support, and evaluation of all teachers and school leaders in New York State. Chapter 21 of the Laws of 2012 amended Education Law §3012-c to fundamentally change the way teachers and principals are evaluated. The purpose of the evaluation system is to ensure that there is an effective teacher in every classroom and an effective leader in every school. The evaluation system will also foster a culture of continuous professional growth for educators to grow and improve their instructional practices. (New York State Department of Education, 2012, p. 6)

This reads with such noble purpose and apparent commitment to "educational" goals; the concepts of growth and development, success and effectiveness are woven into this paragraph, which lies at the beginning of Education Law §3012-c. It sounds like such a good idea: Who doesn't want

Left Behind in the Race to the Top, pages 23–36
Copyright © 2013 by Information Age Publishing
All rights of reproduction in any form reserved.

a successful and effective teacher in every classroom? Who doesn't want our teachers to continue to learn and grow as professionals?

As a scholar and an educator, the red flags raised by this paragraph are difficult to ignore. I am a critical scholar, which means that I look differently at the world. I ask more questions, and I see society as interconnected to power relations that tend to serve the interests of the most powerful. I am also an educator; I have the duty (and pleasure) of working with young women and men who hope to enter the world of teaching in the not-so-distant future. I care very much for them, and for the children whom they will serve and nurture in times to come. I also have a deep-seated objection to standardization, tests, and placing people into rubric boxes (which I will explore further throughout this paper). I am therefore very suspicious of educational laws that originate in legislative bodies—far from the hands (and worlds) of educators.

A strong example of this would be the No Child Left Behind legislation, enacted in 2001, with the purported goals of increasing student achievement. Many critiques of this particular law have arisen, due to alarming factors such as higher levels of standardized testing, disparate and unequal impacts on students of color, disproportionate amounts of time spent on test preparation (while sacrificing non-tested subjects), the lack of financial support for districts and teachers, the labeling and closing of "failing" schools, and an increased focus on "accountability" (Darling-Hammond, 2007; Gay, 2007; Hursh, 2007; Kearns, 2011; Kohn, 2004).

Linda Darling Hammond summarizes some of the major challenges with this form of legislation:

> Dubbed *No Child Left Untested, No School Board Left Standing* and *No Child's Behind Left,* among other nicknames, the law has been protested by more than twenty states and dozens of school districts that have voted to resist specific provisions. One state and a national teachers association have brought lawsuits against the federal government based on the unfunded costs and dysfunctional side effects of the law. Critics claim that the law's focus on complicated tallies of multiple-choice-test scores has dumbed down the curriculum, fostered a "drill and kill" approach to teaching, mistakenly labeled successful schools as failing, driven teachers and middle-class students out of public schools and harmed special education students and English-language learners. (2007, p. 2)

When we begin to analyze teachers, students, and the entire profession through certain perspectives, we need to ask deeper questions about what these laws will mean in the everyday worlds of teachers and our students; the NCLB legislation is a prime example of this. The *intentions* and *implementation* of educational laws are often quite divergent (Darling-Hammond, 2007). Additionally, larger forces have become increasingly involved in the control and measurement of public education and educators, and this has been seen as deeply problematic by many critical scholars (Davies, 2005; Leistyna, 2007).

Examples of this include increased length and frequency of standardized tests for students from first grade onward; punitive measures such as publishing data on schools and individual teachers' "performance" (also based solely on standardized test scores); legislation such as No Child Left Behind and Race to the Top, which involve high levels of solely quantitative measures of "success"; and frequent, expensive tests for preservice teachers that may or may not evaluate their abilities to teach effectively.

When new educational policies are implemented, it is important to critically examine them to understand their origins. This approach assists in gaining perspective on the ramifications of new legislation for students, teachers, and our society. Edmonson (cited in Bartolomé, 2008) argues that educators must critically engage with educational policies by examining their origins, the creators of the legislation, the (potential and actual) consequences of the policy, and the benefits and disadvantages. This chapter critically explores Educational Law §3012-c in an effort to inspire greater awareness and concern about the Annual Professional Performance Review (APPR) that has recently become law in New York State.

APPR is designed to evaluate public schools and the teachers and administrators within them. Teachers' assessments are based on their students' test achievement (40%) as well as classroom observations. The new evaluation system involves large amounts of money, as well very difficult decisions about teachers' performance, promotion, hiring and termination of employment. In addition, third party suppliers are offered the potential to create evaluative rubrics (which require training and potentially retraining) and may generate substantial amounts of money for those companies or organizations that submit successful applications and thus become part of the "approved list" (NYSED.gov, 2013). On the New York State Education's Race to the Top website (nysed.gov), there is a specific section that discusses eligibility for rubric-creation, as well as the general guidelines for the APPR process, including plans created by districts to meet these new levels of standardization and control.

I will begin my examination of this new law with the historical contexts of educational reforms in connection to the philosophical standpoints that are important to consider when examining this legislation. I will then move to the law itself, and the different elements that can be analyzed critically and problematized as a result of this. My conclusion will bring these themes together in an exploration of deeper questions and problems within this approach to reform.

HISTORICAL CONTEXTS

It is important to distinguish between children as *human beings* and children as *products* of a capitalist society. As a critical scholar, I believe that education should serve to develop individuals deeply and broadly into strong, mature, critical, thoughtful, caring, and ethical beings. However, narrow concepts of numerical measurement and standardization contradict this standpoint and create a reductionist vision of our children, teachers, and education.

In the early twentieth century, scientific curriculum production became fashionable. At this time, authors such as Franklin Bobbitt and Frederick Taylor urged educators and the public toward the "scientific" development of the curriculum under very distinctive perceptions of education and its purposes that were based within the time and the limitations of their particular standpoints. Bobbitt contributed greatly to the development of the field of curriculum studies, but interspersed throughout his writings is an orientation that focuses on the efficiency of *production*, very much like a factory. In Bobbitt's world, resources must be "managed" and "controlled," and class time and space must be organized down to the specific minute in order to eliminate "waste" (Bobbitt, 1912). Bobbitt also believed that education should target skills necessary for work. This is not surprising, but it violates Deweyian principles of education, in which education is intended to be for the child in the moment, not preparation for becoming something or someone else. In Bobbitt's approach, education prepares children to become workers, instead of more fully developed human beings, demonstrating a production mentality as opposed to a nurturance, growth, and development model.

It is important to note that Bobbitt believed very strongly that science was the answer to every challenge, and measurement and control were crucial factors for success. He states:

> The technique of scientific method is at present being developed for every important aspect of education. Experimental laboratories and schools are discovering accurate methods of measuring and evaluating different types of educational processes. Bureaus of educational measurement are discovering scientific methods of analyzing results, of diagnosing specific situations and of prescribing remedies. Scientific method is being applied to the fields of budget-making, child-accounting, systems of grading, promotion, etc. (1918/2004, p. 11)

This approach to education as precision, control, and measurement was designed with the management of factories as the core goal. Kliebard (2004) points to the *social efficiency movement* in education, which arose as educational reform in response to Industrialization. He states:

> It was social efficiency, that for most people, held out the promise of social stability in the face of cries for massive social change, and that doctrine claimed the now-potent backing of science in order to insure it.... It was a science of exact measurement and precise standards in the interest of maintaining a predictable and orderly world. (p. 76)

The contemporary allure of the rubric to be used in the rating, testing, and evaluation of teachers is based within this production-focused mentality, which emerged in the late 19th and early 20th Century (Au, 2008, Kliebard, 2004). During this time, the management of schools and human beings focused on the efficiency of control. Au (2008) argues that within our educational system, inequality and capitalist approaches to education result in "means to end" education, where "the endpoints of predetermined objectives and/or standards alone drive the educational process (the production of educated students)" (p. 23).

Control and precision, as well as oversimplified concepts of learning contexts and output, were important facets of these developments. As the United States proceeded rapidly into industrialization, the factory became a central metaphor (and life experience) for many people, and the multiple changes within society increased stress as well as the desire to seek easy answers. For example, the transition from small, local economies to larger, industrialized, fast-paced and dehumanizing environments shifted the forms of work that our society practiced as well as valued. Economics, productivity, and the "bottom line" became the predominant factors. Taylorism (on which Bobbitt based much of his work) stresses the "inherent stupidity" of the worker (Littler, 1978). This perception of workers results in simplified tasks, increased monitoring of behaviors, and the encouragement of monetary rewards for expected *production* goals. This is eerily similar to the language regarding APPR, which clearly reflects a factory-oriented view of the educational process. If workers need simplified, organized, and unimaginative tasks because of their "stupidity," what does this say about teachers and children when this perspective is taken into education and the classroom? Isn't there more to educating a child than production skills and goals?

In addition, the concepts of production, evaluation, analysis, and "prescription of remedies" are disturbing when examining children and learning. An orientation based on these concepts implies that children, teachers, and schools are products in need of analysis and "remediation." It implies that a scientific application of a formula or a rubric can produce greater understanding about teachers, children, and education than educators *themselves* can. Furthermore, it dehumanizes students and teachers into "products" of standardized assessment.

Unfortunately the current approach to educational reform epitomized by Education Law §3012-c mirrors this historical standpoint: Measurement, "effectiveness," numerical evaluation, and performance become the sole focus, and the individuals who are deeply involved in and committed to education become byproducts. In the following section, I will discuss the specifics of the law in more depth, and the aspects that cause concern when considered more deeply.

EDUCATION LAW §3012-C

In New York, the Board of Regents is comprised of 17 individuals, elected by the state legislature, who serve five-year terms. The board is comprised of very few K–12 educators, and is elected by the state legislature (which is not generally composed of educators either). The experiences and specialty areas can be examined in more depth on their site: http://www.regents.nysed.gov/members/. To critically analyze educational policies, it is important to understand their origin as well as their influences.

Notes from the June 18, 2012 Board of Regents meeting indicate support for the statement that "every educator has a fair chance to do well on these measures regardless of the composition of his/her class or school" (retrieved from the New York State Board of Regents site: http://www.regents.nysed.gov/meetings/2012Meetings/June2012/GrowthModel.pdf). This is an overly optimistic proclamation because, historically, increased standardization has led to increased inequalities. The belief that standardized test scores, combined with observation, can provide accurate and complete teacher evaluation is flawed. This belief represents an obsession with standardized evaluation formats which claim to "simplify" the assessment process, but do not question the genuine validity and inherent biases in all forms of assessment. In this instance, we must consider the ways in which personalities, histories, and biases will affect observers who claim to be "objective," as well as the ways in which children's backgrounds, abilities, experiences, and school funding will affect their test scores. Classrooms, students, teachers, principals, and schools are unique; all are affected by context. Standardized testing is neither fair nor equal. It is particularly detrimental to historically marginalized students and districts that have fewer resources (Gay, 2007; Ladson-Billings, 2006).

New York State's APPR policy is an attempt to provide common standards and means of evaluation, but this result is unlikely. As mentioned earlier, organizations can create rubrics to evaluate teachers' effectiveness, and rubrics can be "approved" through an application process. While approved rubrics may generate income for sponsoring organizations, the evaluation system generates additional costs for school districts. Rubrics need evaluators, and evaluators need training, and then retraining due to scoring "drift" that occurs over time. In addition, principals require training, and the law states that all teachers must be evaluated on a yearly basis. How will this be implemented in large, complex districts with multiple needs and challenges? Where will the burden fall? What kinds of stresses and demands will emerge?

Teachers and principals should be evaluated and encouraged to develop professionally, but the standardization of the system ignores the disparate realities and social inequalities that persist within our society. It also relegates teachers to a subordinate role—to a place of stress, narrow evaluations, and decontextualized judgment. Teaching is becoming less of profession when it is exposed to extreme levels of monitoring and control. Therefore, the law encourages current concepts of Taylorism, as it promotes the belief in the "stupidity" of the worker as well as the need to evaluate and control "production."

The law is written to divide the evaluations into percentages by year of implementation, 40% of which involves student achievement data (http://public.leginfo.state.ny.us/LAWSSEAF.cgi?QUERYTYPE=LAWS+&QUERY DATA=$$EDN3012-C). For example, the law states that 20% of teachers' performance will be based on standardized tests given by the state, while the other 20% will be evaluated based on "locally selected measures of student achievement" (even more tests?).

The remaining 60% of the evaluation process is determined by visits, observations, surveys, or locally negotiated assessments. The fact that 40% of the teachers' effectiveness relies on test scores does not take into consideration the many factors that can impact student achievement on standardized tests (such as social class, school resources, race, gender, ability, health, access to external resources and support) nor does it consider research that points to the inequalities and biases within the tests themselves. The additional 60% is tremendously profitable for those organizations and individuals that create rubrics for evaluation. It also simultaneously drains human and financial resources from school districts. It will most likely cause challenges, stresses, and issues for the teachers as well as the principals who will be forced to enact it (Larsen, 2009). Below, I delve into further critiques of this problematic legislation. Through these critiques, I hope to enact some discord with the unthinking acceptance of such laws, as they do and will continue to impact students and teachers in negative ways.

CRITIQUING APPR

Under the new law, New York State will differentiate teacher and principal effectiveness using four rating categories – Highly Effective, Effective, Developing, and Ineffective. Education Law §3012-c(2)(a) requires annual professional performance reviews (APPRs) to result in a single composite teacher or principal effectiveness score that incorporates multiple measures of effectiveness. *The results of the evaluations shall be a significant factor in employment decisions, including but not limited to promotion, retention, tenure determination, termination, and supplemental compensation, as well as teacher and principal professional development (including coaching, induction support, and differentiated professional development).* (NYS Department of Education, June, 2012, emphasis added)

This excerpt from the new law implementing APPR states that crucial decisions will be based on annual assessments of teachers. The intention of the new law may be good (I am being generous here, as I believe that laws such as this have more problematic origins such as teacher dominance); however, once again, *implementation* is not the same as *intention*. Educational regulations must take into account the fact that schools and classrooms are complex human spaces that change and alter on a daily basis. Schools are entities of their own; they often are fraught with issues impacting the larger social world. For instance, poverty, emotional issues, relationships, illness, moods, tests, abilities, and racial and gender aspects all influence classrooms.

Because of these challenges and nuances, several issues of concern emerge with legislation such as this. With the historical difficulties surrounding legislation like NCLB, funding and equity are primary concerns with this new round of legislation. As mentioned previously, the laws may sound good, but in actuality may not be implemented in positive ways. In addition, when large amounts of money are exchanged to test and evaluate, there is a need to question whose interests are genuinely being served, and who is profiting from these laws, literally.

Teaching is intricately connected to local context. When a child, a teacher, a parent, or an administrator has a bad day, this will impact the classroom (this is a minor instance—there are much more powerful issues within schools such as lack of resources and funding, children who have needs that are not being met, racist institutions, and violence). Because of this, it is tremendously problematic to observe a teacher on a one-time basis and make powerfully life-changing decisions (as mentioned above in Education Law §3012-c). In addition, standardized test achievement is not necessarily a strong indicator of student growth or learning. Research has consistently revealed the standardized tests have disproportionately harmful effects on students with special needs, English language learners, and students from different socioeconomic statuses. Moreover, these effects result in negative, ineffective classroom practices (Altshuler & Schmautz, 2006; Kearns, 2011; Kohn, 2000; Rothstein et al., 2010).

Another problematic element is that standardized testing alters the core meaning of education. Education becomes an economic stepping stool, where students and teachers are "better products" or "worse products," rather than a source to engage people in the process of growth, understanding and transformation.

Both historically and contemporarily, scholars have struggled with this concept. There are scholars who argue that education can be a place for transformation, criticality, and the development of human beings (Darder, 2002; Freire, 2005; Kincheloe, 2007). There are others who think that education is the place to learn the basic skills, to be socialized properly, and to learn "core" knowledge (Hirsch, 1987). This struggle has been examined as part of larger forces of globalization, neoliberalism, and corporatization (Davies, 2005; McLaren & Kincheloe, 2007; Lipman, 2011; McLaren & Hursh, 2007), as it has been occurring in international contexts. The battle for the meanings and purpose of education has become sharply divided, with those clamoring for "tougher standards" and increased evaluations influencing and creating policies such as APPR in an attempt to simplify the complexities of teaching and schools. The critical standpoint interrogates this false claim. It recenters the discussion on the growth and humanity and the many nuances involved in education. As critical scholars, we point to the necessity of resisting discourses that silence our realities and attempt to assess our practices with faulty and suspect approaches. If all that "counts" is the evaluative test, then most other aspects of the classroom become lost. When we consider the dreams we hold for our youth, expertise at standardized tests, and robotic teachers, are not what we imagine.

By putting teachers and schools so firmly in the grip of narrowed and standardized evaluations, we will hasten the death of creative teaching, of human relationships, and of all of the other facets of growth we hope for our children.

SOLUTION OR PROBLEM?

Teaching involves skill, perception, techniques, relationships, moods, knowledge, heart, humor, and the many nuances of everyday instances. It is stubbornly difficult to measure, and anyone proposing a nice, simple set of boxes by which to evaluate it has either limited understanding of these complexities or a deliberate belief in the monetary benefits accruing to those evaluators who have been "sanctioned" to train and evaluate teachers. This originates in profit-based motives, and neoliberal approaches to "improving" education (or destroying it). As argued by Berliner (2002) regarding educational research,

> Context is of such importance in educational research because of the interactions that abound. The study of classroom teaching, for example, is always about understanding the 10th or 15th order interactions that occur in classrooms. Any teaching behavior interacts with a number of student characteristics, including IQ, socioeconomic status, motivation to learn, and a host of other factors. Simultaneously, student behavior is interacting with teacher characteristics, such as the teacher's training in the subject taught, conceptions of learning, beliefs about assessment, and even the teacher's personal happiness with life. But it doesn't end there because other variables interact with those just mentioned—the curriculum materials, the socioeconomic status of the community, peer effects in the school, youth employment in the area, and so forth. (p. 19)

In the APPR world of assessment, I argue that the evaluation of teachers is over-simplified and the quantitative rubrics will consistently fail to take into account the multiple differences and nuances mentioned above. The impacts of this legislation will lead to greater levels of stress, monetary expenditures, and imperfect evaluations and decisions based on imperfect forms of assessment, and there are additional concerns. If we connect this legislation to a larger social picture regarding the neoliberal involvement in education, this law becomes decidedly less "supportive" and describes more accurately another level of control and surveillance of education, teachers, and students. McLaren, Martin, Farahmandpur, and Jaramillo (2004) argue:

> Whereas one of the basic premises of neoliberal market forces is "small government," educators and community members across the country are experiencing a relentless assault on their autonomy when it comes to participating in purported democratic decision-making processes. Federally engineered testing and accountability systems, instructional program mandates, and the forced militarization of our public high schools point towards highly regulated and controlled governing systems. "At the end of the year, every public school child in grades 3–8 will experience standardized testing that was developed with an estimated pricetag of 2.7 to 7 billion dollars" (Metcalf, 2002). (p. 133)

APPR opens further spaces for the entrance of the corporate model of education, and through legislated surveillance it will continue the attacks on public education at even more levels than previously imagined.

TIGHTENING THE NOOSE: APPR COMES TO COLLEGE

The excerpt provided here is a personal story regarding APPR. It is mean to demonstrate some of the potential challenges and insights via my individual experience within a teacher education program which heartily embraces New York State mandates. Though it is not "data" in the strict sense, stories such as these will become evident and multiply as the process continues. My personal experience with this topic involved an unfortunate workshop which I attended. This event provided rich fodder for my research into this topic. The workshop I attended inspired a strong reaction to APPR because of the many unexamined issues within this legislation. The presenter (who was well paid for his two-day workshop) claimed to come from a standpoint of "supporting" teachers in their development. How can an axe hanging over one's head "support" one's development?

The rubrics presented were complex, and despite "good intentions," frustratingly difficult to imagine in implementation due to all of the human complexities that I have mentioned previously. People are involved in evaluations and people have past histories, prejudices, bad days, grudges, and imperfect evaluative skills (even after training). In fact, within the workshop, the "drift" of numerical assessments was mentioned—as something to retrain (and reprofit from). The presenter mentioned the fact that many principals don't want to rate teachers as "Developing" or "Ineffective" and will tend to err on the side of "niceness" instead of doing so. The presenter also became defensive when I posed written questions that challenged the profit motives within this new law. He laughed when he read my well-phrased question on the problems of neoliberal attacks on schools and teachers, and the problems inherent within the APPR approach. The approach, the underlying capitalism, and the destructive nature of this law were not brought up for genuine discussion or questioning. Instead, uncritical acceptance seemed to be the dominant reaction within the room.

My strong reactions were caused by the language and approach to evaluation, which had none of the aforementioned issues surfaced, examined or discussed, it all sounded too good to be true. This was troublesome to me, because all of this "good" language serves to tighten the noose around the necks of teachers, and potentially dismiss those who don't "uphold policy" and "comply" (this language on upholding policy and compliance is a direct quote from the presentation as well as New York State standards). These are powerful and disturbing words, harkening back to episodes in our collective history where dissenters have been punished for challenging an oppressive system. This is decidedly *not* what education should be about.

Creativity, genuine reflection, thinking, and supportive growth seem to be missing from this process; the human elements are not a facet, they are merely accomplishments or failures. APPR, when examined more critically, does not seem to come from a place of support, but more a space of domination and control. The conclusion will draw together these threads to speak further of the complexities involved.

CONCLUSION

How are we to resist engaging in the neoliberally induced surveillance of ourselves and each other, surveillance that limits, that holds us neatly packaged within economic and utilitarian discourses. How can we dare to ask, in the face of that discourse and its constraints, the questions that unsettle, the questions that disrupt the certainties and securities. (Davies, 2005, p. 7)

In the quote above, the author attests to the importance of questioning, of maintaining contact with our inner voice, especially when it hums with uncertainty and doubt regarding policies that emerge from suspicious standpoints and powerful hands. She also raises the points that I hope to address here, that when we confront these challenges, we may choose to be disturbed, and to speak up and out about what we see.

In fact, the New York Principal's website offers a powerful response to the problematic aspects of APPR. On this site, concerned educators can add their signature to the position paper on APPR and support the resistance to and reexamination of APPR. The paper's author, Sean Feeney, speaks eloquently about the ways in which APPR is being implemented and raises three concerns: the negative impacts on students, the issue of taking tax dollars and using them for trainers and testing companies, and finally the problems with taking student achievement as directly and solely connected to a particular teacher. For more details on this please see: http://www.newyorkprincipals.org/appr-paper. This is a form of resistance and activism when we are confronted with problematic legislation.

We must struggle with important questions about our society, our children, and the multiple meanings of education, as I have explored throughout this chapter, especially if (or when) we need to take action. If we begin to look deeper, and pull back the veil, policies that seem benign may have powerfully negative unintended consequences. They subtract from the main purposes and goals of a socially just education. Questions to revisit: Who originated APPR and who profits most from Education Law§3012-c? Whose knowledge and performance do we trust, and whose are we suspicious of? What is education really for and whom does it serve? Whom should it serve? What does the discussion herein speak to, in terms of children's needs, wants, growth, and abilities as human beings? What is being left out? What does it mean when we purport to "support" teachers, yet rely heavily on economic and factory-based models on the work of teaching, which is changeable, variable, inherently complex and multifaceted, and perhaps not so easily measured? What about testing and the problems with this as "evidence"? All of the factors about our society that are represented in our educational institutions are conveniently ignored through this legislation. Race, class, gender, sexuality, ability, language dominance are all important variables in the educational lives of students and teachers. This law ignores and negates the realities of students and teachers. It is suspiciously limited in its scope and dependent on standardized measurements that ignore the diverse realities that educators operate within. It is also uncomfortably corporate and "scientifically efficient" in the ways in which human beings in complicated contexts are seen as products and evaluated as such. "Success" and "effectiveness" are seen as wedded to tests, rather than environments, relationships, growth, creativity and curiosity, to the detriment of all.

Finally, considering standardized, problematic legislation as a form of encouraging professional growth is akin to forcing physical exertion on 100 degree days; it may "do the trick" or it may cause people to faint from the heat, or stop their hearts in the process. Stress, suffering, and narrow definitions of success are not forms of motivation; they are forms of oppression. As teachers become investigated, assessed, monitored and controlled, the possibilities, spontaneity and deeper learning which our children deserve will suffer. Closely examine your cup before drinking the New York State APPR legislation.

REFERENCES

Altshuler, S. J., & Schmautz, T. (2006). No Hispanic student left behind: The consequences of "high stakes" testing. *Children and Schools, 28*(1), 5–14.

Au, W. (2008). *Unequal by design: High stakes testing and the standardization of inequality.* New York, NY: Routledge.

Bartolomé, L. (2008). Understanding policy for equity in teaching and learning: A critical historical lens. *Language Arts, 85*(5), 376–381.

Berliner, D. D. (2002). Education research: The hardest science of all. *Educational Researcher, 31*(8), 18–20.

Bobbitt, F. (1912). The elimination of waste in education. *The Elementary School Teacher, 12(6),* 259–271.

Bobbitt, F. (2004). Scientific method in curriculum making. In D. J. Flinders & S. J. Thornton (Eds.), *The curriculum studies reader* (2nd ed., pp. 9–16). New York, NY: Routledge. (Original work published in 1918)

Darder, A. (2002). *Reinventing Paulo Freire: A pedagogy of love.* Boulder, CO: Westview Press.

Darling-Hammond, L. (2007). Evaluating 'No Child Left Behind'. *The Nation.* Retrieved from: http://www.thenation.com/doc/20070521/darling-hammond/print?rel=nof

Davies, B. (2005). The (im)possibility of intellectual work in neoliberal regimes. *Discourse: studies in the cultural politics of education, 26*(1), 1–14.

Freire, P. (2005). *Teachers as cultural workers: Letters to those who dare teach.* Boulder, CO: Westview Press.

Gay, G. (2007). The rhetoric and reality of NCLB. *Race, Ethnicity and Education, 10*(3), 279–293.

Hirsch, E. D., (1987). *Cultural literacy: What every American needs to know.* New York, NY: Houghton Mifflin.

Hursh, D. (2007). Assessing No Child Left Behind and the rise of neoliberal education policies. *American Educational Research Journal, 44*(3), 493–518.

Kearns, L. L. (2011). High-stakes standardized testing and marginalized youth: An examination of the impact on those who fail. *Canadian Journal of Education, 34*(2), 112–130.

Kincheloe, J. (2007). Critical pedagogy in the twenty-first century: Evolution for survival. In P. McLaren & J. Kincheloe (Eds.), *Critical pedagogy: Where are we now?* (pp. 9–42). New York, NY: Peter Lang.

Kliebard, H. (2004). *The struggle for the American curriculum: 1893-1958.* New York, NY: RoutledgeFalmer.

Kohn, A. (2000, September). Standardized testing and its victims. *Education Week.* Retrieved from: http://www.alfiekohn.org/teaching/edweek/staiv.htm

Kohn, A. (2004). The case against "tougher standards". Retrieved from http://www.alfiekohn.org/standards/rationale.htm

Ladson-Billings, G. (2006). From the achievement gap to the education debt: Understanding achievement in U.S. schools. *Educational Researcher, 35*(7), 3–12.

Larsen, M. A. (2009). Stressful, hectic, daunting: A critical policy study of the Ontario Teacher Performance Appraisal system. *Canadian Journal of Educational Administration and Policy, 95*, 1–44.

Leistyna, P. (2007). Neoliberal non-sense. In P. McLaren & J. Kincheloe (Eds.), *Critical pedagogy: Where are we now?* (pp. 98–123). New York, NY: Peter Lang.

Littler, C. R. (1978). Understanding Taylorism. *British Journal of Sociology, 29*(2), 185–202.

Lipman, P. (2011, July/August). Neoliberal education restructuring: Dangers and opportunities of the present crisis. *Monthly Review, 63*(3), 114–127.

McLaren, P., Martin, G., Farahmandpur, R., & Jaramillo, N. (2004, Winter). Teaching in and against the empire: Critical pedagogy as revolutionary praxis. *Teacher Education Quarterly, 31*(1), 132–153.

McLaren, P. & Kincheloe, J. (Eds.). (2007). *Critical pedagogy: Where are we now?* New York, NY: Peter Lang.

New York State Education Department. (2012). *Guidance on New York State's annual professional performance review for teachers and principals to implement Education law §3012-c and the commissioner's regulations.* Retrieved from engageny.org/wp-content/uploads/2012/.../APPR-Field-Guidance.pdf

NYSED.gov. (2013). Request for Qualification (RFQ)—Teacher and principal practice rubric providers. Retrieved from http://usny.nysed.gov/rttt/rfq/rubric.html

Rothstein, R., Ladd, H. F., Ravitch, D., Baker, E. L., Barton, P. E., Darling-Hammond, L., Haertel, E.,. . . Shepard, L. A. (2010). *Problems with the use of student test scores to evaluate teachers.* Economic Policy Institute. Retrieved from http://www.epi.org/publication/bp278/

CHAPTER 4

COST-BENEFIT ANALYSES OF HUMAN CAPITAL

Are Value-Added Measures Valid?

Fred Floss
Buffalo State College

Value added models (VAMs) have a long tradition in economics dating back to the early 1960s. Generally, as a part of any undergraduate Cost Benefit Analysis course, students look at the value of human capital and its relationship to education. In these classes, time is spent looking at how to measure both benefits and costs that may not be directly observable (see Gramlich, 1999).

A traditional case study used for analyzing benefits and costs of VAMs is "The Effects of the Perry Preschool Program on Youths through Age 19" (Berrueta-Clement, Barnett, & Weikart, 1984), published using 1963–1967 data regarding disadvantaged students from Ypsilanti, Michigan. The study looked at two groups of children. One group was enrolled in Perry Preschool Program; the other was a control group who featured similar characteristics but did not experience the program. The authors followed students until they were 19 years of age and then analyzed data about the

Left Behind in the Race to the Top, pages 37–47
Copyright © 2013 by Information Age Publishing
All rights of reproduction in any form reserved.

educational achievement of each group with respect to several attributes. Data analysis indicated that students who had participated in the program had earned better grades and had graduated from high school at a greater rate—both positive effects. Next, researchers calculated the net benefits (benefits minus costs) from the program. After conducting the analysis, researchers found a positive net value of approximately $25,000 per student in 1981 dollars. Benefits described included elements such as increased life-time earnings, reduced crime rates, and reductions in welfare costs; costs were the salaries of the teachers and staff, costs of materials, and costs of the facilities. VAMs look at education from the standpoint of net benefits; however, the benefits in this case involve student performance as measured by increased test scores.

Numerous foundations, educational institutions, and policymakers have considered the possibilities and implications of the application of economic principles to the evaluation of social endeavors and policy initiatives. Both Rand and the Brookings Institute, for example, have done similar cost-benefit studies over the last fifty years looking at project evaluation to determine whether various public policies are cost effective.[1] Jacob Mincer first proposed a production function model for evaluating human capital in 1958, and Gary Becker added to the theory in a number of publications.[2] The difference with value added models as applied to the evaluation and ranking of primary and secondary teachers is the scope and complexity of the evaluation, which is much more difficult than these original models.

No Child Left Behind (NCLB) added a greater sense of urgency to the argument for cost-benefit approaches to evaluating teaching and learning in public schools because it asked for measures of average yearly progress (AYP) for students. The implementation of NCLB and AYP intensified attention to standardized assessments for two reasons: In general, AYP reports were based on student performance on standardized tests; furthermore, AYP results determined whether states would maintain federal education funds. Pressure to improve AYP logically led to the question: *How can schools measure and improve AYP?* Since VAMs or cost benefit studies are a traditionally respected means of evaluating different types of policies, they became one of the obvious choices for research. Proponents of VAM, therefore, argue that their individual models represent the best way to measure AYP.

Given this long history, strong beliefs about the efficacy of value added models and their appropriate use for policy have surfaced. Couple this perspective with the availability of vast amounts of public and private funding for these approaches, and it is no wonder researchers with different methods and theories have been attracted to this issue. Groups from Stanford, Virginia, Albany, and Columbia Universities, as well as organizations such as SAS[3] are proposing their own individual models, which they claim to be superior to all others. Other organizations like Educational Testing Services (ETS), Rand, and Brookings have also weighed in on various aspects of the debate surrounding value added models.[4]

Since these models are surrounded by competing claims and campaigns, it is unsurprising that average policymakers, teachers, and parents are confused about what these models show and whether they should be used to rank teachers. To break through some of this confusion, the following sections of this chapter consider a number of questions and how value added models have been used to answer them. Understanding the differences *in the questions asked* will shed light on the major issues surrounding VAMs and their use in ranking teachers and schools. To accentuate the major issues and to not "get lost" in the statistics, the sections below will illuminate complex issues using simple examples. For those seeking to understand more about the statistical analysis, McCaffery, Lockwood, Koretz, and Hamilton (2003) provide a useful explanation of the different models.

WHAT ARE VALUE ADDED MODELS (VAM)?

Value added models or value added growth models are linear, reduced-form equations that purport to show the relationship between a set of variables. In the field of education, these variables typically include individual teachers and the change in test scores of students from one period to the next. As such, VAM is not a single model but a set of models each with unique sets of variables, assumptions, and estimation techniques.

An example of a simple model is:

$$A_t = T_i + \alpha A_{t-1} + \beta X_t + \varepsilon_t$$

where:

- A_t is the current test score;
- A_{t-1} is last periods test score;
- X_t are a set of student characteristics;
- T_i is the teacher effect, one for each teacher;
- ε_t is an error term; and
- α, β are parameters that measure the growth in test scores (α) or the importance of a characteristic (β)

To generate reportable results, the model estimates T_i (the teacher effect), α (the parameters that measure test score growth), and β (the importance of a particular characteristic), using different statistical methods. Next, teachers (T_i) are ranked from high to low and, based on their ranking, assigned to one of five categories known as "quintiles." Teachers' positions in this ranking are then used to determine whether teachers are rewarded with additional pay or punished by being required to participate in remediation plans, for example. In some cases, teachers are promoted or terminated based on rankings. In addition, school effectiveness is often evaluated through VAM, so entire schools are ranked as successful or failing on the basis of VAM results. Therefore, it is important to understand the strengths and weaknesses of these models before these high-stakes tests are used in models that generate results that become public and drive educational policy.

TWO QUESTIONS

The initial question asked by these value added models is: Does teacher quality matter? (Hanushek & Kimbo, 2000; Rubin, 1974). In statistical terms, the question can be phrased as: Is the T_i coefficient statistically different from zero in the model above? If so, teaching matters and enhancing teacher quality is an important educational goal. If T_i is *not* statistically significant, then teacher quality is a statistically insignificant variable. It follows directly that teacher quality does not matter and, plausibly, anyone can teach, regardless of their preparation or experience. To complicate matters further, it is important to consider this question: Even if T_i is statistically significant, does it have a *practical* difference? For example, an effective teacher could add two points to a student's test score, which—from a statistical standpoint—might be important, but this improvement may neither cause nor reflect a significant difference in authentic student achievement. So, not only do these models have to show statistical significance, but they must also show that good teachers make a real life difference in students' lives. Most studies looking into whether teacher quality matters have found that it does (Hanushek & Kimbo, 2000).

The first question, regarding whether teacher quality matters, is very different from the second question: Can VAM be used to rank individual teachers? (Sanders, Saxton, & Horn, 1997). First, if teacher quality does not matter, then ranking cannot matter either. So evaluating the validity of the first question is a critical starting point. The second question requires additional conditions, including the development of a logical ranking system. In essence, to have a fair ranking, like situations must be compared. Comparing student test scores for a teacher who teaches an honors class with a teacher who has a class of special needs students' gives very little information about which teacher is better. In fact, both may be very good at teaching their particular groups, despite their relative rankings. Most models try to take these types of issues into account, and it is in these contexts where most of the disagreement about VAMs occurs.

While most research shows that teacher quality matters, there is less certainty about whether consistent rankings of teachers are achievable (Rothstein, 2010). Rankings must also be stable; if one year a teacher is ranked near the top, then next year that teacher should not be ranked near the bottom. If rankings are not stable, this indicates a high probability that the rankings are misclassifying teachers as high- or low-performing. This state of affairs will lead to policies that create conditions under which high-quality teachers are fired because of poor rankings. Furthermore, it is important to note it is at this point in the VAM implementation process wherein different groups differentiate their models. Each group attacks the others' models as being inaccurate in order to be better positioned to sell their competing model to states and school districts. These conflicts and competitions create confusion about which models are superior—as well as whether any of these models should be used.

Both overarching questions (*Does teacher quality matter?* and *Can VAM be used to rank individual teachers?*) are important and depend on models' effectiveness with respect to their purposes. To be clear, the first question, does teacher quality matter, leads to policy recommendations such as improving pedagogy, developing teacher centers to share effective practices, and developing systems of master teachers to mentor novices in the profession. No ranking system is needed for these initiatives. The second question, whether VAM can effectively rank teachers, leads to recommendations such as firing the bottom 10% of low-performing teachers, closing schools, and shuttering teacher education program that graduate out low-ranking teachers.

The United States public education system must not become confused about these two questions. It would be a costly mistake to use the statistical analysis that supports the first question to implement the reforms coming out of the second question—a contention that has far less support.

THEORIES OF LEARNING AND VAM

There is no underlying theory of learning or instructional method behind these models. VAMs are simply a ranking device for teachers that holds student characteristics (the X) and past test scores constant. Without an underlying theory of *how students' learning occurs* there is no way to understand what the ranking are actually measuring—not to mention the significance or influence of teachers in this (undefined) process. Therefore, the second question, *can VAMs be used for ranking teachers in a fair and stable way,* cannot generate a definitive answer.

Scholarly literature in the field of education has a long history of studying learning theory. How children learn and understanding how to work with children who have different learning styles are critical components of most teacher education program curricula. Therefore, one essential problem for those proposing VAMs is that it is hard to quantify in a single set of measures that reflect various and diverse styles of learning. Students may naturally learn at different rates regardless of the learning environment; once again, because there is no theory behind VAMs, it is hard to craft and interpret models that reflect the diversity and variations of "natural" learning rates. But why is this important in evaluating and ranking teachers? If they are good teachers, shouldn't they be able to get good test scores no matter what learning styles their students have?

A simple example reveals the problem the VAM modeler must take into account in order to generate an unbiased ranking of teachers when different learning styles exist. Table 4.1 shows two groups of students. The example includes Group A, constant learners, who add 10 points to their scores each year; and Group B, students who have a geometric learning style. For the purpose of this example, let us assume that both teachers are exactly the same and that one teaches Group A and the other teaches Group B. However, no one knows this because the learning styles have not been measured. Now, going from year 2 to year 3 in Table 4.1, AYP is the same for both teachers: a 10 point growth in scores. These teachers would be ranked the same by a VAM. Now examine the trend going from year 5 to 6. During this time frame, the AYP of group B is twice that of Group A (22 to 10). Teacher B now is considered twice as good as Teacher A. The obvious question that will arise is *what has happened to Teacher A?* Administrators and policymakers might also wonder whether Teacher A should be subject

TABLE 4.1   Student Test Scores by Learning Style Group

Year	Student Test Scores A	Student Test Scores B	AYP A	AYP B
0	10	0		
1	20	2	10	2
2	30	8	10	6
3	40	18	10	10
4	50	32	10	14
5	60	50	10	18
6	70	72	10	22
7	80	98	10	26
8	90	128	10	30
9	100	162	10	34
10	110	200	10	38

to a remediation plan, or whether additional professional development is warranted. But continued examination of data indicates that test scores in year 6 are essentially the same: group A has a score of 70 and Group B a score of 72. If we look at year 2 to make the comparison, the results would be exactly the opposite. So who should be ranked the better teacher?

In a more realistic world, there would be many more groups and they would be mixed at different years in any given class. Looking at the two-group example, if more Group B students who were at year 6 are added, this would tend to raise a teacher's ranking and vice versa. Remember, both teachers are assumed equal in quality and effectiveness in this example, but under different groupings of students, teacher A can be ranked higher, lower, or the same as teacher B. This type of issue will surface over and over again; the ranking measures are, in mathematical terms, inconsistent.

The issue is fundamental: Without an underlying theoretical model and appropriate system of structural equations, there is no way to understand *what VAMs actually model* or *whether the rankings are based on teacher quality*. Having a theory of learning styles and how teacher impact different styles of students might have a profound impact on how well students learn. Not connecting the underlying theory with the individual model will only lead to incorrectly interpreting any VAM.

To circumvent this issue, modelers make certain statistical assumptions. One assumption is that students are considered to be randomly selected or homogeneously grouped. If correct, these would be the conditions that must be true for students to be aggregated into a single class taught by the teacher. But this calculation misses the point; without modeling learning theory explicitly, there is no way to test whether these assumptions hold. Instead, data based on erroneous assumptions become a way of deflecting criticism and justifying a particular VAM (see Table 4.1).

There are examples outside the VAM literature that do look at the impact of changing methodology and pedagogy on student outcomes. Spector and Mazzeo (1980) model the effectiveness of teaching economics using new methods. These studies look at different groups who employed the new method as compared to a control group. This is much more difficult to do than a VAM without control groups, because most VAMs use data that are already being collected. The added value of looking at methodology directly is that results of the models can be used to improve teacher quality for all levels of teachers.

EDUCATION POLICY AND VAM

What is the appropriate role of VAMs, and how should they be used in determining who should teach? In almost all concluding sections of VAM studies, the authors suggest that these models should not be used by themselves as the sole evaluation method for a given teacher. They then go on to give a long list of additional research that should be done because of problems associated with VAMs.

Given this explicitly complex context, why have policymakers rushed to impose VAMs as the central evaluation method? Part of the answer may be that with the push for accountability, the appearance of scientific accuracy makes VAMs an easy sell with the public. VAMs also offer a relatively straightforward turnkey implementation process that can be purchased from a university or testing company. VAMs look like a simple solution with very little downside, since the statistical arguments are so complex and the discussions on assumptions are so easy to hide.

Demographic shifts in the United States are also playing a role in the need for tangible proof that taxpayers are getting a good value from their public education system. When the baby boom generation was in school, most taxpayers had a direct connection to their public schools and those teachers who taught their children and grandchildren. This is less true today, as most taxpayers have little connection with schools and are, therefore, more open to the idea of asking for proof.

A major problem policymakers face is that the simple solution of just using a VAM ranking may lead to misclassifying teachers and firing high-quality teachers. As shown in the graphic, depending on the case, either teacher A and B may be deemed underachieving and fired even though they are of equal effectiveness. If this discrepancy becomes clear to college students who want to become teachers, they may stop going into teacher education programs and a teacher shortage may ensue. Instead of improving the quality of teachers, VAMs will have the opposite effect.

Before a policy on VAMs can be propagated, clarity must be sought with respect to two key questions: *Do teachers matter?* and *Can VAMs rank individual teachers?* If VAMs are used to help put together programs to improve teaching or create better methods over diverse sets of students, then VAMs could make an important contribution to educating our children. On the other hand, if the rankings are published and used only to punish low-ranking teachers or used to attack funding for public education, VAMs will have a detrimental impact. Like so many things, VAMs are nothing more than a tool whose impact depends on the care and purposes with which they are used.

NOTES

1. For example, see King and Smith (1988) and Haycock, Lankford, and Olson (2004).

2. Mincer (1958) and Becker (1964) study how an individual's labor value can be increases. The value added models that use a regression model based on variables which explain increases in test scores are just a variation on these original models.
3. SAS stands for Statistical Analysis System and is owned by SAS Inc. which also does consulting work in a number of areas including VAMs.
4. Braun, H. (2005) is a good review of these models.

APPENDIX

1. Checklist of Major Issues with VAMs
   a. VAMs are trying to measure teacher quality quantitatively in a linear manner when the underlying reality is that qualitative issues and nonlinearity are the hallmark of the educational system.
   b. VAMs single out teachers as the only important input into the process; therefore, curriculum, funding, or learning styles do not matter in these models.
   c. VAMs, other than the set of characteristics, assume students are homogeneous in how they learn and how they test and the rate at which they learn.
   d. VAM results are dependent on the test and test design, so rankings are dependent on which test is used and what year the test is given. If the research using NYC data is the only measure of issues used, these results may not hold in the rest of the state.
   e. VAM rankings will change with the cohort chosen to compare teachers, so this choice is important.
   f. VAMs are all partial equilibrium in nature. They do not take into account the dynamic impacts on the supply of new teachers. If teachers are risk-averse, then good college students may not enter the profession.
   g. One important nonlinearity is the matching of teachers or sets of teachers with certain groups of students. Do these teachers get better results because of their personality or the personalities of their students?
   h. VAMs will rank teachers lower who keep low-performing students in school.
   i. VAMs are only a part of the overall evaluation, but they will influence the rest of the process. For example, if a principal knows of a low ranking, this will color the qualitative part of the evaluation.

    j. No one has tested or researched VAM methodology with high-stakes tests; the results may be very different.

2. How are VAMs Related to Teacher Preparation?

    a. The implications for academic freedom are unclear, how will the use of VAMs affect the ability for faculty to teach students in the most appropriate way if they have no input into the review system.

    b. How will VAMs change curriculum over time? Will the test cause stagnation in curriculum development?

    c. What is the relationship between training and education in teacher education programs, and will the VAM decide the mix?

    d. How will VAMs relate to the evaluation of teacher education programs given the concerns above and the fact that little research in this area has been done?

REFERENCES

Becker, G. (1964). *Human Capital.* New York, NY: NBER.

Berrueta-Clement, J., Barnett, W. S., & Weikart, D. P. (1984). *The effects of the Perry Preschool Program on youth through age 19.* Ypsilanti, MI: High Scope Educational Research Foundation.

Braun, H. (2005). *Using student progress to evaluate teachers: A primer on value-added models.* Princeton, NJ: Educational Testing Service.

Gramlich, E. (1990). *A guide to benefit-cost analysis* (2nd ed.). Englewood Cliffs, NJ: Prentice Hall.

Hanushek, E., & Kimbo, D. (2000). Labor force quality and the growth of nations. *American Economics Review, 90*(1), 1184–1208.

Hanushek, E., & Rivkin, S. G. (2010). *Using value added measures of teacher quality.* London, UK: Calder.

Haycock, K., Lankford, H., & Olson, L. (2004). The elephant in the livivng room. *Brookings Papers on Education Policy, 7,* 229–263.

King, E., & Smith, J. P. (1988). *Computing economic loss in cases of wrongful death.* Santa Monica, CA: Rand.

McCaffrey, D., Lockwood, J., Koretz, D., & Hamilton, L. S. (2003). *Evaluating value added models for teacher accountability.* Santa Monica, CA: Rand.

Mincer, J. (1958). Investment in Human Capital and Personal Income Distribution. *Journal of Political Economy, 66*(4), 281–302.

Rothstein, J. (2010). Teacher quaility in educational production: Tracking, decay and student achievement. *Quarterly Journal of Economics,* 175–214.

Rubin, J. (1974). Estimating causal effects of treatments in randomized and non-randomized studies. *Journal of Education Psychology, 66,* 688–701.

Sanders, W. L., Saxton, A., & Horn, B. (1977). The Tennessee Value Added Assesment System: A Quantitative Approach to Educational Assesment. In J.

Millman (Ed.), *Grading teachers, grading schools: student achievement a valid evaluational measure?* (pp. 137–162). Thousand Oaks, CA: Corwin Press.

Spector, L., & Mazzeo, a. M. (1980). Probit Analysis and Economic Education. *Journal of Economic Education, 11*, 37–44.

CHAPTER 5

THE NATIONAL COUNCIL ON TEACHER QUALITY

Judges With an Agenda

Anthony Cody

ORIGINS

Schools of education have traditionally been responsible for preparing the next generation of teachers, but not everyone is happy with that. For more than a decade, efforts have been under way to weaken or displace them, for mostly ideological reasons. The National Center for Teaching Quality (NCTQ) has emerged as a leading critic of schools of education. The NCTQ has positioned itself as a judge issuing reports and "grades" reflecting its appraisal of schools of education. One might expect a judge to be an impartial arbiter, but this nonprofit organization has its origins in a decidedly partisan corner of the battle over the future of our schools.

Diane Ravitch has shared with us her story of the National Council on Teacher Quality. Ravitch is an unusual informant; she was on the inside of the conservative movement, so she has a perspective few of us share. According to Ravitch, NCTQ was created by the Thomas B. Fordham (TBF) Foundation because

Left Behind in the Race to the Top, pages 49–61
Copyright © 2013 by Information Age Publishing
All rights of reproduction in any form reserved.

We thought [schools of education] were too touchy-feely, too concerned about self-esteem and social justice and not concerned enough with basic skills and academics. In 1997, we had commissioned a Public Agenda study called "Different Drummers"; this study chided professors of education because they didn't care much about discipline and safety and were more concerned with how children learn rather than what they learned. TBF established NCTQ as a new entity to promote alternative certification and to break the power of the hated ed schools. (Ravitch, 2012, para. 11)

To understand NCTQ, we need to understand the agenda behind those who invented it. Here is how the Fordham Institute's president, Chester Finn, described its approach back in 2001:

For years, the conventional wisdom about how to boost teacher quality has been to tighten the regulatory screws: impose more requirements, demand longer training programs, and generally focus on inputs. We've been promoting a different approach, one that relies on less regulation, greater freedom and more accountability for results. (Finn, 2002, p. 18)

This drive for results-based accountability is familiar to everyone who has lived in the environment created by No Child Left Behind at around this same time. NCLB was designed to highlight the supposed weaknesses of public schools by the use of standardized tests, and ever-rising annual proficiency goals. Schools that did not meet their targets were labeled, and subject to closure. The NCTQ has applied this test-centered approach in its efforts to transform (or replace) schools of education in a parallel fashion.

Mr. Finn explains what might be called a strong-arm approach to reform:

We shun two other popular theories of education reform that, in our experience, simply do not work to change institutions, alter behavior, or boost academic achievement. More money—absent standards and markets—won't make a difference. It's just paying the same people more to do the same things. And we've seen little evidence that the addition of more "expertise" to the present system will by itself bring about the needed reforms. That's because, with rare (and happy) exceptions, the present system does not much want to change. Hence we favor strategies that, in effect, force it to. (Finn, 2002, p. 6)

In this statement, Mr. Finn states the hallmark objectives of those seeking to "reform" the teaching profession. Funding is to be cut, because money is not the problem, and teacher expertise is irrelevant. The intent is to force change by using the power of the market. The grand vision is to use test scores to create a means of measuring, rewarding, and punishing all aspects of the educational system, including schools of education. The Fordham report cited above repeatedly characterizes their work as part of a "war of ideas." If this is a war, then NCTQ is a decidedly partisan player—a small battalion even. But the group takes pains to draw a different picture. Their website states: "Our Board of Directors and Advisory Board are composed of Democrats, Republicans and Independents, all of whom believe that the teaching profession is way overdue for significant reform in how we recruit, prepare, retain and compensate teachers" (http://www.nctq.org/p/about/index.jsp).

Press reports often echo NCTQ's description of themselves as "non-profit, nonpartisan." They are "nonpartisan" in the narrow Democrat vs. Republican dichotomy, but in the war of ideas launched by conservatives at the Fordham Foundation, they are surely among the warriors.

The NCTQ receives funding from dozens of wealthy philanthropies, such as the Broad Foundation and Gates Foundation (http://www.nctq.org/p/about/funders.jsp).

The thrust of the work of NCTQ is through reports that it issues. These reports are the bread and butter of the nonprofit think tank world. They are used to influence the public and policymakers and to give legislators clear talking points to support policy initiatives they wish to advance.

The first major report issued by NCTQ, "Teacher Certification Reconsidered, Stumbling for Quality," was released in 2001. This report criticized many aspects of teacher preparation programs. The authors criticized the research supporting the value of certification and claimed that there was no evidence that certified teachers were any better than uncertified ones. They suggested that the state of Maryland should "devolve its responsibility for teacher qualification and selection to its 24 public school districts."

After surveying the coursework, the authors decided that much of it was unrelated to what they termed "teacher effectiveness." It is important to note that the term "teacher effectiveness" is used to describe the ability of a teacher to raise student test scores. The executive summary of the report states:

> The teacher attribute found consistently to be most related to raising student achievement is *verbal ability*.
>
> Most researchers understand verbal ability, usually measured by short vocabulary tests, to be a measure of a teacher's general cognitive ability. Recent research has altered significantly our understanding of cognitive ability or intelligence. A person's cognitive ability is no longer understood to be an exclusively innate quality that depends entirely on our genetic composition at birth. Verbal ability is to some degree plastic in nature, capable of being improved at all levels of schooling, including college.
>
> Not surprisingly, the importance of verbal ability aligns with similar findings that teachers who have attended selective colleges are more likely to raise student achievement. (Walsh, 2001, p. v)

The report recommended that the state it focused on "should eliminate the coursework requirements for teacher certification, in favor of much simpler and more flexible rules for entry." This corresponds with their stated lack of confidence in "expertise."

It also suggested, "As an accountability measure, the Maryland Department of Education should report the average verbal ability score of teachers in each school district and of teacher candidates graduating from the State's schools of education" (Walsh, 2001). According to the authors, verbal ability is "usually measured by short vocabulary tests" (Walsh, 2001). Thus, in their view, the primary means we ought to use to determine who has promise as a teacher is a vocabulary quiz. Once again, test scores are the determining factor, no matter the challenge.

The report is hard to take seriously in part because of the blinkered definition of teacher effectiveness—and this flaw is apparent in all of NCTQ's work. The only effect ever addressed is "student achievement," which, in turn, is only ever measured by an annual standardized test score. There are many "effects" that we hope our teachers have on students that are not captured by a test score. As Richard Rothstein pointed out in his book, *Grading Education, Getting Accountability Right*, society has a host of goals it expects our schools and teachers to achieve. He offers this list:

> Basic academic skills and knowledge
> Critical thinking and problem solving
> Appreciation of the arts and literature
> Preparation for skilled employment
> Social skills and work ethic
> Citizenship and community responsibility
> Physical health
> Emotional health (Rothstein, 2008)

Of these, we only even attempt to measure the first through our very imprecise standardized tests. To use these test scores as the source of our definition of teacher effectiveness is to commit a colossal error, and it is one that plagues all of NCTQ's work. The use of test scores is the means by which "market forces" can be used—so that "ineffective" public schools and teachers can be identified and driven out, to be replaced by more efficient charter schools, and more "effective" teachers.

One part of No Child Left Behind was the idea that every child ought to have a "highly qualified teacher." One might think that this definition would include some form of formal teacher training, but the report from the NCTQ was actually used to discredit such formalities in favor of "alternative certification" of the sort practiced by Teach For America.

Linda Darling-Hammond authored a response to this report, in which she noted:

> Although these ideas might seem preposterous to those who are engaged in research regarding teacher preparation and recruitment, the U.S. Secretary of Education echoed these recommendations in his Annual Report on Teacher Quality (USDOE, 2002), a report on the national state of teacher quality required under the 1998 reauthorization of Title II of the Higher Education Act. In this report, the Secretary argued that teacher certification systems are "broken," imposing "burdensome requirements" for education coursework that make up "the bulk of current teacher certification regimes" (p. 8). The report argues that certification should be redefined to emphasize higher standards for verbal ability and content knowledge and to de-emphasize requirements for education coursework, making attendance at schools of education and student teaching optional and eliminating "other bureaucratic hurdles" (Darling-Hammond, 2002, p. 2)

As a teacher in Oakland, I saw the effects of this shift away from traditionally certified teachers firsthand. At the same time we became ever more focused on test scores, our district expanded the use of poorly trained teachers from Teach For America and other alternative certification programs. The rationale was laid out by NCTQ. We should get people into classrooms from "selective colleges," and formal teacher preparation should not be a barrier.

This was not a winning strategy for our high-poverty students. Since, according to one study, 57% of TFA corps members do not intend to make teaching their career, the vast majority left after working just two or three years (Donaldson & Moore Johnson, 2011). There were many reasons that classrooms in Oakland were hard to staff—mostly related to inadequate pay and resources and tough teaching conditions. These conditions were left unchanged, and the federal government allowed teachers with "intern credentials" to be designated as "highly qualified," even though they arrived with only about five weeks of training.

Effective teachers have a solid grasp of both their subject matter and a range of instructional strategies to draw upon to challenge and engage their students. They are able to manage the classroom well and set a solid environment for learning. It takes several years to develop these skills, so creating a revolving door in high-poverty schools is no help. Furthermore, recent research has highlighted the high cost of turnover. A report in *Education Week* provided a summary of the findings:

- For each analysis, students taught by teachers in the same grade-level team in the same school did worse in years where turnover rates were higher, compared with years in which there was less teacher turnover.

- An increase in teacher turnover by 1 standard deviation corresponded with a decrease in math achievement of 2% of a standard deviation; students in grade levels with 100 percent turnover were especially affected, with lower test scores by anywhere from 6% to 10% of a standard deviation based on the content area.
- The effects were seen in both large and small schools, new and old ones.
- The negative effect of turnover on student achievement was larger in schools with more low-achieving and Black students (Sawchuck, 2012).

I created a program in my urban district to attempt to stem the turnover tide among new teachers, but it was tough going for several reasons. Oakland has been among the lowest-paid districts in the area for years, so if you wish to remain in the classroom, it is to your advantage to shift to a better paying district. Conditions in many Oakland schools are challenging, due to the high level of poverty and violence that afflicts these neighborhoods. Added to this, the majority of our new teachers, who were either from TFA or other alternative certification programs, had not made a career choice. They made a short-term commitment, and once their two years were up, they were gone (Cody, 2011).

THE BATTLE OVER NCLB

In the middle of the last decade, criticism of NCLB was becoming more and more widespread. The Department of Education began searching for allies in the public arena. The federal government is not supposed to use public funds to conduct "propaganda" to sway public opinion about its policies. An investigation was conducted by the Inspector General into the use of public funds granted to NCTQ in 2005, and it provides us with a window on a very cozy relationship at work. NCTQ partnered with the Oquirrh Institute to receive a Department of Education grant in the amount of $677,318. The rules include something called the Education Department General Administrative Regulations (EDGAR), which require a disclaimer to accompany any publication paid for with public funds.

The Inspector General's report said that the Oquirrh Institute and NCTQ received funding for publishing op-eds "on teacher quality issues," aligned with the Department of Education's policies. The Inspector General's report did not find that these op-eds were "covert propaganda," although they did not include the required disclaimers. I do not know if any action was ever taken to recover these funds (Higgins, 2005).

NCTQ Grades the States on Teacher Quality

The NCTQ set itself the task of serving as the judge and jury for policies affecting teacher quality across the country, and began issuing reports and letter grades on a state by state basis. The organization issues an annual "State of the States" report that awards letter grades to each state according to how well they align with NCTQ's policy objectives. The 2011 report makes these objectives clear:

> The move to rethink how to evaluate a teacher's performance and explicitly tie assessments of teacher performance to student achievement marks an important shift in thinking about teacher quality. The demand for "highly qualified" teachers is slowly but surely being replaced by a call for highly effective teachers. This change is significant because policymaking around improving teacher quality to date has focused almost exclusively on a teacher's qualifications—i.e., teacher credentials, majors, degrees and licensing. Those criteria would be all well and good if they were associated with positive gains in student learning. Unfortunately, by and large, they are not. (State of the States, NCTQ, 2011, p. 2)

Of course, "positive gains in student learning" sounds better than "increased test scores." But in just about every case, test scores are the indicator being used. The yearbook also singles out Florida for praise because it "connects student achievement gains [test scores] to teacher preparation programs."

In the section on "Identifying Effective Teachers," NCTQ states as its goal:

> The state should either require a common evaluation instrument in which evidence of student learning is the most significant criterion or specifically require that student learning be the preponderant criterion in local evaluation processes. Evaluation instruments, whether state or locally developed, should be structured to preclude a teacher from receiving a satisfactory rating if found ineffective in the classroom. (State of the States, NCTQ, 2012, p. 7)

They go on to explain, "Teacher evaluations should consider objective evidence of student learning, including not only standardized test scores but also classroom-based artifacts such as tests, quizzes and student work" (ibid).

In practice, however, "effectiveness" is almost always reduced to the ability of a teacher to produce test score gains. And every dimension of education, from teacher preparation, to teacher evaluation and to the decisions to grant tenure, is driven to measure and reward "effectiveness."

Individual states also were the focus of specific reports that reviewed how well their programs and policies matched up with NCTQ's criteria. The findings of these reports were often then carried by local newspapers as authoritative. Schools of education were often the focus of these reports, and in some cases they responded.

A publication that represents a collaborative of schools of education, Eduventures, offered its own critique of the NCTQ report on Illinois:

> The majority of NCTQ's standards are not supported by evidence and appear to be broadly subjective. In its *Guide to Ratings Methodologies*, NCTQ frequently couches its rationale with nuances such as "While there is no research basis for this..." (rationale provided for Standard 9), or "While there is no research evidence..." (rationale provided for Standard 13 and 25A). Rather than providing evidence, the rationale NCTQ provides for many standards appears to be opinion-based, and, in some cases, the rationale includes broad generalizations that many experts would recognize as untrue. One example of this might be found in NCTQ's rational for Standard 2: "Teacher preparation programs are...perceived to be the easiest major or program on any campus." Stating such a claim in a rationale for the standard "The coursework has a seriousness of purpose" seems to highlight NCTQ's inherent bias and unique viewpoint. Such subjectivity and generalizations in each standard's stated rationale should be taken into consideration when reviewing NCTQ's findings. (Eduventures, 2010, p. 3)

A publication called Catalyst Chicago interviewed authors Kate Walsh and Julie Greenburg about the controversy over the report, and one of the answers was especially revealing.

> **Catalyst:** You also noted an overabundance of personal reflection activities that seem disconnected from teaching practice.
>
> **Greenberg:** You want to have a reflective professional. There's reflection, and then there's using data, collaborating with colleagues...all those real indicators that somebody is actually going to be modifying their practice. There's no sitting down with data from an Illinois standardized test and saying, "You just found out that your students are one standard deviation below the mean. How is that going to affect your instruction?" That's what reflection means to us. (Harris, 2010, para. 16)

Once again we see that test data is the *only* thing NCTQ sees as worthy of consideration. In my own preparation as a teacher, it was hugely important for me to reflect on and discuss many issues beyond my students' test score data. My goal was to fight social inequity—to give my students a chance in a society that has, in many ways, set them up for failure. The path to their academic success requires us to deal with many issues beyond test performance. Teachers, especially novices, must reflect on all sorts of social and cultural dynamics that are at play in the classroom. Why are some of our students angry? How can we make sure the girls are participating in class discussions? How about our English learners? How do our students perceive the discipline system we are using? How am I, as a middle-class, white male teacher, going to create a nurturing environment for all my students? These are deep questions, not easily answered. Part of our journey as teachers is to reflect on these sorts of things continually, and it is crucial that this be included in our preparation process.

NCTQ EVALUATES SCHOOLS OF EDUCATION

The work of NCTQ continues to seek to reshape schools of education. Their current project is to "evaluate" 180 schools of education in the country, to be released in the fall of 2012, lent weight by their partnership with *US News and World Report*. In advance of this evaluation, they released a report in May of 2012 titled: "What Teacher Preparation Programs Teach About K–12 Assessment." The report highlights as models districts that have won the Broad Prize, such as Charlotte-Mecklenburg (North Carolina):

> All educators in CMS are trained in Data Wise, a structured system to improve instructional and organizational practices based on data, and every school has a data team. Teachers, administrators and coaches can access a wide variety of learning data on the district's online learning portal, which gives them the capacity to meaningfully track student performance and adapt quickly to learning difficulties. (Greenberg & Walsh, 2012, p.3)

The reports states, "It is fair to say that the school districts in the nation that do the best in the face of the challenge of educating disadvantaged students have become obsessive about using data to drive instruction" (ibid).

In spite of this unequivocal statement, the report describes the research that might support this approach as "emerging," and only finds one study that offers very weak evidence of success. The authors must have missed the recent report from the National Research Council, "Incentives and Test-Based Accountability" (Hout & Elliott, 2011), which found little to no growth has resulted from becoming obsessive over test data.

The lack of encouraging research does not stop them from defining three dimensions of assessment on which schools of education are to be rated. These are:

> Domain #1: Assessment Literacy: An understanding of the taxonomy of assessment and a familiarity with the different types of classroom and standardized assessment.
> Domain #2: Analytical Skills: Understanding how to dissect, describe, and display the data that emerge from assessments.
> Domain #3: Instructional Decision Making: An understanding of how to derive instructional guidance from assessment data.

The report complains that most education school programs do not develop these domains adequately, and in particular, they favor classroom assessment practices, neglecting data from standardized tests.

One gets an idea of how political this has become when one hears how NCTQ founder and report author Kate Walsh characterizes the results: "A lot of schools of education continue to become quite oppositional to the notion of standardized tests, even though they have very much become a reality in K–12 schools. The ideological resistance is critical" (Resmovits, 2012, para. 8). It is apparent that since high-stakes tests have become the norm in our schools, Ms. Walsh believes schools of education ought to fall into line and drop any resistance. The evaluations NCTQ is preparing are one piece of pressure.

Though the administration has changed in Washington since 2001, the Department of Education under Arne Duncan has continued to follow the same pattern as the NCTQ. For the next iteration of Race to the Top, Duncan wishes to create a system to measure the Value Added scores for graduates of teacher preparation programs and reward programs that yield high-scoring teachers and punish those that fail to make the grade (Duncan, 2012).

Our schools of education ought to be in a position to think clearly and freely about the challenges our schools face. They are certainly not perfect, but their ability to take an independent stance on education policies and practices is crucial for us to avoid a complete groupthink. In particular, skepticism about the wisdom of obsessing over test data is a very healthy thing, and efforts to forcefully suppress this are a threat to academic freedom, as well as the true quality of education.

THE ROLE OF THE THINK TANK

Schools of education are only loosely connected to the public education system as a whole, and thus have not been directly impacted by sweeping reforms such as NCLB. However, their position is vulnerable, because they depend on support from legislators and policymakers. These decision-makers are the targets for the think tanks such as NCTQ, as Kevin Welner explains here:

> Think tank reports have become widely influential for policymakers and the media. Their influence is due not to the superiority of their research but rather to the think tanks' proficiency at packaging and marketing their publications—many of which are of very weak quality. We have found that these advocacy reports have often attained greater prominence than the most rigorously reviewed articles addressing the same issues published in the most respected research journals. This should be a matter of concern. If all documents la-

beled "research" are indiscriminately received and reported as of equal worth, without review or critique by independent experts, their value is obviously not dependent on quality or rigor. These attributes are beside the point. Value is instead tightly linked to the ability of the researchers to gain attention and influence policy. Private think tanks, which produce their own in-house, non-refereed research, accordingly become sensible investments for individuals and groups hoping to advance their agendas. (Welner, 2011, p. 41)

Several years ago, I interviewed Stanford professor emeritus J. Myron Atkin about the role research plays related to educational policy. He said,

Education policy, like all social policy, is undergirded by a set of values. Scientifically based educational research seldom addresses the often conflicting underlying values. It can't. Yes, education research can inform a decision about whether a particular method of teaching Newton's Laws seems more effective than another, but only if there is agreement about what should be taught about Newton's Laws. . . . And different people bring different values to the table. Scientific research alone is insufficient. What works is a different matter from what is of worth. Scientifically driven research can sometimes contribute to deciding the former. It is of little value with the latter. (Cody, 2009, para. 4)

In the case of NCTQ, we have an organization that has been built to be a partisan vehicle in the war of ideas within education—but it covers itself in the nonpartisan, objective garb of social science. Those that fund NCTQ also fund other groups that advance the same test-driven education reform education reform agenda. There are core values that are embedded in the criteria NCTQ uses to evaluate policies related to teacher quality, but these values are not subject to question. Teacher "effectiveness" is invariably presented as the only conceivable goal, and the role of tests in driving education is never questioned. Ironically, while the NCTQ positions itself as an advocate of teacher quality, it has supported the expansion of programs like Teach For America that specialize in bringing poorly trained novices to low-income schools.

NCTQ is part of the broad campaign to establish test scores as the primary means of ranking students, teachers, and schools. This ranking is then used to manage people and schools in a top-down fashion and to justify rewards and punishments. The use of test scores in this manner undermines the many other goals we have for our schools, and although advocates of this approach often include greater access to equitable outcomes for the poor and disenfranchised, in practice, these policies often have the opposite result.

The landscape has changed a bit since NCTQ issued its first report more than a decade ago. Advocates for public education have become far more aware of the threat that standardized tests and "market-based" solutions pose. Conservative think tanks such as NCTQ face a far greater level of skepticism, and critics have begun to educate the media and public so that their claims are not taken at face value. The war of ideas regarding what we should value in our schools is far from over, but the judges' robes of NCTQ have been torn away to reveal the partisan uniform beneath.

REFERENCES

Cody, A. (2009, October). Interview with Dr. Atkin: Why is research trumped by politics? *Living in Dialogue.* Retrieved from http://blogs.edweek.org/teachers/living-in-dialogue/2009/10/interview_with_dr_atkin_why_is.html

Cody, A. (2011, January). TeamScience tames teacher turnover. *Living in Dialogue.* Retrieved from http://blogs.edweek.org/teachers/living-in-dialogue/2011/01/teamscience_tames_teacher_turn.html

Darling-Hammond, L. (2002). "Research and rhetoric on teacher certification: A response to "Teacher Certification Reconsidered." *Education Policy Analysis Archives, 10*(36). Retrieved from http://epaa.asu.edu/epaa/v10n36.html.

Donaldson, M., & Moore Johnson. (2011). TFA Teachers: How Long Do They Teach? Why Do They Leave? *Phi Delta Kappan.* Retrieved from http://www.edweek.org/ew/articles/2011/10/04/kappan_donaldson.html?intc=mcs

Duncan, A. (2012, February). Teachers get R-E-S-P-E-C-T. Retrieved from http://www.ed.gov/news/speeches/teachers-get-r-e-s-p-e-c-t

Eduventures. (2010, September). Review and critique of NCTQ and Advance Illinois study on Illinois teacher preparation programs. Retrieved from http://www.eduventures.com/services/learning-collaboratives/schools-of-education/illinois-teacher-preparation-programs

Finn, C. E. (2002). *Thomas B. Fordham Foundation Five-Year Report 1997–2001.* http://www.edexcellencemedia.net/publications/2002/200205_tbfffiveyear/report.pdf

Greenberg, J., & Walsh, K. (2012). What teacher preparation programs teach about K–12 assessment: A review. Retrieved from http://www.nctq.org/edschoolreports/assessment/report.jsp

Harris, R. (2010). *Q&A with National Council on Teacher Quality.* Catalyst Chicago. Retrieved from http://www.catalyst-chicago.org/notebook/2010/11/15/qa-national-council-teacher-quality

Higgins, J. (2005). Review of department identified contracts and grants for public relations services, final inspection report. Retrieved from http://www.ed.gov/about/offices/list/oig/aireports/i13f0012.doc

Hout, M., & Elliott, S. (Eds.). (2011). Incentives and test-based accountability in education. Retrieved from http://www.nap.edu/catalog.php?record_id=12521

Paige, R. (2002). *Meeting the Highly Qualified Teachers Challenge: The Secretary's Annual Report on Teacher Quality.* Retrieved from: http://www2.ed.gov/about/reports/annual/teachprep/2002title-ii-report.pdf

Ravitch, D. (2012, May 23). What is NCTQ? [blog]. Retrieved from http://dianer-avitch.net/2012/05/23/what-is-nctq/

Resmovits, J. (May, 2012). Education schools' training on standardized tests found lacking in new report. *Huffington Post.* Retrieved from http://www.huffington-post.com/2012/05/22/education-schools-standardized-tests_n_1536921.html

Rothstein, R. (2008). *Grading education, getting accountability right.* New York, NY: Teachers College Press.

Sawchuk, S. (2012, March). Teacher turnover affects all students. achievement, study indicates. *Teacher Beat.* Retrieved from http://blogs.edweek.org/edweek/teacherbeat/2012/03/when_teachers_leave_schools_ov.html

State of the States (2011). *Trends and Early Lessons on Teacher Evaluation and Effectiveness Policies, NCTQ.* Retrieved from http://www.nctq.org/p/publications/docs/nctq_stateOfTheStates.pdf

State of the States (2012). *Teacher Effectiveness Policies, NCTQ.* Retrieved from http://www.nctq.org/p/publications/docs/Updated_NCTQ_State%20of%20the%20States%202012_Teacher%20Effectiveness%20Policies.pdf

Walsh, K. (2001). Teacher certification reconsidered, stumbling for quality. Retrieved from http://www.nctq.org/p/publications/docs/ed_cert_1101_20071129024241.pdf

Welner, K. (2011). Free-market think tanks and the marketing of education policy. *Dissent.* Retrieved from http://www.colorado.edu/education/faculty/kevin-welner/Docs/Welner%20Dissent%20Original.pdf

PART II

PRIVATIZATION AND MILITARIZATION:
REDEFINING SCHOOLS

CHAPTER 6

THE NEW MARKET BUREAUCRACY IN U.S. PUBLIC SCHOOLING[1]

Kenneth J. Saltman
DePaul University

INTRODUCTION

One of the most important foundational metaphors for public school privatization and neoliberal educational restructuring (or corporate school reform) that has been promoted since the early 1990s involves claims of the "natural efficiencies of markets" and cutting through bureaucratic red tape. This argument against the alleged bureaucratic inefficiency of the public sector and for the alleged managerial efficiency of the private sector was launched by Chubb and Moe's *Politics, Markets, and America's Schools* in 1990.[2] Since the publication of Chubb and Moe's neoliberal educational bible, the de-bureaucratizing force of privatization has been promoted relentlessly in educational policy, despite a lack of evidence for it. Yet corporate school reforms, rather than decreasing bureaucracy and increasing efficiencies in public schooling, have in fact vastly expanded bureaucracy and created economic and operational inefficiencies.[3] That is, corporate school reform has produced a *privatized bureaucratic infrastructure* that has

Left Behind in the Race to the Top, pages 65–84
Copyright © 2013 by Information Age Publishing
65

yet to be identified as such. Moreover, the question of expanding or shrink-
ing bureaucracy to a great extent conceals the ways that corporate school
reforms achieve the redistribution of control and governance over policy
and practice, curriculum and administration as well as the redistribution of
control over educational resources by creating a new two-tiered system that
is privatized at the bottom and undermining the public and critical possibilities of public schools.

This chapter details the new market bureaucracy in corporate school
reform to show that not only has corporate school reform failed at the central aim of bureaucracy reduction but that it smuggles into schooling an
entirely new, largely unstudied kind of privatized bureaucracy with high
social costs. The chapter provides new conceptual tools by reviving the educational literature critiquing the ideology of positivism and social and cultural reproduction in the 1970s and 1980s. The first section elaborates on
the new market bureaucracy, explaining what is new and different about
positivist ideology and social and cultural reproduction in today's rising
culture of irrationalism and dialectically related embrace of positivist rationality in contrast to the positivism in the era of the hidden curriculum and
reproduction under Fordism. The second section focuses on how the new
market bureaucracy is found in contemporary educational reforms that are
aggressively promoted by the venture philanthropists. The third section
explains how the new market bureaucracy is involved in producing a new
kind of privatized, two-tiered educational system that rejects the egalitarian
aspirations of the Civil Rights movement and the Great Society, not to mention more radically democratic visions for the economy, culture, and political system. The chapter aims to identify what has yet to be named as the
"new market bureaucracy" at the center of corporate school reform and
to encourage empirical research into the new market bureaucracy so that
citizens have a better grasp of how to smash the private bureaucracies and
expand public, egalitarian, and democratic forms of control and oversight
over public schooling.

While corporate school reform has failed on its own terms of test-based
performance, costs, and bureaucracy reduction, and while it threatens critical and public education, corporate school reformers have succeeded spec-
tacularly in reframing debates about education in the academic, policy, and
public realms in privatized ways. Like the series of pro-privatization, anti-
union propaganda films *Waiting for Superman, The Lottery,* and *The Cartel*
and the steady stream of the same on NBC television, claims do not follow
from evidence.[4] These examples suggest more than a stunning irrational-
ity and hypocrisy at the core of the corporate educational reform agenda. Instead the championing of privatization relies centrally on business
metaphors of "efficiency" through "debureaucratization," "competition,"
"choice," "monopoly," and "failure," the intersecting discourses of "market

discipline" and "corporeal discipline." This chapter challenges the use of the metaphors of "market efficiency" achieved by cutting through "bureaucratic red tape." Corporate school reformers have justified numerous forms of privatization, including chartering, contracting, and vouchers, on the basis of cutting through the bureaucratic inefficiencies of the public sector.

The most crucial transformation to the public school in the last thirty years is the overt dominance of economic rationales for all educational practices and policies. For liberals and conservatives, nearly everything is justified through two economic promises: the possibility of upward economic mobility and the necessity of global economic competition, which demands educational improvement defined by improvements in numerically quantified test scores. In one sense this has continued the problematic conception of educational equality defined throughout the twentieth century as the equality of opportunity for access to competition. As Stanley Aronowitz has pointed out, the Deweyan progressive tradition has problematically shared in this attribution of educational opportunity defined as the opportunity of the individual to compete for economic inclusion.[5] In a sense, the economization of education simply has made more overt and "honest" the hidden curriculum of capitalist schooling. But at the same time, select liberal humanist referents that founded the public school system have largely been eradicated in the neoliberal era. Gone (with the exception of lip service) is the liberal ideal of the citizen educated as a well-rounded and thoughtful person capable of individual edification, public engagement, and collective self-governance. A different part of the liberal philosophical tradition coming from utilitarianism has won out. This is the triumph of *homo oeconomicus*, whose icy calculation for rational self-interest in the marketplace trumps all. Education suffers from a hardened cynicism about the future that Mark Fisher has described as Capitalist Realism and that Margaret Thatcher described as the TINA thesis—that is, "there is no alternative" to the market.[6] Fisher insightfully discusses how in the neoliberal UK educational system, new corporate-style bureaucratic constraints have been imposed on the justification of increased efficiency. The same is true in the U.S. context.

On the basis of efficient delivery of educational services, "deregulation" of public controls has been enacted. Yet these so-called deregulatory reforms have introduced a vast new regulatory architecture. For example, charter schooling was supposed to free schools and administrators from the bureaucratic constraints of districts to allow for greater accountability (typically this means increased standardized test scores) and decreased costs. Not only have studies of charters found lower standardized test-based performance than comparative traditional district schools, but the EMOs that manage charters have higher costs allocated to administration.[7] Also, the charter movement (and "choice" more generally), bankrolled disproportionately by the Gates Foundation, has introduced entirely new layers of bureaucracy into the school system, such as public relations schemes to market schools to parents; entire new organizations at the local, state, and national level to grease the entry of charters into districts; and "research" centers churning out dubious advocacy, reports, and "studies" to push the various aspects of the privatization agenda.[8] This is to say nothing of the vast new in-school bureaucratic impositions on teachers and administrators who have been transformed into paper-pushing "edupreneurs" encouraged to be constantly hustling for private money to maintain basic operations. The crucial insight to be gleaned from this is that in the name of efficiency, bureaucracy has not been eliminated or necessarily even reduced, but rather it has resulted in a shift in governance and control of school operations and policy formation, subjecting teachers and administrators to an entirely new array of market-oriented bureaucracy. The utterly obvious cost of this shift is that teachers spend their time doing an overwhelming amount of paperwork rather than preparing for lessons or developing as intellectuals. Less obvious are the ways that teaching becomes deskilled and degraded as curriculum is not to be developed but rather delivered. Teaching becomes robotic, less about intellectual development and more about adhering to prescribed methodological approaches. Such prescriptive methodologies also disallow a focus on the specific educational context and student experience, rendering critical pedagogical approaches impossible.[9] Critical pedagogies ideally begin with student experience and educative contexts to foster interpretation of how broader social forces produce these contexts and experiences. While critical pedagogies aim to expand understanding of the production of both knowledge and subjective experience, prescriptive methodologies aim to decontextualize knowledge and reduce comprehension of experience to the individual. Even less obvious are the ways that such deskilling becomes the means for installing conservative ideologies at odds with public and critical forms of schooling.

THE NEW MARKET BUREAUCRACY IN PUBLIC SCHOOLING

The new market bureaucracy in public schooling can be divided into at least three categories for conceptual clarity. First, the new market bureaucracy involves the shift to what I'm calling the "new market positivism"—that is, numerically quantifiable performance outcomes and the bureaucratic apparatuses put in place to control teachers, administrators, and students and to transform curriculum and pedagogy. Second, the new market bureaucracy involves linking the new market positivism to the institutionalization and the funding of entirely new strata of bureaucratic organizations dedicated to furthering the corporate agendas of privatization, deregulation, and standardization; charter support organizations, venture philanthropies;[10]

district support organizations; and lobbying infrastructure. Third, the new market bureaucracy imports into public schooling business expenses and rationales that have financial and social costs such as public relations and advertising required of both public and privatized schools and real estate deals with chartering organizations, funding for market-style competitions for private funds or public funds to implement corporate reforms such as Race to the Top, the Broad Prize, the Milken Prize, and so on. This third form of the new market bureaucracy involves the use of billions of dollars in private foundation money, especially from the large venture philanthropists Gates, Broad, and Walton, to influence and steer public policy. This foundation wealth which is only possible through tax incentives effectively redistributes control over public policy to private super rich individuals. Thus the public pays to give away control over public institutions.[11]

Though the criticism of positivism in Fordist public schooling came and largely went at the end of the Fordist era and the transition to post-Fordism, the culture of positivism (what I am calling here "the new market positivism") has been at the center of the new forms of market-based educational restructuring in the last twenty years.[12] The new market positivism is typified by the reinvigorated expansion of longstanding positivist approaches to schooling: standardized testing; standardization of curriculum; the demand for policy grounded exclusively in allegedly scientific, empirically based pedagogical reforms that (unlike science) lack elaborated framing assumptions or adequate theorization; and the drumbeat against educational theory and in favor of a practicalism that insists that "facts" speak for themselves and that untheorized experience is the arbiter of truth. The new market positivism signals the use of these longstanding approaches towards the expansion of multiple forms of educational privatization. The institutionalization of high-stakes standardized tests offers the promise and the sheen of solidity and certainty in a world rendered abstract through the principle of capitalist exchange applied everywhere.[13] Under the sway of neoliberal ideology, the suggestion that there is no alternative to the market has produced what Mark Fisher calls "market Stalinism," in which the appearance of market efficiency trumps real efficiency.[14] Such market Stalinism represents a world in which all that is solid melts into public relations—a world in which, as David Simon's television series *The Wire* accurately captured, the game of "juking the stats" (creating foremost an appearance of ever improving numerical measures of efficiency) comes to supersede reason or rationale grounded in public interest for the policies and practices of teachers and administrators, police officers, politicians, business people, and public workers. As the numbers game seeks to produce ever better numbers, the pursuit of numbers above all else results in multiple perversions of institutional values and purpose foreclosing the potential for democratic social relations. This is happening in public education under the guise of promoting "market-based efficiencies" by cutting through "public sector bureaucratic red tape."

In part, what is new and different now is the use of positivism in coordination with corporate/corporeal control: (1) the use of positivism to justify various forms of public school *privatization*—a shift in the ownership and control of public schools but also a shift in the culture of schools, their curricula and pedagogies; and (2) repression in schools such as militarized and prisonized schooling, efficiency models for poor students, and schools that aim at *total control of the body* and that justify expulsion through the failure of the student to be totally controlled—this is the flip side of the singular promise of economic freedom and choice and self-realization through consumption and work. These forms of control are typified by the use of drugs in schools for educational competition.

For richer students, the corporeal/corporate controls take the form largely of pharma-control, medicating students into attention (ADD/ADHD upper drugs such as Ritalin and Adderall), which is coordinated with educational competition and economic competition. Pharma-control also is used to medicate students out of depression/panic/anxiety (various anti-depression anti-anxiety downer drugs such as Prozac, Paxil, Zoloft, Xanax, etc.). The logic of charter schools is shared by these control approaches: loosen up controls (de-democratize, privatize, de-unionize) but then demand test-based accountability defined through testing (positivism). The new market positivism evinces a new relationship between freedom and unfreedom. The student is promised the chance to be disciplined into being an entrepreneurial subject, to compete educationally in order to compete economically. Pharma-control drugs, when not given medically, are being used illicitly by students for the very same ends: in order to compete educationally to compete economically.

What is crucially different between the old positivism and the new market positivism is the ways that the old positivism neutralized, naturalized, and universalized social and cultural reproduction under the guise of the public good, the public interest, but also individual values of humanist education. During the Fordist "hidden curriculum" era, the economic role of schooling as a sorting and sifting mechanism for the capitalist economy was largely denied. As Bourdieu and Passeron pointed out, mechanisms such as testing simultaneously stratify based on class while *concealing* how merit and talent stand in for the unequal distribution of life chances.[15] The new market positivism still neutralizes, naturalizes, and universalizes the reproduction of the class order through schooling. But the new market positivism also openly naturalizes and universalizes a particular economic basis for all educational relationships (schooling for work, schooling for economic competition) while justifying a shift in governance and control over educational institutions to private parties. Testing, database projects designed to boil down the allegedly most efficient knowledge delivery systems and reward and punish teachers and students—these are not only at the center of pedagogical, curricular, and administrative reform but, unlike during the era of the hidden curriculum, they are openly justified through the allegedly universal benefits of capitalism. The new market positivism subjects all to standardization and normalization of knowledge, denying the class and cultural interests, the political struggle behind the organization and framing of claims to truth. The trend rejects critical pedagogies that make power, politics, history, and ethics central to teaching and learning and that accord with the values of democratic community. *The new market positivism links its denial and concealment of the politics of knowledge to its open and aggressive application of capitalist ideology to every aspect of public schooling.* The positivism of the hidden curriculum era concealed the politics of knowledge to conceal the capitalist ideology structuring public education. Put bluntly, the reproduction of the stratified workforce, the unequal distribution of life chances, and so on were made to appear natural, neutral, and unquestionable in the era of the hidden curriculum, undermining the capacity of public schools to function as critical public spheres. The new market positivism still conceals the politics of knowledge, but it does so while redefining individual and collective opportunity strictly through open reference to a supreme value on capitalism. The intensified testing, control of time, and standardization regimens of the new market positivism further threaten the possibilities for teachers to teach against the grain (as Roger Simon describes it) and to engage in critical pedagogical practices. The new market positivism effects a kind of deep privatization in the sense that it renders public schools places that are less open to struggle for public values, identifications, and interpretations, thereby reducing the social space of noncommercial values, ideas, and ideologies.

Jeff Edmondson, president of the Strive Together—National Cradle to Career Network that "partners" with public schools to do turnarounds is, according to writer David Bornstein, leading a national effort for establishing "data war rooms" in schools for "data driven instruction," "data-driven administration," and so on. As Edmondson explains in the *New York Times*, "The key to making a partnership work is setting a common vision and finding a common language. You can't let people get focused on ideological or political issues. You need a common language to bring people together and that language is the data."[16] Edmondson concisely and powerfully describes the denial of politics behind the new market positivism. On the one hand there is a universal assumption that the aim of such reform is to increase student test scores towards "global economic competition," that is, capitalist inclusion. On the other hand, there is a denial that such an agenda for education is of course profoundly political. Take a particularly glaring class example. Those who own industry and seek to maximize profit by minimizing labor costs do not share a common set of interests, for example, with those workers who will be forced to sell their time and labor power to the owners in a position to exploit it. The politics of labor is perhaps more concretely understood by the fact that Strive Together is affiliated with the organization Stand for Kids that advocates limiting public teachers' collective bargaining rights in Cincinnati Public Schools and is linked to Michelle Rhee's New Teacher Project (and National Council on Teacher Quality [NCTQ]) that aims for privatization, union busting, pay for test scores, the end of teacher job security, less educated and less experienced teachers, and so on. Data can be creatively manipulated or utterly ignored when in the service of this ideological agenda pushed by Rhee and the New Teacher Project, NCTQ, Hanushek, Finn, Peterson and the usual cast of corporate school reformers affiliated with Hoover, Fordham, AEI, Heritage, and the other rightist think tanks.[17] Data as "the common language" provides a way actively to deny the sometimes incommensurably different values, histories, and interests of different groups.

As Mark Fisher details in his book *Capitalist Realism: Is There No Alternative?*, the new market bureaucracy that has overtaken public schooling installs an audit culture in which it is not performance of teachers and students that is compared but rather "comparison between the audited representation of that performance and output" pp. 42–43).

> The idealized market was supposed to deliver 'friction free' exchanges, in which the desires of consumers would be met directly, without the need for intervention or mediation by regulatory agencies. Yet the drive to assess the performance of workers and to measure forms of labor which, by their nature, are resistant to quantification, has inevitably required additional layers of management and bureaucracy. . . . Inevitably, a short circuiting occurs, and work becomes geared towards the generation and messaging of representations rather than to the official goals of the work itself. (p. 42)

As numerical test output targets become the end of schooling in the new market bureaucracy, as Fisher puts it, "if students are less skilled and knowledgeable than their predecessors, this is due not to a decline in the quality of examinations per se, but to the fact that all of the teaching is geared towards passing the exams. Narrowly focused 'exam drill' replaces a wider engagement with subjects" (pp. 43–44). As Fisher observes, more effort ends up expended on generating and representing the "outputs," which in education take the form of manipulated test data than on improving the quality and depth of instruction—that is, the process of teaching itself.

Theodor Adorno's concept of what drives the allure of positivism is the promise of the concrete in the world of abstraction/alienation produced by a social world characterized by market exchange in which everything is turned into equivalences.[18] What we have now is a new, evermore

control- and output-oriented educational system in which numbers allegedly dictate. Yet we have policy implementation that is utterly at odds with
both empirical evidence for reforms (charters and EMOs) within the positivist assumptions, and we have the public purposes of schooling being
elided by these control- and output-oriented bureaucratic reforms. Along
with an explicit justification of all policy on the basis of individual participation in capitalism—a system represented as the only game in town not
just economically, but politically and culturally as well. The triumph then,
as Fisher points out, is an ascendancy of schooling as public relations in
which everyone knows the lie but plays along anyway. As charters and EMOs
show worse to par test scores with traditional public schools in comparisons,
those at the center of the audit culture (such as the venture philanthropists
like the Gates and Broad Foundations) change the audit criteria from standardized test scores to graduation and college enrollment rates.[19] What is
crucial to the public assenting to such policies is the ongoingly produced
pedagogies that educate subjects ideologically and that also foster a culture
of cynicism about intervening to challenge the audit culture and the new
market positivism.

We need to rethink the accusations of bureaucratic "red tape" that have
been a core part of the corporate reform agenda. What most teachers and
administrators experience in schools is a new market bureaucracy that has
been installed and expanded under the guise of market efficiencies. Fisher
offers a succinct and powerful antidote to the new market bureaucracy. He
calls for demanding fulfillment of the promises for de-bureaucratization
instilled through neoliberalism. In other words, for Fisher we should take
the neoliberal imperative for cutting bureaucratic red tape seriously but direct this imperative towards market-driven audit culture. In education this
means aiming to dismantle the market bureaucracy and its frenzied pursuit
of ever more numerical representations of educational progress.

The new market positivism appears in the "global knowledge economy"
mantra in a two part argument. First the allegedly universally valuable test
scores (such as the OECD PISA international comparisons in reading, math,
and science) are used to claim that the public school system has failed and
that educational failure both explains the current failure of capitalism to
provide employment adequate growth and green tech development, and
the failure portends a bleak future as other nations competing against the
U.S. on tests threaten U.S. economic and technological hegemony. Yet, as an
atypical article "U.S. Schools Are Still Ahead—Way Ahead" in the business
press points out, these stereotypes about the failures of U.S. public schooling do not stand up to evidence, including the ones about international
test score comparisons, the quality of science and engineering preparation,
and worries about U.S. students socializing instead of studying hard.[20] As
Vivek Wadhwa rightly argues in *Businessweek*, the differences between U.S.

and other nations are negligible, while the U.S. has the greatest diversity in student population ("disadvantaged minorities and unskilled immigrants") and still produces more higher-performing students in science and reading than any other country, while in math it comes second only to Japan. The second part of the "global knowledge economy" argument says that this supposed failure demands radical market reforms (charters and other privatizations, linking teacher pay to test scores, crushing teacher unions) despite the fact that no evidence exists for such reforms on the same terms of test-based improvement or in terms of cost savings. Such assertions rely on the alleged objectivity of tests for the first part, and then when it comes to prescription, abandons all recourse to alleged objectivity by failing even to respect the need for evidence for policy. Such arguments, which are being rehearsed by the U.S. Secretary of Education, the venture philanthropists, and the mass media, suggest that what is at play in the new market positivism is a change in the relationship between truth and authority with regard to evidence and empirical data. Flagrant disregard for evidence extends to other neoliberal education cheerleaders such as *New York Times* columnist Thomas L. Friedman who leads the public scapegoating of education, suggesting that high unemployment rates in the U.S. are caused by the failure of teachers and schools to make adequately entrepreneurial workers.[21] If only, he contends, schools could promote such entrepreneurialism, then those workers would not have been fired. In this view, the expansion of the "knowledge economy" depends only on creativity and knowledge production. In reality, economic development and entrepreneurialism also requires capital—a vast amount of which was destroyed by the speculative economy produced by the neoliberal policies of privatization and deregulation of the last 30 years.

While the logic of empiricism has overtaken educational debates, demanding that everything be justified with an evidentiary basis, in reality the reforms are being implemented principally through the justification of market ideologies and metaphors that most often run contrary to the evidence of proponents. Whether it is charter schools, for-profit management companies, vouchers, so called "portfolio districts," NCLB, or competitions like RTTT, implementation is based not on evidence but on market-based advocacy. The new market positivism is characterized by a triumph of irrationalism under the guise of rationality, a new bureaucracy under the guise of efficiency, audit culture and unaccountability at the top masquerading as accountability, extension of repressive bodily and hierarchical institutional controls defended through reference to freedom and opportunity, anti-intellectualism and destruction of the conditions for creativity pushed on the basis of the need to produce creatively minded workers and entrepreneurs, and a denial of intellectual process, curiosity, debate and dialogue justified on the basis of intellectual excellence. There is a kind of emptiness at the core of the new market positivism in that it is seldom about making decisions based in the imperative for empirical evidence and conceptual justification but rather about using evidence when convenient for the ends of amassing elite control. In education corporate bureaucracy is being installed and expanded, yet as Wall Street is discovering, corporate bureaucracy may have seen its best days. The editor of the *Wall Street Journal*, Alan Murray, in August of 2010 argued that "corporate bureaucracy is becoming obsolete."[22] Wall Street subjects teachers and students, administrators and citizens to the sloughed-off detritus of corporate culture. Meanwhile, business prescriptions for education are exactly what business is discarding for business.

THE NEW MARKET POSITIVISM
IN THE DOMINANT EDUCATIONAL REFORMS

Positivism is at the center of dominant educational reforms that are modeled on corporate culture and a private sector vision of management, growth, and quality. Standardized testing is at the center of No Child Left Behind and its blueprint for reauthorization, Race to the Top, the push for value added assessment, the creation of database tracking projects to longitudinally measure teacher "performance" on students' standardized tests, the linkage of teacher evaluation and pay to such standardized test-based measures, the imposition of "urban portfolio districts," legislative moves to stifle the power of teachers unions, the unbridled entry of corporate managers into school reform bypassing professional educators and educational scholarship, and the use of corporate media to frame educational problems and solutions. Standardized testing has also been at the center of the push for charter school expansion and the expansion of for profit management companies running schools.

These dominant reforms share a common logic with regard to standardized testing. Test scores that are low in relation to the norm are used to justify policies such as regressive funding formulas (NCLB), imperatives for corporate reforms like "turnarounds" (NCLB and RTTT), school closures (NCLB and RTTT), and school privatizations. Corporate reformers use the alleged objectivity of the standardized tests to champion corporate reforms that lack scholarly or empirical justification. The alleged objectivity of the standardized tests dooms the public schools under scrutiny, but the reforms put forward by the corporate reformers are not held to the same standards. For example, charter schools, No Child Left Behind, and for-profit management of schools can be fairly described as "failed" corporate educational reforms that do not increase standardized tests, while no evidence for the success of "turnarounds" and "portfolio districts" exists.[23] Indeed, the proponents of portfolio districts, which model districts on a stock portfolio and the superintendent as a stock investor, contend that it is impossible to measure the success of such models in terms of the same standardized testing that they use to justify implementation.

As the corporate reforms have failed to succeed on the proponents' grounds (higher test scores), proponents have responded with two strategies. One strategy is willful ignorance. Policy elites such as the Secretary of Education, the venture philanthropists, charter school associations, and the right wing think tanks have continued, for example, wrongly asserting the success of charters and for-profit management companies and insisting on the need to continue NCLB (albeit slightly tweaked). The other strategy has been to change the rules of the game. This has been most evident with the failure of the charter movement to prove itself in terms of test score improvements that justified its corporate backers. With a lack of test-based evidence, a number of policymakers have come out suggesting other measures to determine charters a success. Eugenicist, Harvard professor, and co-author of the *Bell Curve*, Charles Murray, wrote explicitly about the need to change the measure in a *New York Times* op-ed.[24] Charters, it seems, were justified for implementation based in the low test scores of public schools but the same criteria should not be used to justify their continuation. Likewise, Paul Hill, who leads the pro-privatization Center for Reinventing Public Education at University of Washington, explained in his reports on creating "portfolio districts" that the measure of the success of charters and other privatizations should be the implementation of these reforms rather than the rise in test scores.[25] The Bill and Melinda Gates Foundation has been the single largest funder of charter school expansion for schools, districts, and numerous charter "support" organizations at the local, state, and national level. Since succeeding in getting the dubious charter movement made a central element of the federal education agenda in RTTT and NCLB, the Bill and Melinda Gates Foundation's reauthorization efforts have never admitted that evidence does not back its billions in spending. Instead, it continues to pour money into charters and more and more into other reforms more closely tied to standardized testing. For example, it is pushing for expanding value added assessment and linking value added assessment to teacher pay, and linking value added assessment to video surveillance. The aims of these reforms will be to deduce a methodology for teaching practice that will raise test scores and that can be forced on numerous teachers.

The new market positivism can also be found in the market based rearticulation of the language of schooling for social justice. While Secretary of Education Arne Duncan regularly describes education as the most important social justice and civil rights issue today, he then asserts that the imperatives for test-based measures of educational quality and privatizations are the solution to the historical injustices he registers. Duncan is not alone. The Gates and Broad Foundations explain their push for test-based reforms, especially database tracking of student tests scores, as intended to "close the achievement gap." Duncan, Gates, Broad, and other proponents of the new market positivism share a number of related assumptions about knowledge, the self, and the society. Knowledge in this view is to be efficiently delivered and does not need to be comprehended in relation to its conditions of production or interpretation. In other words, the subjective positions of the claimant of truths do not need to be investigated, nor do the objective conditions that give rise to particular interpretations need to be comprehended. The self in this static view of knowledge ought to accumulate ever more knowledge towards the end of "measurable achievement" and instrumental action linked to economic utility. Within this view, social justice is not to be achieved by collective action and aspirations for reconceptualizing and impacting the social world. Instead, social justice for the new market positivists becomes an individualized pursuit in which disciplined consumption of preordained knowledge creates the possibilities for inclusion into a social order presumed to be fundamentally just. This, of course, has little to do with social justice in the sense of transforming the economy either by ameliorating the devastating effects and dire inequalities of wealth and income of capitalism through social democratic welfare state controls. Nor does it have to do with more fundamentally transforming the political governance of capitalism through democratizing relations of production and consumption. As well, this conception of social justice has no sense of transforming the culture to value dissent, disagreement, difference, and dialogue, which are the lifeblood of democratic social relations. Instead, this version of social justice imposes a singular value of individual economic inclusion in a corporate economy.

The ubiquitous concepts of "student achievement," the "achievement gap" and the call across the political spectrum to "close the achievement gap" all presume that achievement is measured by standardized testing. "Student achievement" naturalizes, neutralizes, and universalizes class and culturally specific knowledge establishing norms, comparing and ranking in relation to the norm, all the while disavowing the politics of knowledge informing the selection and framing of knowledge on the tests. The denial of the politics of knowledge is then further deepened by the concept of the "achievement gap," which suggests that the test outcomes indicate how racial and ethnic groups fare in relation to the norm. In the spirit and legacy of cultural imperialism and colonialism, racial and ethnic cultural differences are ignored and denied in the making of the standardized tests, but then differences are invoked to demand that the ordained knowledge be consumed and displayed on the tests.[26] In this view, cultural differences and struggles over their meaning are not at the center of teaching and learning, an object of analysis that could form the basis for emancipatory pedadgogies that comprehend claims to truth in relation to the social positioning of individuals and groups. Instead, cultural differences in the new market positivism are only to be registered as something to be overcome as all students are required to take in the dogma.

THE NEW MARKET POSITIVISM IN THE NEW TWO-TIERED EDUCATIONAL SYSTEM

As David Hursh, Sandra Mathison, and Mark Garrison,[27] among others, powerfully emphasize, we must understand the emphasis on standardized testing as both utterly central to historical struggles over public education and as central to the current neoliberal school reforms. What is afoot in the current privatization initiatives is an attempt to do nothing short of transform public education into a private market, essentially ending public education.

The transformation of public education into a private market is being done by what Naomi Klein calls "disaster capitalism" and David Harvey describes as "accumulation by dispossession" and in education I have termed "capitalizing on disaster" or "smash and grab privatization," in which declarations of disaster, failure, and crisis are used to implement longstanding privatization initiatives that could not be otherwise enacted. This broader privatization trend is particularly evident in the rapidly expanding charter movement (which is a frontal assault on teachers unions, teacher work, and teaching as a critical and intellectual endeavor, and the speartip of the privatization movement), the continuing voucher movement, Race to the Top, the organized efforts of the "venture philanthropies" [28] such as the Gates, Broad, and Walton foundations as well as numerous neoliberal think tanks, associations, and political organizations as well as back to back U.S. Departments of Education dominated by bureaucrats with a corporate view of school reform.

These organizations and individuals are rapidly succeeding in smashing teachers unions, overrunning local school boards in order to put in place privatized school networks, as in New Orleans after Katrina.[29] Indeed, New Orleans, that great neoliberal experiment in privatization that was remade with privatized charter networks, has been expanded statewide in Louisiana as the Louisiana Governor Jindal, Louisiana Board of Education Superintendent Pastorek (since this writing Pastorek has left the position to work for military contractor EADS), and Recovery School District CEO Vallas seek to ratchet up school failure scores to declare more and more public schools as "failed" and subject to closure and replacement by privatized schools. The privatizers have a profound antipathy for teacher education and academically grounded certification, local school boards and community governance, and an outspoken hostility for educational theory in favor of anti-intellectual practicalism, teacher de-skilling, and a relentless penchant for radical experimentation especially with unproven market-based reforms.

What the teachers unions, education scholars, teachers, and everyone concerned about strengthening public education has to grasp is that *as long as the framing of educational quality remains trapped within the current frame of allegedly neutral and allegedly objective quantifiable "student achievement," public education stands to be dismantled.*

The kind of schooling pushed by the privatization advocates aims to transform a current dual system of public schooling into another dual system of public schooling. In the current dual system, elite public schools in rich, predominantly White communities prepare managers, leaders, and professionals for the top of the economy and the state, while the underfunded public schools in poor, working class, and predominantly non-White communities prepare the docile, disciplined workforce for the bad jobs at the bottom of the economy and for exclusion from the economy altogether. Despite the ceaseless neoliberal and liberal rhetoric of crisis and failure, the public schools as Freire, Bourdieu, Ollman, and others recognize do exactly what they are supposed to do: They produce the stratified workforce while sanctifying inequality as a matter of individual merit or talent.[30] The neoliberal privatization reforms maintain the dual system, leaving in place the elite public schools but targeting poor schools and predominantly students of color to turn them into *short-term* profit opportunities in numerous ways: contracting, testing, and tutoring schemes[31] but also for-profit management, charters, as well as all the ancillary profits that can be generated through privatization, like the public funds that will pour into marketing charter schools to prospective "customers" through advertising and PR, the lucrative real estate deals through charters, etc.[32] At present, the lower end of the dual system provides a *deferred* investment in low-pay, low-skill disciplined workers and fodder for the for-profit prison industry and the military. Privatization targets the low end of the dual system and pillages the public sector for short-term profits benefitting most the ruling class and professional class (poverty pimping) while doing nothing to transform the dual system of public education into a single system as good as its best parts throughout. For investors in privatization, the benefits are double: money can be made in the short run by draining public tax revenue while the future exploitable workforce can still be produced for the long run. And, as the investors are benefitting twice, they can feel good that they are giving poor students "every opportunity" to benefit themselves. Of course, class mobility is declining, unemployment is rising, and the shifting of economic inequality and exclusion onto school kids who will need to be—in the words of Thomas Friedman—more entrepreneurial to get and keep scarcer jobs. This displaces the violence of the capitalist economy onto the weakest and most vulnerable citizens, children. As I write this, one in five U.S. children is on food stamps with ballooning rates of child homelessness.[33] The goal should not be to see how we can all help to subsidize the rich getting richer by replicating a more lucrative system of dual education—the rich part still public and the poor part privatized. The goal must be ending the dual education system, but the new market positivism is at the core of creating the new privatized dual education system by making standardized testing, database tracking, and standardization of curriculum and pedagogy the measure of good teaching and learning. The alternative to these positivist approaches to teaching and learning are democratic approaches to education such as critical pedagogy.

NOTES

1. This chapter has been adapted and revised from Kenneth J. Saltman *The Failure of Corporate School Reform* "White Collar, Red Tape: The New Market Bureaucracy in Corporate School Reform" Boulder: Paradigm Publishers 2011, pp. 54–79. The larger original article includes sections that discuss the new market positivism in relation to a rising culture of irrationalism and an expanded discussion of the historical educational theorizing of educational positivism under the Fordist economy.
2. John Chubb and Terry Moe, *Politics, Markets, and America's Schools* Washington, DC: Brookings Institution 1990.
3. For empirical study of how this has played out with the largest corporate component of corporate school reform of chartering see Miron, G. & Urschel, J.L. (2010). *Equal or fair? A study of revenues and expenditure in Americancharter schools.* Boulder and Tempe: Education and the Public Interest Center & Education PolicyResearch Unit. Retrieved from http://epicpolicy.org/publication/charter-school-finance http://epicpolicy.org/publication/charter-school-finance. Empirical study has yet to be done that accounts for and aggregates all of the new market bureaucracy spending on advertising, public relations, venture philanthropy expenditures, Astroturf lobbying to expand privatization, and contracting.
4. I detail the empirical studies of numerous neoliberal restructuring plans and the lack of evidence for them in Kenneth J. Saltman *The Failure of Corporate School Reform* Boulder: Paradigm 2012.
5. See Stanley Aronowitz, *Against Schooling and For An Education That Matters* Boulder: Paradigm 2007.
6. Mark Fisher, *Capitalist Realism: Is There No Alternative?* Washington: Zero Books 2009. Fisher writes that capitalist realism, " . . . is more like a pervasive atmosphere, conditioning not only the production of culture but also the regulation of work and education, and acting as a kind of invisible barrier constraining thought and action."(16).

7. The majority of studies of charter school effects on academic achievement show on par to negative effects in comparison with traditional public schools. Two of the most extensive and significant studies were the 2004 NAEP results as analyzed by Martin Carnoy and colleagues [Carnoy, M., Jacobsen, R., Mishel, L., & Rothstein, R. (2005). *The Charter School Dust Up: Examining the Evidence on Enrollment and Achievement.* Washington, DC: Economic Policy Institute] and the Stanford CREDO study of 2009. Available at http://credo.stanford.edu/reports/MULTIPLE_CHOICE_CREDO.pdf], *Disparities in charter school resources—the influence of state policy and community.* Other studies include:

Bodine, E., Fuller, B., González, M., Huerta, L., Naughton, S., Park, S., & Teh, L.W. (2008, January). TITLE. *Journal of Education Policy, 23* (1), 1-33.
Finnigan, K., Adelman, N., Anderson, L., Cotton, L., Donnelly, M. B., & Price, T. (2004). *Evaluation of the Public Charter Schools Program: Final evaluation report.* Washington, DC: US Department of Education.
Ladd, H.F. & Bifulco, R.P. (2004). *The impacts of charter schools on student achievement: Evidence from North Carolina.* Working Paper SAN04-01. Durham, NC: Terry Sanford Institute of Public Policy, Duke University.
Nelson, F.H., Rosenberg, B., &Van Meter, N. (2004). *Charter school achievement on the 2003 National Assessment of Educational Progress.* Washington, DC: American Federation of Teachers.
What Works Clearinghouse (2010) *WWC Quick Review of the Report "Multiple Choice: Charter School Performance in 16 States."* Washington, DC: Author.
Center for Research on Education Outcomes. (June 2009). *Multiple choice: Charter school performance in 16 states.* Stanford, CA: Author.

On the higher administrative cost of charters see, Miron, G., & Urschel, J. L. (2010). *Equal or fair? A study of revenues and expenditure in American charter schools.* Boulder and Tempe: Education and the Public Interest Center & Education PolicyResearch Unit. Retrieved from http://epicpolicy.org/publication/charter-school-finance http://epicpolicy.org/publication/charter-school-finance

8. I take this up in detail in Saltman, K. (2010). *The gift of education: Public education and venture philanthropy.* New York, NY: Palgrave.
9. The centrality of context and student experience to critical pedagogy can be found elaborated in for example Paulo Freire *Pedagogy of the Oppressed*, a number of books by Henry Giroux including *Theory and Resistance in Education, Border Crossings*, and *Teachers as Intellectuals.*
10. See Saltman, K. (2010). *The gift of education: Public education and venture philanthropy.* New York, NY: Palgrave.
11. I detail this as the "circuit of privatization" in *The Gift of Education.*
12. For the most important criticisms of positivism in the fordist era of the hidden curriculum see Henry A. Giroux's early work particularly his article "Schooling and the Culture of Positivism: Notes on the Death of History" republished in *On Critical Pedagogy* New York: Continuum 2011, pp. 19–47 originally published Henry A. Giroux (1979) "Schooling and the Culture of Positivism: Notes on the Death of History" *Educational Theory, 29*(4), 263–284.

13. Theodore Adorno, *Introduction to Sociology* Stanford: Polity 2000.

14. Mark Fisher, *Capitalist Realism: Is There No Alternative?* U.K. Zero Books 2008.

15. Pierre Bourdieu and Jean Claude Passeron, *Reproduction in Education, Society, and Culture* Second Edition Thousand Oaks: Sage 1990.

16. David Bornstein, "Coming Together to Give Schools a Boost," *The New York Times* March 7, 2011. Available at http://opinionator.blogs.nytimes.com/2011/03/07/coming-together-to-give-schools-a-boost/

17. For a plethora of research reviews that reveal the extent to which ideologically driven data manipulation is employed by corporate school reform ideologues see the National Education Policy Center Think Tank Review Project available at: http://nepc.colorado.edu/think-tank-review-project. See for example, Pecheone, R. L. & Wei, R. C. (2009). Review of "The Widget Effect: Our National Failure to Acknowledge and Act on Teacher Differences." Boulder and Tempe: Education and the Public Interest Center & Education Policy Research Unit. Retrieved from http://epicpolicy.org/thinktank/review-Widget-Effect. For deception by Hanushek see also Kilpatrick, J. (2011). Review of "U.S. Math Performance in Global Perspective: How Well Does Each State Do at Producing High-Achieving Students?" Boulder, CO: National Education Policy Center. Retrieved from http://nepc.colorado.edu/thinktank/review-us-math. For deception by Finn see Barnett, W.S. (2009). Special Review of "Reroute the Preschool Juggernaut." Boulder and Tempe: Education and the Public Interest Center & Education Policy Research Unit. Retrieved [date] from http://epicpolicy.org/thinktank/Special-Review-Reroute-Preschool-Juggernaut. And for a nice example of deception by Peterson see: Lubienski, C and S. (2006). *Review of "On the Public-Private School Achievement Debate."* Boulder and Tempe: Education and the Public Interest Center & Education Policy Research Unit. Retrieved [date] from http://epicpolicy.org/thinktank/review-on-public-private-school-achievement-debate

18. See Theodor Adorno, *Introduction to Sociology.* Stanford, CA: Polity 2000.

19. Both Gates and Broad foundations have massively funded various forms of privatization especially chartering but also database tracking projects to measure student test scores and teacher "performance" relative to the scores. When the charters were not showing promise on raising the test scores Gates shifted the criteria to focus on graduation rates and college enrollment rates. Similarly for the Center for Reinventing Public Education's Paul Hill the standardized test scores should be used to justify closing traditional public schools but not for evaluating the contractors who take their place.

20. See Vivek Wadhwa, "U.S. Schools Still Ahead—Way Ahead" Bloomberg *Businessweek* January 12, 2011 available at www.businessweek.com

21. Thomas L. Friedman, "The New Untouchables" *The New York Times* October 21, 2009, A31.

22. Alan Murray, "The End of Management" The *Wall Street Journal* August 21, 2010 available at www. Wsj.com.

23. Kenneth J. Saltman, "Urban School Decentralization and the Growth of Portfolio Districts" National Education Policy Center June 2, 2010. Retrieved from http://nepc.colorado.edu/publication/portfolio-districts

24. Charles Murray, "Why Charter Schools Fail the Test" *The New York Times*, May 5, 2010, A31.
25. Hill, P., Campbell, C., & Menefee-Libey, D. (2009). *Portfolio School Districts for Big Cities: An Interim Report*. Seattle: Center on Reinventing Public Education, University of Washington.
26. This way of thinking about difference as needing to be registered in order to overcome such difference can be found exemplified in the speaking and writing of Vickie Philips head of the Bill and Melinda Gates Foundation and books such as *Abigail Thernstrom and Stephen Thernstrom, No Excuses: Closing the Racial Gap in Learning* New York: Simon & Shuster 2003. Racial, ethnic, linguistic, and cultural difference is positioned in this discourse of the "achievement gap" as an obstacle and sometimes as a pathology that needs to be overcome. The way to overcome difference is to enforce the learning of prescribed knowledge which is alleged to be of universal value. This is diametrically opposed to critical pedagogy in which difference needs to be engaged for how individuals and groups are positioned materially and symbolically in subordinate or superordinate ways and how such social positioning informs the claims to truth made by different parties. Such critical interrogations of difference form the basis for reconstructing individual and group experience and ideally form the basis for collective action towards equality.
27. For an excellent historical account of the political struggles over standardized testing see Mark J. Garrison's *A Measure of Failure: The Political Origins of Standardized Testing* Albany: SUNY Press 2009. For an excellent contemporary take on the relationships between standardized testing and neoliberalism see David Hursh *High Stakes Testing and the Decline of Teaching and Learning* Lanham, MD Rowman & Littlefield 2008.
28. My book *The Gift of Education: Venture Philanthropy and Public Education* New York: Palgrave 2010 details this largely ignored radical market based transformation of educational philanthropy.
29. See Kristen Buras, "Review of The Louisiana Recovery School District: Lessons for the Buckeye State" National Education Policy Center 2012 available at http://nepc.colorado.edu/thinktank/review-louisiana-recovery-buckeye See also Kristen Buras, *Pedagogy, Policy, and the Privatized City* New York: Teachers College Press 2010 and Kenneth J. Saltman, *Capitalizing on Disaster: Taking and Breaking Public Schools* Boulder: Paradigm 2007.
30. See Paulo Freire, Pedagogy of the Oppressed New York: Continuum 1970; Pierre Bourdieu and Jean Passeron, Reproduction in Education, Society, and Culture Thousand Oaks: Sage 1990; Bertell Ollman, "Why So Many Exams?: A Marxist Response" October 2002 Z Magazine available at < http://www.nyu.edu/projects/ollman/docs/why_exams.php>.
31. See Patricia Burch, *Hidden Markets: The New Educational Privatization* New York: Routledge 2010.
32. For-profit real estate investment cashing in on the charter boom include numerous banks and corporations (Intel, movie companies) and even celebrity athletes like Andre Agassi. See for example, Tierney Plumb (The Motley Fool), "Movie House Investor Dives into Charter School Space" Daily Finance 8/16/11 Retrieved from http://www.dailyfinance.com/2011/08/16/

movie-house-investor-dives-into-the-charter-school/>; Roger Vincent, "Agassi to Invest in Charter Schools" The Los Angeles Times June 2, 2011. Retrieved from http://articles.latimes.com/2011/jun/02/business/la-fi-agassi-fund-20110602>;

33. According to the National Center for Children in Poverty 15 million or 21% of U.S. children live below the poverty line. See http://www.nccp.org/topics/childpoverty.html. According to the campaign to end childhood homelessness 1.5 million U.S. children are homeless. That is, 1 in 50 or 2% of American children are homeless in the richest country. See http://www.homeless-childrenamerica.org/

CHAPTER 7

MISSING THE MARK

Neoliberalism and the Unwarranted Rise of Charter Schools

Richard Mora and Mary Christianakis
Occidental College

INTRODUCTION

Presently, there are over 5,500 charter schools in 41 states, in the District of Columbia, and Puerto Rico, with most in low-income urban communities, serving over 1.8 million students (Center for Research on Education Outcomes, 2009; National Alliance for Public Charter Schools, 2012; National Center for Educational Statistics, 2010), with tens of thousands more students on waiting lists (U.S. Department of Education, 2008). A wide array of institutions, some public and some not, manage charter schools: social service agencies, universities, philanthropic organizations, religious schools (that remove religious symbols), previously tuition-charging privates, for-profit firms, parents, community members, and educators. These diverse stakeholders underscore the structural and economic changes that have resulted from the expansion of charter schools. Proponents of charter schools contend that traditional public education

Left Behind in the Race to the Top, pages 85–102
Copyright © 2013 by Information Age Publishing
All rights of reproduction in any form reserved.

is overly bureaucratized and politicized and unsalvageable in its traditional form (Chubb & Moe, 1990).

Despite President Barack Obama's invested hope, charter schools have not given children greater access to quality education, nor have they closed the achievement gap. Research strongly suggests that the consequences of Obama's charter policies will continue well beyond his presidency, leaving the most vulnerable of our students underserved. The future of public education in capitalized school markets looks grim. Charter schools appear to be an intermediary step in the larger neoliberal and conservative agenda to privatize schools and funnel tax dollars into the market.

In this chapter, we discuss the expansion of charter schools, particularly of for-profit schools, and examine their impact on public schooling. We begin by situating the school choice discourse within the U.S. neoliberal economic practices of the last decade. We then examine Arne Duncan's legacy in Chicago's public schools, and what that means for the Race to the Top initiatives that have incentivized charter schooling. Finally, we expose the failed promises of charter schools and the conflicts of interest that keep them alive.

NEOLIBERALISM AND SCHOOL CHOICE

For decades now, neoliberal economics has invoked market discourses (e.g., choice) to frame both the problems and utility of public schools (McLaren & Farahmandpur, 2001). According to neoliberalism, public education is an economic drain linked to an unsustainable welfare state (Burchell, 1996). The only way to address the costs associated with public education, neoliberals argue, is to marketize it like any other service so that the markets can make schools more productive and efficient (Peters, 1999).

Market-oriented thinking has won charter schools support across the political spectrum. Neoliberals and conservatives alike favor them for operating semiautonomously from unions and state and district mandates. Neoliberals maintain that unions protect incompetent teachers and perpetuate mediocrity. They also argue that curricular independence holds the promise of closing the racialized achievement and graduation gaps. For conservatives, a main selling point of charter schools is that they are not required to employ unionized teachers. The convergence of neoliberal and conservative ideologies on the issue of public education has created a sociopolitical climate in which traditional public schools are assailed as a failing public good and charter schools are trumpeted as entrepreneurial innovations.

The school choice movement gained a strong foothold within public education during the Bush presidency. Along with doling out annual federal funds for charter schools, the Bush administration encouraged school choice programs as a solution for underperforming school systems. After Hurricane Katrina in 2005, for example, the White House provided New Orleans with $1.9 billion in school aid, of which $500 million dollars went to school vouchers and $24 million to charter schools (Saltman, 2007). The marketization of public education in New Orleans led to both a drastic expansion of charter schools, which now account for over 50% of the city's public schools (U.S. Department of Education, 2008), and to two-thirds of New Orleans children attending either private or charter schools (Henderson, 2010). Additionally, during Bush's presidency, the charter school movement was aligned with privatization through the growth of education management organizations (EMOs) (Molnar & Garcia, 2007).

For most of their 20-year history, charter schools have enjoyed access to federal funds along with political support. In 1994, at end of President Bill Clinton's first term in office, the Department of Education (DOE) started funding charter school conferences, state programs, and charter school research through the Public Charter Schools Program (PCSP). The PCSP was subsequently amended by the Charter School Expansion Act of 1998 and by President George W. Bush's No Child Left Behind Act of 2001 in order to provide "support for the planning, program design, and initial implementation of charter schools" (U.S. Department of Education, 2004, p. 2). In 2001, the DOE also established the Credit Enhancement for Charter School Facilities Program to provide competitive grants for entities seeking to secure loans for the acquisition, construction, renovation, and/ or operation of charter school facilities (Temkin, Hong, Davis, & Bavin, 2008, p. xi).

ARNE DUNCAN AND THE MARKET-BASED REFORM OF CHICAGO PUBLIC SCHOOLS

Obama's choice of Arne Duncan as Secretary of Education, over progressive educator Linda Darling-Hammond (2010), made clear that he intended to advance free-market models of school choice. As CEO of Chicago Public Schools, Duncan championed Renaissance 2010, a plan to shutdown underperforming city schools and open new, autonomous schools (as possible charters) by 2010. Renaissance 2010, which Duncan and Chicago Mayor Richard Daley launched in 2004, was developed in collaboration with the Commercial Club of Chicago (CCC), a group of leaders from corporate, financial, philanthropic, and civic sectors.

During Duncan's tenure, 44 traditional schools failed to meet the academic standards and were shut down (Gwynne & de la Torre, 2009). Chicago experienced an increase in both public and private charter schools and militarized public schools (Au, 2009). The closing or turning around of schools also resulted in experienced teachers losing their jobs and being replaced at the new schools by younger, cheaper, and less-experienced teachers (Brown, Gutstein, & Lipman, 2009). Renaissance 2010 has destabilized working-class and low-income communities (Brenner & Theodore, 2002). Children experienced school closings as a crisis of displacement as they transferred to other schools, which led to instability and correlated to an increase in youth violence (Brown et al., 2009). Thousands of residents, including many in public housing, were displaced as middle class families were lured to the city with offers of privatized choice through a lottery-based charter system (Brown, et al., 2009). Critics of Renaissance 2010 charge that charter schools are both the outgrowth of and stimulus for urban gentrification (Brown et al., 2009; Lipman, 2009).

Under Renaissance 2010, Charter schools in Chicago handed public moneys to more private corporate sponsors than ever before. Of the first 57 charter schools in Chicago, 42 are corporate, three are teacher initiated, nine are community centered, and three are university based (Lipman, 2009). Two years after Renaissance 2010 was initiated, Ayers and Klonsky (2006), two renowned educational scholars and developers of the small schools movement, cautioned that existing research did not justify having educational management organizations (EMOs) or profit-oriented companies run new Renaissance charter schools. The funding of EMOs is especially telling given that Renaissance 2010 provided no funds for traditional CPS schools or support for CPS teachers (Lipman & Hursh, 2007).

Overall, students' achievement at the charter schools was not significantly different from matched comparison students in traditional schools (Booker, Gill, Zimmer, & Sass, 2009; Young et al., 2009). Also, the Consortium on Chicago School Research, a nonpartisan group at the University of Chicago, found that closure of low-performing schools reshuffled eight out of every ten students into similarly low-performing schools, and that when math scores were compared with other urban school districts, charter students were not among the highest performers (Gwynne & de la Torre, 2009).

A RAND study found that Chicago charter schools attracted and served students who performed at higher achievement levels prior to entering charter schools than their counterparts enrolled in traditional schools (Booker et al., 2009). Also, a 2006–2008 study comparing traditional public schools with Renaissance 2010 schools found that the latter had a smaller proportion of bilingual students attending (24% versus 36%) (Young et al., 2009). A similar pattern emerged with special needs students—with 11% at Renaissance 2010 schools compared to the 15% in traditional public schools. Furthermore, when controlled for grade level, the students attending traditional public schools were older—a demographic that is statistically more likely to perform lower and to drop out—than those attending Renaissance 2010 schools.

It is also worth noting that by its very design, Renaissance 2010 gave the impression of far greater improvement than was actually the case. As Saltman (2007) explains, "By closing and reopening schools, Renaissance 2010 allows the newly privatized schools to circumvent NCLB AYP progress requirements, thus making the list of Chicago's 'need improvement' schools shorter. This allows the city to claim improvement by simply redefining terms" (p. 135). All this evidence challenges Duncan's claim: "For students trapped in chronically struggling schools...cutting-edge new schools under Renaissance 2010 hold out the most promise" (Duncan, 2006, p. 458).

RACE TO THE TOP AND THE EXPANSION OF CHARTER SCHOOLS

Following in his predecessors' footsteps, Obama allocated $4.35 billion to the Race to the Top grant competition to entice states into adopting, among other policies, the expansion of charter schools primarily in urban neighborhoods. During both Race to the Top competition rounds, state applications "receive[d] points based on the extent to which their laws do not prohibit or effectively inhibit increase of the number of high-performing charter schools" (U.S. Department of Education, 2010, p. 24). Early on, Obama made it clear that states with restrictions or caps on the total number of charter schools would be at a competitive disadvantage for federal funds: "[R]ight now, there are many caps on how many charter schools are allowed in some states, no matter how well they're preparing our students. That isn't good for our children, our economy, or our country" (White House Office of the Press Secretary, 2009, para. 30). A total of 41 states and the District of Columbia submitted applications, and only 11 states and DC receiving funds. The states that received federal funds had heeded the administration's warnings and eliminated or raised their caps considerably. Given that nearly all of the states that applied for the federal funds relaxed restrictions on charter schools, the Race to the Top is the most far-reaching federal policy enacted on behalf of charter schools.

It seems Obama's educational policies are contributing significantly to the growing number of charter schools. According to the National Alliance of Public Charter Schools, the leading national nonprofit organization advocating for and supporting the expansion of charter schools, the total number of charter school in the U.S. went from 4,913 in the fall of the 2009–2010 academic year to 5,611 in the fall of the 2011–2012 school year—a 12% increase that raised the percentage of charter schools to public schools from 5.0% to 5.8% in that two-year span. In addition, numerous

EMOs are actively planning to expand their school networks. Over the next decade, Knowledge Is Power Program (KIPP) intends to double the number of schools to 200 throughout the country and Aspire Public Schools, the largest EMO in California, also plans to operate twice as many schools (Chea, 2011).

Politicians and other public officials are trumpeting charter schools as a panacea and implementing pro-charter school policies and legislations. In Chicago, with the support of Mayor Rahm Emanuel, who previously served as Obama's Chief of Staff, charter schools are the fastest growing part of Chicago Public Schools, using up $300 million in funds (Joravsky & Dumke, 2011). In April 2012, Philadelphia Public Schools and their consultants proposed a reorganization plan that calls for the closure of 64 schools within five years and the establishment of school networks, which the plan estimates will result in 40% of students being enrolled in charter schools by 2017. The state of Tennessee used Race to the Top funds in May of 2011 to establish the "Achievement School District," which put five failing schools under the auspice of the state, which allowed for charter school EMOs to operate the schools. Three months later, Governor Chris Christie of New Jersey approved a pilot program authorizing private EMOs to run failing public schools. In March of 2011, for example, Robert Bobb, the Detroit Public Schools' emergency financial manager charged with reducing the district's deficit, announced the Renaissance Plan 2012, which focuses on converting 41 of Detroit's 141 public schools into charter schools. In the years to come, charter schools will likely have the greatest footprint in many of the neediest communities in our country.

The continued expansion of charter schools is also leading educational entrepreneurs to explore new ways by which to profit from both the marketization and the privatization of education. In this way, education is reduced to "a subsector of the economy" (McLaren & Farahmandpur, 2001, p. 136). Writing about a key entrepreneur in the Renaissance 2010 reform, Ayers and Klonsky (2006) state:

> Chris Whittle, former publisher of *Esquire* and founder of the Edison Schools—one of the companies brought in to manage CPS schools—found that it can be just as profitable to manage public space as to own it. The way Whittle sees it, "If profits cannot be made in education, then here is a partial list of things that should be removed from schools immediately: textbooks, computers, desks, milk, pencils, paper, and all athletic supplies and uniforms. And let's not forget to tear all school buildings down." (p. 463)

Edison Schools, which became a publicly traded company in 1999, had financial difficulties in 2001 after "its track record emerged—years in the red, unremarkable academics, accounting irregularities that led to a SEC investigation, and trouble retaining teachers" (Goldstein, 2008, para. 3).

Two years later, Edison became a private corporation again after former Governor Jeb Bush of Florida, along with two other state Republicans and fellow proponents of school choice, authorized the use of Florida Retirement System (FRS) funds, which included the savings of retired public school teachers, to purchase the struggling corporation (Bracey, 2004). With the highly criticized deal signed, Whittle's salary as head of Edison went from $345,000 to $600,000 (Bracey, 2004).

Other entrepreneurs have moved beyond the limitations of brick-and-mortar schools to the internet, where for-profit companies operate virtual (or cyber) charter schools. Presently, cyber schools operate in at least 27 states (Glass & Welner, 2011). Like physical charter schools, cyber charter schools are receiving the support of both Democrats and Republicans.

In August of 2011, Oregon passed legislation authorizing the expansion of cyber charter schools up to 3% of school districts' student enrollment. On May 15, 2012, Michigan Governor Rick Snyder signed a bill to expand cyber charter schools in the state to no more than 2% of the state's total public school enrollments. Months prior, in December of 2011, Synder had signed legislation removing the cap on the number of charter schools that can operate throughout the state, ensuring that the number would rise beyond the 255 charter schools operating at the time—80% of which are run by for-profit outfits (Landon, 2011). Even more interesting, Snyder had been repeatedly lobbied by Jeb Bush, former governor of Florida and proponent of online charter schools, prior to signing the legislation (Fang, 2011). The confluence of marketized legislation and the increased support for marketized for-profit schools is bad for public education.

The marketization of public education is being driven by the close ties between government officials and the charter school industry. In 1999, William J. Bennett, the U.S. Secretary of Education under Ronald Reagan, established K12 Inc., the most prominent outfit in the cyber charter school industry. Under Governor Arnold Schwarzenegger, Ted Mitchell, the CEO of the NewSchools Venture Fund and board member of the National Alliance for Public Charter Schools (NAPCS), served as president of the California State Board of Education, California's governing and policy-making body. The New Jersey pilot program discussed above is overseen by Christopher Cerf, the former president of Edison Schools (renamed EdisonLearning), the largest private-sector EMO in the country, whom Christie appointed as New Jersey's acting education commissioner. The Achievement School District in Tennessee is run by Chris Barbic, a successful charter school organizer (Resmovits, 2011). The revolving door between government and the private educational sector raises serious questions about the existence of conflicts of interest and/or the lack of necessary checks and balances to ensure educational policies are rooted in sound educational research and not business calculations.

BLURRING THE LINE BETWEEN PRIVATE
AND PUBLIC INTERESTS

Along with the support from politicians, charter schools have garnered the support of private foundations with large sums of money at their disposal, including some of the most well-known partisan and bipartisan organizations: the Annenberg Foundation, the Ely and Edith Broad Foundation, the Lilly Endowment, the David and Lucile Packard Foundation, the WK Kellogg Foundation, the Walton Foundation, the Gates Foundation, the Heritage Foundation, the Bradley Foundation, the John M. Olin Foundation, and the Lynde and Harry Bradley Foundation. Moneys from foundations have funded both start-up and operating costs of individual charter schools and nonprofit organizations dedicated to the nationwide expansion of charter schools. Using venture capitalist models, some foundations call for charters to be managed like financial portfolios. The Gates Foundation, for one, supports a portfolio management system to "ensure a supply of quality school options that reflects a community's needs, interests, and assets ... and [to ensure] that every student has access to high-quality schools that prepare them for further learning, work, and citizenship" (Gates Foundation, 2005, p. 3). The central role of these venture philanthropists, or "philanthrocapitalists" (Ravitch, 2010, p. 199), is startling. They are involved in one of the most sweeping educational reforms and yet cannot be held accountable by voters.

Additionally, charter schools benefit from the work of the National Alliance for Public Charter Schools (NAPCS), the leading national nonprofit organization supporting the expansion of charter schools. In 2010, the NAPCS, whose board members have ties to public school districts, philanthropic foundations, and charter school operators, released a report that provided proponents of the charter school movements with a comparative assessment to be used as states establish or modify charter laws to improve their chances in the Race to the Top competition. The report also gauged each state "with respect to its commitment to the full range of values in the public charter school movement: quality and accountability, funding equity, facilities support, autonomy, and growth and choice" (NAPCS, 2010, p. 3). As part of its campaign to promote charter schools, the NAPCS also holds an awards dinner during the National Charter Schools Week—the first week of May—called Champions for Charters, at which they honor public officials for supporting charter school legislation. Additionally, by sponsoring the Alliance of Public Charter School Attorneys (APCSA), an organization that was established in 2008 to provide lawyers with charter school-related information and networking opportunities, the NAPCS has access to a cadre of lawyers to advance the charter school agenda on the legal front.

CHARTER SCHOOL MYTHS:
INNOVATION, ACHIEVEMENT, AND EQUITY

In public comments, U.S. Secretary of Education Arne Duncan has referred to charter schools as "laboratories of innovation" that produce better classroom practices that can benefit traditional schools (Diamond, 2009, para. 5). Given all the political and philanthropic support charter schools are receiving, one would think that there is overwhelming evidence indicating the schools' success. However, this is not the case. Even as Duncan announced the first round of Race to the Top winners, there was plenty of mounting evidence that charter schools as a whole were neither innovative nor better schooling options. Research suggests that classroom strategies at charter schools are not innovative, but rather much the same as those developed and used at traditional public schools (Lubienski, 2003). The few innovations observed at charter schools had to do with self-marketing (Lubienski, 2003). Even more telling, multinational data indicate that educational innovation results from "public-sector policies" and *not* from the competition among schools encouraged by charter school proponents (Lubienski, 2009).

Students attending charter schools are not faring any better than peers at traditional schools. In a 2007 study, the North Carolina Center for Public Policy Research (NCCPPR), a nonpartisan, nonprofit group, found that charter schools in the state perform no better than traditional public schools and concluded "choice" was not a good enough reason to authorize expanding public charter schools (Manuel, 2007). Similarly, a RAND study of Philadelphia's public schools found that between 1997–2007 children in charter schools did not outperform their traditional school counterparts and that competition from charter schools did not improve traditional public schools (Zimmer, Blanc, Gill, & Christman, 2008). Additionally, the data from the 2007 National Assessment of Educational Progress (NAEP) report indicate that when compared to charter school students, traditional public school students in fourth grade scored higher in both reading and mathematics, and that eighth grade traditional public school students scored higher in mathematics and the same in reading (Robelen, 2008). More telling yet, a 2009 Stanford University study of 2,403 charter schools in 15 states found that 37% of the charters had learning gains that were significantly below those of traditional public schools, 46% showed no difference, and only 17% showed significantly better gains (CREDO, 2009). Worse, research shows that cyber charter schools perform worse on every measure (CREDO, 2011; Glass & Welner, 2011).

An extensive analysis by the Civil Rights Project at UCLA found that charter schools isolate students by class and race and may be contributing to white flight (Frankenberg, Siegel-Hawley & Wang, 2010). While nearly one in four charter schools do not provide data on low-income students, available data show that charter schools with high minority student enrollments have high rates of low-income students. Additionally, the UCLA study finds that charter schools are more racially segregated than traditional schools. Black students attending charter schools face far greater segregation than other students. Latino charter students, on the other hand, experience less segregation than Black students, but are under-enrolled in some Western states where they account for the majority of public school students.

Studies also suggest that many charter schools under-serve students who are English language learners (ELLs). Studies of charter schools in New York show that they enroll fewer ELLs and fewer special needs students than the traditional schools they replaced (Advocates for Children, 2002; Pallas & Jennings, 2009). Betts, Rice, Zau, Tang, and Koedel (2006) found that ELLs in San Diego had less access to charter schools because of language barriers in the dissemination and translation of registration materials. The educational level of the parents included in the study correlated with choice, in effect advantaging better-educated and wealthier parents. In a study of Washington, DC charter schools, Buckley and Schneider (2007) document that ELLs were proportionately underrepresented in 28 of the 37 charters (and special education students in 24 of the 37 charters). In Boston, while ELLs comprised one-fifth of the public school enrollment, they comprised only 4% of charter enrollment, and over one third of the Boston charters did not have a single ELL (Ravitch, 2010). Consequently, the relative academic success of many Boston public charter schools (Kane et al., 2009) may be due to their unrepresentative student populations. More recently, a March 2011 study finds that Knowledge is Power Program (KIPP), which operates nearly 100 schools throughout the country and serves over 25,000 students, enrolled lower rates of ELL students (11.5%) than traditional public schools (19.2%) (Miron, Urschel, & Saxton, 2011).

Unfortunately, large-scale examinations of charter schools' ELL enrollments are difficult because many charter schools do not provide the federal government with data, resulting in "major gaps in federal data sources" (Frankenberg et al., 2010, p. 5). The lack of data is so extensive that the available "Federal data on charter schools in California, arguably the country's most significant gateway for immigrants, describe just *seven* ELL students attending its state charter programs" (Frankenberg et al., 2010, p. 5). Some of the available data suggest that those California charters that serve ELLs do not provide enough qualified and specialized teachers to fulfill ELL needs (Fuller, Gawlik, Gonzales, Park, & Gibbings, 2003). By not providing qualified teachers, charter schools violate Lau v. Nichols, which guarantees equal access to the core curriculum. The fact that charter schools do a poor job of providing data on ELL students and of hiring qualified teachers raises the question of just how committed they are to serving ELL students.

School choice is also resulting in the exclusion of students with special needs, undoing decades of progress toward mainstreaming (Howe & Welner, 2002). Some charter schools are "counseling out" children with disabilities (Rhim & McLaughlin, 2007; Estes, 2006; Fierros & Blomberg, 2005; Grant, 2005; Howe & Welner, 2002). In a survey, 3% of charter schools admitted telling parents of children with disabilities they could not admit their children, and 44% of the schools admitted informing parents that their children would be better served at another school (Rhim & McLaughlin, 2007). Additionally, a study finds that KIPP schools have lower rates of disabled children (5.9%) than traditional public schools (12.1%) (Miron et al., 2011). In 2011, a news investigation team found that "more than 86 percent of Florida's charter schools do not serve a single child with a severe disability—compared to more than half of district schools that do" (O'Connor & Gonzalez, 2011). Lastly, a recent General Accountability Office (2012) report finds that charter schools enroll students with disabilities at rates lower than those of public schools.

Many charters employ inexperienced and uncredentialed teachers, who are "are less likely to be knowledgeable about the Individuals with Disabilities Education Act (IDEA), the Least Restrictive Environment (LRE), and Free and Appropriate Education (FAE) requirements of the law" (Grant, 2005, p. 71). These teachers are more likely both to teach racial minority students and to refer them for special education services (Cartledge, 2005). Also, a study of 502 charter schools in California found that charter schools have fewer students with special needs than traditional public schools, and that Black students were overrepresented in classes for the severely learning disabled and the emotionally disturbed (Fierros & Blomberg, 2005). The study also found that ethnically diverse students receiving special education services were more likely to be segregated. Given such findings, special education scholars argue that charters only be given to applicants who demonstrate how they will provide the necessary accommodations to students with special needs (Davis, 2005; Obiakor, Beachum, & Harris, 2005).

Given such data, leading educators and scholars question the role of charter schools. Bob Peterson, a teacher and founding editor of *Rethinking Schools*, asserts "[W]e're setting up a two-tier system . . . the most difficult-to-educate kids, a higher percentage of special needs, English language learners, kids who are counseled out of charter schools and voucher schools because of discipline problems—they end up in the public schools, while there's a self-selected group in the charter schools" (Democracy Now, 2009a). Deborah Meier, who began the small schools movement, concludes that though some charter schools are quality schools, nearly all charter schools are "just alternative private systems within the public sector" (Democracy Now, 2009b, para. 20). Lastly, Ravitch (2010), a prominent educational historian and a one-time influential proponent of school choice, argues that business-driven educational policies, including the expansion of charter schools, are unlikely to result in meaningful reform and efficiency.

Scaling up good charter schools, as neoliberal and conservative proponents recommend, is likely to prove difficult, if not impossible. Many charter schools operate by relying on parents' "help labor" (Christianakis, 2011) to keep their costs down and are highly dependent on the financial support of philanthropists (Education Sector, 2009). For example, a predominantly middle-class charter school in Atlanta saved money by having parents contribute 15–40 hours of labor per week (Hankins & Martin, 2006). Additionally, a study found that $500 million in private donations was needed over the course of a decade for networks of nonprofit operators to open approximately 350 charter schools (Education Sector, 2009). More recently, research found that KIPP schools, which George W. Bush and Obama have praised for their standardized test outcomes, receive much more funding from the federal government and private donors than other charters or traditional public schools, resulting in thousands of dollars more in per-pupil spending (Miron et al., 2011). Such dependence on private donations, as well as federal funds, raises serious questions about the feasibility and sustainability of charter school expansion.

When charter schools are closed due to their low-test scores, cheating scandals (see, e.g., Blume, 2011), or financial malfeasance (see Blume, 2010), students and parents must turn to the available school options, which in low-income communities may be limited to other schools in danger of being closed. Consequently, in the not too distant future, it may be that in entire communities children's educational experiences are defined not by innovative instruction, but rather by their matriculation in a series of struggling charter or traditional schools. Adding insult to injury, neoliberals and conservatives will likely hold these children and their families solely responsible for their poor consumer choices within the education market.

CONCLUSION

Obama has correctly stated on numerous occasions that education is the civil rights issue of our time. While education is at the center of struggles for civil rights, there is a befuddling disconnect between Obama's words and his educational policy. If he truly believes that education is our generation's civil rights concern, why is he subjecting it to market pressures? When has the corporate world been out front on civil rights issues?

Obama's educational policy has resulted in the greatest increase of charter schools to date. The increase marks the convergence of politics, money, and neoliberal market rationalism in support of school choice, a fact that Duncan knows all too well. In his address at the 2009 National Alliance for

Public Charter School Conference, he stated, "We may never have an opportunity like this again—this president, this Congress, $100 billion, and a
broad and growing consensus around the importance of education. So this
is our time and this is our moment. This is our chance to transform the one
thing in society with the power to transform lives. The path to success has
never been clearer" (Duncan, 2009, p. 6). With all that has been discussed
in this chapter, it bears asking: Whose time? Whose success?

Obama's educational policy is furthering neoliberal and neoconservative
agendas to undermine the welfare state and hand over the public sector to
market capitalism. In a market economy, charter school expansion will likely increase social inequalities by encouraging capitalist Darwinism, which
leaves urban minority youth, special needs students, and English language
learners at less than a competitive disadvantage. Though Obama places his
hope on a market-driven education, research indicates that such hope demands blind faith in the sort of neoliberal audacity that nearly toppled the
financial market.

Eduardo Galeano (2000) reminds us that capitalist discourse "wear[s]
the stage name 'market economy'" (p. 40) to disguise offenses carried out
in the public arena. In closing, we borrow Galeano's analogical style, which
reveals how euphemisms mask and normalize neoliberal lexicons, to highlight the emerging marketing language in public schooling:

- Shutting down schools without community input bears the name
  "Renaissance."
- Displacing students is called "restructuring."
- Turning away students is the luck of the draw in a "lottery."
- School choice is dressed up as "civil rights."
- Requiring parents to donate time and labor in order to stay within
  lean budgets falls under "parent involvement."
- Re-titling superintendents as portfolio-managing CEOs is called
  "Reform."
- Funneling public money into "for profit" schools is called
  "innovation."
- Revolving doors and potential conflicts of interest between business-
  es, philanthropies, schools, nonprofits, and government officials is
  termed "collaboration."
- Teacher bashing goes under the name "merit pay," "added value,"
  and "accountability."
- Learning a foreign language is a must for "global competition," yet
  children who are English Language Learners are "low performers."
- Rejecting special needs children is called "counseling out."
- Federal coercion goes under the competitive title "Race to the Top."
- Children are so-called investments—subject to elastic market pressures.

- The rich who are co-opting public services are praised as philanthropists who "give generously."
- Ill-prepared, inexperienced teachers are heralded as, "altruistic, bright, recent college graduates."

REFERENCES

Advocates for Children. (2002). *Pushing out at-risk students: An analysis of high school-discharge figures—a joint report by AFC and the Public Advocate.* Retrieved from http://www.advoatesforchildren.org/pubs/pushouts-11-20-02.html

Au, W. (2009). Obama, where art thou? Hoping for change in U.S. educational policy. *Harvard Educational Review, 79*(2), 309–320.

Ayers, W., & Klonsky, M. (2006). Private management of Chicago schools is a long way from Mecca. *Phi Delta Kappan, 87*(6), 461–463.

Ball, S. (1998). Big policies/small worlds: An introduction to international perspectives in educational policy. *Comparative Education, 34*(2), 119–130.

Bartlett, L., Frederick, M., Bulbrandsen, T., & Murillo, E. (2002). The marketization of education: Public schools for private ends. *Anthropology & Education Quarterly, 33*(1), 1–25.

Betts, J., Rice L., Zau, A., Tang, Y., & Koedel, C. (2006). *Does school choice work? Effects on student integration and achievement.* San Francisco, CA. Public Policy Institute of California.

Berlowitz, M. (2000). Racism and conscription the JROTC. *Peace Review, 12*(3), 393–398.

Blume, H. (2010, August 31). L.A. Unified moves to close charter school over alleged misuse of $2.7 million. *Los Angeles Times.* Retrieved from http://articles.latimes.com/2010/aug/31/local/la-me-charter-20100831

Blume, H. (2011, March 5). Founder of Crescendo charter schools fired. *Los Angeles Times.* Retrieved from http://articles.latimes.com/2011/mar/05/local/la-me-crescendo-20110305

Booker, K., Gill, B., Zimmer, R., & Sass, T. (2009). *Achievement and attainment in Chicago charter schools.* Santa Monica, CA: The Rand Corporation.

Bracey, G. W. (2004, October). The 14th Bracey Report on the condition of public education. *Phi Delta Kappan,* 149–167.

Brenner, N., & Theodore, N. (2002). Cities and the geographies of "actually existing neoliberalism." *Antipode, 34*(3), 349–379.

Brown, J., Gutstein, E. R., & Lipman, P. (2009). Arne Duncan and the Chicago success story: Myth or reality? *Rethinking Schools Online, 23*(3). Retrieved from http://www.rethinkingschools.org/archive/23_03/arne233.shtml

Burchell, G. (1996). Liberal government and the techniques of the self. In A. Barry, T. Osbourne, & N. Rose (Eds.), *Foucault and political reason: Liberalism, neoliberalism, and rationalities of government* (pp. 19–37). Chicago, IL: The University of Chicago Press.

Cartledge, G. (2005). Restrictiveness and race in special education: The failure to prevent or return. *Learning Disabilities: A Contemporary Journal, 3*(1), 27–32.

Center for Research on Education Outcomes (CREDO). (2009). *Multiple choice: Charter school performance in 16 states.* Stanford, CA: Stanford University.

Center for Research on Education Outcomes (CREDO). (2011). *Charter school Performance in Pennsylvania.* Stanford, CA: Stanford University. Retrieved from http:// credo.stanford.edu/reports/PA%20State%20Report_20110404_FINAL.pdf

Chea, T. (2011, January 21). Charter schools expand with public, private money. Associated Press. Retrieved from http://www.huffingtonpost.com/2011/01/21/ charter-schools-expand_n_812183.html?utm_hp_ref=charter-schools

Christianakis, M. (2011). Parents as help labor: Inner-city teachers' narratives of parent involvement. *Teacher Education Quarterly, 38*(4), 157–178.

Chubb, J., & Moe, T. (1990). *Politics, markets, & America's schools.* Washington, DC: The Brookings Institute.

Darling-Hammond, L. (2010). *The flat world and education: How America's commitment to equity will deter our future.* New York, NY: Teachers College Press.

Davis, C. (2005). Restrictiveness and race in special education: Access to a special education infrastructure. *Learning Disabilities: A Contemporary Journal, 3*(1), 57–63.

Democracy Now!: The War and Peace Report. (2009a, June 23). Education Secretary Arne Duncan pushes to aggressively expand charter schools while admitting problems. Retrieved from http://www.democracynow.org/2009/6/23/ education_secretary_arne_duncan_pushes_to

Democracy Now!: The War and Peace Report. (2009b, May 21). Teaching pioneer Deborah Meier on Obama's education policy and the future of charter schools. Retrieved from http://www.democracynow.org/2009/5/21/schools

Diamond, L. (2009, March 15). Cash-strapped charter schools struggle. *The Atlanta Journal Constitution.* Retrieved from http://www.ajc.com/hotjobs/content/ printedition/2009/03/15/charterschools03153dot.html

Duncan, A. (2006). Chicago's Renaissance 2010: Building on school reform in the age of accountability. *The Phi Delta Kappan, 87*(6), 457–458.

Education Sector. (2009, November) Growing pains: Scaling up the nation's best charter schools. *Education Sector Report.* Retrieved from http://www.educationsector.org/usr_doc/Growing_Pains.pdf

Fierros, E. G., & Blomberg, N. A. (2005). Restrictiveness and race in special education placements in for-profit and non-profit charter schools in California. *Learning Disabilities: A Contemporary Journal, 3*(1), 1–16.

Frankenberg, E., Siegel-Hawley, G., & Wang, J. (2010). *Choice without equity: Charter school segregation and the need for civil rights standards.* Los Angeles, CA: The Civil Rights Project/Proyecto Derechos Civiles at UCLA. Retrieved from www.civilrightsproject.ucla.edu

Fuller, B., Gawlik, M., Gonzales, E., & Park, S. with Gibbons, G. (2003). *Charter schools and inequality: National disparities in funding, teacher quality, and student support.* Working Paper Series 03-2. Berkeley, CA: Policy Analysis for California Education.

Galeano, E. (2000). *Upside down: A primer for the looking glass world.* New York, NY: Picador/Henry Holt.

General Accountability Office. (June 2012). *Charter schools: Additional federal attention needed to help protect access for students with disabilities.* Washington, DC: Author.

Glass, G. V., & Welner, K. G. (2011, October 25). *Online K–12 schooling in the U.S.: Uncertain private ventures in need of public regulation.* Boulder, CO: National Education Policy Center.

Goldstein, D. (2008, August 5). Business schools. *The American Prospect.* Retrieved from www.prospect.org//cs/articles;jsessionid=aIx0OLvmcvHgvyH5uK?article=business_schools

Grant, P. A. (2005). Restrictiveness and race in special education: Educating all learners. *Learning Disabilities: A Contemporary Journal, 3*(1), 70–74.

Gwynne, J., & de la Torre. (2009). When schools close: Effects on displaced students in Chicago Public Schools. Consortium on Chicago School Research. Retrieved from http://ccsr.uchicago.edu/publications/CCSRSchoolClosings-Final.pdf

Hankins, D., & Martin, D. (2006). Charter schools and urban regimes in neoliberal context: Making workers and new spaces in metropolitan Atlanta. *International Journal of Urban and Regional Research, 30*(3), 528–547.

Howe, K., & Welner, K. (2002). School choice and the pressure to perform: Déjà vu for children with disabilities. *Journal of Remedial and Special Education, 23*(4), 212–221.

Kane, T., Abdulkadiroglu, A., Angrist, J., Cohodes, S., Dynarski, S., Fullerton, J., & Pathak, P. (2009). *Informing the debate: Comparing Boston's charter, pilot, and traditional schools.* Boston, MA: Boston Foundation. Retrieved from http://www.gse.harvard.edu/%7Epfpie/pdf/InformingTheDebate_Final.pdf

Landon, S. (2011, December 15). Michigan house votes to lift charter school cap. *The Huffington Post.* Retrieved from http://www.huffingtonpost.com/2011/12/14/michigan-house-lift-charter-school-cap_n_1149911.html?utm_hp_ref=charter-schools Lau v. Nichols. (1974). 414 US 563.

Lipman, P. (2009). Making sense of *Renaissance 2010* school policy in Chicago: Race, class, and the cultural politics of neoliberal urban restructuring. Great Cities Institute Publication Number: GCP-09-02.

Lipman, P., & Hursh, D. (2007). Renaissance 2010: The reassertion of ruling-class power through neoliberal policies in Chicago. *Policy Futures in Education, 5*(2).

Lubienski, C. (2003). Innovation in education markets: Theory and evidence on the impact of competition and choice in charter schools. *American Educational Research Journal, 40*(2), 395–443.

Lubienski, C. (2006). School diversification in second-best education markets international evidence and conflicting theories. *Educational Policy, 20*(2), 323–344.

Lubienski, C. (2009). *Do quasi-markets foster innovation in education? A comparative perspective.* Education working paper, 25. Paris, France: Organisation for Economic Co-operation and Development.

McLaren, P., & Farahmandpur, R. (2001). Teaching against globalization and the new imperialism: Toward a revolutionary pedagogy. *Journal of Teacher Education, 52*(2), 136–150.

Manuel, J. (2007). *Charter schools revisited: A decade after authorization, how goes the North Carolina experience?* Raleigh, NC: North Carolina Center for Public Policy Research.

Miron, G., Urschel, J. L., & Saxton, N. (2011, March). *What makes KIPP work? A study of student characteristics, attrition, and school finance.* National Center for the Study of Privatization in Education, Teachers College, Columbia University and the Study Group on Educational Management Organizations at Western Michigan University.

National Center for Educational Statistics. (2010, September). Table 100. Number of traditional and public charter elementary and secondary schools and percentages of students, teachers, and schools, by selected characteristics: 2007–2008. Retrieved from http://nces.ed.gov/programs/digest/d09/tables/dt09_100.asp

National Center for Educational Statistics. (n.d.). Table A-32-1. Number and percentage distribution of charter schools and students, by selected characteristics: Selected school years 1999–2000 through 2007–08. http://nces.ed.gov/programs/coe/2010/section4/tablecht-1.asp

Obiakor, F., Beachum, F., & Harris, M. (2005). Restrictiveness and race in special education: Practicalizing the laws. *Learning Disabilities: A Contemporary Journal, 3*(1), 52–55.

O'Connor, J., & Gonzalez, S. (2011, December 14). Florida charter schools failing disabled students. *NPR.* Retrieved from http://www.npr.org/2011/12/14/143659449/florida-charter-schools-failing-disabled-students

Pallas, A., & Jennings, J. (2009). New York city's progress reports. In L. Haimson & A. Kjellberg (Eds.), *New York City schools under Bloomberg and Klein: What parents, teachers, and policymakers need to know* (pp. 77–86). Raleigh, NC: Lulu.

Peters, M. (1999). Neoliberalism. *The Encyclopedia of Philosophy of Education.* Retrieved from http://www.vusst.hr/ENCYCLOPAEDIA/neoliberalism.html

Public Law 94-142, Education for All Handicapped Children's Act of 1975, 89 Stat 773.

Ravitch, D. (2010). *The death and life of the great American school system: How testing and choice are undermining education.* New York, NY: Basic Books.

Resmovits, J. (2011, July 13). Tennessee's state-controlled school district puts reform to the test. *Huffington Post.* Retrieved from http://www.huffingtonpost.com/2011/05/13/tennessee-state-controlled-school-district_n_860324.html?utm_hp_ref=charter-schools

Rhim, L. M, & McLaughlin, M. J. (2007) Students with disabilities in charter schools: What we now know. *Focus on Exceptional Children, 39*(5), 1–13

Robelen, E. W. (2008). NAEP gap continuing for charters: Sector's scores lag in three out of four main categories. *Education Week, 27*(38), 1–14.

Saltman, K. J. (2007). Schooling in disaster capitalism: How the political right is using disaster to privatize public schooling. *Teacher Education Quarterly, 34*(2), 131–156.

Saul, J. R. (2005). *The collapse of globalism and the reinvention of the world.* New York, NY: Penguin Books.

Scoppio, G. (2002). Common trends of standardization, accountability, devolution and choice in the educational policies of England, U.K., California, USA., and Ontario, Canada. *Current Issues in Comparative Education, 2*(2), 130–141.

Tareen, S. (2007, November 2). Chicago leads in public military schools. *Associated Press.* Retrieved from http://www.usatoday.com/news/nation/2007-11-02-2738760309_x.htm

Temkin, K., Hong, G., Davis, L., & Bavin, W. (2008). Implementation of the credit enhancement for charter school facilities program. Washington, DC: U.S. Department of Education, Office of Planning, Evaluation and Policy Development Policy and Program Studies Service Implementation.

United States Department of Education. (2004). Charter schools program, title v, part b, non-regulatory guidance. Retrieved from http://www2.ed.gov/policy/elsec/guid/cspguidance03.doc

United States Department of Education. (2008). *A commitment to quality: National charter school policy forum report.* Washington, DC: Author.

United States Department of Education. (2010). *Race to the Top program guidance and frequently asked questions.* Washington, DC: Author.

White House Office of the Press Secretary. (2009, March 10). Remarks by the president to the Hispanic Chamber of Commerce on a complete and competitive American education. Retrieved from http://www.whitehouse.gov/the-press-office/remarks-president-united-states-hispanicchamber-commerce

Whitty, G., & Edwards, T. (1998). School choice policies in England and the United States: An exploration of their origins and significance. *Comparative Education, 34*(2), 211–228.

Young, V. M., Humphrey, D. C., Wang, H., Bosetti, K. R., Cassidy, L., Wechsler, M. E., Rivera, E., Murray, S., & Schanzenhack, D. W. (2009). *Renaissance schools fund supported schools: Early outcomes, challenges, and opportunities.* Stanford Research International and Chicago Consortum on Chicago School Research. Retrieved from http://ccsr.uchicago.edu/publications/RSF%20FINAL%20April%2015.pdf

Zimmer, R., Blanc, S., Gill, B. P., & Christman, J. B. (2008). *Evaluating the performance of Philadelphia's charter schools.* Santa Monica, CA: RAND Education.

CHAPTER 8

GATES OF HELL

Abandon all Hope, Ye Who Enter Here

by Susan Ohanian

If they can get you asking the wrong questions,
they don't have to worry about the answers.
—Thomas Pynchon, *Gravity's Rainbow*

In 1996, Stuart Cheifet, executive producer and host of "The Computer Chronicles" on Public Television, told "All Things Considered" listeners why Bill Gates would make a good president,[1] which was in line with the era's media Gates worship. Everybody loves a rich man. Over the next couple of years, however, things changed dramatically. Maureen Dowd started out 1998[2] by calling Gates a "spoiled, rich brat." The media turned on Gates because after the U.S. Department of Justice sued Microsoft for anti-trust violations, Gates thought he could stonewall his way out of it. This was nothing new. In 1993, the Federal Trade Commission had turned complaints over to the Department of Justice. One of the ensuing rules was that Microsoft couldn't throw out any documents: "In Building 8, where Gates' office was, the hallways were lined floor to ceiling, for two corridors and wings, with file boxes full of paper collected for the DoJ. . . . The DoJ estimated its

Left Behind in the Race to the Top, pages 103–127
Copyright © 2013 by Information Age Publishing
All rights of reproduction in any form reserved.

investigation took 14,000 attorney hours, 5,500 paralegal hours, and 3,650 economist hours.[3]

The imbroglios over the next 4 years are fascinating but a bit too abstruse to summarize here. Just know that attorney generals from a number of states filed their own suits, the Microsoft second-in-command said to heck with US Attorney General Janet Reno and Justice Department officials accused Microsoft of hubris and of deliberately thumbing its nose at the Government and the Federal bench. Anyone who believes what Mr. and Mrs. Gates claim about teacher excellence should read John Heilemann's account[4] of the disastrous Gates deposition: "He was the sort of CEO who would profess not to recall countless emails he'd written and who would claim to be ignorant of his company's strategies—strategies he himself had masterminded. Who would quarrel stubbornly over the meanings of words like *concern, compete, definition, ask,* and *very....*" In those days, even the press took note: A CNN headline[5] reads "Gates deposition makes judge laugh in court."

Probably the most telling thing a teacher can glean from studying the anti-trust action against Microsoft is that Gates and the people around him all believed he was smarter than the lawyers—his own lawyers and the opposing lawyers. A Microsoft senior manager told John Heilemann,[6] "This is not a normal client who just sits across from his lawyers and takes their advice. No way." One can hardly expect that it would occur to such a man to consult veteran educators.

When the United States Department of Justice sued Microsoft for anti-trust violations, *Time* noted,[7] "Power in the nation's capital isn't about right and wrong. It's about making nice." By 1998, the Gates machine had figured out if he wasn't going to make nice with the Department of Justice, he'd better do it in public. And so, from singing his daughter's favorite song "Twinkle, Twinkle, Little Star" to a gushing Barbara Walters on "20/20"[8] in January to a December gift of $100 million for child immunizations—plus a chat on potty training[9] with Rosie O'Donnell (where Natalie Imburglia, ranked #90 on VH1's Top 100 Sexiest Artists, was also a guest), 1998 was the year of the Bill Gates attempt at a media makeover. February's *New York Times* report that "the Microsoft mogul was nailed with a good old vaudevillian custard pie in the face with cameras catching him awkwardly wiping goo from his hair and glasses"[10] was just a temporary glitch in the plan.

Not everyone was signing on to the plan. *New York Times* columnist Frank Rich observed,[11] "As a hard-knuckled tycoon he was at least true to his arrogant self. Now he is morphing into another phony full-time actor in the sentimental PR pageant that has become American public life. He must turn himself into a lovable character that the entire populace will adore, if that's what it takes to deflect the Feds." This list of headlines from 1998 reveals that a few others also had some doubts about Mr. Gates.

- "Liberties: Revenge on the Nerds"[12]
- "Of Mice and Men, Release 2.0[13]"
- "Gates Helped Draft Microsoft's Response to Judge" [14]
- "Gentlemen, Choose Your Sausage"[15]
- "See Gates Lobby"
- "Love that Bill"[16]
- "Clash of the Titans"[17]
- "Windows 98, The Tuneup"[18]
- "What Antitrust Is All About"[19]
- "Bill Gates Buys Homer Painting for Record Price"[20]
- "Rich Man, Richer Man"[21]
- "United States v. Microsoft"[22]
- The Nation—"Rating the Bigshots: Gates vs. Rockefeller"[23]
- "Microsoft's World: A special report: How Software's Giant Played
- Hardball Game"[24]
- "Microsoft: Looking Out for Number One,"[25]
- "Gates Quoted as Seeing Case 'Blow Over'"[26]
- "On Day 1, U. S. Targets Gates; Government Portrays Microsoft
- Chairman as Cagey, Ruthless"[27]
- "The Microsoft Mafia"[28]
- "Influence"[29]
- "Microsoft's 'Jihad' Jam"[30]
- "Bill Gates donating $100 million for child immunizations"[31]
- "Bill Gates: Software Strongman" [32]
- "Publicists spin as MS seeks AOL-Netscape papers. And the kinder, gentler Gates answers three questions. Take it easy, Bill . . ."[33]
- "A Kinder, Gentler Bill"[34]
- "Video Dominates Microsoft Trial Before Recess"[35]
- "The Right Thing; Bosses Beware When Bending the Truth"[36]
- "Microsoft's Big Browser"[37]

When *New York Times* reporter Allen Myerson[38] compared Gates to John D. Rockefeller, he noted that while Gates was richer, Rockefeller had more fancy houses; but Gates had market power that Rockefeller would envy. In terms of who was "more a rapacious monopolist," it was probably a draw. Gates may well have felt flattered. Former *New Yorker* and *Wired* staff writer John Heilemann offers a deadpan and riveting description[39] of a ritzy Silicon Valley enclave where the "geeked out" Gates regales the table with tales of programs he'd written in Microsoft's early days and speaks admiringly about the just-published *Titan*, Ron Chernow's biography of Rockefeller. Heilemann also quotes bulldog antitrust lawyer Gary Reback's observation, "The only thing J. D. Rockfeller did that Bill Gates hasn't done is use dynamite against his competitors!"

Can you imagine anyone talking about Bill Gates this way today? Gates must have known he was in trouble when Maureen Dowd quoted[40] the Reback observation in January and *The New Yorker* did likewise[41] in May.

Teachers may well ask: Where are these reporters today?

If you want to read about the Gates who bragged that he had "as much power as the president" and who burst into tears at a Microsoft board meeting, then you need to buy Heilemann's book.

Even though Microsoft was found guilty, the story does not have a happy ending. And the education community should take notice of why this happened. Once Microsoft had been found guilty, the judge asked its victims to offer suggestions of a suitable punishment. Heilemann describes the chilling silence that ensued. As much as Silicon Valley hated Bill Gates, as much as they felt threatened by him, they were scared into silence by the threat of his power.

These days, the lure of Gates Foundation money combines with the fear, real and imagined, of local reprisals to keep educators silent. But we could look to a conservative jurist for a lesson. While University of Chicago free-market economist Milton Friedman was decrying the lawsuit as "government interference," conservative jurist Robert Bork, whose *The Antitrust Paradox* was sacred text for Chicago School economists, stunned bystanders. Writing in the May 1998 *New York Times*, "What Antitrust Is All About,"[42] Bork made the point that should be made today about the Gates education monopoly:

> There seems to be a widespread impression that the Microsoft controversy should be resolved by an ideological litmus test: liberals are bent on punishing success, and conservatives must defend Bill Gates's company from any application of the antitrust laws. But the question is not one of politics or ideology; it is one of law and economics. And that is why an outspoken free marketeer like me can be found arguing against Microsoft.

Who would guess that Ralph Nader and Robert Bork would ever be on the same side of anything? Can we hope that Parents Across America and unions and progressive groups fighting for public education will drop litmus tests and hold hands with Jay P. Greene, the Heritage Foundation, and the market-based think tank Washington Policy Center[43] in opposition to the Common Core?

Closing out 1998, Bill/Monica made *Advertising Age's* December recap of the ten notable people of 1998.[44] And so did Gates. Described as "omnipresent," Bill Gates appeared just below Jesse Ventura. In the United Kingdom, *The Register* noted[45] that the $100 million gift for children's vaccines seemed conveniently timed, also pointing out that Microsoft's full-page advertisements in the *WSJ*, the *New York Times* and the *Washington Post* pleading its case would be "unthinkable in England."

While Gates was promoting his "nice guy" image, some remembered what happened in 1993 when the Federal Trade Commission opened an inquiry into Microsoft's business practice. Gates responded by accusing then-commissioner, "soft spoken" Dennis Yao, of harboring communist-like views on how the New Economy should work.[46]

But 1998 had taught the hard-knuckled tycoon something. In 1999, Gates the philanthropist comes on strong. No longer are we reading about the bully, the socially-inept predator, the despotic potentate, the guy with "the emotional make-up of a petulant 10-year-old," "egomaniacal and dangerous," or even the "nerd king." Preeminent descriptive adjectives in the press become "Philanthropist," "creator of the country's largest charitable foundation," "the world's richest man," and these epithets continue to this day. In September 1999, the *New York Times* was explicit, calling Gates's transformation "a metamorphosis from businessman to philanthropist." The media was no longer getting the March 16, 1994, Bill Gates who could tell Connie Chung (off air), "Connie, I just can't believe how fucking stupid you are!"[47]

So the press went gaga over a carefully staged $100 million contribution to speed the delivery of four vaccines for child immunization in developing countries, with hardly anybody noticing what Gates spent on decorations for that mega-million dollar, 66,000-square-foot house (variously described as costing somewhere between $35 and $100 million). In 1994, Gates paid $30.8 million for *Codex Leicester*, a 72-page manuscript compiled by Leonardo da Vinci. Then came the paintings:

> 1996: Andrew Wyeth's "Distant Thunder," $7 million
> 1997: William Merritt Chase's "The Nursery," $10 million
> 1998: Frederick Childe Hassam's "Room of Flowers," $20 million
> (Hassam's "The Avenue in the Rain" hangs in Obama's Oval Office.)
> 1998: Winslow Homer's "Lost on the Grand Banks," $36 million
> 1999: George Bellow's "Polo Crowd," $28 million

The point here is not to begrudge a man worth $65 billion a few collectibles but to bring some perspective to the $100 million contribution. And remember: When Attorney General Janet Reno announced in October1997 that the Department of Justice was not only seeking an injunction against Microsoft for violating the consent decree, but was asking a federal court to impose a fine of $1 million a day—the largest civil fine in Justice Department history (until the company stopped tying its browser to Windows)—Bill Gates' sneering response was, "These people have no idea who they're dealing with,"[48] bragging, "Every two and half hours I make a million!"[49]

BILLIONAIRE FOUNDATIONS

The William H. Gates Foundation was formed in 1994 and renamed in 1999. In mid-2008, Bill Gates announced his plan to reduce his work at Microsoft and devote more time to the foundation. Between 2008 and mid-2010, the Bill and Melinda Gates Foundation put something like $650 million into projects that advanced their educational priorities—things like charter schools, testing and "teacher effectiveness," standardized curriculum, and a national test. This beneficence might bring John D. Rockefeller to mind. His gifts to the American Baptist Education Society endowed the University of Chicago and Rockefeller Institute for Medical Research, which became Rockefeller University, paid off the debt of Atlanta Baptist Female Seminary, which became Spelman College (W. E. B. DuBois had a few words to say about how "the great dominating philanthropic agency" trained the Negro according to the needs of the white South, but that's another story), and so on and so on. There's no record that Rockefeller launched a nationwide film campaign telling the faculty how to teach.[50]

And Henry Ford might be a more apt comparison. The man Edmund Wilson called "the despot of Dearborne" provides a showcase for what happens when unlimited money meets arrogance, hubris, and ignorance. In 1927, needing rubber for the tires on his cars, Henry Ford decided to grow his own rubber trees in Brazil. At that time, Ford was the richest man in the world and he was buying up significant Americana artifacts for his personal museum in Greenfield: the homes of such notables as Noah Webster, the Wright Brothers, William McGuffey; the 1840 Logan County, Ill. Courthouse where Abe Lincoln practiced law; Harvey Firestone's Ohio farm, transplanted from Ohio; Walter P. Chrysler's 1932 custom limousine painted red to match a Ming Dynasty vase he owned.[51]

Ford extended his reach—from establishing this museum in Greenfield to building a model American village in the Amazon jungle. In *Fordlandia: The Rise and Fall of Henry Ford's Forgotten Jungle City*[52] Greg Grandlin offers a mind-boggling account of Ford's ideal village, complete with Cape Cod-style shingled houses (their asbestos-lined tin roofs totally inappropriate for the Amazon climate), time clocks, square dancing, recitations of poetry by William Wordsworth and Henry Wadsworth Longfellow, and of course Model Ts rolling down the paved streets. The press was ecstatic. Grandlin notes[53] that in 1931 the *Washington Post* described Ford's venture as bringing "white man's magic" to the wilderness. *Time* magazine gushed about industrializing the whole jungle, with the Black Indians using their heavy blades to slash down "their one-time haunts to make way for future windshield wipers, floor mats, balloon tires."[54] Even as the ill-conceived real Fordlandia was crumbling in Brazil, the American press "kept up their drumbeat celebration." Sounds like today's education reformers and the media celebrating hapless programs that claim to prepare children to be workers in the Global Economy, trying to reform teachers while ignoring the fact that a growing number of schoolchildren are homeless and poverty is increasing for the rest.[55]

Henry Ford, who conceived of Fordlandia as a showcase of his vision of the capitalist American dream of combining high wages, automation, and moral improvement to bring prosperity to backward people, never set foot in the place. Walt Disney did visit—as part of Nelson Rockefeller's Office of Inter-American Affairs mission to promote the commercial, cultural, and scientific integration of the Americas[56]—and soon after started his own namesake make-believe place. Fordlandia suffered from blight and bugs; it failed both as a rubber plantation and as Cape Cod capitalism. Greg Grandin's details of this enterprise in *Fordlandia* are so mind-boggling they are at once laugh-out loud funny and sobering. As we laugh at the situation of jungle residents being forced to listen to Henry Longfellow, what do we make of the Gates Foundation methods for judging effective teaching. Here's one Gates grant:

To: Clemson University

Purpose: to work with members of the Measuring Effective Teachers (MET) team to measure engagement physiologically with Galvanic Skin Response (GSR) bracelets which will determine the feasibility and utility of using such devices regularly in schools with students and teachers.

Amount: $498,055

This is the stuff of neuromarketing, where consumers' sensorimotor, cognitive, and affective response to marketing stimuli are studied. So the Gates Foundation joins Google, CBS, and Frito-Lay in looking for ways to measure consumer reactions to stimulus. Put a Galvanic Skin Response (GSR) bracelet on every kid in the class and supposedly you can measure teacher effectiveness in improving their test scores. Maybe the next step is for the bracelet to zap kids with electric current when their attention wanders. And then the step after that will be the Galvanic Skin Response bracelet on every teacher—to zap her when she veers from the prescribed Common Core curriculum. Then . . . bring on the drones to eliminate such teachers.

Glen Ford at *Black Agenda Report* has seen the handwriting on the wall for years. He warned that the goal of corporate education reform is to turn teaching into a service industry. In "The Corporate Dream: Teachers as Temps,"[57] Ford pointed out that "Teachers are the biggest obstacle in the way of the corporate educational coup, which is why the billionaires, eagerly assisted by their servants in the Obama administration, have made demonization and eventual destruction of teachers unions their top priority." The Gates approach to this theme is to offer to identify the excellent teachers (by student standardized test scores), put more kids in their classes, get rid of the less excellent, and the reduction in staff enables districts to save money.

And then there are those Tennessee teachers forced to wear earbuds so "experts observing from the back of the room"[58] can critique their lesson in real time according to the model shipped in from the Bill and Melinda Gates Foundation. They call this earbud thing *tailoring professional development*. BZZZZ. Big Brother calling. From the coach's mouth to teachers' ears. "Once a teacher understands what it feels like to be successful, it takes root immediately," Monica Jordan, coordinator of teacher professional development in Memphis City Schools, told a gullible reporter from *The Commercial Appeal*. From Memphis, coaches can deliver instructions to teachers worldwide, helping them *understand what it feels like to be successful*.

I asked a class of high schoolers what they thought the effect of the earbudded teacher would be. They thought the very idea was a hoot, and when they stopped laughing, they said kids would be totally intent on watching the teacher—not paying any attention to the lesson she was presenting—but trying to figure out when she'd gotten a message and just how negative the message was. "They wouldn't be sending positive messages," one kid declared. And everybody agreed.

In Fordlandia, nurseries experimented with giving soy milk to babies because Henry Ford hated cows. We don't know just what Bill Gates hates that would cause this earbud experimentation. A priest who ministered in Fordlandia observed that Ford managers "never really figured out what country they were in."[59] One can wonder what country the PBS NewsHour is in when they give Melinda Gates, (valedictorian from Ursuline Academy of Dallas, B.A. from Duke in computer science, and M.A. from Fuqua School of Business) great quantities of air time to pontificate on teacher effectiveness. Of course the fact that the Bill and Melinda Gates Foundation is a major underwriter of the PBS Newshour is just coincidental.

EDUCATION BY MORSE CODE

Does anybody know if Bill Gates is a baseball fan? On Aug. 15, 2011, the *New York Times* published an obituary for Nat Allbright, 87. Mr. Allbright gained fame for broadcasting 1,500 Brooklyn Dodgers games without seeing a single one

> [H]e took bare-bones telegraph messages transmitted by Morse code ("B1W" for Ball One Wide); embellished them with imagination and sound effects; and then broadcast games that sounded as if he were in the ballpark hearing,

smelling and seeing everything, from steaming hot dogs to barking umpires to swirling dust at second base.

Surely, Nat Allbright's talented masquerade provided inspiration for Bill Gates' education policy. Yes, Bill Gates, the wealthiest entrepreneur of the personal computer revolution, could use something more sophisticated than Morse code to receive signals from schools. But for him any signals are irrelevant. What he reports on education does not come from the clutter and ambiguity of actual classrooms. He's already decided that what's going on there needs to be reformed.

In *Notes on Cooking*,[60] Lauren Braun Costello and Russell Reich offer important information that applies to the classroom as much as the kitchen, but it is advice education reformers can't tolerate: *Twenty-four cooks assigned to the same mayonnaise recipe—the same bowls, same spoons, same eggs, same mustard, same oil, same whisks, same peppermills, same measuring cups, same room, same time of day, same marching orders—will create twenty-four different mayonnaises.*

Got That?

But let's change the scenario. Bring in a mayonnaise consultant, someone who may not have ever made mayonnaise but who has written a 200-page book detailing the four domains of mayonnaise-making, a book that spells out the 22 components of those domains, including the 76 descriptive elements that further refine our understanding of what mayonnaise making is all about." Using this consultant's rubric for mayonnaise making, coach those 24 cooks—through earbuds, of course. If the cooks still end up producing 24 different mayonnaises, then rate them as "not meeting standards." In the Denver Public Schools, they call this the *Framework for Effective Teaching Evidence Guide.* [61] Produced with money from the Bill and Melinda Gates Foundation, the rubric for evaluating teachers is twenty-nine pages long. In 2010–11, it was 28 pages long, but then they added a page. Try reading it aloud. That's what I did at the annual meeting of the British Columbia Teacher Federation. Reaction? Loud, incredulous laughter. I had to assure teachers that it was real, that when talking about education reform you never have to make anything up to get a laugh.

As long as we're talking about some similarities between cooking and teaching, consider "the chefs who rule."[62] One New York City bistro, for example, known for its fries, has a strict rule: No ketchup. A gastropub refuses to serve a burger with any cheese other than Roquefort, and although Murray's Bagel will put almost anything on top of the bagels, it won't toast them. My favorite is the San Francisco restaurant that does not supply salt and pepper because the chef "seasons things perfectly." These pigheaded, doctrinaire chefs seem to have a lot in common with the Common Core State (sic) Standards, whose over-the-top rule in teaching literacy is that students must rely strictly on textual analysis and the teacher must not allow students to bring in their own background knowledge or express personal opinion. David Coleman, Common Core leading author and architect and major consultant until he abandoned ship to become president of the College Board, told an audience at the New York State Department of Education that kids need to understand that "When you grow up in this world you realize people don't give a shit about what you feel or what you think."[63]

Don't Argue: The Chef Seasons Things Perfectly

Nathan Myhrvold can't be blamed for the Common Core, but as former Microsoft chief technology officer, he gives us the Microsoft connection and another look at someone who takes science and technology so far over the top it's breathtaking. And crazy. Myhrvold wrote a 2,438 page cookbook, *Modernist Cuisine: The Art and Science of Cooking*. It comes in six volumes and has a price tag of $625 and, depending on which press account one reads, weighs somewhere between 40 and 52 pounds. (How hard is it to weigh a book?) The Gates Foundation puts galvanic bracelets on school kids? Myhrvold gives us a recipe that makes watermelon look like meat and a recipe for macaroni and cheese based on wheat beer, sodium nitrate, and iota carrageenan, a gelatin from red seaweed.[64] The book's list of "must-have" kitchen implements includes liquid nitrogen, a centrifuge, and a tabletop homogenizer. The *Wall Street Journal* featured Myhrvold's hamburger,[65] which takes 30 hours to prepare. Myrvold wouldn't tell *BusinessWeek* how much he spent in producing the book but acknowledged "millions of dollars."[66] To avoid arguing with publishers who might have wanted him to cut back a bit, he published it himself. He who has money answers to no one.

Now Bill Gates isn't responsible for Nathan Myhrvold and vice versa, but it is instructive to look at the mindset these billionaires bring to their enterprises. Myrhvold and his co-authors say their cooking reform brings a "deeper understanding of science and advances in cooking technology." Ah, science and technology. The Bill and Melinda Gates Foundation's enterprises use these terms more than any other to justify what they're doing. Both the Bill and Melinda Gates Foundation and *Modernist Cuisine* have the idiosyncrasies of one man at their core, but there are a couple of big differences. For starters, Myhrvold, who seems to be a genuine polymath, worked for two years as a stagier in Seattle's French restaurant

Rovers and trained with a chef at the Ecole de la Varenne before writing the book. We might well ask just whose science gives us grey mustard ice cream with red cabbage gazpacho and a 30-hour hamburger, but are free to ignore both the science and the ice cream. But the Gates version of scientific teaching is uninformed, intrusive, and unavoidable. Teachers have no notion of how to avoid or refuse it. Joyce Wadler tells the story in the *New York Times*[67] of cooking in simpler times. A man who knew Julia Child well enough to make an emergency call when a clam chowder he was making for a dinner for thirty people curdled and looked awful, but tasted all right, cried for help. Julia's advice: "Dim the lights." It's worth repeating: Dim the lights. In simpler times, we teachers used to be able to shut our doors. Those days are gone.

"SOMETHING HAPPENS TO A GUY WHEN HIS NET WORTH PASSES $100 MILLION"

In *Pride Before the Fall: The Trials of Bill Gates and the End of the Microsoft Era*, former *New Yorker* and *Wired* staff writer John Heilemann reminds us[68] of what we need to know: "Microsoft is a company run by engineers. Engineers like simplicity. They don't like nuance. That's how Bill sees the world. And if it's how Bill sees the world, it's how Microsoft sees the world." And the U.S. press, who can't seem to conceive of arguing with a billionaire, choose to describe Bill Gates through his own lens. Even though it seems absolutely un-American to criticize the man who heads the company that has created 5,000 millionaires and three billionaires—and who is out to rid the world of polio and malaria—I admit that when discussing Bill Gates, I'd like to borrow what Joe Queenan said *in Red Lobster, White Trash, and the Blue Lagoon* when he offered an analysis of Tom Clancy's work: "Frankly, I think Clancy is completely full of shit." All evidence—and I've researched tons of matter pertaining to the Gates version of education reform and enough matter about his health agenda to know there's plenty of controversy there too—provokes me to say the same about Bill Gates: completely full of it. I mean, what can you say about a guy who, while talking about the deadly scourge of malaria at a TED conference, releases a glass full of mosquitoes into the audience.

"Malaria is spread by mosquitoes," Gates intoned while opening a jar onstage at the Technology, Entertainment, Design Conference—a gathering known to attract technology kings, politicians, Hollywood stars, and wannabes who can come up with the minimum $7,500 registration fee. Gates continued, "I brought some. Here I'll let them roam around. There is no reason only poor people should be infected."[69] He opened the jar and tossed out mosquitoes. Fox News reported it as an "unusual presentation on malaria prevention." MSNBC.com reported that the mosquito incident was confirmed by the media office of the Bill and Melinda Gates Foundation, which also noted that the insects released were not carrying malaria. Not so enamored by the billionaire, *The Telegraph* reported, "Delegates at the elite Technology, Entertainment, and Design conference, which is being held in Long Beach, California, were left stunned by Gates's stunt. . . ."[70]

A blogger wrote, "Remind me never to sit in the front row of anywhere this guy is making an appearance. Another blogger suggested that next time Gates should take a page from the Ozzy Osbourne handbook and bite the head off a bat. But we know that Gates would prefer decapitating a teacher.

Wall Street Journal reporter David Bank writes[71] that Gates himself mused that "Something happens to a guy when his net worth passes $100 million." Victims of what passes for school reform in the 21st century are learning what happens when a guy's net worth passes $15 billion and then $50 billion. Not only is he unwavering in his certainty that he has The Solution, the U.S. Department of Education, the *New York Times* editorial board, Thomas Friedman, NBC, and Oprah think so too. In the computer wars, Microsoft treated PC makers less as partners and more as mere distributors for Windows. This is exactly how the Gates Foundation sees teachers: distributors of Common Core curricula.

Microsoft's bell-curve grading-system[72] wherein "every manager ranks one-fifth of his employees as below average each year to help the company weed out chronic underperformers" plays out in Arne Duncan's Title I School Improvement Grant Program wherein 5% of schools in the state must dump either the principal or the faculty. Never mind that the "low performing" students at the school highly rated by parents, such as one in Burlington, Vermont, include a high percentage of immigrants from Somalia who haven't yet learned English. No excuses.

David Bank reports[73] that at Microsoft, "Overt aggression was cultivated . . . for those who could play the game, the meritocracy was thrilling." No one touting the Gates education agenda asks if this is the sort of culture in which young schoolchildren will thrive. The media keeps playing the Gates/Duncan tune that we must start in pre-K to produce competitive workers for the Global Economy. Noted literacy scholar and USC Professor Stephen Krashen offers[74] a tongue-in-cheek recommendation of prenatal phonics training for prelinguistic children. These days, a lot of people don't get the joke.

In *Hard Drive: Bill Gates and the Making of the Microsoft Empire*, James Wallace and Jim Erickson note, "With Gates, everything turned into some form of competition." As one programmer put it,[75] "We were driven to the edge all the time." Microsoft fomented "a mystique about the long hours employees worked, with an unstated job requirement that everyone had to be at the office late into the night and on weekends, regardless of how much work there was to do on a given day. No one wanted to be the first to leave." Gates himself boasted a seven-hour turnaround—meaning that from the time he left Microsoft to the time he returned in the morning was a mere seven hours. Count 'em: That's 17 hours a day on the job. Baldino Professor of Sleep Medicine at Harvard Medical School, Dr. Charles Czeisler, terms this kind of behavior "Sleep Machismo,"[76] arguing that "contemporary work and social culture glorifies sleeplessness in the way we once glorified people who could hold their liquor." Czeisler added that this kind of corporate behavior is the antithesis of high performance.

Under Bill Gates' leadership, employee e-mail records at Microsoft were inspected—to determine how many hours of overtime each employee racked up. Bonuses were tied not to how effectively one worked, how much was accomplished, or how important a specific project was, but rather on how many hours of overtime an employee put in late at night or on the weekends.[77] Leo Nikora, marketing manager for Windows, said,[78] "Bill required everyone to devote their entire life to Microsoft, like he did." In a *Vanity Fair* excerpt from his memoir *Idea Man: A Memoir by the Cofounder of Microsoft*, Paul Allen writes[79] of Gates prowling the parking lot on weekends to see who was in. Allen tells of an employee who had been a Harvard classmate of Gates who had "put in 81 hours in four days, Monday through Thursday" to finish an important job. When Gates touched base toward the end of this marathon, he asked,

> "What are you working on tomorrow?"
> "I was planning to take the day off."
> And Bill said, "Why would you want to do that?"

Allen also gives this example of the Gates style of voicing disagreement, almost identical to the one he used with Connie Chung: "That's the stupidest fucking thing I've ever heard!" Admittedly, this is the one Gates praxis I wish teacher unions and professional organizations would adopt: Give up on being polite and/or subservient. Every time Gates or his acolyte Arne Duncan—or any camp followers from Jonathan Alter to the Walton Family opens their mouth, just repeat, "That's the stupidest fucking thing I've ever heard!" Let this become a Gates/Duncan rebuttal ringing loud and clear across the land.

Make your own enemies list. Mine is alphabetized and numbers about 100 people and organizations. I collect silly and dangerous things they say.

Teachers are too damn polite, and so, in absence of any real opposition from teacher unions or professional organizations and operating in a fusion of the Marquis de Sade and *The Little Engine That Could*, Bill Gates has joined up with the U.S. Department of Education, encouraging his pal Arne Duncan to transplant the Microsoft culture of nastiness, frenzied competition, and terror to teachers. *Who is coming to get us tomorrow?!* is the question hanging over every faculty room in the land. With hundreds of thousands of public school teachers getting pink slips while at the same time the Democrats in the U. S. Congress earmark $50 million for Teach for America and another $50 million for KIPP,[80] it's hard to call public school teachers paranoid. And with professional organization silence and union capitulation, Gates and Duncan seem more than half-way home in convincing teachers that their paycheck should be tied to student scores on tests that have less regulation than dog food.

ENTER THE COMMON CORE STATE (SIC) CURRICULUM STANDARDS

Very few people, even those working in public education, are aware that the Bill and Melinda Gates Foundation financed the Common Core State (sic) Standards. The National Governors Association Center for Best Practices has received over $39 million, the Council of Chief State School Officers over $68 million. Not many people know what the AFT, American Enterprise Institute, ASCD, James B. Hunt, Jr. Institute for Educational Leadership and Policy Foundation, Inc., the Khan Academy, Military Child Education Coalition, National Indian Education Association, National Writing Project, the PTA, Scholastic Inc., and the Teaching Channel have in common. They all received Gates money to promote the Common Core. Massachusetts Institute of Technology, The University of the State of New York, University of North Carolina at Chapel Hill, University of Michigan, Stanford University, and University of Arizona have all received big money from Gates to deliver some goods on the Common Core.

In 2011, Harvard scholar Henry Louis Gates was effusive about Bill Gates's appearance as keynote speaker at the Urban League National conference. "Not only is Bill Gates a cousin, Bill Gates is a brother." Then Bill Gates told the audience what Arne Duncan and the Business Roundtable keep telling newspaper editors and TV pundits—end the myth that "that poverty needs to be eradicated before reforming education." Bruce A. Dixon, managing editor of *Black Agenda Report*, commented, "the billionaire lectured the assembled on education and poverty, although Gates is not qualified to teach an hour in any classroom in the land, and has certainly never been poor."[81] Note: In 2009, the Bill and Melinda Gates Foundation gave the Urban League $900,000; in 2011, $2,900,000. As Dixon observes, "Like school districts, the National Urban League, the NAACP, the National Council of LaRaza, and more are dependent on corporate donations to keep going." So the result is they become cheering sections "for corporate experiments on black school children."

The U.S. Department of Education serves as an echo chamber for Bill and Melinda Gates Foundation education policy, but the press rarely mentions this. Here are the three mentions I found in over 700 articles on Race to the Top and the Common Core Standards appearing between 2009 and mid-2010:[82] "The Gates program and the Arne Duncan program are pretty much the same program," Nancy C. Detert, chair of the Education Committee in the Florida Senate, told the *New York Times*.[83] Mike Petrilli, vice president of the Thomas B. Fordham Institute, agrees, telling the *Puget Sound Business Journal*,[84] "It is not unfair to say that the Gates Foundation's agenda has become the country's agenda in education." Exceptionally, *The Business Journal* noted that as of that date, the Fordham Institute itself had received nearly $3 million in Gates Foundation grants. This is exceptional because the Gates money dumped into education policy is almost never mentioned. Pulitzer Prize journalist Daniel Golden, reporting in *Bloomberg Businessweek*[85] is the other exception. In addition to noting that "the Gates Foundation and Education Secretary Duncan move in apparent lockstep" on an agenda Golden calls "an intellectual cousin of the Bush administration's 2002 No Child Left Behind law," Golden notes the tidy sum that the Thomas B. Fordham Institute received from Gates to provide analysis of the Common Core standards.

People working for the Bill and Melinda Gates Foundation don't appear much in the media. Other people do it for them: academics, think tank entrepreneurs, nonprofits. The Gates Foundation disperses monies to make this happen. For example, in 2012, Stanford and Harvard received two Gates Grants, $30,000 each, "to support development of a chapter" for the edited volume of the Measures of Effective Teaching project, a heavily subsidized Gates notion. Educational Testing Service received $45,000 and $50,000 for two chapters on the same thing; the Rand Corporation and University of Texas at Austin $30,000 each. These are all grants of one month duration. How will the other chapter authors feel when they find out that the University of Virginia received $49,864 for the development of one chapter? And how about Rutgers, who received only $10,000? University of Michigan received a two-year grant of $1,297,627 "to house and make available to qualified researchers the data collected by the Measures of Effective Teaching project." And on and on and on.

In 2010, Stanford received $2,024,234 for a capacity building project, "to help develop and test the next generation of district and school diagnostic systems that incorporate and respond to a wider range of student supports than existing systems" and so on. In early 2012, some of this seems to have come to fruition. The Stanford University School of Education launched a website in April 2012: Understanding Language.[86] Each of the 13 "commissioned papers" one can download at this website offers advice on making the Common Core Standards more efficient for English Language Learners and each comes with this acknowledgement: *The Understanding Language Initiative would like to thank the Carnegie Corporation of New York and the Bill and Melinda Gates Foundation for making this work possible.* And you can bet your bippy that these folk will speak up for the Gates agenda when the media calls.

On the very rare occasion when reporters in the twenty-first century even notice that Bill Gates orchestrates school policy on a variety of topics, they quote no naysayers but seem poised to hand him scepter and crown. Here's Steven Levy,[87] introducing his last column for *Newsweek*: "Even the most virulent Microsoft hater, I believe, has to admire the fact that he's going to be spending the bulk of his time now working for beyond-reproach causes such as eradicating diseases that strike poor people and improving high school education."

There you have it: You can't quarrel with money. Money is beyond reproach. Never mind that this should be labeled "vulture philanthropy." After all, if the tax breaks Bill Gates gets for his munificence went into public coffers where it belongs, local school boards could choose how their schools should be run. Read Kenneth Saltman's *The Gift of Education: Public Education and Venture Philanthropy*,[88] documenting how venture philanthropy "treats schooling as a private consumable service and promotes business remedies, reforms, and assumptions with regard to public schooling." Nonetheless, even though he's operating with taxpayer dollars, *beyond reproach* is the almost-universal mantra for what Bill Gates does in education. Governors, desperate for any money they could get, signed on. Not wanting to jeopardize their mythical "place at the table," teachers unions pocket the handouts and keep quiet, and professional organizations, quick to see the possibilities of publishing books and professional development for the new Common Core, also keep quiet. And when Mr. and Mrs. Gates announce that teacher experience isn't worth a hill of beans, we see this maxim repeated in articles, editorials, and in prepackaged sound bites ready for T-shirt slogans for Pearson employee picnics.

Except for a few bloggers, nobody informs the teachers of the real stakes here. For starters, in the fully implemented Gates plan, complete with earbuds, Charlotte Danielson rubrics, David Coleman's imposition of an ill-informed bastardized version of New Criticism, the National Governors Association declaring computers better at choosing books than teachers,[89] and galvanic bracelets, children are pawns to the testing industry, and teachers are left without a profession.

The Microsoft crew regarded Judge Thomas Penfield Jackson, a conservative whose heroes are Barry Goldwater and John McCain, as a technological caveman, but, as *New Yorker* writer Ken Auletta observes,[90] "Jackson didn't need an engineering degree to understand Microsoft's alleged intent to harm competitors or to punish companies that did business with rivals." Jackson identified the Gates "crime" as hubris, a refusal to acknowledge that the nation's antitrust laws applied to him. Auletta writes that Jackson "was only half joking when he told me, 'If I were able to propose a remedy of my devising, I'd require Mr. Gates to write a book report.' The assignment, Jackson said, would be a recent biography of Napoleon, and he went on, 'Because I think he has a Napoleonic concept of himself and his company, an arrogance that derives from power and unalloyed success, with no leavening hard experiences, no reverses.'"

We could wish that Ken Auletta wrote about education and that the U.S. Department of Education would hire Judge Thomas Penfield Jackson as an advisor.

EPILOGUE

I was going to refrain from commenting about Bill Gates declaring in print that he "enjoyed greatly" *The Bridges of Madison County*. But Dan Kennedy uses this[91] in his review of Gates's book *Road Ahead*, which, he says, offers a passive sentenced, "dumbed-down rehash of MIT Media Lab head Nicholas Negroponte's book *Being Digital*." Kennedy notes that along the way Gates spices things up with insensitivity, crypto-fascism, and the numbingly obvious. Kennedy adds, "The banality of this isn't that surprising, for Gates, despite his media image, really isn't a technology maven at all. Instead, he's a ruthless businessman who got where he is the same way the robber barons of the 19th century did: by pursuing and either buying out or destroying the competition." Besides that $30.8 million *Codex Leicester* manuscript by Leonardo da Vinci, the Gates home library has a quote from *The Great Gatsby* engraved on the ceiling: "He had come a long way to this blue lawn, and his dream must have seemed so close that he could hardly fail to grasp it." A more sensitive billionaire might have realized that mentioning *The Great Gatsby* would reminds us of a much more famous quote: "They were careless people, Tom and Daisy—they smashed up things and creatures and then retreated back into their money or their vast carelessness or whatever it was that kept them together, and let other people clean up the mess they had made. . . ."

Writing a 1980 book review in *Playboy*,[92] John Leonard revealed that Hugh Hefner's favorite writer was F. Scott Fitzgerald. Leonard also mentioned that Hefner was "disinclined to publish advertisements referring to such male frailties as baldness, obesity, acne, halitosis, athlete's foot, or hernias." This reminds me that I've read in a number of places, including *The*

Telegraph,[93] that Bill Gates has dandruff. Surely, reading this will make a few million public school teachers smile.

NOTES

1. Wertheimer, L. (1996 March 18). Microsoft's Bill Gates for president in 1996. *All Things Considered.* Washington, D. C.: National Public Radio. Retrieved from http://www.highbeam.com/doc/1P1-28474201.html
2. Dowd, M. (1998 Jan 1). Liberties; revenge on the nerds. *New York Times.* Retrieved from http://www.nytimes.com/1998/01/21/opinion/liberties-revenge-on-the-nerds.html
3. Edstrom, J., & Eller, M. (1998). *Barbarians Led by Bill Gates: Microsoft from the Inside: How the World's Richest Corporation Wields Its Power.* New York: Henry Holt. 182.
4. Heilemann, J. (2001). *Pride Before the Fall: The Trials of Bill Gates and the End of the Microsoft Era.* New York: Collins Business. 126–128.
5. Wasserman, E. (1998 Nov. 17). Gates deposition makes judge laugh in court. CNN. Retrieved from http://web.archive.org/web/20091124024726/http://www.cnn.com/TECH/computing/9811/17/judgelaugh.ms.idg/index.html
6. Heilemann, 129.
7. Dickerson,J.F.,&vanVoorst,B.(1998March9).ClashoftheTitans.*Time.*Retrieved from http://www.time.com/time/magazine/article/0,9171,987959,00.html #ixzz22QmCmGyF
8. Staff. (1998 Jan 30). Bill Gates Sings Lullaby on '20/20.' *Chicago Sun-Times.* Retrieved from http://www.highbeam.com/doc/1P2-4432192.html Transcript. (1998 Jan 30). *20/20.* New York: ABC. Retrieved from http://www.highbeam.com/doc/1P1-28659061.html
9. O'Donnell, R. (1998 Dec. 8). Bill Gates chats with Rosie O'Donnell about REALLY important matters! YouTube. Retrieved from http://www.youtube.com/watch?v=4FUCf_DVeqY
10. Asimov, E. (1998 Feb. 14). Gentlemen, choose your sausage. *New York Times.* Retrieved from http://www.nytimes.com/1998/02/15/weekinreview/gentlemen-choose-your-sausage.html
11. Rich, F. (1998 March 7). Love that Bill. *New York Times.* Retrieved from http://www.nytimes.com/1998/03/07/opinion/journal-love-that-bill.html
12. Dowd, M.
13. MacGregor, J. (1998 Jan. 3). Of mice and men, Release 2.0. *New York Times.* Retrieved from http://www.nytimes.com/1998/01/03/opinion/of-mice-and-men-release 2.0.html?pagewanted=all&src=pm
14. LaBaton, S. (1998 Jan. 15). Gates helped draft microsoft's response to judge. *New York Times.* Retrieved from http://www.nytimes.com/1998/01/15/business/gates-helped-draft- microsoft-s-response-to-judge.html
15. Asimov, E.
16. Rich, F.
17. Dickerson,J.F.,&vanVoorst,B.(1998March9).Clashofthetitans.*Time.*Retrieved from http://www.time.com/time/magazine/article/0,9171,987959,00.html #ixzz22QmCmGyF

18. Lewis, P. H. (1998 April 30). Windows 98: the tuneup. *New York Times*. Retrieved from http://www.nytimes.com/1998/04/30/technology/windows-98-the-tuneup.html?pagewanted=all&src=pm
19. Bork, Robert H. (1998 May 5). What antitrust is all about. *New York Times*. Retrieved from http://www.nytimes.com/1998/05/04/opinion/what-antitrust-is-all-about.html
20. Vogel, C. (1998 May 6). Bill Gates buys Homer painting for record price. *New York Times* news service. Retrieved from http://www.chron.com/CDA/archives/archive.mpl/1998_3053074/bill-gates-buys-homer painting-for-record-price.html
21. Cassidy, J. (1998 May 8). Rich man, richer man: behind the comparisons of John D. Rockfeller and Bill Gates. *The New Yorker*. Retrieved from http://archives.newyorker.com/?i=1998-05-11#folio=098
22. Editorial. (1998 May 19). United States v Microsoft. *New York Times*. Retrieved from http://www.nytimes.com/1998/05/19/opinion/united-states-v-microsoft.html
23. Myerson, A. R. (1998 May 24). The Nation; rating the bigshots: Gates vs. Rockefeller. *New York Times*. Retrieved from http://www.nytimes.com/1998/05/24/weekinreview/the- nation-rating-the-bigshots-gates-vs-rockefeller.html?pagewanted=all&src=pm
24. Lohr, S., & Karkoff, J. (1998 Oct. 8). Microsoft's world: a special report: how software's giant played hardball game. *New York Times*. Retrieved from http://www.nytimes.com/1998/10/08/business/microsoft-s-world-a-special-report-how- software-s-giant-played-hardball-game.html?pagewanted=all&src=pm
25. Cocoran, E. (1998 Oct. 18). Microsoft: looking out for number one. *Washington Post*. Retrieved from http://www.washingtonpost.com/wp- srv/business/longterm/microsoft/stories/1998/microsofta101898.htm
26. Foster, D. (1998 Oct. 19). Gates quoted as seeing case 'blow over.' Associated Press.
27. Chandrasekaran, R. (1998 Oct. 20). On day 1, U. S. targets Gates; government portrays Microsoft chairman as cagey, ruthless. *Washington Post*. Retrieved from http://www.highbeam.com/doc/1P2-698232.html
28. Taylor, C. (1998 Oct. 21). Microsoft mafia. *Time*. Retrieved from http://www.time.com/time/nation/article/0,8599,15355,00.html#ixzz22QjPxlzm
29. Novack, V. (1998 Nov. 2). Influence. *Time*. Retrieved from http://www.time.com/time/magazine/article/0,9171,989489,00.html#ixzz22QfrwyGM
30. Taylor, C. (1998 Nov. 16). Microsoft's Jihad jam. *Time*. Retrieved from http://www.time.com/time/nation/article/0,8599,15926,00.html#ixzz22QeXyAXG
31. Harpaz, B. J. (1998 Dec. 2). Bill Gates donating $100 million for child immunizations. Associated Press. Retrieved from http://www.highbeam.com/doc/1P1-19423374.html
32. Gelernter, D. (1998 Dec. 7). Bill Gates: software strongman. *Time*. Retrieved from http://www.time.com/time/magazine/article/0,9171,989792,00.html
33. Lea, G. (1998 Dec. 9). Publicists spin as MS seeks AOL-Netscape papers. And the kinder, gentler Gates answers three questions. Take it easy, Bill.... *The Register* (UK). Retrieved from http://www.theregister.co.uk/1998/12/09/publicists_spin_as_ms_seeks/

34. Staff. (1998 Dec. 15). A Kinder, Gentler Bill. *Newsweek.* Retrieved from http://connection.ebscohost.com/c/interviews/1384016/kinder-gentler-bill

35. Coatne, M. (1998 Dec. 15). "Video dominates Microsoft trial before recess." *Time.* http://www.time.com/time/nation/article/0,8599,16957,00.html#ixzz22Qc6ijvl

36. Seglin, J. L. (1998 Dec. 20). The right thing; bosses beware when bending the truth. *New York Times.* Retrieved from http://www.nytimes.com/1998/12/20/business/the-right-thing-bosses-beware-when- bending- the-truth.html

37. Hedrick, L. (1998 Dec. 28). Microsoft's big browser." *The Nation.* Retrieved from http://web.ebscohost.com/ehost/pdfviewer/pdfviewer?sid=a7501fa4-f1a8-4861-86ad- 46289cf5e8d7%40sessionmgr14&vid=11&hid=9

38. Myerson, A. R.

39. Heilemann, J. 125

40. Dowd, M.

41. Cassidy, J.

42. Bork, R. H. (1998 May 5). What antitrust is all about. *New York Times.* Retrieved from http://www.nytimes.com/1998/05/04/opinion/what-antitrust-is-all-about.html

43. Washington Policy Center. Website. Retrieved from http://www.washington-policy.org/search/apachesolr_search/%22common%20core%22

44. Staff. (1998 Dec. 21). Strange bedfellows abound In 1998: People: Denis Beausejour Bill Clinton/Monica Lewinsky Jesse Ventura Tina Brown Dan Snyder Bud Paxson Tom Ryder Brad Ball Bill Gates Mel Karmazin." *Advertising Age.* Retrieved from http://www.highbeam.com/doc/1G1-53482450.html

45. Lea, G. (1998 Dec. 9). Publicists spin as MS seeks AOL-Netscape papers. And the kinder, gentler Gates answers three questions. Take it easy, Bill . . .' *The Register* (UK). Retrieved from http://www.theregister.co.uk/1998/12/09/publicists_spin_as_ms_seeks/

46. Hedrick, L. (1998 Dec. 28). Microsoft's big browser. *The Nation.* Retrieved from http://web.ebscohost.com/ehost/pdfviewer/pdfviewer?sid=bd5fe5e4-9aaa-44bd-bee7- 6b9d55a36330%40sessionmgr4&vid=13&hid=10 Taylor, S. Jr. (1993 Nov. 1). What to do with the Microsoft monster. *American Lawyer.* Retrieved from http://stuarttaylorjr.com/content/what-do-microsoft-monster

47. Rohm, W. G. (1998). *The Microsoft File: The Secret Case Against Bill Gates.* New York: Times Books/Random House. 157.

48. Heilemann, J. (2000 Nov.). The truth, the whole truth, and nothing but the truth: the untold story of the Microsoft antitrust case and what it means for the future of Bill Gates and his company. *Wired.* Retrieved from http://www.wired.com/wired/archive/8.11/microsoft_pr.html

49. Rohm. 275

50. Bill and Melinda Gates Foundation grant to James B. Hunt Jr. Institute for Educational Leadership and Policy Foundation, Inc. (2009). retrieved from http://www.gatesfoundation.org/Grants-2009/Pages/James-B-Hunt-Jr-Institute-for-Educational-Leadership-and-Policy-OPPCR055.aspx

51. Borcover, A. (1986 July 27). The Ford legacy of wonderful `stuff.' *Chicago Tribune.* Retrieved from http://articles.chicagotribune.com/1986-07-27/travel/8602240576_1_greenfield-village- henry-ford-museum-mcguffey-readers

52. Grandin, G. (2009). *Fordlandia: The Rise and Fall of Henry Ford's Forgotten Jungle City*. New York: Metropolitan Books.
53. Grandin, 5
54. No author. (1927 Oct. 24). Ford rubber. *Time*. Retrieved from http://www.time.com/time/magazine/article/0,9171,736942,00.html
55. Christ, L. (2012 Aug 20). NY1 Exclusive: DOE finds almost 70 percent of city students live in poor households.*NY1*. Retrieved from http://www.ny1.com/content/news_beats/education/166790/ny1-exclusive—doe-finds-almost-70-percent-of-city-students-live-in-poor-households
56. Grandin. 346
57. Ford, G. (2011 May 29). The corporate dream: teachers as temps. Black Agenda Report. *Common Dreams*. Retrieved from https://www.commondreams.org/view/2011/05/29-2
58. Roberts, J. (2011 Feb. 22). Memphis city schools teachers get an earbud-ful of class coaching. *The Commercial Appeal*. Retrieved from http://www.commercialappeal.com/news/2011/feb/22/lend-me-your/
59. Grandin. 274–275
60. Costello, L. B., & Reich, R. (2009). *Notes on Cooking: A Short Guide to an Essential Craft*. New York: RCR Creative Press. 3.
61. Denver Public Schools. (2011). Framework for Effective Teaching Evidence Guide. Retrieved from http://leap.dpsk12.org/LEAP/media/Main/PDFs/Framework-EVIDENCE-GUIDE-v3-184- 2011-COLOR.pdf
62. Cardwell, D. (2011 March 4). Have it your way? purist chefs won't have it. *New York Times*. Retrieved from http://www.nytimes.com/2011/03/05/nyregion/05puritans.html
63. Coleman, D. (2011 April 28). Bringing the Common Core to life. New York State Education Department webinar. Retrieved from http://usny.nysed.gov/rttt/resources/bringing-the- common-core-to-life.html
64. no author. (2011 Nov. 11). Billionaire Nathan Myhrvold's $625 cookbook. *BloombergBusinessweek*. Retrieved from http://www.businessweek.com/magazine/content/10_47/b4204089237326.htm#p2
65. no author. (2011 March 5). Making a 21st-century hamburger, with interactive graphics. *Wall Street Journal*. Retrieved from http://online.wsj.com/article/SB10001424052748704615504576172610668896674.html
66. no author. (2011 Nov. 11). Billionaire Nathan Myhrvold's $625 Cookbook. *BloombergBusinessweek*. Retrieved from http://www.businessweek.com/magazine/content/10_47/b4204089237326.htm#p2
67. Wadler, J. (2012 Aug. 16). Scrap mansion. *New York Times*. Retrieved from http://www.nytimes.com/2012/08/16/garden/an-ever-expanding-house-of-architectural- salvage.html
68. Heilemann, J. (2000 Nov.).
69. Gates, B. (2009 Feb. 2). Mosquitoes, malaria and education. TED. Retrieved from http://tinyurl.com/7mxpxjo Staff. (2009 Feb 5). "Bill Gates unleashes swarm of mosquitoes on crowd." FoxNews.com. Retrieved from http://www.foxnews.com/story/0,2933,488348,00.html#ixzz21D8CDWdv
70. Beaumont, C. (2009 Feb. 5). "Bill Gates unleash swarm of mosquitoes at TED 2009. *The Telegraph*. Retrieved from http://www.telegraph.co.uk/technology/

microsoft/4524578/Bill-Gates-unleash-swarm-of-mosquitoes-at-TED-2009. html

71. Bank, D. (2001). *Breaking Windows: How Bill Gates Fumbled the Future of Microsoft.* New York: The Free Press. 69.
72. Ibid. 183.
73. Ibid. 13-14.
74. Krashen, S. D. (1998 Winter). Phonemic awareness training for prelinguistic children: Do we need prenatal PA? *Reading Improvement* 35: 4. 167–71. (ERIC Document Reproduction Service BED198035099).
75. Wallace, J., & Erickson, J. (1992). *Hard Drive: Bill Gates and the Making of the Microsoft Empire.* Hoboken, N.J.: John Wiley & Sons. 161.
76. Fryer, B. (2006 Oct.). Sleep deficit: the performance killer, a conversation with Charles A. Czeisler. *Harvard Business Review.*
77. Wallace and Erickson. 276.
78. Ibid. 304
79. Allen, P. (2011 May). Microsoft's odd couple. *Vanity Fair.* Retrieved from http://www.vanityfair.com/business/features/2011/05/paul-allen-201105.
80. Dillon, S. (2010 Aug.). Education Department Deals Out Big Rewards. *New York Times.* Retrieved from http://www.nytimes.com/2010/08/05/education/05grants.html
81. Dixon, B. A. (2011 Aug. 10). Corporate funding of Urban League, NAACP & civil rights orgs has turned into corporate leadership. *Black Agenda Report.* Retrieved from http://blackagendareport.com/corporate-funding-urban-league-naacp-civil-rights-orgs-has turned-corporate-leadership.
82. Ohanian, S. (2010 Sept.). 'Race to the Top' and the Bill Gates connection: who gets to speak about what schools need? *Extra!* Retrieved from http://www.fair.org/index.php?page=4147
83. Dillon, S. (2009 Oct. 27). After complaints, Gates Foundation opens education aid offer to all states. *New York Times.* Retrieved from http://www.nytimes.com/2009/10/28/education/28educ.html
84. Holtzman, C. (2009 May 14). Growing D.C. presence for Gates Foundation. *Puget Sound Business Journal.* Retrieved from http://www.bizjournals.com/seattle/stories/2009/05/18/story2.html
85. Golden, D. (2010 July 15). Bill Gates' latest mission: fixing America's schools. *Bloomberg Businessweek.* Retrieved from http://www.msnbc.msn.com/id/38282806/ns/business- bloomberg_businessweek/#.UCkjO6O8GSo
86. Understanding Language website. http://ell.stanford.edu/policy-news/understanding-language- initiative-launch
87. Levy, S. (2008 June 22). My last Newsweek article. *Newsweek.* Retrieved from http://www.stevenlevy.com/index.php/06/22/my-last-newsweek-article
88. Saltman, K. (2010). *The Gift of Education: Public Education and Venture Philanthropy.* New York: Palgrave-McMillan.
89. Ohanian, S. (2012 Aug. 18). With the help of Student Achievement Partners, National Governors Association and Council of Chief State School Officers declare computers better than teachers at choosing books. blog. Retrieved from http://www.susanohanian.org/core.php?id=323

90. Auletta, K. (2001 Jan. 15). Final offer. *The New Yorker.* Retrieved from http://www.newyorker.com/archive/2001/01/15/2001_01_15_040_TNY_LIBRY_000022502#ixzz22XPma77n

91. Kennedy, D. (1995 Dec.). Bill Gates Fights to Keep the World Safe for Microsoft. *Boston Phoenix.* Retrieved from http://bostonphoenix.com/alt1/archive/books/reviews/12-95/BILL_GATES.html

92. Leonard, J. (1980 May). Thy neighbor's wife, *Playboy.* 56–58; Leonard, J. (2012). *Reading for My life,* edited Sue Leonard. New York: Viking. 50–56

93. Highfield, R. (20007 Nov. 5). Dandruff microbe's DNA cracked. *The Telegraph.* Retrieved from http://www.telegraph.co.uk/science/science-news/3313152/Dandruff-microbes-DNA cracked.html

REFERENCES

Advertising Age Staff. (1998, December 21). Strange bedfellows abound in 1998: People: Denis Beausejour, Bill Clinton/Monica Lewinsky, Jesse Ventura, Tina Brown, Dan Snyder, Bud Paxson, Tom Ryder, Brad Ball, Bill Gates, Mel Karmazin. *Advertising Age.*

Allen, P. (2011, May). Microsoft's odd couple. *Vanity Fair.*

Asimov, E. (1998, February 14). Gentlemen, choose your sausage. *New York Times.*

Auletta, K. (2001, January 15). Final offer, *The New Yorker.*

Bank, D. (2001). *Breaking Windows: How Bill Gates Fumbled the Future of Microsoft.* New York: The Free Press. 69.

Beaumont, C. (2009, February 5). Bill Gates unleash swarm of mosquitoes at TED 2009." *TheTelegraph.*

BloombergBusinessweek. (2011, November 11). Billionaire Nathan Myhrvold's $625 Cookbook. *Bloomberg Businessweek.*

Bork, Robert H. (1998, May 5). What antitrust is all about. *New York Times.*

Borcover, A. (1986, July 27). The Ford legacy of wonderful 'stuff.' *Chicago Tribune.*

Cassidy, J. (1998, May 8). Rich man, richer man: behind the comparisons of John D. Rockfeller and Bill Gates. *The New Yorker.*

Cardwell, D. (2011, March 4). Have it your way? purist chefs won't have it. *New York Times.*

Chandrasekaran, R. (1998, October 20). On day 1, U.S. targets Gates; government portrays Microsoft chairman as cagey, ruthless. *Washington Post.*

Chicago Sun-Times staff. (1998, January 30). Bill Gates sings lullaby on '20/20.' *Chicago Sun-Times.*

Christ, L. (2012, August 20). DOE finds almost 70 percent of city students live in poor households. *NY1.*

Coatne, M. (1998, December 15). Video dominates microsoft trial before recess. *Time.*

Cocoran, E. (1998, October 18). Microsoft: looking out for number one. *Washington Post.*

Coleman, D. (2011, April 28). Bringing the Common Core to life. New York State Education Department webinar.

Costello, L. B., & Reich, R. (2009). *Notes on Cooking: A Short Guide to an Essential Craft.* New York: RCR Creative Press.

Denver Public Schools. (2011). Framework for Effective Teaching Evidence Guide.

Dickerson, J. F., & van Voorst, B. (1998 March 9). Clash of the titans. *Time.*

Dillon, S. (2009, October 27). After complaints, Gates Foundation opens education aid offer to all states. *New York Times.*

Dillon, S. (2010, August). Education department deals out big rewards. *New York Times.*

Dixon, B. A. (2011, August 10). Corporate funding of Urban League, NAACP & civil rights has turned into corporate leadership. *Black Agenda Report.*

Dowd, M. (1998, January 1). Liberties; revenge on the nerds, *New York Times.*

Edstrom, J., & Eller, M. (1998). *Barbarians Led by Bill Gates: Microsoft from the Inside: How the World's Richest Corporation Wields Its Power.* New York: Henry Holt, 182.

Ford, G. (2011, May 29). The corporate dream: teachers as temps. Black Agenda Report. *Common Dreams*

Foster, D. (1998, October 19). Gates quoted as seeing case 'blow over.' Associated Press.

Fox News staff. (2009, February 5). Bill Gates unleashes swarm of mosquitoes on crowd.

FoxNews.com.

Fryer, B. (2006, October). Sleep deficit: the performance killer, a conversation with Charles A. Czeisler, *Harvard Business Review.*

Gates, B. (2009, February 2). Mosquitoes, malaria and education.TED conference.

Gelernter, D. (1998, December 7). Bill Gates: software strongman. *Time.*

Golden, D. (2010, July 15). Bill Gates' latest mission: fixing america's schools. *Bloomberg Businessweek.*

Grandin, G. (2009). *Fordlandia: The Rise and Fall of Henry Ford's Forgotten Jungle City.* New York: Metropolitan Books.

Harpaz, B. J. (1998, December 7). Bill Gates donating $100 million for child immunizations. Associated Press.

Hedrick, L. (1998, December 28). Microsoft's big browser. *The Nation.*

Heilemann, J. (2000, November). The truth, the whole truth, and nothing but the truth: the untold story of the Microsoft antitrust case and what it means for the future of Bill Gates and his company. *Wired.*

Heilemann, J. (2001). *Pride Before the Fall: The Trials of Bill Gates and the End of the Microsoft Era.* New York: Collins Business.

Highfield, R. (2007, November 5). Dandruff microbe's DNA cracked. *The Telegraph.*

Holtzman, C. (2009, May 14). Growing D.C. presence for Gates Foundation. *Puget Sound Business Journal.*

Krashen, S. D. (1998, Winter). Phonemic awareness training for prelinguistic children: do we need prenatal PA? *Reading Improvement* 35:4, 167–71.

Kennedy, D. (1995, December). "Bill Gates fights to keep the world safe for Microsoft." *Boston Phoenix.*

LaBaton, S. (1998, January 15). Gates helped draft Microsoft's response to judge. *New York Times.*

Lea, G. (1998, December 9). Publicists spin as MS seeks AOL-Netscape papers. And the kinder, gentler Gates answers three questions. Take it easy, Bill . . . *The Register* (UK).

Leonard, J. (1980, May). Thy Neighbor's Wife. *Playboy.* 56–58.

Leonard, J. (2012). *Reading for My life,* ed. Sue Leonard. New York: Viking.

Levy, S. (2008, June 22). My last Newsweek article. *Newsweek.*

Lewis, P. H. (1998, April 30). Windows 98: the tuneup. *New York Times.*

Lohr, S., & Karkoff, J. (1998, October 8). Microsoft's world: A special report: how software's giant played hardball game. *New York Times.*

MacGregor, J. (1998, January 3). Of mice and men, release 2.0. *New York Times.*

Myerson, A. R. (1998, May 24). The nation; rating the bigshots: Gates vs. Rockefeller. *New York Times.*

Newsweek Staff. (1998, December 15). A kinder, gentler Bill. *Newsweek.*

New York Times editorial. (1998, May 19). United States v Microsoft. *New York Times.*

Novack, V. (1998, November 2). Influence. *Time.*

O'Donnell, R. (1998, December 8). Bill Gates chats with Rosie O'Donnell about REALLY important matters! YouTube.

Ohanian, S. (2010, September). 'Race to the Top' and the Bill Gates connection: Who gets to speak about what schools need? *Extra!*

Ohanian, S. (2012, August 18). With the help of student achievement partners, National Governors Association and Council of Chief State School Officers declare computers better than teachers at choosing books. www.susanohanian. org. blog.

Rich, F. (1998, March 7). Love that Bill. *New York Times.*

Roberts, J. (2011, February 22). Memphis city schools teachers get an earbud-ful of class coaching." *The Commercial Appeal.*

Rohm, W. G. (1998). *The Microsoft File: The Secret Case Against Bill Gates.* New York: Times Books/Random House.

Saltman, K. (2010). *The Gift of Education: Public Education and Venture Philanthropy.* New York: Palgrave-McMillan.

Seglin, J. L. (1998, December 20). The right thing; bosses beware when bending the truth. *New York Times.*

Taylor, C. (1998, November 16). Microsoft's Jihad jam. *Time.*

Taylor, S. Jr. (1993, November 1). What to do with the Microsoft monster. *American Lawyer.*

Time. No author. (1927, October 24). "Ford Rubber." *Time.*

Vogel, C. (1998, May 6). Bill Gates buys Homer painting for record price. *New York Times* news service.

Wadler, J. (2012, August 16). Scrap mansion. *New York Times.*

Wall Street Journal. (2011, March 5). Making a 21st-century hamburger, with interactive graphics. *Wall Street Journal.*

Wallace, J., & Erickson, J. (1992). *Hard Drive: Bill Gates and the Making of the Microsoft Empire.* Hoboken, N.J.: John Wiley & Sons, 161.

Wasserman, E. (1998, November 17). Gates deposition makes judge laugh in court. CNN.

Wertheimer, L. (1996, March 18). Microsoft's Bill Gates for president in 1996. *All Things Considered.* Washington, DC: National Public Radio.

CHAPTER 9

THE SECRETARY
AND THE SOFTWARE

On the Need for Integrating Software
Analysis into Educational Spaces

Tom Liam Lynch
Pace University

secretary: (1) One who is entrusted with private or secret matters; a confidant; one privy to a secret; (2) One whose office it is to write for another; spec. one who is employed to conduct or assist with correspondence, to keep records, and (usually) to transact various other business, for another person or for a society, corporation, or public body.

software: The programs and procedures required to enable a computer to perform a specific task, as opposed to the physical components of the system.

—*Oxford English Dictionary*

Learning technologies are not new. They're surprisingly old. Technology, by which I mean the use of an instrument to extend human beings' natural ability (Ong, 1982), has informed education not for many decades but for thousands of years (Havelock, 1986). As Buckingham (2008) reminds us, "Education inevitably uses technologies of many kinds, and it has always

Left Behind in the Race to the Top, pages 129–142
Copyright © 2013 by Information Age Publishing
129

done so: the book, the pencil and the chalkboard are technologies just as much as the computer, the video camera or the latest mobile communication device" (p. 176). Still, despite a lack of newness, the speeches of policymakers and the promises of companies offering the latest "innovative" resources to schools seem to indicate that recent technologies, by their very nature, improve teaching and learning. This conclusion is utterly inaccurate. The learning technologies to which education reformers increasingly refer are beyond the books, pencils, and chalkboards of which Buckingham speaks. These new technologies are powered by software, making software something which we must discuss openly and critically. Software can no longer be a frightening technical word lost on educators. It must roll off the tongue lightly and be the subject of heavy inspection.

T.H.E. ARGUMENT FOR LEARNING TECHNOLOGIES

The expanding popularity of software-powered technologies is not accidental. This expansion is fueled by an education reform agenda that encourages many kinds of applications that rely on software and gather data on teaching and learning. In addition to the monetary encouragement realized in the $4 billion tied to Race to the Top, venture capitalists have, by one conservative estimate, increased their funding of educational technology products to over $300 million dollars in 2011, a nearly 40% increase compared to the previous year (Ash, 2012). One of the more compelling and ubiquitous cases for the use of learning technologies in education reform might be referred to as *T.H.E.* argument: a justification for the use of learning technologies based on techno-historical-economic (T.H.E) grounds.

T.H.E. argument begins with what appear to be simple statements about the current state of education. President Barack Obama's Secretary of Education, Arne Duncan, utters the following simple statement in two separate speeches framing his education reform agenda: "Schools adopted the factory model that was popular to produce graduates that mirrored the needs of the workforce at that time" (Duncan, 2009a, para. 16; 2009b, para. 16). This one sentence contains all three elements of T.H.E. argument, by evoking technology ("factory model"), history ("at that time"), and economics ("needs of the workforce"). The effectiveness of this kind of sentence is that it positions the administration's reform agenda as an economic imperative, suggesting that the country's economic woes are due in no small part to the fact that its schools are not preparing young people for the workforce (see Apple, 1996, 2000, for counterarguments to this position). In short, schools should adopt models of operation that mirror those of the private sector, which today means relying on technology.

Duncan's use of T.H.E. argument continues in a speech given to a conservative think-tank, the American Enterprise Institute (AEI), where he is more explicit about the need for reform and the interplay between technological, historical, and economic forces. In his own words:

> Our K–12 system largely still adheres to the century-old, industrial-age factory model of education.... Technology can play a huge role in increasing educational productivity, but not just as an add-on or for a high-tech reproduction of current practice. Again, we need to change the underlying processes to leverage the capabilities of technology. The military calls it a force multiplier. Better use of online learning, virtual schools, and other smart uses of technology is not so much about replacing educational roles as it is about giving each person the tools they need to be more successful—reducing wasted time, energy, and money. (Duncan, 2010, para. 29)

Again, Duncan underscores an interdependent relationship between education and economy. He suggests that whereas industry has developed away from the assembly lines of yore, schools still look very similar to the way they did over a century ago. When this logic is accorded—that schools fail because they did not "evolve" the way industry has—it is a small step to say that if technological innovations helped pave the way for commerce, the same innovations will improve schools. T.H.E. argument presents a simple, believable story that both diagnoses a problem and prescribes the pharmakon.

In addition to leveraging education as an economic remedy, T.H.E. argument is also used to make a case for the investment in "innovative" technologies that can help propel schools out of their 19th-century internment, which Duncan describes above as the "century-old, industrial-age factory model of education." It is this approach that undergirds Secretary Duncan's launch of Race to the Top, a reform program that is at the heart of the Obama administration's education agenda. Here is how Duncan explains Race to the Top on a Sunday morning political show:

> We want to reward those states, those districts, those nonprofits that are willing to challenge the status quo to get dramatically better, close the achievement gap and raise the bar for everybody. And what's been so encouraging is before we spent a dollar, a dime, of Race to the Top money we've seen 48 states come together to raise the bar, higher standards for everyone, to stop lying to children. You've seen states remove barriers to creating new innovative charter schools, you've seen folks get rid of firewalls separating student achievement data from teachers'. There's been this extraordinary movement in the country before we spent one dollar. (NBC News, 2009)

Race to the Top, as Duncan describes, takes an unusual tack in realizing the administration's reform goals. It frames a competition for states, districts, and nonprofits to battle each other for a piece of the hefty prize.

As he mentions in passing, Race to the Top values particular kinds of re-form efforts, including the subscription to certain standards, easing the paperwork for charter schools, and ensuring that student and teacher per-formance data become more strategically available. Linking student and teacher data recurs throughout Duncan's speeches, as in this excerpt from a speech delivered at Teachers College, Columbia University:

> The draft Race to the Top criteria would also reward states that publicly re-port and link student achievement data to the programs where teachers and principals were credentialed. And the federal government has funded a large expansion of teacher residency programs in high-need districts and schools, including one to be run out of the Teachers College. (Duncan, 2009c, para. 42)

The criteria referring to "firewalls separating student achievement data from teachers'" and "publicly report and link student achievement data to the programs where teachers and principals were credentialed" are of particular interest to the current discussion. These criteria are echoed in the formal language on the USDOE's web site, where the Race to the Top application requirements ask applicants to "advance reforms around four specific areas," one of which is "building data systems that measure student growth and success, and inform teachers and principals about how they can improve instruction" (U.S. Department of Education, 2010, n.p.). The use of data systems to measure student and teacher performance *requires* that districts and schools rely on technologies to capture, analyze, and share information. In order for this kind of information to be captured, however, the very social and complex actions that comprise teaching and learning must be distilled into discrete tidbits that can be neatly housed in databases. This is something easily lost in the metaphors that comprise Duncan's lan-guage. "States" do not "report and link" data. Representatives from the state, often in close partnership with salesmen and project managers from commercial IT companies, create customized software solutions to do the job. It is all driven by software.

In the above excerpts, Secretary Duncan implies two main ways in which technologies can be leveraged to improve learning, which might be called (1) informational and (2) instructional. While these two are not easily separa-ble, there is something to be gained from considering them distinctly. Infor-mational uses of technology (like "data systems") refers to the exchanging of batches of data associated with certain aspects of education. It might include names, home addresses, ID numbers, birthdays, race/ethnicity, income lev-els, and official test scores. Instructional uses of technology (like "online learning and other smart uses of technology") begin with pedagogical con-siderations, meaning the role of the use of technology is primarily about sup-porting students in learning content and skills relevant to a specific area of study. In the case of both informational and instructional uses of technology, it is what is done with technology that makes technology useful and worthwhile. This is something researchers of educational technology have declared repeatedly: that the use of technology outweighs the commercial or political hype that preludes its adoption (Buckingham, 2008; Cuban, 2001; Menchik, 2010; Zhao, Pugh, Sheldon, & Byers, 2002). Still, what too often escapes our attention as a field is the fact that what we mean by learning technologies has changed drastically in recent years. It is not just about wires and computers. It is about software. And we must begin to see that informational and instructional uses of software-powered technologies can sometimes become entwined, fused so seamlessly by imprecise language that moving batches of data across servers becomes confused with teaching and learning.

THE SILENT ROLE OF SOFTWARE

In the sections above, I argue that our technologies increasingly rely on software. This is true in our everyday lives and in education. When it comes to the latter, however, it is important to note that software both inhibits and enables certain pedagogical practices, whether in online learning platforms, e-Readers, the latest web-based app, or automatic essay scoring (AES) products. This section proposes the establishment of what we might call educational software analysis, a method for analyzing the pedagogical implications of software that borrows concepts from the fields of software studies, new media, and spatiality theory. For modeling purposes, I draw upon two of Lev Manovich's (2001) five principles of new media: the concepts of *automation* and *transcoding*. Though Manovich does not focus on education, his ideas serve dual purposes. They ground the current analysis in the field of software studies, which currently is underrepresented in educational research, with some exceptions (Adams, 2006; Lane, 2008), and they also provide a conceptual framework for critically discussing the pedagogical impact of software.

Automation

An example from video gaming can help define *automation* and the hidden role of software. Imagine a computer game where the lead character can seemingly do whatever the player wishes. The character can run quickly or slowly, jump, grab, dance, turn to the player and suggest strategies, or even communicate with other characters. These capacities seem to indicate that computer programming has achieved some pinnacle of pure artificial intelligence. It appears that the player has uninhibited freedom, able to make the characters behave however he wishes. Such freedom is an illusion. The illusion is made possible because the gaming software has been tightly programmed to limit the interactions a player can input. As Manovich (2001) explains, "computer characters can display intelligence and skills only because programs place severe limits on our possible interactions with them. Put differently, computers can pretend to be intelligent only by tricking us into using a very small part of who we are when we communicate with them" (p. 34). There is a limit to software: It can only do automatically what it is programmed to do. Manovich refers to this as "automation." In schools, for instance, when students take an online quiz that immediately generates their scores, this is possible because the software that powers the quiz was programmed with "correct" answers and students are only able to input certain kinds of information. Automation occurs because "severe limits" on students' possible learning interactions are preset. Student input is right *or* wrong.

Transcoding

Later Manovich discusses another principle of new media called *transcoding*, which spatiality theorists Kitchin and Dodge (2011) helpfully define in their discussion of software-powered social spaces thus:

> To transcode is to translate meaning and function from one media to another. The technicity of code enables the translation of important aspects of culture into a framework defined by the software ontology, epistemology, and pragmatics, in so doing meaning and language become translated into code or transcoded, with the resulting shift having an effect on how people understand and act in the world. (p. 124)

The word *transcode* has its roots in computer science, referring to the loss of quality when converting one type of media file to another. Manovich adapts this notion to apply to the ways in which human culture also undergoes a kind of translation when converted to code. For purposes of illustration, consider how the complexities of face-to-face human interaction compare to interaction via software-powered media with the "resulting shift having an effect on how people understand and act in the world." There are degrees of difference, for instance, between (1) taking a friend to a concert, (2) meeting another friend face to face for dinner and *showing her pictures of the concert*, (3) *showing that friend a video* of the concert face to face, and (4) *posting a picture or video* to a social network online. In these different cases, the nuance of human experience is transcoded into kinds of information that computer systems can understand, whether through a picture and video shared face to face or a picture and video shared distantly online. With each kind of transcoding act, the relationship between the subject, the friend, and the experience of concert-going undergoes shifts that are technical, cultural, and social. When we apply Manovich's ideas to educational settings, we must note that transcoding teaching and learning experiences effects an additional shift in pedagogy as well. When students learn how to write via submitting assignments to software rather than in dialogue with peers and teachers, something is lost and something is gained. What is lost and what is gained requires further unpacking.

Taken together, Manovich's principles of automation and transcoding offer us a way to consider software-powered learning technologies, raising the following question: How do the characteristics of software, especially automation and transcoding, affect pedagogy? In order to respond to this question, we now turn our attention to a kind of educational software that, as briefly suggested above, is the subject of much enthusiasm and investment in this Race to the Top climate. It is a widely used software program that automatically assesses students' writing.

AN EXAMPLE IN WRITING

Automated essay scoring (AES) software has been in use for decades (Grimes, 2008). Recently, attention has been rekindled after a study claimed that computer programs were as accurate in scoring writing as human scorers (Shermis & Hammer, 2012). With AES software, students can submit a piece of writing and receive both quantitative and narrative feedback automatically—in just a few seconds. Interest in such software is spurred by promises of savings in both time and cost. Let's consider an example.

One popular automated essay scoring product, which I will call Auto-Assess, is offered for licensing to K–12 schools by a major international educational publisher. When using Auto-Assess, students log in to its web site. There, the student finds a particular prompt chosen by her teacher. Below the prompt is a large text box where the student is instructed to write a response to the prompt. As a precaution, Auto-Assess does not permit a student to copy and paste text into the box. Students are expected to write on-demand and a sort of stopwatch tracks the amount of time students work on the written response. The student composes her response. When complete, she submits her response and a few seconds later the student sees feedback automatically generated by the software. The feedback scores the student on a scale using six traits of writing as criteria (Ideas, Organization, Word Choice, Sentence Fluency, Voice, and Conventions). Accompanying each numeric score is a piece of narrative feedback such as, "Your essay received a Sentence Fluency score of 1. It may be hard to read because some sentences are put together in the wrong way. Your essay is very choppy to read out loud because you did not write different kinds of sentences." The student can, depending on the settings established by the teacher, resubmit her response in a second attempt.

PEDAGOGICAL IMPACT

In order to understand the pedagogical implications of AES, it helps to make explicit some of the actions the software takes as part of what I've just described. When a student submits a response to a prompt, the software generates automatic feedback to the writing by transcoding the written text into quantitative elements. That is, software can quickly determine the average number of letters in words, words in sentences, sentences in paragraphs, and so on. Software can identify the presence of key words that it has been programmed to recognize (i.e., characterization, simile, Milton), including transitional words (such as "however," "finally," and "in conclusion"). Software can also conduct syntactical analyses similar to what popular word processing programs do when they underscore parts of sentences in squiggly green lines. When a prompt is predetermined, it is also possible for software to compare a student's writing to a database of carefully scored anchor essays on the same topic. "Anchor essays" commonly refer to a collection of human-scored and "aligned" essays that are used as a benchmark for large-scale writing evaluation. Software can present what *appears* to be personalized feedback to students whose writing characteristics match those in its database.

AES software like Auto-Assess has both enthusiasts and opponents. Those who oppose its use claim that software cannot assess writing with any depth, can be manipulated by savvy students, and can overlook the nuances in students' thinking (Perelman, 2008; Winerip, 2012). On the other hand, proponents of AES argue that some kinds of writing assignments occur in contexts (such as introductory courses or standardized tests) where assessors are inundated by large samples of writing at once, making it difficult to respond in a timely or cost-effective way (Shermis & Burstein, 2003). AES, they claim, makes the assessment of such writing assignments expeditious and economical. At first glance AES seems to be a cheap and fast way to grade large numbers of papers without needing to pay educators. It would be reasonable to anticipate educators resisting AES loudly. This is not necessarily the case.

Literacy education scholar Miles Myers (2003) makes a compelling case in favor of AES. Myers argues that researchers in the fields of composition studies and English education have known for some time that the project-based approach, coupled with frequent and timely feedback, is a high-leverage "best practice" in the teaching of writing. One of the challenges of this approach, however, is that it is logistically difficult to manage (i.e., multiple drafts by over one hundred students who are all at different places in their writing development) and that time can be swallowed up in responding perfunctorily to students' common, relatively simple writing needs. AES, Myers thinks, offers a solution

> AES can help K–12 teachers overcome these difficult problems of time, cost, and generalizability in assessment . . . computer-scored (and analyzed) essays, using one of the automated essay scorers, can produce a score and some analysis in a few seconds, and for a secondary student looking for a first or second opinion on an essay, computer-scored essays is a very helpful and a relatively cheap addition. (2003, p. 15)

Myers' claim is rooted, admirably, in a firm sense of what the realities of writing instruction consist of for teachers. I say this as a teacher who, myself, struggled for years with meaningfully assessing students' writing. Myers, however, fails to interrogate the *way* AES software performs its assessment of student writing. He leaves the reader with the impression that such software is merely mechanical, like a piece of chalk in a teacher's hand. In fact, software contains the ideologies, pedagogies, and epistemologies of those who commission and code it.

I think Myers both hits and misses the pedagogical potential of this kind of software. He captures the most essential component of using AES and any other learning technology: it is the pedagogy, not the technology, that primarily matters. If a teacher who is well-versed in project-based writing processes can find ways to use AES to give students more frequent and useful feedback while easing the paper load—excellent. In that case, the use of the learning technology enhances already sound practice. If, however, the use of a software-powered learning technology like AES supplants the teaching of writing, it will disappoint. In my experience working with schools, I have seen—time and time again—administrators purchase software like Auto-Assess in order to compensate for the professional learning needs of a teacher. Or, due to the way in which budgets in urban districts are distributed and reduced, school leaders sometimes find themselves purchasing products like AES because they know that students need help with writing and are enchanted by the technological allure of new software. Beleaguered, beguiled administrators often hand technologies to teachers without providing meaningful pedagogical support.

Myers does not explicitly consider the degrees to which AES software's ability to provide automatic feedback necessitates the transcoding of the writing process. Failure to recognize automation and transcoding (as discussed earlier) can result in software being used for *informational* purposes and never reaching its *instructional* potential. When AES is programmed to recognize certain syntactical features or key words, it is performing a useful informational action. It transcodes language into quantities and binaries in order to be processed by computer systems. When the software gives feedback to students, however, it does so in a way that appears to be instructional when in fact it is *still* informational. Recall Manovich's warning that "computers can pretend to be intelligent only by tricking us into using a very small part of who we are when we communicate with them." The feedback generated by software is the product of automation, of an algorithm, and not as authentic as it is made to appear. This suggests that there are at least two types of transcoding that AES's automation enacts: (1) transcoding alphabetic language into quantities and (2) transcoding the relationship between writer and reader.

Transcoding Alphabetic Language into Quantities

As described above, software can only recognize and evaluate certain kinds of characteristics of writing. When a student's writing is transcoded into quantities and binaries in order for software to process it, elements of style become lost. As an example, consider the opening proem to *Paradise Lost*, which begins "Of man's disobedience and the fruit of that forbidden tree..." When I enter the entire passage into some basic text analysis software fundamentally similar to AES software, a report is generated that gives us insight into how language is transcoded. The report tells us that the famous passage consists of 199 words, 2 sentences, 4.3 characters per word on average, 1.3 syllables per word on average, and 99.5 words per sentence on average. Milton, if he had been writing his epic with Auto-Assess, might well have been automatically told to "write different kinds of sentences."

To be clear, I am not saying that such text analyses are not useful. There are strong cases made for the use of such software in the humanities. Ramsay (2011) puts it well when he discusses the fact that literary criticism has many qualities aligned with those of computer software. In his words, "the narrowing constraints of computational logic—the irreducible tendency of the computer toward enumeration, measurement, and verification—is fully compatible with the goals of criticism" (p. 16). The transcoding of language into "enumeration, measurement" makes possible new kinds of entry points into both reading and writing. In the hands of a thoughtful and supported pedagogue, textual analytical software can be invaluable. However, if the transcoding of a writer's craft into quantities ends with a litany of numbers and pseudo-narrative feedback, then Manovich's warning from earlier will have gone unheeded. The software—including those who developed and marketed it—will have tricked us into using only a small part of who we are.

Transcoding the Relationship Between Writer and Reader

As the act of teaching writing becomes transcoded, the student-writer's relationship to her audience shifts. Traditionally, when a student writes for her teacher or peer, she imagines her reader with some confidence. This imagining of the reader might lead the student to write in a particular style, integrate personalized ideas, and even forecast how her teacher might respond to this word or that punctuation mark (Lynch & McKibbin, 2010). This ability for a writer to imagine and empathize with an audience has been argued to be a hallmark of college-ready writers (Schorn, 2006).

When a student writes for Auto-Assess, her relationship to her audience shifts. This new audience can recognize only certain kinds of characteristics. It can easily process transitional words, even if used awkwardly. It can pick up on key words it has been programmed to recognize. The software-reader can be programmed to give greater value to anything quantifiable, such as polysyllabic words. A danger of this kind of transcoding is not, as some would have us think, that it will mechanize the writing process. The writing process, in too many contexts, is already well on its way to mechanization (Kohn, 2006). The danger of this new software-reader lies in the possibility that we won't teach students the importance of writing for many different kinds of audiences, in many different kinds of genres. I am less worried about the idealized relationship between the student-writer and teacher-reader being somehow corrupted than I am that technophobic rants against products like Auto-Assess will distract us from a lesson of immense import to our students' lives as writers: imagine your audience.

The growing use of the automation in the assessment of student composition is transcoding the teaching of writing. This may or may not portend a grave pedagogical future, but we must begin to speak about the role of software differently. When a product like Auto-Assess is used in schools without due attention to pedagogy, we are unknowingly choosing to use software for informational rather than instructional purposes. In a case where students "learn" writing in a computer lab with a fledgling educator using Auto-Assess, without an intentional pedagogical context, the software will still generate data-filled spreadsheets and analytic reports about students' use, strengths, and needs. It will produce batches and batches of data—some of which might be used to evaluate teachers' effectiveness. However, opportunities to enhance instruction will have been squandered because the professional learning necessary to integrate such software will have been ignored, unknown, or unfunded.

IMPLICATIONS FOR THE FIELD

There are unique and interlocking ways in which educators can leverage software to deepen teaching and learning. First, educators need a language for critiquing educational software. While there are some frameworks for assessing the content of software or the way in which it is instructionally designed, these kinds of resources do not look critically or thoroughly enough at the more subtle ways software steers pedagogy. Education scholars can help fill this need by studying the ways in which software studies and media and spatiality theory can inform and reform current thinking across fields. Secondly, school leaders and educators can make more intentional efforts to critique and discuss both why technology has been positioned in schools the way it has been and how the way software is designed affects teaching and learning. In addition to the content or instructional design of educational software, question explicitly how the nature of software itself—like automation and transcoding—is at play. Thirdly, professional organizations that support subsets of teachers can do more to engage in the discourse surrounding the use of educational software. The International Association of K–12 Online Learning (iNACOL) and the International Society of Technology Education (ISTE) have many resources to assist schools in the integration of learning technologies. These resources, however, offer little guidance or language to help educators more deeply understand the ways in which software itself both enables and inhibits certain kinds of practices. What's more, organizations like the National Council of Teachers of English (NCTE) should have resources to assist schools in critically examining the pedagogical impact of products like Auto-Assess. These materials appear to be lacking greatly. Finally, policymakers must do more to observe the distinctions between informational and instructional uses of learning technologies. Extinguishing firewalls between student and teacher data is primarily an informational use of technology and, in and of itself, does not necessitate any difference in instructional practice. Moving data across servers does not constitute an innovation in pedagogy.

While enthusiasm for learning technologies is nothing new, the ubiquity of software is, which makes it important that we begin to better understand how software can impact pedagogy. As discussed above, the way in which policymakers, specifically Arne Duncan, discusses education reform makes use of what I call T.H.E. argument, which ties educational ends to economic ends and sets up technology as a key lever for "improving" schools. The resulting focus on technology, however, is often too broadly conceived—confusing informational and instructional uses of technologies—and makes us blind to the nuances of the role of software. By calling attention to the ways in which research and theories from other fields can be used to frame our own thinking in education, my hope is that we can collectively shift our discourses to account for the secrets of software.

REFERENCES

Adams, C. (2006). PowerPoint, habits of mind, and classroom culture. *Journal of Curriculum Studies, 38*(4), 389–411.

Apple, M. W. (1996). *Cultural politics and education.* New York, New York, NY: Teachers College Press.

Apple, M. W. (2000). *Official knowledge: Democratic education in a conservative age.* New York, NY: Routledge.

Ash, K. (2012, February 1). K–12 marketplace sees major flow of venture capital. *Education Week.* Retrieved from http://www.edweek.org/ew/articles/2012/02/01/19venture_ep.h31.html

Buckingham, D. (2008). *Beyond technology: Children's learning in the age of digital culture.* Maldan, MA: Polity Press.

Cuban, L. (2001). *Oversold and underused: Computers in the classroom.* Cambridge, MA: Harvard University Press.

Duncan, A. (2009a, August 20). From compliance to innovation. Retrieved from http://www.ed.gov/news/speeches/compliance-innovation

Duncan, A. (2009b, October 7). Make no small plans. *Secretary Arne Duncan's Remarks at the Grantmakers for Education Conference in Chicago.* Retrieved from http://www.ed.gov/news/speeches/make-no-small-plans

Duncan, A. (2009c, October 22). Teacher preparation: Reforming the uncertain profession. Retrieved from https://www.ed.gov/news/speeches/teacher-preparation-reforming-uncertain-profession

Duncan, A. (2010, November 17). The new normal: Doing more with less. Retrieved from http://www.ed.gov/news/speeches/new-normal-doing-more-less-secretary-arne-duncans-remarks-american-enterprise-institut

Grimes, D. C. (2008). *Middle school use of automated writing evaluation: A multi-site case study* Unpublished doctoral dissertation, University of California, Irvine, Irvine, California.

Havelock, E. A. (1986). *The muse learns to write: Reflections on orality and literacy from antiquity to the present.* New Haven, CT: Yale University Press.

Kitchin, R., & Dodge, M. (2011). *Code/Space: Software and everyday life.* Cambridge, MA: MIT Press.

Kohn, A. (2006). The trouble with rubrics. *English Journal, 95*(4), 12–15.

Lane, L. (2008). Toolbox or trap? Course management systems and pedagogy. *Educause Quarterly, 2,* 4–6.

Lynch, T. L., & McKibbin, K. (2010). When writers imagine readers: How writing for publication affects students' sense of responsibility to readers. In P. Sullivan, H. Tinberg, & S. Blau (Eds.), *What is "college-level" writing? volume 2: Assignments, readings, and student writing samples (online).* Urbana, IL: NCTE.

Manovich, L. (2001). *The language of new media.* Cambridge, MA: MIT Press.

NBC News. (2009, November 15). *Meet the press.* Retrieved from http://www.msnbc.msn.com/id/33931557/ns/meet_the_press/

Menchik, D. A. (2010). Placing cybereducation in the UK classroom. *British Journal of Sociology of Education, 25*(2), 193–213.

Myers, M. (2003). Automated essay scoring: A cross-disciplinary perspective. In M. D. Shermis & J. C. Burstein (Eds.), *What can computers contribute to a K–12 writing program?* (pp. 3–20). New York, NY: Routledge.

Ong, W. (1982). *Orality and literacy: The technologizing of the word.* New York, NY: Methuen.

Perelman, L. (2008). Information illiteracy and mass market writing assessments. *College Composition and Communication, 60*(1), 128–141.

Ramsay, S. (2011). *Reading machines: Toward an algorithmic criticism.* Urbana, IL: University of Illinois Press. Retrieved from http://books.google.com/books?id=14KPI0ORQigC

Schorn, S. E. (2006). A lot like us, but more so: Listening to writing curriculum across the curriculum. In P. Sullivan & H. Tinberg (Eds.), *What is "college-level" English?* (pp. 330–340). Urbana, IL: NCTE.

Secretary. 2013. In OED Online. Retrieved April 20, 2013, from http://www.oed.com/view/Entry/174549?isAdvanced=false&result=1&rskey=ZAzJ7R&

Shermis, M. D., & Burstein, J. C. (2003). *Automated essay scoring: A cross-disciplinary perspective.* New York, NY: Routledge. Retrieved from http://books.google.com/books?id=JIR6ihd7ZA4C

Shermis, M. D., & Hammer, B. (2012). *Contrasting state-of-the-art automated scoring of essays: Analysis.* Akron, OH: University of Akron. Retrieved from http://dl.dropbox.com/u/44416236/NCME%202012%20Paper3_29_12.pdf

Software. 2013. In OED Online. Retrieved April 20, 2013, from http://www.oed.com/view/Entry/183938?redirectedFrom=software#eid

U.S. Department of Education. (2010). *Race to the top.* Washington, DC: Author. Retrieved from http://www2.ed.gov/programs/racetothetop/index.html

Winerip, S. (2012, April 22). Facing a robo-grader? Just keep obfuscating mellifluously. *New York Times.* Retrieved from http://www.nytimes.com/2012/04/23/education/robo-readers-used-to-grade-test-essays.html?pagewanted=all

Zhao, Y., Pugh, K., Sheldon, S., & Byers, J. L. (2002). Conditions for classroom technology innovations. *Teachers College Record, 104*(3), 482–515.

CHAPTER 10

THE ERA OF RECRUITMENT

The Militarization of Everything

William M. Reynolds
Georgia Southern University

*During the last decade, the language and ghostly shadow of war
became all-embracing, not only eroding the distinction between war and peace,
but putting into play a public pedagogy in which nearly every aspect of the culture
was shaped by militarized knowledge, values, and ideals.*
—(Giroux, 2011, p. 138)

It's not just a job; it's an adventure
—United States Navy recruiting slogan 1976–1986)

Army Strong!
—United States Army recruiting slogan 2006–present[1]

Left Behind in the Race to the Top, pages 143–157
Copyright © 2013 by Information Age Publishing
All rights of reproduction in any form reserved.

INTRODUCTION

Where have all the young men gone?
Long time passing
Where have all the young men gone?
Long time ago
Where have all the young men gone?
Gone for soldiers every one
When will they ever learn?
When will they ever learn? (Seeger, 1960/2012)

Picture yourself as a young man or woman sitting at home and you are taking a pause from playing your favorite video game and watching television. You might be watching the Military Channel. This channel was launched in 2005. It is 24-hour "militainment": "The new channel promised to take viewers to the front lines, showcase new gadgets, and deliver the standard military history fare" (Stahl, 2010, p. 144).

The frequent commercial interruption occurs. This scene unfolds in one such commercial. Two young men, one Black and one White, are vigorously playing a video game, hands clutched around their controllers. Flash to the screen of their monitor. We see soldiers in the game moving in on a house in some Middle Eastern land. The troops have their rifles held out in front of them ready for action. The sounds of war are ringing all around them. All of a sudden one of the techno gear-laden soldiers in the game turns and knocks on the screen. "You look like you are really into this. You guys want the real challenge?" (goArmy.com/courage, 2007). The 30-second commercial proceeds to discuss the opportunities available in the Army. It concludes with the web address where the two young men and those watching can send for the free official video game of the United States Army, *America's Army*. The web site allows you to download the video game for free. This video game is actually two games in one. The first is about military life and how it progresses.

> There's Soldiers, a single-player 2D RPG in which you guide a soldier from enlistee to high ranking officer, periodically tweaking the character's values and goals to shape the soldier's final outcome. You'll help your soldier settle upon a career, get an education, visit the recruiter, and advance through the ranks; all while "progress[ing] through the Army and see[ing] for yourself what a rich life experience the U.S. Army offers." The game will play like an interactive movie, as its Story Engine software drives a Movie Generation System, which assembles and plays video and audio based upon your input. The game holds and espouses values central to the Army: loyalty, duty, respect, selfless service, honor, integrity, and personal courage. Your job is to coordinate six resources and input the decisions that reflect the Army's values. Resources are health, strength, knowledge, skills, finances, and popularity. You win if your soldier becomes a Sergeant. (Cockeram, 2005, p. 1)

The second part of the game will, no doubt, be the more popular section with youth. It is in the shooter game tradition.

Squad-based multi-player missions will comprise the bulk of game play; though there will be solo training missions. Multiple environments like indoor, swamp, desert, and forest will add variety, while soldier BDUs (battle dress uniforms) will update for fuller realism. In an interesting pro-America twist, no matter what squad you play on, your teammates will appear to you as the U.S. Army, while your opponents appear as the enemy. In one mission, for example, you're a group of elite Army soldiers sneaking into a terrorist camp to retrieve important intelligence from their computers. Or you're a group of elite Army soldiers protecting sensitive government intelligence from an invading band of terrorists. (Cockeram, 2005, p. 1)

The commercial and the video game are examples of the new public military pedagogy that pervades our society, the lives of our youth, and all of us. The military knows that today's youth are immersed in the techno-culture and offering up a free video game is a way into their everyday lives. And it is a not-so-subtle recruitment device.

This is one small example of not only the current historical conjuncture, but part of the era of recruitment made necessary by the all-volunteer army established in 1973. Ironically, this militarization is indirectly a result of the post-Vietnam era. The protests against the draft and the so-called Vietnam Syndrome were in many ways responsible for ending the draft (see Baily, 2007, p. 48). But moving to the all-volunteer army (and other armed services) has resulted in an all-out push to recruit as many youth as possible into military service. The percentage of federal budget for defense is approximately 36%.[2] Figures for the increase in defense spending post-9/11 are just as staggering. The budget for defense/military spending for the period between 2001 and 2009 rose from $358.1 billion to $494.3 billion.[3] These figures do not include the Iraq and Afghanistan Wars. The cost the Iraq War increases by the second, but is $806 billion at the time of the writing of this chapter, and the Afghanistan War comes in at $557 billion.[4] The amount spent by the Federal government for recruiting and retention is $7.7 billion. This figure has more than doubled since 2004. The result is an all-volunteer Armed Services whose racial make-up is as follows (these percentages of total recruits are taken from the conservative Heritage Foundation study in 2008. I am using their categories)[5]: White = 65.50%, African-American/Black = 12.82%, Hispanic = 12.93%, Asian/Pacific Islander = 3.25%, American Indian/Alaskan Native = 1.96% and Racial Combination = .66% (Watkins & Sherk, 2008). The percentage of women in the Army varies in reports from 14% to 20%. It is interesting that the South is overrepresented in the numbers of recruits. According to the Heritage Foundation Report, this is likely due to the rich military traditions in the

South. As we will see, it may also be a result of a more "military friendly" atmosphere in the public schools and universities in the South. Although these figures are approximations, the point is clear that the United States is focused on military spending and recruitment. In fact, the United States defense spending represents 46% of the world's military expenditures.[6]

The amounts of money spent on military agendas, wars, and recruitment are only part of the framework of our increasingly militarized culture. We will take a brief look at the way militarization has increased its connection to a movement in popular thinking from a suspicion of the military to an all-out embrace of the military. This allows us to understand the movement toward greater fetishization of the military and hence a type of military hegemony. This hegemony was ironically foreshadowed in Dwight D. Eisenhower's farewell speech in 1960:

> In the councils of government, we must guard against the acquisition of unwarranted influence, whether sought or unsought, by the military-industrial complex. The potential for the disastrous rise of misplaced power exists and will persist. We must never let the weight of this combination endanger our liberties or democratic processes. We should take nothing for granted. Only an alert and knowledgeable citizenry can compel the proper meshing of the huge industrial and military machinery of defense with our peaceful methods and goals, so that security and liberty may prosper together. (Eisenhower, 1960, p. 1037)

It is now a larger phenomenon than just the military-industrial complex. This has morphed into the military/militainment, corporate, prison complex. There is a sense in our current milieu that to speak against the military is tantamount to blasphemy. This notion of the heresy of critique and therefore the lack of it is one of the consequences of a deficit of critical thinking in the schools. And one result of the lack of critique is that there is this troubling militarization of the public schools and universities. This deficit will be discussed in a following section.

After suffering through the disastrous Vietnam conflict and the death of over 58,193 Americans and over 1 million North Vietnamese and Viet Cong (Smith, 2000), Americans were tired of war, despite the fact that Vietnam was never officially a war. Rachel Maddow in *Drift: The Unmooring of Military Power* (2012) claims that in every war in United States history and even in the Cuban Missile Crisis, the National Guard and Reserves had been called up to serve. President Johnson avoided "war" by not doing so and relying on the draft. If Americans were ever going to support war again, we had to win one. President Reagan had an up-to-the-last-minute, covert debacle in Grenada. But we won, apparently, and "rescued" some medical students. This was placed, by the Reagan administration, in contrast to President Carter's miserably failed attempt at rescuing the hostages in Iran. The Reagan administration emphasized that difference constantly. Then

George H.W. Bush went to war over Saddam Hassan's invasion of Kuwait. The neoliberals were satisfied at this point that this "victory" put to rest the haunting syndrome of Vietnam. Of course, executive privilege at waging war had become permanent. Then came 9/11. After this horrific and devastating terrorist attack, Americans wanted patriotic heroes again. At least they were told they wanted the return of the patriotic hero (see Reynolds & Webber, 2009, pp. 145–149). Susan Faludi in *The Terror Dream: Fear and Fantasy in Post 9/11 America* (2007) discusses the return of the patriotic hero (man). She cites a *New York Times* article that characterizes the desire or yearning to return to a time when we had manly heroes: "In contrast to past eras of touchy-feeliness (Alan Alda) and the vaguely feminized, rakish man-child of the 1990s (Leonardo DiCaprio), the notion of physical prowess in the service of patriotic duty is firmly back on the pedestal" (Leigh Brown, 2001, p. 5).

Rugged firemen, policemen, and soldiers became our heroes. And they were ubiquitously portrayed by the media as men. The desire of the neoliberal agenda was to return women to their rightful and secondary role in society. This media trend completely ignored the fact the women were also an important part of the military, police, and fire personnel. Besides the iconic *Time Magazine* patriotic cover photo of three firemen raising the American flag over the rubble of the Twin Towers, there were numerous photos of brave policemen and fireman rescuing women and children. It raised our military patriotic fervor to engage with the terrorists in Afghanistan and led President George W. Bush to declare a preemptive and unjustified war in Iraq.

This brief history of our progress toward a militarized society is the backdrop to the major topics that this chapter addresses. First, there is a discussion of the ways in which this militarized society leads to increasingly militarized schools. Second, we look at the ways in which schools and universities are now military friendly and sites for recruitment of youth from elementary schools to colleges. Third, throughout the rest of the chapter there will be continual connections made between the entertainment industry and the military.

MILITARY RECRUITMENT

The most blatant indication of military recruiting on campus [public school] is the regular presence of uniformed recruiters. In many schools recruiters have unchecked access—unlike most adults and organizations, which must schedule appearances in campus cafeterias and classrooms. Recruiters pull students from class and take them out to lunch or to other off campus activities, without their parents' permission.

—Allison & Solnit, 2007, p. 9)

*The federal No Child Left Behind law of 2002 requires schools to release names
and telephone numbers of their students to military recruiters, if they wish
to continue to receive federal aid.*
—Seefeldt, 2012, p. 1

When we take a close look at public schools the consistent presence of recruiters and other intrusions of the military are astonishingly evident presence. In their book, *Army of None: Strategies to End War, and Build a Better World,* Allison and Solnit (2007) investigated the military's presence in
public schools. Their study brings to our consciousness the ever-increasing
presence of the military. The topics they cover can be emphasized and
explained. We can look at some key elements of the military presence in
the schools: recruiters, JROTC, cadet corps, magazines, video games, and
commodities.

There is a sharp contrast to forty years ago when active recruiting and the
presence of recruiters in schools was actively protested and fought against.
In the hallways of contemporary public schools at all levels—elementary
schools, middle schools and high schools—it is not unusual to view the
presence of uniformed recruiters calling students over to them so they can
explain the advantages of military service. These recruiters are notorious for
taking students to lunch off campus and using this as a friendly recruiting
tool. It is interesting, as Allison and Solnit (2007) discuss, that any other
organization or individual entering the school would have to pass through
a host of legal barriers in order to take a student off campus, but in many
districts across the country this is not problematic for the military recruiters.
There is an open-door policy when it comes to the military. This, of course,
is not publicized or widely known, and schools district prefer to keep it that
way. Again, this intrusion of the military into public schools is occurring at
all levels, even elementary schools. In these schools, programs exist such as
buddies for lunches and pen-pal programs. "Military partners routinely take
young children on field trips to military bases or appear in the classroom or
on campus in uniform" (Allison & Solnit, 2007, p. 26). Apparently rather
than Big Bird it is Sergeant Friendly. In Horton Elementary School in San
Diego County, during a career fair the military drove a tank on campus
(Allison and Solnit, 2007, p.26). So, the military is an option for the career
of choice. The parents at the school protested this action. And, of course,
the military has its assortment of embossed pencils, pens, stickers, and so
on, which are distributed to kids at all levels of schooling. Apparently the
military recruiters and the recruitment policy consider that recruitment
should start with the very young. And recruiters since 2005 are having a
difficult time recruiting. "The problem is that no one wants to join," the
recruiter said "We have to play fast and loose with the rules just to get by"
(Cave, 2005, p. 1).

In middle schools there is a military presence as well. A type of pre-JROTC exists. It is the Cadet Corps. Allison and Solnit (2007) discuss the fact that recruiters have even used the middle school Cadets to go into elementary schools to sign up fifth graders for the Cadet Corps. The Cadet Corps continues to be a strong presence, and it is a nation-wide presence. Students as young as 11 are allowed enroll in the Army's Cadet Corp. They do have to have their parents' permission.

> The USAC is a career-exploration program, providing young people with a very realistic view of Army life. Statistically, 65% of those Cadets who stay in USAC 18+ months have gone into the Armed Forces. Most importantly, a young person must want to become a Cadet. Under no circumstances will USAC accept a recruit who is court-ordered into the program, or forced by their parents to participate. (http://goarmycadets.com/qualificaitons.php, 2013, paragraph 2)

The Cadet Corps also has a Cadet Creed. Some of the statements in the Cadet Creed concern loyalty, good citizenship, and patriotism. Cadets also pledge to "seek the mantle of leadership and stand prepared to uphold the Constitution and the American way of life" (Army Cadet Website). The cadets also have a required uniform. This is at the age of 11: "Cadets will wear the Army combat uniform (ACU) with camouflage cap and authorized boots. Cadets will not wear a beret of any color. Cadet rank will not be worn except when the Cadet is serving in a leadership position" (U.S. Army Cadet Command, 2012, p. 87).

This is just a precursor to the military's most important recruitment program, the Junior Reserve Officer Training Corp (JROTC) in the nation's high schools. The public's understanding of JROTC is that this program recruits students who eventually will assume leadership positions in the military as officers. But, on the contrary, JROTC recruits students into the lowest enlisted levels in the military (Allison & Solnit, 2007). There are over 500,000 students enrolled in the over 3,200 JROTC programs across the country, and every branch of the armed services has a JROTC program. These programs are partially funded by the federal government; in recent years the budget has reached $340 million. School districts pick up the remaining costs. The cost for many school districts is staggering. Of course, the funds spent on JROTC programs by school districts takes away funds from other programs and resources. So as the schools become progressively more militarized, other programs and resources suffer or are simply cut.

The instructors for JROTC do not need to have a college degree initially to be qualified as a JROTC instructor. To be an Army Instructor you must possess an associate's degree or be making progress toward the degree, and to be a Senior Instructor you need a bachelor's degree. The type of degree is not specified. So these JROTC instructors do not have to have degrees that are specific to the subjects they are teaching. The curriculum that is taught in the courses is "designed by the Pentagon and regulated by the national JROTC Cadet Command" (Allison & Solnit, 2007 p. 17). Many times JROTC courses are substituted for regular school course offerings if they are filled. So some students are put into the military curriculum not by choice but by accident. The military presence in high schools is widespread, but JROTC instructors are not the only way that the military is gaining access to the public schools. Schools are now getting teachers who are from the Department of Defense Program known as Troops to Teachers, which began in 1994. In 2000, the oversight of the program was transferred to the U.S. Department of Education.

> The Troops to Teachers program provides funds to recruit, prepare, and support former members of the military services as teachers in high-poverty schools. Successful program candidates obtain certification or licensing as elementary school teachers, secondary school teachers, or vocational or technical teachers and become highly qualified teachers. The program also helps these individuals find employment in high-need local education agencies (LEAs) or charter schools. (U.S. Department of Education, 2012, paragraph 1)

Troops to Teachers (TTT) increases the presence of the military in the public schools. This program assists former military personnel on their pathway to becoming a teacher in the public schools. The program is housed under the Defense Activity for Non-traditional Education Support. Their website states the goal and objectives of Troops to Teachers.

> Reflecting the focus of the No Child Left Behind Act of 2001, the primary objective of TTT is to recruit eligible military personnel to become highly qualified teachers in schools that serve students from low-income families throughout America. TTT helps relieve teacher shortages, especially in math, science, special education and other critical subject areas, and assists military personnel in making successful transitions to second careers in teaching. (DANTES, 2013, paragraph 2)

It is interesting that the focus of these former military personnel and their transition to teachers is in low-income neighborhoods. This is where "accidental" recruitment can and does take place. The percentage of youth of color who are middle school cadets is 54%, although the composition of the services is predominately White. Recruitment efforts are targeted for youth of color and in areas of low income. This gives an interesting option to low-income youth of color. It appears that it becomes a choice between the prison system and the military.

The militarization of educational institutions is not limited to the public schools at all levels but moves into colleges and universities as well. That is where we turn next.

MILITARY FRIENDLY SCHOOLS[7]

"Military friendly schools are defined as institutions which constantly recruit military students and focus on establishing military friendly programs that encourage these non-traditional students to complete their education" (DDST, 2011, paragraph 1; Military friendly schools, 2010a, b). Teachers, professors, students, and all others involved in schools and universities face an ever-increasing military presence in the halls of educational institutions on the websites of their institutions; on the screens of their televisions, computers, and video games; and on the movie screens.[8] It is not just the overt presence of the military in these places, but also how the presence is demonstrated in more subtle ways, as will be discussed. The connection between the military and colleges and universities Turse (2008) calls the "military–academic complex" (p. 39).

One of the ways in which universities and colleges are becoming more militarized, in addition to having recruiters on campuses and the traditional ROTC programs, is achieving the status of a military-friendly campus. The military-friendly schools website has a list of all colleges and universities by state that are judged to be military friendly. This is a program that takes a look at how these various institutions are treating veterans. "These schools offer military students the best services, programs, discounts, scholarships, clubs, networking and staff" (Victory Media, 2012). The judgment as to whether universities are military friendly are made by a Military Friendly Schools Academic Advisory Board; this board is comprised of higher education administrators (12), a representative from the Student Veterans Association, and the 2011 Military Spouse of the Year (Victory Media, 2012). This panel determines the criteria and how those various criteria will be weighted. Colleges and universities strive to be on this list. There are a host of events, resources, and places that are constructed to achieve the status. The status is usually announced on a university's web page, in hard copy brochures, and so on. Universities often construct special military resource centers (including lounges, outreach coordinators, computer labs, and game rooms) for the exclusive use of military affiliates. Special ceremonies at commencement to specifically honor graduates with ROTC endorsement are frequently held on many campus. All of these events and activities assist universities in getting on the list, so it is not only about recruitment into the military but it also concerns increasing student enrollment in general. The more military friendly, the more veterans and ROTC candidates come to a particular campus and the more students attend a university. Campuses also enhance the facilities for their ROTC programs. These often include specific building(s) for ROTC students. Training facilities or special locker rooms within those training facilities are dedicated for ROTC students. Elaborate outside training courses can also be seen on campuses. And the trend is that enrollment in ROTC is on the rise. Since the United States is in economic crisis, one could speculate that because tuition and additional funding is available through ROTC and these are provided on military-friendly campuses these programs have an added appeal to lower-income students across the country.

PLAYING GAMES

Video games, various forms of technology, and military logos are issues that further the overall presence of the military in the youths' everyday lives. This chapter opened with the description of a commercial that targets youth and their attachment to video game culture. The military is keenly aware of the tie that youth have to video games, and it uses that interest to further its recruitment efforts with youth. The use of video games helps the military make the face of war and military involvement as easy and detached as playing a game. There are countless examples of the ways in which video games and war are interrelated. In this chapter I will focus on two examples that accentuate this connection. Drone warfare and military training are two uses of the video game phenomenon that deserve attention when it comes to attracting youth to military service. The connection that is lost in all this techno-warfare is that real people become casualties despite the fact that killing takes on characteristic unreal quality.

In her book *Drone Warfare: Killing by Remote Control* (2012), Medea Benjamin discusses drone surveillance and predator drones. Drones, according to Benjamin, come in all shapes and sizes from drones as small as hummingbirds to the more infamous predator drones that are as big as a commercial airplane. The interesting and eerie phenomenon, however, concerns the piloting of these drones. The piloting of the drones, such as the ones that are targeting terrorist leaders in Afghanistan, is accomplished not in Afghanistan or even anywhere in the Middle East, but in control/pilot rooms in states like New Jersey. Most of the young pilots—nineteen- or twenty-year-olds—sit in a secluded room, in a padded office chair, at a computer station, and fly the drones like they are playing a video game. The controllers for the drones are modeled after Playstation controllers. This gives those video pilots a sense of remoteness to the targeting and destruction in which they are engaged and more of the feeling that they are at home playing the latest video game. This notion that flying drone aircraft will be like your favorite video game is an excellent recruitment tool. It will be just like the AR Pursuit–AR Drone Video game where you actually fly a scale model drone and hunt targets on your screen. This AR drone can also be controlled from an iPad. The Air Force has been quick to catch on to the video game/military/ militainment connection for the purposes of recruitment. "The Air Force is developing a new video game designed to attract young recruits to a crucial, growing career field: drone piloting" (Weinberger, 2010, p. 1).

Not only are video games useful for recruiting drone pilots, but they are also interconnected as was previously discussed with *America's Army* to general recruiting efforts and training as well. There are also a plethora of games focusing on the War on Terror, such as *Operation Desert Storm* (1991) and *Fugitive Hunter: War on Terror* (2006). Another aspect of Video War Games is that they are being used for actual military training (see Reynolds, 2012). One example is being used by the United States Marines. "A modified version of the interactive computer game *Operation Flashpoint: Game of the Year Edition (2003)*, with the assistance of some Operation Iraqi Freedom veterans, is training Marines preparing to deploy to Iraq" (Rhodes, 2005, p. 1).

Paul Virilio in *War and Cinema: The Logistics of Perception* (1989) discussed the notion that the nuclear deterrence that characterized war in the past would be replaced by a type of ubiquitous surveillance. Of course, this certainly is characteristic of drone warfare. He also discussed the type of video imaging and training for war that is ever-present in the current historical moment:

> Thus alongside the army's traditional "film department" responsible for directing propaganda to the civilian population, a military "images department" has sprung up to take charge of all tactical and strategic representations of warfare for the solider, the tank, or aircraft pilot, and above all the senior officer who engages combat forces. (Virilio, 1989, p. 2)

The armed services have learned and developed the lessons of a young generation brought up on video games and technology and are effectively using that technology to entice, recruit, train, and retain young men and women for the armed services.

Finally, one other aspect of militarization is the commodification of the military. In many ways the Army, Navy, Air Force, and Marines have become commodified. They have become logos. First, anyone can purchase name-brand clothing with the various military logos. It is possible to buy Under Armour performance wear with the logo of the various armed services emblazoned across the front of the shirt or the shorts. You can lift weights, run, and cycle wearing the logo of your favorite branch of the armed services. Run as a Marine, even if you are not one. But logo t-shirts and performance wear are only a small part of the commodities available for purchase and consequently advertising for the military. There are websites I visited, investigating recruiting and other aspects of the militarization of everything that were exclusively about shopping. When I clicked on *topmilitaryshop.com*[9] I was confronted with a series of pages where you could buy stickers, games, Swiss army knives embossed with the various logos, Humvee posters, a sniper motivational poster, World War II posters, military movies, t-shirts, Zippo lighters with a military insignia, a tactical combat knife, a military carbide sharpener, dog tag silencers, a camouflage lamp shade, a military uniform display case, video games, and on and on. The commodification of the military is another way that the full impact of joining the military and heading off to war is diffused. Youth begin viewing the military as just another object for purchase. This is not just limited to youth but it affects all ages.

FINAL COMMENTS

The chapter has demonstrated that the times we are living in are increasingly militarized. In an effort to demonstrate this 21st century occurrence, several subjects have been covered. First, the general milieu has been discussed. Recruitment in the elementary schools, middle schools, high schools, and universities was analyzed. Other current programs that connect the military and education were discussed, such as Troops for Teachers and military-friendly universities. Finally, the connection has been made that the techno-generation is seduced by the military by their use of video games and commodities, consequently blurring the line between actual war and its video screen/t-shirt version. As I was finishing this chapter, Senator John McCain was making his speech at the Republican convention in Tampa, Florida. It was a frighteningly militaristic speech. McCain advocated United States military intervention in several countries in the Middle East, including Syria and Iran, and maintaining our military presence in Afghanistan. Of course, McCain's status as a prisoner of war and an American hero appeals to some listeners and gives his comments an air of credibility, but it reminds us that militarization is always already present. It is part of the neoliberal political agenda.

This analysis draws a fairly bleak assessment of the dominance of military power. None of this militarization, particularly in terms of recruitment of the young into the military, occurs without resistance and activist counter-recruitment work. There are a number of websites, books and chapters devoted to helping parents and their children resist the draw of the current militarization. The hope of this particular chapter is to make citizens aware of the issues and problems of the increasing militarization of our everyday lives and that it will no longer persist as undisturbed and uncontested. It is the hope of critical public pedagogy. That critical thinking about militarization will lead to more discussion, and action concerning attempts to change this dangerous and disturbing use of education/schooling.

NOTES

1. Selected recruiting slogans:
   United States Army
   1971–1980: Today's Army Wants You
   1980–2001: Be All That you Can Be
   2001–2006: Army of One
   2006–present: Army Strong
   United States Navy
   1976–1988: It's Not Just a Job, It's an Adventure
   1988–1990: You Are Tomorrow–You are the Navy
   1990–1996: You and the Navy Full Speed Ahead
   1996–2001: Let the Journey Begin
   2001–2009: Navy Accelerate Your Life
   2009–present: America's Navy—A Global Force for Good
   Navy SEALS
   The Only Easy Day Was Yesterday
   United States Marines
   1798–2007/present: Looking for a Few Good Men
   2007–present: The Few, The Proud, The Marines
2. This figure of 36% is taken from the War Resisters League (http://www.warresisters.org/pages/piechart.htm)
3. These figures are taken from Infoplease (http://www.infoplease.com/ipa/a0904490.html).
4. These figures are taken from the National Priorities Project. Retrieved from http://costofwar.com/
5. A search of other sources for racial and ethnic demographics for the United States Military are within 2 or 3 percentage points from those reported the Heritage Foundation Study. But we must be somewhat suspicious of any statistical reporting.
6. This figure is taken from Largest Military Expenditures. Retrieved from http://www.infoplease.com/ipa/A0904504.html
7. I will be focusing primarily on the United States Army for this section.
8. For a discussion of the military in film see Reynolds, W. M. (2012; in press).
9. The website is http://www.topmilitaryshop.com/

REFERENCES

Allison, A., & Solnit, D. (2007). *Army of none: Strategies to counter military recruitment, end war and build a better world.* New York, NY: Seven Stories Press.

Bailey, B. (2007). The army in the marketplace: Recruiting an all-volunteer force. *The Journal of American History, 4*(1), 47–74.

Benjamin, M. (2012). *Drone warfare: Killing by remote control.* New York, NY: Verso.

Cave, D. (2005, May 3). Army recruiters say they feel pressure to bend rules. *New York Times.* Retrieved from http://www.nytimes.com/2005/05/03/national/03recruit.html?pagewanted=2

Cockeram, P. (2005). *America's army preview (PC).* Retrieved from http://www.games-first.com/index.php?id=933

Codemasters. (2003). *OPeration flashpoint: Game of the year edition.* Birmingham, UK: Codemasters Birmingham.

DDST. (2011, November 17). Military friendly schools [Web log comment]. Retrieved from http://getcollegecredit.com/blog/article/military_friendly_schools

Defense Activity for Non-traditional Education Support. (2013). Retrieved from http://www.dantes.doded.mil/programs/ttt_overview.html

Eisenhower, D. D. (1960). *Public Papers of the Presidents* (pp.1035–1040). Retrieved from http://coursesa.matrix.msu.edu/~hst306/documents/indust.html

Faludi, S. (2007). *The terror dream: Fear and fantasy in post 9/11 America.* New York, NY: Metropolitan Books

Giroux, H. A. (2011). *Zombie politics and culture in the age of casino capitalism.* New York, NY: Peter Lang.

GoArmyCadets.com. (2013). Retrieved from http://goarmycadets.com/qualificaitons.php

GoArmy.com/courage. (2007). Retrieved from http://www.youtube.com/watch?v=XkKF4ZcqW14.

Jones, J. (1991). *Operation: Desert storm.* Chicago: Bungie Software

Leigh Brown, P. (2001, October 28). Heavy lifting required: The return of manly men. *The New York Times* section 4, p. 5.

Maddow, R. (2012). *Drift: The unmooring of American military power.* New York, NY: Crown.

Military Friendly Schools. (2012a). *2013 Guide to Military Friendly schools.* Retrieved from www.militaryfriendlyschools.com

Military Friendly Schools. (2012b). *Recruiting military students.* Retrieved from www.militaryfriendlyschools.com

PLaystation. (2006). *Fugitive hunter: War on terror.* Gardena, CA: Encore Software.

Rhodes, S., C. (2005, March, 10). Training marines with video games. Retrieved from http://usmilitary.about.com/od/marinetrng/a/videogame.htm

Reynolds, W. M. (2012). The way of the soldier—Jarheads and hurt lockers: Perpetual war, identity and critical media literacy. In P. R. Carr & B. Porfilio (Eds.), *Educating for peace in a time of permanent war: Are schools part of the solution or the problem?* (pp. 115–133). New York, NY: Routledge.

Reynolds, W. M. (in press). Militainment and war: How long must we sing this song? *Peace Studies Journal.*

Reynolds, W., & Webber, J. A. (2009). *The civic gospel: A political cartography of Christianity.* Boston, MA: Sense Publishers.

Seefeldt, R. (2012). *About military recruiting in high schools.* Retrieved from http://www.ehow.com/about_6393846_military-recruiting-high-schools.html

Seeger, P. (2012). Where have all the flowers gone? On *The Rainbow Quest* [CD]. Washington, DC: Smithsonian Folkways Records. (Originally recorded in 1960)

Smith, R. (2000). *Casualties—US vs. NVA/VC.* Retrieved from http://www.rjsmith.com/kia_tbl.html

Stahl, R. (2010). *Militainment, Inc: War, media, and popular culture.* London, UK: Routledge.

Turse, N. (2008). *The complex: How the military invades our everyday lives.* New York, NY: Metropolitan Books.

U.S. Army Cadet Command. (2012). *Organization, administration, operations, training and support.* Fort Knox, KY: Author.

U.S. Department of Defense, Defense Activity for Non-traditional Education Support. (2012, February 9). *Troops to teachers: Program Overview.* Retrieved from http://www.dantes.doded.mil/Sub%20Pages/TTT/TTT_Overview.html

U.S. Department of Education. (2012). *Troops-to-teachers-program* (CDFA No. 84.815). Retrieved from http://www2.ed.gov/programs/troops/index.html

Virilio, P. (1989). *War and cinema: The logistics of perception* (P. Camiller, Trans.). New York, NY: Verso.

Victory Media. (2012). *About military friendly schools.* Retrieved from http://www.militaryfriendlyschools.com/article/about-us

Watkins, S., & Sherk, S. (2008). Who serves in the U.S. military? The demographics of enlisted troops and officers. In *The Heritage Center for Data Analysis Report #08-05.* Retrieved from http://www.heritage.org/research/reports/2008/08/who-serves-in-the-us-military-the demographics-of-enlisted-troops-and-officers

Wedekind, J. (2005, June 3). The children's crusade: Military programs move into middle schools to fish for future soldiers. *In These Times.* Retrieved from http://www.inthesetimes.com/article/2136/

Weinberger, S. (2010 August 19). Will video games help air force recruit drone pilots? *AOL News.* Retrieved from http://www.aolnews.com/2010/08/19/air-force-working-on-video-game-to-recruit-drone pilots/

PART III

ALIENATION:
DISPLACING STUDENTS AND TEACHERS

CHAPTER 11

TEACHER AND STUDENT LABOR IN TWENTY-FIRST CENTURY SCHOOLS

Joshua Garrison
University of Wisconsin–Oshkosh

INTRODUCTION

Schools are institutions in which teachers and students labor. In return for a wage, teachers provide instruction, assess students, and maintain control over the classroom, while students earn grades and scores by completing assignments and taking examinations. The fundamental question that must be posed regarding student and teacher labor is one of purpose: For whom does the worker labor, and for what reasons? Critical pedagogues and progressive educators have long believed that learning should be meaningful, fulfilling, and purposeful, yet all too often we find that teachers and students labor in meaningless tasks and complete unfulfilling activities without sufficient purpose to arouse their interests. With greater frequency, external agencies are imposing upon workers in the schools social, political, and economic demands that have little to do with student learning, inner wellbeing, community life, or the cultivation of creative or critical capacities. In this chapter I examine how some of these forces are impoverishing

Left Behind in the Race to the Top, pages 161–172
Copyright © 2013 by Information Age Publishing
All rights of reproduction in any form reserved.

the professional lives of teachers and the academic lives of young people, and I explore how Karl Marx's notion of alienation can help us to understand some of the core issues facing schools today.

TEACHER LABOR

In 2007, the United States' Seventh Circuit Court of Appeals issued a ruling in which elementary school teacher Deborah Mayer was denied the right to speak freely in the workplace. Mayer was fired after making an ostensibly controversial remark regarding the war in Iraq, and she sued the Monroe County School Corporation for violating her First Amendment rights. The Seventh Circuit subsequently upheld her termination, prompting critics of the decision to complain that the court "has created a per se rule that teachers have no right to express opinions in the classroom" (Nemunaitis, 2007, p. 779). But this was precisely the court's intention, a point made clear in the decision's concluding passage: "the First Amendment does not entitle primary and secondary teachers, when conducting the education of captive audiences, to cover topics, or advocate viewpoints, that depart from the curriculum adopted by the school system" (*Mayer v. Monroe*, 2007). More interesting, perhaps, is the court's justification for the denial, which defines teacher speech as a *commodity* that is exchanged for a wage. In entering an employment contract, a teacher exchanges her right to speak freely for a wage; consequently, she is allowed to speak only the curriculum that has been adopted by the school board, without diverging from it or adding any opinions or "idiosyncratic perspectives" (*Mayer v. Monroe*, 2007). As the court put it, "the school system does not 'regulate' teachers' speech as much as it hires that speech. Expression is a teacher's stock in trade, the commodity she sells to her employer in exchange for a salary" (*Mayer v. Monroe*, 2007).

Critical scholars of educational policy frequently employ the ideas of nineteenth-century German philosopher and economist Karl Marx to make sense of "the social context of education, and the social struggles in and surrounding it" (Anyon, 2011, p. 1). Marx can help us to better understand the Seventh Circuit's decision, as well as how all schools utilize and regulate teacher labor. Two central themes from Marx's work are important here: commodification and wage labor.

For Marx, a commodity is "a thing which through its qualities satisfies human needs of whatever kind" (Marx, 1990, p. 125). People purchase commodities every day, from the food they eat, to the clothes they wear. In their working hours, most people are also involved in the production of commodities, whether these be goods or services. A commodity is useful, and has "use value," when it meets a consumer's needs, and when a consumer desires a commodity she can exchange other commodities (including money) in order to get it. How much she must give to own the commodity is determined by its exchange value, which is comprised of the thing's material value and, more importantly, the amount and kind of labor that has been expended during its production. All commodities, goods, and services contain "congealed quantities of homogenous human labour" (Marx, 1990, p. 128) and their value is based on "the amount of labour-time socially necessary for its production" (p. 129).

The value contained in a material commodity, such as fabric, nails, or wheat, is relatively easy to establish, since one can make a quantitative determination as to how much labor time was expended during the production of any given article. The value of a service commodity, however, is more difficult to ascertain, since we are dealing with something that is immaterial and abstract. The Seventh Circuit's decision to regard the act of teaching as a commodity begs a Marxian reading, as Marx has written the most thoughtful analysis on the process by which an object or act is transformed into a commodity. Like any other service, teachers engage in socially useful labor that can be exchanged with their employers for a wage. As Marx writes,

> [L]abour-power can appear on the market as a commodity only if, and in so far as, its possessor, the individual whose labour-power it is, offers it for sale or sells it as a commodity. . . . He must constantly treat his labour-power as his own property, his own commodity, and he can do this only by placing it at the disposal of the buyer, i.e., handing it over to the buyer for him to consume, for a definite period of time, temporarily. (Marx, 1990, p. 271)

Read in this way, teaching is the labor-power that a properly trained and certified individual possesses, and the labor that the school expects in return for a wage is the transmission of the knowledge, skills, and dispositions that are contained within the curriculum. As the Seventh Circuit so clearly notes, the teacher labors when she speaks the curriculum, and should she speak something that is not in the curriculum, then she is not performing the labor for which she is being paid. For the period during which she is working for the school, the teacher temporarily loses ownership over the commodity— speech—which she is selling, a point made clear in reading *Mayer v. Monroe* and Marx's *Capital*, two very different texts that express the same point.

Teacher-labor is exchanged for a wage, but how is the value of a teacher's work determined? First and foremost, the labor offered by the worker to the employee must be socially useful. Teacher-labor, defined as the transmission of an established curriculum, is useful in that it promises to create law-abiding and civically engaged citizens who possess skills that can be used in the workplace; when "properly" educated, graduates of the school system will benefit the social whole. Second, the economic value of teaching labor is determined by the period of preparation and training that teaching candidates must complete prior to entering the classroom. One's opportunity to "speak" the school's curriculum comes only after a significant outlay of labor and time, and the extent of this investment, as well as the candidate's relative success during her program of studies, determines the wage that the she will receive.

In capitalist societies, wage labor "exhibits two characteristic phenomena." First, the worker labors under the direction and supervision of the capitalist, to whom the worker's labor belongs; second, the goods or services being produced are the property of the capitalist, not the worker (Marx, 1990, pp. 291–292). Public, nonprofit systems of education are not "capitalistic" in the strict sense—their purpose is not to generate surplus profits by selling goods and services for more than the combined cost of materials and labor. Public schools do, however, serve the capitalist economy by providing workers, consumers, and law-abiding citizens who will contribute to the economy and not challenge the inequalities that are fundamental to the capitalist order. Nor do we need to review the literature of "radical" Marxist scholars to illustrate this point. Horace Mann, the nineteenth-century Massachusetts school reformer, and history's most influential advocate for free and universal public schooling, wrote in his "Fifth Annual Report" that educated workers will enhance the profits of industrialists and save society from the economic burdens incurred by having a large class of "paupers" (Mann, 1891a, p. 97). In his "Twelfth Annual Report," he makes the unsupported claim that public education can mitigate class conflict by providing all citizens with an equal opportunity to share in society's wealth. In this, his final report to the Massachusetts legislature, Mann states clearly that the primary aim of education is economic: "The greatest of all the arts in political economy is to change a consumer into a producer; and the next greatest is to increase the producer's producing power—an end to be directly attained by increasing his intelligence" (Mann, 1891b, p. 260).

That the state's primary interest in providing public education is to increase the productive capacities of its workforce has been documented by numerous educational historians (Katz, 1968; Nasaw, 1981; Spring, 1973). In recent decades, federal educational policy has focused on creating a competitive global labor force that will enhance the nation's economic standing. During the Regan administration (1981–1989), the National Commission on Excellence in Education [NCEE] issued its famous report, *A Nation at Risk* (1984), which lamented America's global economic decline and placed the blame squarely on the public schools: "If only to keep and improve on the slim competitive edge we still retain in world markets, we must dedicate ourselves to the reform of our educational system for the benefit of all" (NCEE, 1984, p. 7). More recently, the Obama administration has implemented a series of educational reforms that "encourages and rewards states" that "adopt standards and assessments that prepare students to succeed in college and the workplace and to compete in the global economy" (U.S. Department of Education, 2009, p. 2). Many critical scholars (Gabbard, 2000; McLaren & Farahmandpur, 2001) have argued that the public schools have been transformed into instruments of global capital, a claim supported by numerous policy documents published over the last thirty years, which unabashedly advocate curricular reforms that promise economic growth. In this way, education and capital are inextricably linked—despite the fact that "those who embrace the secular theology of schooling and tacitly agree to maximize their utility within the global economy have no guarantee that their 'investments' in their education will reap 'dividends'" (Gabbard, 2000, p. xxii). It is vital, then, that we understand teacher labor as taking place in a context in which the primary institutional aim is the training of productive workers and creating voracious consumers. With this awareness, we can better recognize just what kind of labor schools expect their hired workers to perform.

The commodity that teachers exchange for a wage is the ability and willingness to speak a curriculum that prioritizes capital while, simultaneously, omitting "opinions" or "idiosyncrasies" (*Mayer v. Monroe*, 2007) that challenge or bring into question the school's overriding aim. Critical pedagogues like Peter McLaren and Henry Giroux argue that teachers should challenge the school's prevailing ideology and seek to effect social change by promoting dissent, collectivist action, and radical intellectual critique. It is important to realize, however, that a Marxian reading of teacher labor teaches us that diverging from the established curriculum is not a freedom that teachers possess. By virtue of entering into a contract in which teachers exchange their First Amendment right to free speech for a wage, the school takes ownership of that speech. Teachers are regularly dismissed from their jobs when speech is exercised in ways that run counter to the curriculum, and there is a well-established legal precedent that provides school boards and administrators with the authority to dismiss teachers who deviate from the standard curriculum while speaking as employees (*Pickering v. Board of Education*, 1968). The free exercise of speech can only be regained when the wage contract is suspended or revoked.

Recalling Marx, labor is of value only insofar as it is useful. In our case, a teacher who challenges the prescribed curriculum by, say, developing with her students a critique of capital or an examination of the destructive consequences of unfettered consumption, would be *useless* to a state-run institution that is beholden to economic interests. Such a teacher might be useful to a host of other interests—human rights and environmental organizations, for instance—but those groups are not contracting her speech. Indeed, when sacrificing speech for a wage, the teacher herself must face the very real possibility that she will be asked to speak against her own beliefs. This was, of course, the point of the *Mayer* decision:

Majority rule about what subjects and viewpoints will be expressed in the classroom has the potential to turn into indoctrination; elected school boards
are tempted to support majority positions about religious or patriotic subjects especially. But if indoctrination is likely, the power should be reposed in
someone the people can vote out of office, rather than tenured teachers. At
least the board's views can be debated openly, and the people may choose to
elect persons committed to neutrality on contentious issues. That is the path
Monroe County has chosen; Mayer was told that she could teach the controversy about policy toward Iraq, drawing out arguments from all perspectives,
as long as she kept her opinions to herself. The Constitution does not entitle
teachers to present personal views to captive audiences against the instructions of elected officials.

Once speech is commodified—transformed into a service that is sold for a
wage—it ceases to belong to the individual. As the above passage illustrates,
the individual's voice effectively becomes the property of elected officials,
who are free to express their positions via the school's curriculum, even to
the point of indoctrination. Teacher labor, then, can be defined as the speaking as the state wishes to speak. A Marxian analysis reveals that this loss of
freedom is embedded in the very structure of public schooling, and the profession has yet to develop the imagination or politics needed to challenge it.

STUDENT LABOR

Scholars who have conducted surveys of pre-service teachers have found that
their primary reasons for entering the teaching profession include making
a positive difference in students' lives, serving as role models, developing
self-esteem among their charges, fostering a love of learning, and finding
a "personally gratifying career [that allows them] to express their creative
abilities" (Hayes, 1990, p. 20; Stiegelbauer, 1992, p. 13). Unfortunately, the
expectations that new teachers bring to their jobs may not be met—the
demands of standards-based curricula, the prioritization of "hard" subjects
over "soft" ones, the introduction of punitive teacher-assessment schemes,
and increasingly draconian student conduct codes may well contradict the
professional goals that the newly hired teacher brings with her to the workplace. And, as the above section demonstrates, teachers may be required
to follow curricula set by elected officials that run counter to best practice,
the interests of students, and their own professional aspirations. This situation—marked by a conflict between workers' internal goals and external
demands placed on them by employers—leads to *alienation,* an idea that is
central to Marx's work. In his "Economic and Philosophical Manuscripts,"
originally published in 1844, Marx defined alienated labor as:

work [that] is *external* to the worker, that it is not part of his nature; and that, consequently, he does not fulfil [sic] himself in his work but denies himself, has a feeling of misery rather than well-being, does not develop freely his mental and physical energies but is physically exhausted and mentally debased. The worker, therefore, feels himself at home only during his leisure time, whereas at work he feels homeless . . . the external character of the work for the worker is shown by the fact that it is not his own work but work for someone else, that in work he does not belong to himself but to another person. (Marx, 1964, pp. 124–125)

And while this language may seem strong, Marx's definition of alienation is strikingly similar to the more common notion of teacher "burnout," which has been characterized by scholars as a state of "emotional exhaustion, depersonalization, and reduced personal accomplishment" (Huberman & Vandenberghe, 1999, p. 1). To better understand the problem of teacher burnout, one may do well to revisit Marx's notion of alienation.

Teachers are not the school's only laborers; students also labor, and they too can "burn out" from the tedium of following an alienating curriculum and experiencing "poor school life quality" (Fimian & Cross, 1986, p. 247). And though students do not work for wages, they do labor for grades, test scores, diplomas, and other awards that are given for the successful completion of their "schoolwork."[1] But, as Alfie Kohn has noted, external rewards and punishments do not guarantee that students will engage in meaningful learning. In fact, Kohn tells us that grades "make students perform better for fear of receiving a bad grade or in the hope of getting a good one" (Kohn, 1993, p. 201). In their famous study from the 1970s, Samuel Bowles and Herbert Gintis also posit that docility is rewarded in the schools:

> Students are rewarded for exhibiting discipline, subordinacy, intellectually as opposed to emotionally oriented behavior, and hard work independent from intrinsic task motivation. Moreover, these traits are rewarded independently of any effect of "proper demeanor" on scholastic achievement. (Bowles & Gintis, 2011, p. 40)

Measures such as grades and test scores are used to promote some behaviors over others, but they are also used for other purposes, such as "sort[ing] students on the basis of their performance" (Kohn, 1993, p. 201). Richard Brosio argues that this sorting based on "test scores and letter grades allow[s] for stratification to continue along a historical head-hand divide. The capitalist class-stratification system needs criteria in order to assign various people to specific places on the ladder" (Brosio, 2003), a claim that critical theorists have made for decades. On this point, Bowles and Gintis draw the important parallel between grade labor and wage labor:

[T]he relationships of authority and control between administrators and teachers, teachers and students, students and students, and students and their work replicates the hierarchical division of labor which dominates the work place. Power is organized along vertical lines of authority from administration to faculty to student body; students have a degree of control over their curriculum comparable to that of the worker of the content of his job. The motivational system of the school, involving as it does grades and other external rewards and the threat of failure rather than the intrinsic social benefits of the process of education (learning) or its tangible outcome (knowledge) mirrors closely the role of wages and the specter of unemployment in the motivation of workers. (Bowles & Gintis, 2011, p. 12)

While grades and test scores—the "fruits" of the student's labor—may indeed be used to mark students with their future roles in the workforce, in recent years policymakers, public officials, and school administrators have put students to work in a variety of other ways. Schoolwork is now regularly used to determine teacher merit and effectiveness (Ballard & Bates, 2008); demonstrate that states, districts, and schools are eligible for federal funding (Austin, 2005); ensure that the United States will retain competitive footing in the "global economy" (Levin, 1998); and bridge the achievement gap between "racial majority and minority students" (Hunter & Bartee, 2003, p. 153). In effect, policymakers and administrators have set students to work for institutional and economic purposes that have little or nothing to do with the individual's intellectual development, personal well-being, or creative or critical capacities.

Even more menacing is the recent and rapid growth of the for-profit educational racket, which exploits student labor in entirely new ways. Privatized, online educational ventures, known as "virtual schools," now operate across the United States, and they are proving to be big business: K12, the company that currently holds the market's largest share, generated $522 million in revenue for the 2011 fiscal year, a nearly 36% increase from 2010; the company predicts another 31% of growth for 2012, increasing revenues to $685 million (K12, 2012). Connections Education, K12's closest competitor and recently acquired by the educational publishing firm Pearson, generated $190 million in revenue in 2011. A *New York Times* investigation of for-profit educational firms "raise[d] serious questions about whether K12 schools—and full-time online schools in general—benefit children or taxpayers, particularly as state education budgets are being slashed. Instead, a portrait emerges of a company that tries to squeeze profits from public school dollars by raising enrollment, increasing teacher workload and lowering standards" (Saul, 2011). The company receives between "$5500 and $6000 per student from state and local governments" and estimates that the market for online high school education could be as high as $15 billion (Saul, 2011). In effect, these companies "channel taxpayer money" from school districts to corporate coffers (Fang, 2011) and are aided by well-connected lobbyists who also promise to get rich from the privatization of public schools. As reported by *The Nation*,

> Lobbyists...have made 2011 the year of virtual education reform, at last achieving sweeping legislative success by combining the financial firepower of their corporate clients with the seeming legitimacy of privatization-minded school-reform think tanks and foundations. Thanks to this synergistic pairing, policies designed to boost the bottom lines of education-technology companies are cast as mere attempts to improve education through technological enhancements, prompting little public debate or opposition. (Fang, 2011)

Despite K12's mission "to provide any child access to exceptional curriculum and tools that enable him or her to maximize his or her success in life, regardless of geographic, financial, or demographic circumstance" studies have shown that only 27.7% of K12's students meet adequate yearly progress measures, while 52% of those attending brick and mortar schools do (Miron & Urschel, 2012, p. 31). Regardless of the relative success or failure of K12's online method of instruction, it must be kept in mind that for-profit educational companies have the legal obligation to place the interests of shareholder *over* those of the students, and this dynamic undermines the logic of the entire enterprise of public education:

> The way in which corporate law is currently constructed requires directors and officers to justify any socially responsible actions under the guise of, or the aim of, their short-term or long-term shareholder wealth maximization.... The corporation can be considered a form of institutionalized self-interest in the sense that the best-interest principle, as it is being interpreted by the courts and by corporate decision makers, is clearly one in which wealth of shareholders is paramount, ignoring all other constituencies. (Bakan, 2004, p. 177)

In his *Economic and Philosophical Manuscripts* Marx poses the following question: "If my own activity does not belong to me but is an alien, forced activity, to whom does it belong? To a being *other* than myself. And who is this being?" (Marx, 1964, p. 129). The answer to this question depends upon for whom the student is laboring. But it should be clear from the preceding paragraphs that students labor for a variety of interests—political, administrative, and corporate—and each of these impose upon students demands that have little to do with their own educational interests, whatever those may be.

The pioneering progressive educator John Dewey condemned schools and teachers that demanded from their students the performance of any academic labor that did not speak to the student's educational interests, and warned against attaching "some external bait that may be hitched to the alien material" (Dewey, 1944, p. 127). For Dewey, interest is what makes education meaningful and purposeful—indeed, having interest in one's own activities is essential to the construction of identity and selfhood. As he writes in *Democracy and Education:* "[S]elf and interest are two names for the same fact; the kind and amount of interest actively taken in a thing reveals and measures the quality of selfhood which exists" (1944, p. 352). Thus, a person who is forced to engage in uninteresting and alien work experiences an impoverishment of the self. And requiring a student to engage in work that has no meaningful connection to her life is to treat her "*only as* a pupil, not as a human being" (p. 156, emphasis in original).

Like Dewey, Marx's philosophical vision is informed by the idea that human happiness and wellbeing is dependent on purposeful activity. For Marx, humans are naturally productive beings—they produce objects, communities, and selves. Production is the "life activity" of the "species-being," and humans fulfill their nature when production is voluntary, free, and spontaneous (Marx, 1976, p. 126). Whereas animals produce only from instinct and need, Marx's ideal human "is motivated by nothing more than the need to create, to express oneself, to give oneself external embodiment" (Schacht, 1970, p. 78). But when productive labor, whether teaching students or completing schoolwork, is done without inner purpose and for the benefit of another, "the poorer [the worker] becomes in his inner life and the less he belongs to himself" (Marx, 1964, p. 122).

In conceiving of teacher and student labor from a Marxian frame, it is necessary to ask for whom the worker labors. When educational regimens are imposed upon teachers and students by outside agencies, we must examine whether or not the school's laborers are being exploited and, if so, for what purposes. Social control, profit maximization, and political indoctrination are ends commonly sought by "stakeholders" operating beyond the classroom walls. And while many critical scholars have argued that the exploitation of teachers and children is undemocratic and unjust, Marx's notion of alienation provides us with a deeper and more fundamental conclusion: It is also inhumane.

NOTE

1. Some school districts and academic have even experimented with paying students for academic achievement; see Fryer, 2011.

REFERENCES

Anyon, J. (2011). *Marx and education*. New York, NY: Routledge.
Austin, G. (2005). Leaving federalism behind: How the No Child Left Behind Act usurps state's rights. *Thomas Jefferson Law Review, 27*, 337–370.

Bakan, J. (2004). *The corporation: The pathological pursuit of profit and power.* New York, NY: The Free Press.

Ballard, K., & Bates, A. (2008). Making a connection between student achievement, teacher accountability, and quality classroom instruction. *The Qualitative Review, 4,* 560–580.

Bowles, S., & Gintis, H. (2011). *Schooling in capitalist America: Educational reform and the contradictions of economic life.* Chicago, IL: Haymarket Books.

Brosio, R. (2003). High-stakes tests: Reasons to strive for a better Marx. *Journal for Critical Education Policy Studies, 2.* Retrived from http://www.jceps.com/print. php?articleID=17

Dewey, J. (1944). *Democracy and education: An introduction to the philosophy of education.* New York, NY: The Free Press.

Fang, L. (2011, November 16). How online learning companies bought America's schools. *The Nation.* Retrieved from http://www.thenation. com/article/164651/how-online-learning-companies-bought-americas-schools?page=full

Fimian, M. J., & Cross, A. H. (1986). Stress and burnout among preadolescent and early adolescent gifted students: A preliminary investigation. *The Journal of Early Adolescence, 3,* 247–267.

Fryer Jr., R.G. (2011). Financial incentives and student achievement: Evidence from randomized trials. *Quarterly Journal of Economics, 126,* 1755–1798.

Gabbard, D. (Ed.). (2000). *Knowledge and power in the global economy: Politics and rhetoric of school reform.* Mahwah, NJ: Lawrence Erlbaum.

Hayes, S. (1990). *Students' reasons for entering the educational profession* (Report No. HE-027-075). Alva, OK: Northwestern Oklahoma State University. Retrieved from ERIC database. (ED366234)

Huberman, A.M. & Vandenberghe, R. (1999). Introduction—Burnout and the teaching profession. In A. M Huberman & R. Vandenberghe (Eds.), *Understanding and preventing teacher burnout: A sourcebook of international research and practice* (pp. 1–11). Cambridge, UK: Cambridge University Press.

Hunter, R. C. & Bartee, R. (2003). The achievement gap: Issues of competition, class, and race. *Education and Urban Society, 2,* 151–160.

Katz, M. B. (1968). *The irony of early school reform: Educational innovation in mid-nineteenth century Massachusetts.* New York, NY: Teachers College Press.

K12. (2012). Investor day presentation. Retrieved from http://investors.k12.com/ phoenix.zhtml?c=214389&p=irol-irhome

Kohn. A. (1993). *Punished by rewards: the trouble with gold stars, incentive plans, A's, praise, and other bribes.* Boston, MA: Houghton Mifflin.

Levin, H. (1998). Educational performance standards and the economy. *Educational Researcher, 4,* 4–10.

Mann, G. C. (1891a). *Life and works of Horace Mann, vol. III.* Boston, MA: Lee and Shepard Publishers.

Mann, G. C. (1891b). *Life and works of Horace Mann, vol. IV.* Boston, MA: Lee and Shepard Publishers.

Marx, K. (1964). *Early writings.* New York, NY: McGraw-Hill. Translated by T. B. Bottomore.

Marx, K. (1990). *Capital, vol. I.* New York, NY: Penguin.

Mayer v. Monroe County School Corp., 474 F.3d 477 (7th Cir. 2007). Retrieved from http://caselaw.findlaw.com/us-7th-circuit/1233551.html [last accessed 4/20/13]

McLaren, P., & Farahmandpur, R. (2001). Teaching against globalization and the new imperialism: Toward a revolutionary pedagogy. *Journal of Teacher Education, 2,* 136–150.

Miron, G., & Urschel, J. L. (2012). *Understanding and improving full-time virtual schools: A study of student characteristics, school finance, and school performance in schools operated by K12 Inc.* Boulder, CO: National Education Policy Center. Retrieved from http://nepc.colorado.edu/publication/understanding-improving-virtual

National Commission on Excellence in Education. (1984). *A nation at risk.* Westford, MA: Murray Printing Company.

Nasaw, D. (1981). *Schooled to order: A social history of public schooling in the United States.* New York, NY: Oxford University Press.

Nemunaitis, J. (2007). Mayer v. Monroe: The Seventh Circuit sheds freedom of speech at the classroom door. *Seventh Circuit Review, 2,* 762–795.

Pickering v. Board of Education , 391 U.S. 563 (1968)

Saul, S. (2011, December 12). Profits and questions at online charter schools. *New York Times.* Retrieved from http://www.nytimes.com/2011/12/13/education/online-schools-score-better-on-wall-street-than-in-classrooms.html?_r=1

Schacht, R. (1970.) *Alienation.* Garden City, NY: Doubleday & Company.

Spring, J. (1973). *Education and the rise of the corporate state.* Boston, MA: Beacon Press.

Stiegelbauer, S. (1992). Why we want to be teachers: New teachers talk about their reasons for entering the profession (Report No. SP-034-033). Toronto, CA. Retrieved from ERIC database. (ED348367)

U.S. Department of Education. (2009). *Race to the top program: Executive summary.* Washington, DC: Author.

CHAPTER 12

SOLDIERS OR STUDENTS?

JROTC, the Military Presence in Schools, and Educating for Permanent War

Shannon K. McManimon,
Brian D. Lozenski, and Zachary A. Casey
University of Minnesota

For thirty years, the U.S. public has been told stories about failing schools, failing students, failing teachers—particularly in low-income districts and communities of color. A frequent response has been to privatize and corporatize education, surveilling students and teachers through metal detectors and video cameras or standardized testing and scripted curricula. Increasingly, as public schools are decreed a failure and students characterized as lacking discipline and motivation, the U.S. military is brought in. While the U.S. military (in nearly 150 countries, with over 650 military bases) maintains U.S. global dominance, the U.S. military is more and more often declared the answer to (manufactured) crises in U.S. public schools.

This is not a new "solution." The 1916 National Defense Act created the high school Army Junior Reserve Officer Training Corps (JROTC) program, which helped to cultivate ideological support for the military prior to

Left Behind in the Race to the Top, pages 173–187
Copyright © 2013 by Information Age Publishing
All rights of reproduction in any form reserved.

U.S. entry into World War I (Bartlett & Lutz, 1998). Subsequently, JROTC has expanded in times of war, changing military needs (including needs for public support and social control—see, for instance, Collin, 2008), and military recruiting shortfalls. For instance, after the end of the Cold War, the Department of Defense began to develop education, health care, and juvenile justice programs (Hanser & Robyn, 2000). These new and expanded joint civilian and military ventures extended the military's role, aiming, for instance, to address a "lack of role models" for young people (Nunn, 1993, p. 5). JROTC was "one of a dwindling set of tools" (Taylor, 1999) seen as bridging a growing disconnect between the military and civilian society. As of 2008, nearly half a million students in the United States were enrolled in JROTC programs in 3,600 high schools (Arnoldy & Lubold, 2008).

JROTC's official purpose is "to instill in students in United States secondary educational institutions the values of citizenship, service to the United States, and personal responsibility and a sense of accomplishment" (Junior Reserve Officers' Training Corps, 10 U.S.C. § 2031). Each military branch— Air Force, Army, Marines, and Navy—has its own units. Through JROTC, (former) soldiers become teachers, and students become cadets. JROTC cadets wear military uniforms to school (at least) weekly; JROTC texts and practices teach about military discipline and leadership, health and fitness, and citizenship, as well as service-specific topics (e.g., aerospace science in Air Force JROTC). Cadets also participate in out-of-school activities, such as parades, community service, and trips to military bases or sites. While high school students have no future military obligation (unlike their collegiate counterparts in ROTC), JROTC functions as an effective recruiting agent. Between 30 and 50% of JROTC cadets enlist after high school (Arnoldy & Lubold, 2008; Barron, 2000).

JROTC, today and historically, has targeted students considered "at-risk," code for students of color or students from low-income families. A raced and classed logic states that these students need military discipline because of personal and community deficits. For instance, a 1990s JROTC expansion offered up to five years of special financial assistance to schools considered educationally or economically disadvantaged, mostly rural or inner-city and many in northern states (where there were fewer JROTC units) (Corbett & Coumbe, 2001). In the last two decades, JROTC units have expanded rapidly, especially in large urban school districts such as Oakland and Philadelphia. For example, Chicago public schools have nearly four dozen military programs, including six public military high schools and a military program in a middle school. The embedding of the military in schools now includes public all-military schools, JROTC Career Academies (schools-within-a-school), after-school programs such as the Young Marines for children as young as 7, military officers appointed as CEOs of major school districts (Saltman, 2012), and more.

Of course, the purpose of the U.S. military is not to solve the difficulties of U.S. schools; it is to train and prepare for war. The military calls the JROTC program "citizenship." But we argue that instilling imperialist values through military drilling, values, and history educates future soldiers (and others) into an uncritical nationalism that maintains U.S. economic, political, cultural, and military dominance across the globe. Further, promoting obedience to hierarchical authority does not allow for examining the devastating effects of U.S. militarism. In this chapter, we address the increasing military occupation of U.S. public schools, specifically through the JROTC program. The official knowledge of JROTC, its militarized curricular ideology, requires cadets—no longer students—to enact an embodied military culture that creates conditions of alienation. While many young people find belonging and success in JROTC, this military occupation turns public schools into sites that embrace an ideology of and educate for permanent war.

THE CURRICULAR IDEOLOGY OF JROTC

All of us are, all the time, caught up in processes and practices of ideology, a political relation and way of seeing and understanding; thus, *all* curricular programs and projects arise from and refer to an ideological viewpoint or viewpoints. Curricular ideology, then, is the ideological substance—the underlying, often unspoken, presuppositions that inform or enable a particular curriculum—of curricular materials, from content and standards to contexts and practices.

Curriculum must be examined in political, economic, and educational contexts. We live in a cultural context beset with neoliberalism,[1] systemic racism, heterosexism, patriarchy, and other violent structural processes that serve to oppress the great majority of humanity. This hegemonic—dominant—ideology structures the ways in which women and men understand themselves and their realities and thus also their struggles over ideas and ideals. In other words, ideology works to make the ruling or dominant class's notions of what is "good" or "best" the "natural" conception of "good" or "best": to become common sense.

Today, "common sense" portrays the U.S. military as inherently benevolent—defending the world, spreading democracy, and so on. This benefits the business of war and military action while ignoring other consequences, such as the devastation experienced by peoples around the world who face military occupation, drone bombings, and other terrible practices of war. The curricular ideology of JROTC mobilizes common-sense beliefs about the military and military training to legitimize a military recruitment program and to glorify the horrific practices of the U.S. military the world over.

To demonstrate how this process of manipulating ideology to serve the interests of the dominant class functions in schools, we refer to two critical conceptions of curricular theory developed by Michael Apple (2000). First is the concept of official knowledge: the named and stated standards that teachers are expected to teach and students to know/learn. Second is mentioning: including content from historically marginalized communities or bodies of knowledge in ways that utilize the dominant class's discourse and values.

Apple (2000) contends that we can understand what counts "officially" as knowledge in schools as that which aligns with or supports the dominant class's conception of knowledge, or, in other words, what supports dominant economic and political interests. In this formulation, the purpose of schools is maintaining and reproducing the status quo (including its various oppressions). In the case of JROTC, a glimpse of a workbook or textbook can tell volumes about what counts as official knowledge. Students move their bodies and exercise in militarized ways, following military protocol. They learn history—military history. The U.S. military is presented in its most commonsensical representation: as "the good guys" throughout history, defending ever-mounting threats to "American" liberties in wars all over the world. But of course, many mainstream U.S. history courses offer little more than the retelling of great military achievements over time, so what makes JROTC especially problematic?

The essential difference is this: in the mainstream class, even if military history is the focus, curriculum norms and standards still require that students learn about social history, about peoples who were not presidents or soldiers, even if those histories are merely "mentioned." JROTC official knowledge, on the other hand, need make no such detours from the rich and noble history of the U.S. military. The fact that cadets may be able to take JROTC in lieu of social studies (substituting JROTC for health or physical education courses is also common) is evidence of the ideological structuring of what counts as official knowledge in schools.

Examining such practices for their "official knowledge" shows the ways in which the dominant social order values a highly skilled military or the possession of military skills. These skills include a rigorous adherence to chain of command, to conformity, and to order. Masked as "citizenship" and "leadership," the skills taught in JROTC mirror those skills that the dominant class demands of the vast majority of working peoples. Such skills are often promoted as "habits of self discipline," implying that young people (or at least those not in JROTC) are deficient, lacking these habits.

In addition to "official knowledge," curriculum always has hidden implications. Here, these include advocating a permanent state of war in the name of "national security" and conflating serving one's community with serving in the armed forces. What these almost endless implications have in common is adherence to dominant ideologies of uncritical and unquestioning nationalism and obedience of mind and body. Examples from a *Marine Corps JROTC Cadet Handbook* can clarify. Under the heading "classroom procedures" is the following: "Do not interrupt the SMI's [Senior Military Instructor] or MI's conversation. Wait for acknowledgment and then say, 'Excuse me, Sir/Ma'am'... All head calls [bathroom breaks] will be made before or after class. No head calls will be authorized during class except in cases of emergency" (Chicago JROTC, n.d.b, p. 6).

Students in these classes, then, are not allowed to ask questions, or at least not in the way they can in other classroom spaces. Their bodies are strictly disciplined. This is perhaps the most clear instance of "banking education" imaginable, wherein the instructor deposits information into the heads of passive learners so that they will in turn demonstrate their learning in ways defined by the instructor (Freire, 1970). Expectations for JROTC Marine Corps cadets continue:

> Cadets will not display any gestures of affection in school or on school grounds.... Affection between a man and a woman should be a private matter.... Cadets who think they are showing off their maturity by kissing and hugging in public are only displaying a lack of maturity and risking a lower Marine Corps JROTC leadership grade for their conduct. (Chicago JROTC, n.d.b, p. 7)

Not only are cadets not allowed to show affection (at the risk of a lower grade), but the curriculum offers a (barely) hidden curricular project of compulsory heterosexuality. But we must go further in our analysis, to the project of "mentioning" that is so common across contemporary curriculum and in particular in JROTC programs.

While some marginalized discourses and knowledges have found their way into mainstream curricula (e.g., an historical anecdote that includes Indigenous people's names for an area), mentioning usually happens by "integrating selective elements into the dominant tradition by bringing them into close association with the values of powerful groups" (Apple, 2000, p. 54). Apple gives the example of teaching about AIDS, but from the standpoint of an "abstinence-only" policy or program.

In JROTC, what are mentioned are not marginalized peoples and knowledges, but rather what JROTC would consider "civilian" knowledges. Official JROTC documents like the *Marine Corps JROTC Cadet Handbook* mention, for instance, curricular concepts such as "instruction on personal finance" and writing "research reports." These concepts are not, however, the aim of JROTC programs. Over and over, JROTC mentions "citizenship." Citizenship education is lauded as a universal good, without context as to the content of "citizenship." In practice, citizenship education is reduced to "promot[ing] an understanding of the basic elements and requirements for national security" and developing "respect" and "understanding" for "the need for constituted authority in a democratic society" (Chicago

JROTC, n.d.b, p. 4). Here, citizenship has value only in its relationship to national security and the need for authority. It is mentioned, brought into the curriculum, and then bent and molded to align with the dominant (in this case militaristic) conception of citizenship.

Of course, what is left out—the null curriculum (Eisner, 1985)—of JROTC programs might be its most instructive curricular ideology. What is left out includes student-centered curricula, problem-posing pedagogies, culturally relevant pedagogy, and often even critical thinking skills. Instead, the curricular ideology of JROTC can be characterized as militaristic nationalism, beset with oppressive rules and regulations, masked as citizenship education and leadership training. JROTC represents an oppressive social order, relying on oppressive means to protect and maintain the oppressive reality in which we live, even if the program may increase individual cadets' self-esteem. While all curricula are rife with ideology, the JROTC curriculum stands in opposition to progressive pedagogies that attempt to center students' "funds of knowledge" (Gonzalez & Moll, 2002, p. 623) and cultures. Instead, the curricular ideology produces an embodied military cultural capital.

THE EMBODIED, MILITARY CULTURAL CAPITAL OF JROTC

A simplistic portrayal of JROTC would be that it lures naïve youth and their families into its clutches through deceptive mechanisms. But we must take seriously how some youth (particularly low-income youth of color) make meaning of such a program and how JROTC can align with their social, cultural, and educational needs and their knowledges. Pierre Bourdieu's (1986) idea of cultural capital can help us explore how the culture of JROTC both aligns and conflicts with certain aspects of youth and school culture. Bourdieu (1986) argues that purely economic analyses of capital limit our understanding of the forms in which capital is accumulated and distributed in society. Instead, he writes, capital has three major forms: economic, social, and cultural. We acquire, distribute, and exchange these types of capital in our social interactions in broader structures; how these interactions are interpreted within the structures that govern society determine whether beneficial outcomes are possible.

Of these, cultural capital is perhaps the most complex form; it is largely hidden and operates in nuanced ways, often tied to social class. Many education researchers (e.g., DiMaggio, 1982; DuMais, 2002; Lareau, 1987) address the workings of cultural capital in schools, particularly how it relates to the academic success or failure of students from non-dominant social classes. For instance, Prudence Carter's (2005) study of black and Latino/a youth in Yonkers, New York, recognizes that cultural capital is accumulated and distributed in multiple directions. She demonstrates how low-income, urban youth produce and exchange forms of cultural capital to denote authentic "Blackness" or Latino/a culture in their own social worlds. These forms of cultural capital often do not conform to teachers' expectations or dominant forms of cultural capital. Because they are instead seen as resistant or re-bellious, students then "experienced school as a sorting and selecting machine, penalizing those with different cultural attributes" (Carter, p. 64). Yet these students make strategic decisions about how and when they choose to dispense these distinct forms of cultural capital to signal belonging, which then impacts how successful they are in school. They are calculating how to use different types of cultural capital. How, then, do we make sense of the cultural capital produced and distributed by military education programs like JROTC? As a distinct and often celebrated entity within a school (see, e.g., Taylor, 1999), JROTC has mechanisms for processing displays of cultural capital that allow for certain possibilities.

While the fluid nature of cultural capital does not allow us to easily dis-tinguish between them, differing forms of cultural capital exist in students' communities, in schools, and in military programs. Further, these forms of cultural capital are embodied—they are taken up in physical ways by physical bodies. As an example, we focus on language. Language development begins at birth and is a process. In schools, language is often the first form of cultural capital used to restrict, sort, and punish children, particularly those students from different racial, ethnic, and social classes than their teachers (Perry & Delpit, 1998). Because students are unable to immediately acquire the em-bodied capital of the language valued in school, Black children who speak African-American English, or Ebonics (Smitherman, 1998), for instance, face more of a challenge acquiring the legitimated linguistic cultural capital of school, or "standard English."

JROTC, and the military in general, use standard English in the same ways schools do. But this language includes both technical accuracy (what) as well as forms of interaction (how). In JROTC, what is said may not be as important as *how* it is said. The cultural capital of language is exchanged in ways that prioritize deference to superior ranked cadets and instructors; a grammatically perfect soliloquy is less important than a succinct response to a command. The military generally makes explicit its rules of human interaction, from eye contact to vocal tone to timeliness of response. The cultural capital of this military exchange of language is easier to acquire than that of traditional school, as the rules of the latter are largely hidden. The rules—the "how"—of language exchange in the military are made explicit (see the above example from the Marine Corps JROTC). We are not, however, suggesting that military cultural capital aligns with commu-nity cultural capital, only that it is easier to acquire for young people who recognize that they are at a disadvantage in how they interact with and are evaluated by official institutions.

Another way of examining this is using Bourdieu's (1977) theory of *habitus*, or the practices that we have developed over time, both historically and in our own lives, that shape our predispositions. Although we usually do not consciously recognize the historical process (and forget it if we do) and instead feel habitus development as natural, each of us has a habitus that is historically constructed as our actions develop into practices. Institutions such as the U.S. military also have forgotten histories that shape their embodied capital. For instance, the military is built for efficiency through a rigid, hierarchical structure. The embodied capital that is of value is to quickly follow commands from higher-ranking officers; general deference to superiors is part of the military habitus. Those who acquire and inscribe this embodied capital into their being have more opportunities for success. In an ironic way, the military actually does work in a much more meritocratic form than most other institutions, particularly schools.

To illustrate this point, we can use Lisa Delpit's (1988) notion of the "culture of power." Delpit contends that codes of power exist in all schools and classrooms and that these codes are typically hidden from students who do not come from the white, middle-class cultural environments that schools seek to replicate. Delpit equates the culture of power to dominant forms of cultural capital. She argues that to create a more equitable society, schools must teach and make explicit these tacit cultural codes, especially for children who are not from and therefore have not internalized the culture of power. Often, the families of these children "want to ensure that the school provides their children with discourse patterns, interactional styles, and spoken and written language codes that will allow them success in the larger society" (Delpit, 1988, p. 285). While traditional schools still do not, for the most part, make the culture of power (dominant forms of embodied cultural capital) explicit, programs like JROTC certainly do. While JROTC does not necessarily make the codes of the broader society explicit, it makes military codes very obvious to students. For many students, this makes achieving success (as determined by JROTC) easier. In a sense, then, JROTC is more interested in creating a successful (non-raced) cadet, who will help maintain the status quo of military hegemony, than traditional schools are in creating a successful student of color, who may seek to disrupt the maintenance of a raced and classed social hierarchy.

As critical educators, though, we cannot ignore the implications of "banking" (Freire, 1970) dominant forms of cultural capital—here, embodied military cultural capital—into students. A pedagogy that exposes power and the underlying roots of inequality must be undertaken in problem-posing, generative ways that honor the historical, cultural, and social identities and experiences of children (Freire, 1970; hooks, 1994;

Ladson-Billings, 1995). Perhaps one reason that critical educators have had such difficulty gaining traction in mainstream education is that we have had to continually promote educational models that require retraining teachers and rethinking pedagogy and curriculum so as not to ask students to sacrifice their cultural integrity for academic success, thereby defying the very nature of the purpose of cultural capital. On the other hand, the military can easily insert JROTC programs in an endless line of schools in predominantly underresourced communities because it does not worry about these concerns. It comes with its own history, culture, codes of power, and strict hierarchies (neatly packaged) that are not to be questioned or critically analyzed. In fact, JROTC gives schools permission to *not* engage in any form of critical or culturally relevant pedagogy because that is explicitly the opposite of its purpose. JROTC has mastered a hyper form of banking education that makes understanding its habitus easy, which in turn makes acquiring its embodied cultural capital easier. But what does this mean for students—cadets?

JROTC AS ALIENATION?

Of course, students want teachers who care, expect rigorous work, and take time with them in clean, safe, well-equipped facilities. They want, in other words, not to be alienated from their education. Obviously, those of us claiming to be interested in student-centered pedagogy must listen to students. And so we must pay attention when JROTC cadets assert that their military high school program is "not like regular high schools; instead of you just wanting to leave, you wanna stay here and then they wanna kick you out 'cuz you're here too late"; or "I started joining teams and it was really fun. And I just stayed in because of the people and, you know, the whole family feeling" (Chicago JROTC, n.d.a). For many students, JROTC counters the alienation of schooling, particularly when schooling in underresourced and overcrowded schools seems irrelevant to their lives. Over and over, cadets praise JROTC for creating a type of family and a sense of belonging, pride, accomplishment, and camaraderie—in other words, helping them overcome alienation. For many students, participating in JROTC means being treated with respect in schools, finding a sense of community and belonging, and having opportunities to excel as well as to participate in extracurricular activities (see, e.g., Chicago JROTC, n.d.a; Pérez, 2006).

But what does JROTC's answer to the alienation of schools look like? Students spend seven to eight hours a day in schools, using their mental and physical capabilities to engage in different tasks. This then is a form of labor. With Marx (1994), we thus consider how JROTC cadets might be alienated from both the process and product of their work (their learning) and from themselves and other workers (students or cadets).

The JROTC classroom aims to instill military values, hierarchy, and discipline, both through the process and in the products of classroom and extracurricular work. One's body is no longer one's own body, but sheathed in a military uniform and called on to perform military rituals. Indeed, in some JROTC or military academies, when the expected product (outcome) of the classroom is breached, cadets are reprimanded and given physical tasks (e.g., running laps). Cadets become objects both in themselves and because they have little control over the product of their work—this is under the control of a higher-ranking person. Learning, in JROTC curricular ideology, is not about self-appropriated knowledge but about strict adherence to military customs and procedures.

Further, military values emphasize an individualism that turns a student into a cadet, alienated from others and from one's own identity as a student. Marx (1994) asks, "If my own activity does not belong to me, if it is an alien and forced activity, to whom then does it belong?" (p. 65). The military is built—of necessity—on unquestioning obedience to hierarchical authority. The answer to Marx's question then is simple: to the next person up the chain of command. An easy example is the iconic drill sergeant in basic training yelling an expletive-laced version of "you belong to me!" In a Philadelphia public military academy, upperclass student platoon leaders direct other students' (cadets') movements around school, asking permission from teachers to enter a classroom and then telling the other students when to sit (Price, 2008). In Chicago, a platoon leader orders another cadet to do push-ups for a uniform infraction. This type of separation and regimentation, activity directed by others according to military values, may even be praised; Pauline Lipman (2011), for instance, writes that administrators at a Chicago public military academy "extol the virtues of a system that requires youth to refuse to compromise military discipline for solidarity with other youth" (p. 84). Commonsense norms of JROTC thus emphasize adherence to military values and commands, in other words, to someone else. And not only is the work of learning controlled by someone else, but so is identity. In JROTC and other public military programs, young people are no longer students but cadets. Marx would argue that this kind of alienation prevents the realization of one's full humanity—what Freire (1970) calls the ontological vocation of becoming fully human.

From a structural and ideological standpoint, it would seem that JROTC alienates cadets from their learning (their labor) and from forming consensual, equitable relationships with their peers. And yet their voices remind us that JROTC may decrease student alienation, just as the easier access to the cultural capital of the military may enable academic success in the program. Holding these in tension is perhaps an example of what

Lois Weis and Michelle Fine (2012) term *critical bifocality*, a "dedicated theoretical and empirical attention to structures *and* lives" (p. 174, emphasis in original).[2] Critical bifocality attempts to connect macro-level structural dynamics such as neoliberalism with the ongoing and daily decision making of students and families, knowing that such a focus will find complexities and contradictions. In the complicated nexus of such forces, JROTC is offered as a choice, particularly for low-income students and students of color. Historical, political, and economic structures have created oppressive conditions that alienate students from schooling; simultaneously, students both reproduce and resist these structural conditions. JROTC provides a mechanism for resisting alienation, even as it reproduces alienation and oppression in other forms. Yet this choice, often offered as the only way out of alienating schooling for low-income students and students of color is, we contend, a false choice, offering belonging and achievement (along with an uncritical nationalism and patriotism) at the expense of critical thinking and autonomy.

JROTC: NEOLIBERAL EDUCATION FOR PERMANENT WAR

Writing and researching with a critical bifocality allows us to examine "how public opportunities, institutions, and resources are being redesigned in law, policy, and academic practices that further tip educational advantage in the direction of children of privileged families, while an array of equally expensive public policies—testing, policing, and surveillance—are being unleashed within low-income communities" (Weis & Fine, 2012, p. 187). Public military education must be added to this array of policies used to discipline the bodies and minds of U.S. students, particularly low-income and students of color.

In addition to serving as a disciplining force, militarizing public education fits well into the neoliberal project of privatization. David Harvey (2005) calls practices that convert formerly public goods or services into individually held goods or services "accumulation by dispossession." Manipulating (and sometimes manufacturing) crises about "failing" students, teachers, and schools while simultaneously ignoring root causes such as poverty and structural racism enables public education to be privatized or turned over to nonpublic entities such as the military, whose curriculum, instructors, policies, and practices are not controlled by local schools and districts. In 2010, for instance, the National Association of the State Boards of Education recommended that state and local education agencies develop "strategic partnerships" and especially "take advantage of possible educational partnerships with all branches of the armed services" (p. 5). But in such processes, students are dispossessed of public education.

The dismantling of the Chicago Public School (CPS) system is an example. *Public* is more and more a misnomer. Over the last two decades, the mayor has taken control of the schools; a chief executive officer has replaced a school superintendent; and neighborhood public schools have been closed (with notable exceptions due to community pressure) and reopened as charter or contract schools, following patterns of gentrification. At the same time, CPS has become home to the nation's largest public school military program (both in numbers of units and of students). (For more, see, Galaviz, Palafox, Meiners, & Quinn, 2011; Lipman, 2011, 2012; Roa, 2009.) In the words of (retired) Colonel Kevin Kelley (2012), CPS Director of Military Instruction, "Chicago Public Schools and the Department of JROTC are on the leading edge of implementing JROTC in urban education and achieving student academic success through military academies, military academies within a school, traditional JROTC programs, middle school cadet corps programs, and corporate/foundation partnerships" (p. 30). In the words of Brian Roa (2009), who taught science at a Chicago high school forced to share space with the Rickover Naval Academy, "Chicago's plan is not a school improvement plan. It is the dismantling of a public good for the benefit of a chosen few. School militarization was accelerated as this plan was being implemented in Chicago." As in other cities, while comprehensive neighborhood schools are closed and smaller magnet schools are opened for wealthier and White students, poor students and students of color are offered the "choice" of military programs or public military schools, often with newer facilities and opportunities for field trips and extracurricular activities. Galaviz et al. (2011) argue that this "is a form of economic coercion, forcing parents and students to make the rational choice of the adequately funded alternative over an obviously neglected school" (p. 33).

We must ask why military programs with their militaristic curricular ideology are offered as a viable educational alternative—especially given the students whom the military targets. What are the costs and consequences? Why does the National Association of State Boards of Education (2010) assert that "[m]ilitary programs manage to succeed where others fail because of their attention to a holistic approach to student education and development" (p. 4)? Doesn't this deny the work of thousands of teachers, teacher educators, and educational researchers whose work emphasizes holistic approaches—but who often have to beg for money, rather than having the financial backing of history's largest and most well-funded military? Why is "military methodology" (retired Brigadier General Frank Bacon of Chicago's Military Academy [in McCann, 1999]) the answer to educating students in underresourced schools?

In our present era of unfettered global capitalism, neoliberalism, and permanent war, students in schools the world over are marginalized and commodified to serve the dominant oppressive order. These practices

materialize clearly in JROTC programs. JROTC's curricular ideology in-
stills a dogmatic need for global (military) security, for fear of Others, and
for continuing permanent wars. JROTC's view of citizenship emphasizes
hierarchical obedience to authority. JROTC's embodied military cultural
capital centers dominant codes of power in explicitly banking ways. This
alienates students by cutting them off from the process and the product of
their labor as learners and from one another while promoting individual
self-preservation as the highest order and ideal. In sum, the military occupation of our schools through programs such as JROTC directly limits
students' agency, autonomy, and humanity; further, it enables utterly aban-
doning culturally relevant or critical pedagogies. The need for ever more
soldiers in ever more wars and for unending increases in military spending
and a global military presence: All are used to justify leading students to believe that their self-worth can best be defined by participating in the global
war machine that is the U.S. military. Students are left behind, changed
forever, into cadets—into commodities in the great capitalist-war industry
that continues to dehumanize and terrorize peoples the world over.

NOTES

1. Critical geographer David Harvey (2005) defines neoliberalism as "a theory
   of political economic practices that proposes that human well-being can best
   be advanced by liberating individual entrepreneurial freedoms and skills
   within an institutional framework characterized by strong private property
   rights, free markets, and free trade" (p. 2).
2. Recognizing that their work attends more to ethnographic research than the
   type of theoretical analysis we are doing here perhaps suggests a direction
   for research on JROTC and other military incursions into public education,
   incursions that are severely understudied and unknown.

REFERENCES

Apple, M. W. (2000). *Official knowledge: Democratic education in a conservative age.* New
    York, NY: Routledge.
Arnoldy, B., & Lubold, G. (2008). Leadership course or recruiting tool? A battle
    over JROTC. *Christian Science Monitor, 100*(226), 1–11.
Bartlett, L., & Lutz, C. (1998). Disciplining social difference: Some cultural politics
    of military training in public high schools. *The Urban Review, 30*(2), 119–136.
Barron, W. (2000, February 18). Junior ROTC eyed as cheaper recruiting tool. *CQ
    Daily Monitor (Congressional Quarterly).*
Bourdieu, P. (1977). *Outline of a theory of practice.* New York, NY: Cambridge Uni-
    versity Press.

Bourdieu, P. (1986). The forms of capital. In J. G. Richardson (Ed.), *Handbook of theory and research for the sociology of education* (pp. 241–258). New York: Greenwood.

Carter, P. (2005). *Keepin' it real: School success beyond black and white.* New York, NY: Oxford University Press.

Chicago JROTC. (n.d.a). JROTC: A promise to keep. (Video). Retrieved from http://www.chicagojrotc.com/apps/video/watch.jsp?v=28522&autoPlay=true

Chicago JROTC. (n.d.b). Marine Corps JROTC Cadet Handbook. Retrieved from http://chicagojrotc.com/pdf/marine_cadet_handbook.pdf

Collin, R. (2008). On the march: Social and political contexts of the expansion of the Junior Reserve Officers' Training Corps. *Educational Policy, 22*(3), 457–482.

Corbett, J. W., & Coumbe, A. T. (2001, January/February). JROTC recent trends and developments. *Military Review,* 40–45, 48.

Delpit, L. (1988). The silenced dialogue: Power and pedagogy in educating other people's children. *Harvard Educational Review, 58*(3), 280–298.

DiMaggio, P. (1982). Cultural capital and school success: The impact of status culture participation on the grades of U.S high school students. *American Sociological Review, 47(2),* 189–201.

DuMais, S. (2002). Cultural capital, gender, and school success: The role of habitus. *Sociology of Education, 75(1),* 44–68.

Eisner, E. W. (1985). *The educational imagination: On the design and evaluation of school programs.* New York, NY: Macmillan.

Freire, P. (1970). *Pedagogy of the oppressed.* New York, NY: Continuum.

Galaviz, B., Palafox, J., Meiners, E. R., & Quinn, T. (2011). The militarization and the privatization of public schools. *Berkeley Review of Education, 2*(1), 27–45.

Gonzalez, N., & Moll, L. C. (2002). Cruzando el puente: Building bridges to funds of knowledge. *Educational Policy, 16*(4), 623–641.

Hanser, L. M., & Robyn, A. E. (2000). *Implementing high school JROTC [Junior Reserve Officers Training Corps] Career Academies.* Santa Monica, CA: National Defense Research Institute.

Harvey, D. (2005). *A brief history of neoliberalism.* Oxford, UK: Oxford University Press.

hooks, b. (1994). *Teaching to transgress: Education as the practice of freedom.* New York, NY: Routledge.

Junior Reserve Officers' Training Corps. (2012). 10 U.S.C. § 2031.

Kelley, K. (2012, 17 April). Service leadership programs: Overview briefing. Chicago: Chicago Public Schools. Retrieved from www.chicagojrotc.com/pdf/overview_2012.pdf

Ladson-Billings, G. (1995). Toward a theory of culturally relevant pedagogy. *American Educational Research Journal, 32*(3), 465–491.

Lareau, A. (1987). Social class differences in family–school relationships: The importance of cultural capital. *Sociology of Education, 60,* 73–85.

Lipman, P. (2011). Cracking down: Chicago school policy and the regulation of black and Latino youth. In K. J. Saltman & D. A. Gabbard (Eds.), *Education as enforcement: The militarization and corporatization of schools* (2nd ed., pp. 73–91). New York, NY: Routledge.

Lipman, P. (2012). Neoliberal urbanism, race, and urban school reform. In W. H. Watkins (Ed.), *The assault on public education: Confronting the politics of corporate school reform* (pp. 33–54). New York: Teachers College Press.

Marx, K. (1994). *Economic and philosophic manuscripts* (selections). In L. H. Simon (Ed.), *Karl Marx: Selected writings* (pp. 54–97). Indianapolis, IN: Hackett Publishing. (Original work published 1844)

McCann, H. G. (1999, September 8). First public ROTC high school opens. *Associated Press News.* http://www.apnewsarchive.com/1999/First-Public-ROTC-High-School-Opens/id-e724e770ebe3206732df35257f22b98d

National Association of State Boards of Education. (2010). *Common ground: Education and the military meeting the needs of students.* Arlington, VA: NASBE.

Nunn, S. (1993, February). *Domestic missions for the armed forces.* Presented at the U.S. Army College Fourth Annual Strategy Conference. Carlisle, PA.

Pérez, G. M. (2006). How a scholarship girl becomes a soldier: The militarization of Latina/o youth in Chicago public schools. *Identities, 13*(1), 53–72.

Perry, T., & Delpit, L. (Eds.) (1998). *The real Ebonics debate: Power, language, and the education of African-American children.* Boston, MA: Beacon Press.

Price, H. B. (2008). About-Face! *Educational Leadership, 65*(8), 28–34.

Roa, B. (2009, July 1). The military invades U.S. schools: How military academies are being used to destroy public education. Retrieved from http://www.alternet.org/story/141034/the_military_invades_u.s._schools%3A_how_military_acadamies_are_being_used_to_destroy_public_education

Saltman, K. (2012). The rise of venture philanthropy and the ongoing neoliberal assault on public education: The Eli and Edythe Broad Foundation. In W. H. Watkins (Ed.), *The assault on public education: Confronting the politics of corporate school reform* (pp. 55–78). New York, NY: Teachers College Press.

Smitherman, G. (1998). Black English/Ebonics: *What it be like?* In T. Perry & L. Delpit (Eds.), *The real Ebonics debate: Power, language, and the education of African-American Children* (pp. 29–37). Boston, MA: Beacon Press.

Taylor, W. J. (1999). *Junior Reserve Officers' Training Corps: Contributions to America's communities.* Final report of the CSIS Political-Military Studies Project on the JROTC. Washington, DC: Center for Strategic and International Studies.

Weis, L., & Fine, M. (2012). Critical bifocality and circuits of privilege: Expanding critical ethnographic theory and design. *Harvard Educational Review, 82*(2), 173–201.

CHAPTER 13

IMPORTING INTERNATIONAL EDUCATORS

A Neoliberal Assault on Public Education as We Know It

S. Books
State University of New York—New Paltz

J. J. R. de Villiers
University of Pretoria

The profession of education has not escaped the currents of neoliberalism now roiling the globe (Giroux, 2004; Gutierrez, 2009; Harvey, 2007; Robertson, 2008). Teachers' unions, which historically have pushed back against the encroachment of market forces into public schooling, have necessarily been a target (Harvey, 2007; Robertson, 2008). The erosion of teachers' and other public-sector workers' collective bargaining rights in 2011 and 2012, most publicly in Wisconsin but in many other states as well, was disheartening, but not surprising. Outside the United States, the International Monetary Fund's structural adjustment policies have required many devel-

Left Behind in the Race to the Top, pages 189–207
Copyright © 2013 by Information Age Publishing
All rights of reproduction in any form reserved.

oping countries to pay teachers far too little (Global Campaign for Education, 2009; Spreen & Edwards, 2011). Meanwhile, chronic underfunding of many central-city and rural schools in the U.S. (Baker, Sciarra & Farrie, 2012; Kozol, 2005) has made these schools not very desirable places to teach or learn (American Federation of Teachers [AFT], 2009; Eaton, 2006; Hadley Dunn, 2011). Underpayment of teachers in developing countries and neglect of many schools in the U.S. support another practice in public education: recruitment of international teachers without a long-term stake in union negotiations to work in U.S. classrooms. This "burgeoning phenomenon in the neoliberal push for alternative teacher recruitment" (Hadley Dunn, 2011, p. 1381) has been justified in large part through undocumented claims of teacher shortages—a politically charged discourse that warrants far more scrutiny than it has received.[1]

In the discussion that follows, we offer an overview of the recruitment of international teachers to work in the U.S., explore the public discourse on the alleged teacher shortage, describe the workings of the H-1B and J-1 visa programs, and then look at the push and pull factors that drive teacher recruitment. We conclude with some recommendations and reflections on the broader political and economic context of the practice of "importing educators" (AFT, 2009)—namely, the neoliberal agenda, a form of late-stage global capitalism that envisions an unrestricted market subsuming all things public, including, and perhaps especially, schools. First, however, a clarification: *Our intention is in no way to challenge the right of workers everywhere to seek—and, we would argue, to find—meaningful and adequately compensated employment.* Rather, we hope to better illuminate the political context in which international teachers are recruited: teacher layoffs, efforts to cripple public employees' unions, and a move towards alternative teacher-certification programs.

THE NUMBERS AND SOME STORIES BEHIND THEM

Although the U.S. Department of Education does not track the number of international teachers in U.S. classrooms (Wolfe, 2007), we estimate that 14,000 are now teaching in U.S. public schools through the H-1B and J-1 nonimmigrant visa programs.[2] Shannon Lederer, associate director of international affairs for the AFT, believes the number is closer to 20,000, at least through 2010 (personal communication, April 1, 2011). In FY (fiscal year) 2011, more than 5,000 H-1B petitions were approved for workers in elementary and secondary schools (U.S. Department of Homeland Security, 2012). In 2010, more than 800 teachers participated in the J-1 program (Interagency Working Group on U.S. Government-Sponsored Exchanges and Training, 2011). (J-1 data are not yet available for 2011.) The H-1B and J-1 trends combined show annual visa issuances to primary and secondary school teachers in the 7,000 to 9,000 range from FY 2004 through FY 2009, before a drop to about 5,000 in FY 2010 (see Figure 13.1). To put this in perspective, this is "two to three times as many teachers as Teach For America [has been] fielding annually" (Noah, 2011, p. 2).

Why is this problematic? As we will discuss in more detail, the recruitment of international teachers is rationalized through questionable, if not blatantly dishonest, assertions. On one hand, the recruitment is justified as a way to address an undocumented teacher shortage, and on the other, to foster cultural and global understanding. Recruitment has led to emotional trauma as well as legal and financial exploitation of often ill-informed international teachers. The practice pits U.S. teachers against teachers recruited abroad in a way that erodes teachers' collective bargaining rights—a neoliberal dream, quickly becoming a reality. Finally, the practice enables political leaders at all levels (national, state, and local) to respond to systemic problems with stop-gap measures that do not address the core problem: that some public schools in the U.S., particularly high-poverty schools in central cities, have become places where many teachers prefer not to teach (AFT, 2009; Hadley Dunn, 2011) and where many students find they cannot learn (Eaton, 2006, Kozol, 2005).

This exploration of international teacher-recruitment practices builds on a substantial foundation provided by the AFT (2009), the National Education Association (NEA) (Barber, 2003), and the Association of International Educators (AIE) (Black Institute, 2011). The NEA (Barber, 2003) and AFT (2009) reports both decried not the right of international teachers to seek work in U.S. schools, but rather the lack of federal data on this trend (or lack of public access to the data) and the inadequate regulation

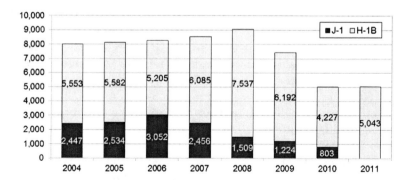

Figure 13.1 H-1B and J-1 visas issued to primary and secondary teachers. *Source:* AFT (2009), U.S. Department of Homeland Security (2010, 2012), and the Interagency Working Group on U.S. Government-Sponsored International Exchanges and Training (2009, 2010, 2011). Data on J-1 visa issuances for 2011 was not yet available.

of the international teacher-recruitment industry. Barber (2003) found that thousands of international teachers were working in U.S. public schools in situations that ran the gamut from acceptable to illegal. Six years later, the AFT (2009) estimated that approximately 19,000 international teachers "from nearly every country in the world" were working in "nearly every state in the union," and offered Baltimore as an example of "the speed with which reliance on international recruitment can take root" (pp. 8–9).

In 2005, the Baltimore City Public Schools hired 108 teachers from the Philippines. Four years later, more than 600 Filipinos (almost 10% of the city's teaching force) were teaching in Baltimore, including more than 25 from one of the top schools in Cebu.[3] "The [school] district incurred no extra costs for hiring [the teachers]. In fact, the recruitment agency paid for multiple trips to Manila for human resources officials, with accommodations in luxury hotels" (AFT, 2009, p. 8). Other counties followed suit, and by 2009, approximately 1,200 Filipinos were teaching in Maryland.

Now, it seems, most of these teachers are disillusioned and preparing to return home. The Baltimore schools announced in 2012 that only 46 of the 154 international teachers who must either gain permanent residency or leave in 2012 will be sponsored, after a market review showed hundreds of U.S. teachers were interested in and qualified for the positions (Green, 2012a). "This whole thing has shown that the American Dream can be a lie," said an angry and disappointed high school senior, the daughter of a Filipino special educator who now plans to move her family back to the Philippines after teaching in Baltimore for six years (Green, 2012b).

Ramona Diaz (2011) produced and directed a documentary film that follows four Filipinos as they leave their families and students in the Philippines and move to the U.S. to work in public schools in East Baltimore, highlights the emotional trauma of teaching in these circumstances. Lured by the promise of much higher pay (one said she earned 25 times more in the U.S. than in the Philippines), the teachers struggle with the pain of separation from husbands, families, and young children; with classroom-management challenges; and with the ongoing need to disabuse family members of the belief that a job in the U.S. can satisfy all wants as well as needs. In short, although many international teachers undoubtedly have provided students in the U.S. with good instruction, the practice is fraught with difficulties (Hadley Dunn, 2011).

The AIE report (Black Institute, 2011) details the experiences and frustrations of hundreds of Caribbean teachers "aggressively recruited" in 2001 by the New York City Department of Education (DOE).

> These skilled professionals were enticed to come to the United States with the clear understanding of a number of commitments. In fact, it was the promises of New York State teacher certification, Master's degrees, housing assistance

and ultimately, a pathway to permanent United States residency for themselves and their nuclear families which prompted them to uproot themselves
and their families to teach in our public schools. By and large . . . these promises were never kept. (p. 4)

One of the teachers recalls the initial interviews in the West Indies in this way:

We were told . . . that the DOE would pay our airfare, pay our rent for the first
three months and for those people needing their Master's degrees, they said
they would assume those costs as well. Everything was very nebulous from
the beginning. The recruiters kept saying things that never came to fruition.
(Black Institute, 2011, p. 7)

The teachers' efforts to obtain green cards, after working under J-1 and
then H-1B visas, have largely been unsuccessful (Black Institute, 2011). Now
saddled with substantial legal fees and threats of termination and deportation, they are protesting what the AIE report suggests was a bait-and-switch
trap. Of the 3,340 international teachers hired to teach in New York City
between 2000 and 2005, less than 20% have gained permanent residency. In
one teacher's view, she and her colleagues' temporary status renders them
vulnerable to "be gotten rid of at their 'whim and fancy'" (Black Institute,
2011, p. 8).

These are not the worst stories. Multiple recruitment agencies have been
fined for extorting wages and threatening international teachers with deportation. "Because their sponsor constructively controls their visa, [inter-
national teachers] are effectively 'at will' employees," which creates "at least
the potential for a degree of intimidation from which permanent employees are shielded" (Barber, 2003, p. 2).

In 2002, 15 mathematics and science teachers from India who were
teaching in Newark charged the Teachers Placement Group (TPG, 2011)
with extortion of wages. With the help of the Newark Teachers Union, the
Indian teachers sought to invalidate a contract they had been forced to
sign that required them to give TPG about $1 million of their earnings
over a three-year period. Finding that TPG had coerced and threatened the
teachers with deportation, the Department of Labor fined the company's
founder and president $120,000 and required TPG and its officers to pay
$187,546 in back wages (Barber, 2003). Despite this history, the Connecti-
cut Department of Education began working with TPG in 2006 to develop a
Visiting International Teachers program to bring Indian mathematics and
science teachers to Connecticut on three-year contracts. The Bridgeport,
Bloomfield, and Hartford school districts subsequently signed up for the
program (AFT, 2009).

In 2004, Omni Consortium, Multicultural Professionals, and Multicultural Education Consultants were indicted on charges of conspiring to

commit alien smuggling, visa fraud, mail fraud, and money laundering in connection with the recruitment of 273 Filipinos who were promised teaching jobs in the U.S. The teachers paid up to $10,000 for the recruiters' services, many by taking loans from the recruiters that carried a compounding interest rate of more than 60% a year. The teachers were not allowed to join trade unions (Chanda, 2011), were housed in unfinished properties in groups of 10 to 15, were forbidden to own cars, and were warned that they would be deported if they tried to find jobs on their own, which they could not do in any case because the recruiters had confiscated their transcripts and certifications (AFT, 2009, p. 17).

In 2010, the AFT and the Southern Poverty Law Center filed a class-action lawsuit in a California federal court against Universal Placement International, Inc. The lawsuit accuses the Los Angeles-based company of running a human-trafficking operation that brought hundreds of Filipinos to teach in public schools in Louisiana. "Teachers were saddled with crippling debts, placed into shoddy housing and threatened with deportation if they complained," according to a lawyer for the AFT (quoted in Deslatte, 2010). Each teacher paid about $16,000 (five times the average annual household income in the Philippines) before leaving home, some by taking high-interest loans from a lender recommended by Universal. More fees and legal entanglements followed once the teachers arrived in the U.S., including contracts requiring them to give a percentage of their monthly pay to Universal, which confiscated their passports and visas (Deslatte 2010).

In 2011 the U.S. Department of Labor ordered Prince George's County Schools in Maryland to pay $1.7 million in fines and to return $4.2 million to Filipino teachers who paid $1,000 in visa fees that the employer legally was required to pay (Green, 2011). The U.S. and the Philippines subsequently signed a Joint Declaration of Migrant Workers Rights, designed to present such abuses (Jaleco, 2012).

TEACHER LAYOFFS AND "SHORTAGES"

Assertions of a teacher shortage have paved the way for recruitment of international teachers (Books & de Villiers, 2011). *The Learning* (Diaz, 2011) opens with an informational session in the Philippines in 2006 in which a recruiter tells his audience, "One of the things we're finding in the U.S. is that we don't have an abundant supply of math teachers and science teachers and special education teachers." In her introduction to a televised showing of the film in 2011, PBS News Hour Anchor Judy Woodruff framed the documentary as "a different take on how to solve teacher shortages in inner-city schools." In 2009, *The New York Times* issued a clarion call, based on a report by the National Commission on Teaching and America's Future (2008) about an impending teacher shortage nationwide, created by retirements and weak retention of new teachers:

> Over the next four years, more than a third of the nation's 3.2 million teachers could retire, depriving classrooms of experienced instructors and straining taxpayer-financed retirement systems.... The problem is aggravated by high attrition among rookie teachers, with one of every three new teachers leaving the profession within five years. (Dillon, 2009, p. A16)

U.S. Department of Labor statistics support this notion of a teacher shortage. The Bureau of Labor Statistics ranks "elementary school teachers, except special education" among the 20 occupations with "the highest projected numeric change in employment" between 2010 and 2020 (U.S. Department of Labor, 2012). The U.S. Department of Education's (2012) *Teacher Shortage Areas Nationwide Listing* reports a teacher shortage in one or more areas for 2012–2013 in every state in the nation. Criteria for teacher shortages vary from state to state. The states report "shortage areas" to the Department of Education, seemingly with no further verification either made or sought.[4]

News reports assert just the opposite: no shortage at all. Rather, large numbers of teachers are losing their jobs. "America's public schools may see the most extensive layoffs of their teaching staffs in decades," *The New York Times* reported in 2011 (Dillon, 2011, p. A13). "States and school districts across the country have fired thousands of teachers, raised college tuition, relaxed standards, slashed days off the academic calendar and gutted pre-kindergarten and summer school programs," the *Los Angeles Times* announced about the same time (Caesar & Watanabe, 2011). Arguing for his jobs bill in the summer of 2012, President Obama cited the loss of some 250,000 teachers over the past three years and told the nation, "It should concern everyone that right now—all across America—tens of thousands of teachers are getting laid off" (Reston, 2012). In California alone, 32,000 teachers, 11% of the workforce, have lost their jobs in the last three years (Hoag, 2012). The Center on Budget and Policy Priorities (Oliff & Leachman, 2011) reported that school districts nationwide cut 278,000 teaching jobs between September 2008 and September 2011.

Multiple explanations potentially could reconcile these contradictory discourses of teacher shortages and K–12 workforce reductions, including budget crises at the federal, state, and local levels that recently have worsened significantly, common practices of school districts handing out pink slips and then rehiring teachers a few months later, and regional differences (teacher shortages in some places but not others) (Books & de Villiers, 2011). Nevertheless, the double-speak calls into question the widespread assumption of a teacher shortage, a discourse being used to rationalize recruitment of international teachers to teach in U.S. classrooms.

THE TICKET: H-1B AND J-1 VISA PROGRAMS

International teachers come to the U.S. through two temporary work visa programs, the H-1B and J-1 programs. The H-1B Specialty Occupation Program, administered by the Bureau of U.S. Citizenship and Immigration Services within the Department of Homeland Security and by the U.S. Department of Labor, is restricted to occupations that require "theoretical and practical application of a body of specialized knowledge" and at least a bachelor's degree in the specialty (U.S. Department of Labor, 2011). The H-1B visa has a three-year term, renewable once for a total of six years. Individuals apply for this visa in concert with an employer authorized by the Department of Labor to hire nonimmigrant workers. In the case of teachers, the authorized school district generally becomes the employer. Although designed to ameliorate shortages in specialized occupations, until recently, school districts have not had to show a critical skills shortage or any other workforce need (Barber, 2003). Among the top 10 H-1B visa sponsors for teachers in 2011 were the Chicago, Los Angeles, Madison Parish (Louisiana), and Roosevelt (New York) public schools as well as Global Teachers Research and Resources Inc. (2011), a placement agency with offices in Morrow, Georgia, and in Bangalore, Chennai, and Mumbai, India.[5]

While many U.S. companies are lobbying to have the current annual cap of 65,000 on H-1B visas lifted (Preston, 2011), the program is facing serious criticism. Immigration scholar Ronil Hira told a U.S. House of Representatives judiciary panel in March 2011 that the H-1B program needs an "immediate and substantial overhaul" to close loopholes that make it "too easy to bring in cheaper foreign workers, with ordinary skills, who directly substitute for, rather than complement, workers already in America" (*H-1B visas*, 2011, p. 2). Because H-1B visas are held by the employer, not the worker, the program gives employers inordinate power over workers, whose legal status is in their hands. Although H-1B visas are temporary, employers can choose to sponsor workers for permanent residence—or not.

The J-1 visa, linked to the Exchange Visitor Program of the U.S. Department of State and administered by its Bureau of Educational and Cultural Affairs, has an explicit mission of promoting intercultural understanding through educational and cultural exchanges. This visa has an initial term of one year, renewable twice for a total of three years. Thereafter, a participant must return to his or her home country for at least two years before applying to return to the U.S. Successful applicants must be qualified to teach in their home countries, must have at least three years of teaching or related professional experience, and must meet the standards of the U.S. state in which they will teach. The J-1 program now has 61 sponsors, including 20 state Departments or Boards of Education; the Chicago, Denver, Olympia (Washington), Philadelphia, and Shawnee (Kansas) Mission Schools; and a range of private schools, foundations, institutes, and nonprofit and for-profit agencies (U.S. Department of State, 2012). Despite the program title, no actual exchange of teachers occurs.

INTERESTS AND OPPORTUNITIES

Profit-driven recruiters are actively working to develop both a demand for and a supply of international teachers in U.S. schools. Recruiting agencies based in the U.S. take in approximately $4 million a year from recruited teachers, Shannon Lederer of the AFT told the Commonwealth Advisory Council on Teacher Mobility, Recruitment and Migration (Chandra & De-gazon-Johnson, 2010). Profit comes from inflated travel costs (which teach-ers pay); placement fees charged both to teachers and to schools; housing, visa processing, and other fees; and sometimes double-charging teachers: having them pay in their home countries and in the United States.

International teachers learn about the possibility of working in the U.S. in part through Web sites maintained by teacher recruitment agencies and organizations, and these sites are sometimes their only sources of informa-tion. Our inquiry into the recruitment of international teachers began five years ago with a study of the online recruiting practices of 43 UK-based teacher-recruitment agencies recruiting in South Africa (de Villiers & Books, 2009). We then looked at 21 U.S.-based agencies that are recruiting globally (Books & de Villiers, 2011). In both cases, we found that recruit-ers are emphasizing opportunities for travel and an exciting experience abroad, and have far less to say about the real costs of living in the UK or the U.S. or about the challenges international teachers likely will face in the public schools in these countries. As the AFT (2009) also found:

> Recruiters have a financial interest in making the "pull" factors seem as tempting as possible and may mislead teachers by encouraging inflated and inaccurate expectations about life in a country like the United States. Poten-tial recruits may learn, for instance, of the comparatively high salaries they could earn...but receive no information about income tax rates or the cost of living. They may also make their decisions to migrate without ever learning about the very different challenges of teaching in American schools. (p. 14)

Much of the recruiting in the U.S. has been done in the Philippines, which, with its high poverty and surplus of well-trained teachers, is regarded as "a fertile recruiting ground."[6] Four of the 21 U.S.-based agencies we reviewed recruit in the Philippines, and three recruit only in the Philippines. English is the language of instruction in the Philippines, and Filipinos "typically see migration to the U.S. as a golden opportunity," the Houston-based Professional and Intellectual Resources Corporation says on its Web site (2011). The migratory path from the Philippines to the U.S. arguably was paved years ago:

> U.S. colonization of the Philippines created the conditions for the current migration of Filipino teachers to the U.S. The U.S. colonial education system in the Philippines mandated English instruction; it was modeled after the U.S. educational system; and it reinforced the superiority of the U.S. Colonial education intended to "civilize" the Filipinos in American ways for the benefit of America. As a result, the education system and other institutions in the Philippines have been oriented to benefit the U.S. over the needs of the Philippines. (Gutierrez, 2009, p. 54)

Indeed, as of 2012, when thousands of Filipinos were teaching in the U.S., the Philippines faced a shortage of 47,000 public school educators ("DepEd Bares Shortage," 2012).

The U.S. teacher-recruitment agency Web sites overall create a picture not of other countries losing some of their best teachers, but rather of hardworking, eager-to-please, and "bargain-priced" educators (i.e., "perfect workers") eager to come to the U.S. to ameliorate a "teacher shortage" and promote "cultural understanding." This rosy picture rests on inaccuracies and distortions. Credible data directly contradict assertions of a teacher shortage, and the sheer numbers of international teachers and their placement in hard-to-staff schools defy a notion of "cultural exchange." Noah's (2011) blunt statement is much to the point: "When 10 percent of a school district's teachers are foreign migrants [as is the case in Baltimore], that isn't cultural exchange. It's sweatshop labor" (p. 2).

Tellingly, almost none of the Web sites include arguments that the international teachers will improve the quality of teaching and learning in a school. Perhaps most crassly, Teachers International Placement (2011) positions teaching in the U.S. instead as "a unique opportunity to work with young students have summers off and competitive starting salaries [sic]." In her review of the scholarship on teacher migration in southern Africa, Brown (2008) notes that the question of educational quality has been largely overshadowed by a focus on "teacher shortages" (p. 283).

Although some international teachers with temporary visas are paid by a third-party agency or organization, most are paid by the school district. The district often pays the recruiter a contractor fee, which generally is less than the cost of benefits and pension contributions. Consequently, employing visa holders can be a way to cut personnel costs (Gutierrez, 2009). H-1B regulations require that visa holders be paid the prevailing wage, and it seems that international teachers generally are paid wages comparable to those of other teachers with similar qualifications and experience. Still, "there is at least anecdotal evidence that, absent a collective bargaining agreement or law or policy, some school districts pay their nonimmigrant employees as new teachers, regardless of their experience and qualifications" (Barber, 2003, p. 2). Nevertheless and despite the sometimes exorbitant fees international teachers pay to recruiters, because teacher salaries are so much higher in the U.S. than in most other parts of the world, these costs can seem like wise investments, as clearly was the case for the Filipinos profiled in the film *The Learning* (Diaz, 2011).

RECOMMENDATIONS

The international teacher-recruitment industry needs to be made more transparent and regulated more diligently to protect everyone involved, especially teachers. Barber (2003) recommended that employers "be required to demonstrate an actual shortage of specific available workforce skills before being granted the authority to employ nonimmigrant workers" and that the federal government "be required to disclose much more extensive data on nonimmigrant work visa certifications and authorizations" (pp. 4–5). Echoing Barber (2003), the AFT expressed concerns not only about limited access to federal data, but also about the lack of almost any regulation of international recruiting, about the loss to host countries of some of their best and brightest teachers, about kickback-type arrangements for school officials, and about "widespread and egregious" abuse of teachers—"often the profit point in the industry" (AFT, 2009, p. 7).

More recently, immigration scholar Ronil Hira told a U.S. House of Representatives judiciary panel that Congress and the Department of U.S. Citizenship and Immigration Services ought to publish full employment data for all H-1B workers to show the scope, consequences, and basic functioning of the H-1B program across occupational sectors (*H-1B visas*, 2011). The AFT (2009) and AIE (Black Institute, 2011) reports include recommendations that international teachers be hired only by school districts and not by third-party agencies or organizations, that they be paid comparably to others in the district, and that they be provided with the same working conditions as well as with special protection against arbitrary revocation of their visas. Further, responsibility for immigration documentation should be taken "out of the hands of school principals"

(Black Institute, 2011, p. 16). We concur with all these recommendations and would add a few more:

- Data on teacher layoffs and shortages should be collected routinely by federal agencies and monitored closely by scholars.
- International recruiters should include such basic information on their Web sites as the costs of living in the U.S. and the realistic challenges international teachers likely will face in hard-to-staff U.S. schools.
- Oversight mechanisms should be established to ensure that recruitment of international teachers is not used to exploit their "legally precarious status" (Barber, 2003, p. 2) or to disempower their U.S. colleagues. The Commonwealth Teacher Recruitment Protocol (Commonwealth Secretariat, 2004), adopted in 2004 by the education ministers of 53 member nations, attempts to establish practices that ensure fair treatment of international teachers in recruiting countries and to protect the interests of source countries. This document could provide a model for the U.S. as well.[7]
- Teacher-education programs should ensure that all practicing and prospective teachers understand teachers' rights, the ideological forces shaping the profession of education, and the international context of the work of teaching.
- Finally, the legal, political, discursive, and human-rights dimensions of international teacher recruitment should receive far more critical scholarly attention than they have.

CONCLUSION: A SHORTAGE OF CANDIDNESS AND COMMITMENT TO PUBLIC SCHOOLS

Recruitment of international teachers allows leaders at all levels of educational governance (national, state, and district) to respond to problems of neglect and underfunding in high-poverty, central-city and rural schools with stop-gap measures that do not address the core reasons that hard-to-staff schools are hard to staff. "The harsh reality is that it is easier and cheaper to hire teachers abroad than to solve the systemic problems" at home (Hadley Dunn, 2011, p. 1401). Taken-for-granted but undocumented assumptions about a widespread teacher shortage, plus promises of promoting cultural understanding, provide a rationale for displacing U.S. teachers with short-term and less expensive international teachers with no long-term stake in union contracts and negotiations. Lured by "broken promises," too many of these "bracero teachers" (Noah, 2011, p. 2) end up, at best, in ambiguous situations, and, at worst, in nightmarish immigration-status limbos (Black Institute, 2011).

As we have noted (Books & de Villiers, 2011), from the perspective of the Heritage Foundation, a self-described conservative think-tank and advocacy group, this displacement is all for the best. The Heritage Foundation advocates raising the cap on H-1B visas (now 65,000 per year) and structuring teaching contracts accordingly "to give local districts more stability and flexibility" (Johnson, 2005, p. 1). By aligning contracts with three-year H1-B visas, a school district furthermore could "eliminat[e] the possibility of [a teacher] moving to another school district or employer without compensation" (Johnson, 2005, p. 4). "This vision of 'captive' teachers perpetually trying to acclimate to a new country is not in the best interest of students or teachers," here or abroad (Books & de Villiers, 2011).

Recruiting abroad to staff hard-to-staff schools not only creates "a migrant class of teachers who shortchange students in their home countries as well as potentially under-educate the students stuck in these . . . schools" (Spreen & Edwards, 2011, p. 32). Worse, this practice turns teachers, and therefore students, into proxy warriors in a high-stakes political battle that ultimately has nothing to do with teaching and learning. Teacher migration overall has hurt the quality of education in sending countries because the teachers who leave generally are the best (Brown, 2008). As a case in point, 25 teachers from one of the best schools in Manila are now working in Baltimore.[8] When experienced teachers leave, the relatively new teachers left behind are often then saddled with larger classes and a skeletal staff of colleagues. Consequences for receiving countries have been mixed. Although international teachers can enrich the curriculum by bringing new perspectives to bear, cultural differences also have led to miscommunication, to clashes in basic approaches to work, and to struggles to adapt a curriculum to unfamiliar local contexts (Brown, 2008; Hadley Dunn, 2011).

Importantly, battles over U.S. teachers' collective bargaining rights and recruitment of international teachers with no stake in those rights are occurring in the context of a public discourse that takes for granted that teachers are both overpaid and in short supply. Indeed, it seems that public-sector workers, including and especially teachers, have become the new "welfare mothers" (Albelda, 2011; Gabriel, 2011; Rice, 2011). This discourse, which flourished in the hard-fought struggles over public employees' collective-bargaining rights, most notably in Wisconsin in the spring of 2011 and then in Ohio in the fall of 2011, ought to be seen as part of a larger battle, the aim of which is to "re-class" (change the social class of) public school teachers (Noblitt, 2011) in line with neoliberal commitments to deregulate markets and to privatize all things public (Harvey, 2007).

Teacher educators and the schools and colleges of education in which they work are being marginalized and devalued as well. Increasingly, fast-track, alternative teacher-preparation programs are put forth as necessary to recruit "the most talented" to teach in the "neediest" public schools (Kumashiro, 2010, p. 56). Federal dollars are supporting such practices, which mark a move away from teacher preparation offered by schools and colleges of education and away from viewing teaching as a professional career. The move instead is towards "solutions" that staff classrooms, often in any way possible and sometimes by pitting teachers worldwide against each other in an unregulated "free market" competition for jobs. Even as traditional teacher-preparation programs are regulated ever more heavily, federal support is offered for fast-track alternatives like Teach for America. These paths are depicted as breath-of-fresh-air alternatives to college-based teacher-preparation programs, characterized by former President George Bush as "unnecessary barriers" keeping qualified candidates out of the classroom (Kumashiro, 2010, p. 61). More harshly, the Heritage Foundation (again) has construed the whole enterprise of state teacher certification as "a cartel operated by the teacher unions and colleges of education to enforce monopolies in what amounts to restraint of trade" (quoted in Imig & Imig, 2008, p. 889).

The current assault on teachers' collective-bargaining rights, the denigrating teacher-bashing and especially teacher-union bashing, the marginalization of schools and colleges of education, and the largely under-the-radar "experiment" in international teacher recruitment—justified through undocumented assertions of a U.S. teacher shortage—all are components of an ideologically driven agenda that is fundamentally redefining what it means to be a teacher in the United States. The stakes are alarmingly high in this neoliberal move to replace tenured teaching positions with short-term work contracts "won" in an international trade in teachers. Quality teaching and learning, hardly the focus of this agenda, may nevertheless be the collateral damage left in its wake.

NOTES

1. This chapter is an updated and abridged version of an article published in the *Journal for Critical Education Policy Studies*: Books, S., and de Villiers, J.J.R. (in press), "Importing educators and redefining what it means to be a teacher in the U.S.," and of commentary published in the *Teachers College Record*: Books, S., and de Villiers, J. J. R. (26 September 2011), "'Teacher shortages' in the U.S. and the politics of recruiting abroad." Retrieved from http://www.tcrecord.org.
2. This figure is derived from the methodology that Barber (2003) and then the AFT (2009) used to estimate the number of nonimmigrant teachers in

2003 and 2009, respectively. The estimate includes the number of J-1 visas for 2009 and the number of new and renewed H1-B visas for 2007, 2008, and 2009 issued to primary and secondary teachers, a total of 21,038. The estimate assumes that approximately two-thirds of all J-1 and H-1B visa holders are teaching in public schools, based on an analysis of FY 2002 H-1B certifications by the U.S. Department of Labor, where 67% of the positions approved for K-12 teaching positions were for applications from public school authorities (Barber, 2003).

3. R. Anthony Japzon, president of Filipino Educators of Maryland, shared this information during a live chat held in conjunction with the PBS broadcast of the film *The Learning* (Diaz, 2011). The transcript, retrieved September 28, 2011, was available at http://www.pbs.org/pov/learning/newshour-chat. php.

4. Asked about the criteria for a shortage, Mary Miller, analyst with the Department of Education, offered this brief response via email on March 4, 2011: "The States determine their Teacher Shortage Area and submit them to the U.S. Department of Education. The criteria vary from state to state."

5. See ranking provided by *Myvisajobs.com*, a job information portal owned by the Mahwah, NJ-based Quant Decisions LLC at http://www.myvisajobs.com/ Teacher-11JT.htm.

6. Sara Neufeld, a freelance journalist whose articles in the *Baltimore Sun* inspired the film *The Learning* (Diaz, 2011), made this observation in a live chat held in conjunction with the PBS broadcast. Transcript Retrieved from http://www.pbs.org/pov/learning/newshour-chat.php [Accessed 10 October 2011].

7. Another positive initiative, to consider the feasibility of extending a voluntary code of conduct for the ethical recruitment of international nurses to other health professionals as well as to teachers, has been undertaken by George Washington University and funded by the John D. and Catherine T. MacArthur Foundation (2011).

8. R. Anthony Japzon, president of Filipino Educators of Maryland, shared this information during a live chat held in conjunction with the PBS broadcast of the film *The Learning* (Diaz, 2011). Transcript Retrieved from http://www. pbs.org/pov/learning/newshour-chat.php [Accessed 10 October 2011].

REFERENCES

Albelda, R. (2011). Teachers, secretaries, and social workers—The new welfare moms? *Dollars and Sense*, May/June. Retrieved from http://www.dollarsand-sense.org/archives/2011/0511albelda.html

American Federation of Teachers. (2009). *Importing educators: Causes and consequences of international teacher recruitment* [Online]. Retrieved from http://www.aft. org/pdfs/international/importingeducators0609.pdf

Baker, B., Sciarra, D., & Farrie, D. (2012). *Is school funding fair? A National Report Card, second ed.* (June). Retrieved from http://www.schoolfundingfairness. org/National_Report_Card_2012.pdf

Barber, R. (2003). *Report to the National Education Association on trends in foreign teacher recruitment* (June). Retrieved from http://www.cwalocal4250.org/outsourcing/binarydata/foreignteacher.pdf

Black Institute. (2011). *Broken promises: The story of Caribbean international teachers in New York City's public schools.* Retrieved from http://www.theblackinstitute. org/announcements/international-teachers-in-nyc

Books, S., & de Villiers, J. J. R. (2011). "Teacher shortages" in the U.S. and the politics of recruiting abroad. *Teachers College Record.* Retrieved from http://www.tcrecord.org

Brown, B. (2008). Teacher migration impact: A review in the context of quality education provision and teacher training in higher education in Southern Africa. *South African Journal of Higher Education, 22,* 282–301.

Caesar, S., & Watanabe, T. (2011, July 31). Education takes a beating nationwide. *Los Angeles Times.* Retrieved from http://articles.latimes.com/2011/jul/31/nation/la-na-education-budget-cuts-20110731

Chanda, C. (2011). *Next steps in managing teacher migration. Report of the Commonwealth Advisory Council on teacher mobility, recruitment and migration.* London, UK: Commonwealth Secretariat. Retrieved from http://www.thecommonwealth.org/files/239060/FileName/Secondmeetingreport.pdf

Chanda, C., & Degazon-Johnson, R. (2010). *Report of the inaugural meeting of the Commonwealth Advisory Council on the teacher mobility, recruitment and migration.* London, UK: Commonwealth Secretariat. Retrieved from http://www.thecommonwealth.org/files/234328/FileName/ReportoftheInauguralMeeting oftheAdvisoryCouncil,June20103.pdf

Commonwealth Secretariat. (2004). *Protocol for the recruitment of Commonwealth teachers.* Retrieved from http://www.thecommonwealth.org/shared_asp_files/GFSR.asp?NodeID=39311

"DepEd Bares Shortage of Public School Teachers." (2012, May 27). *The Philippine Star.* Retrieved from http://www.philstar.com/ArticlePrinterFriendly.aspx?articleId=811187&publicationSubCategoryId=63

Deslatte, M. (2010, August 6). Lawsuit filed against Filipino teachers' recruiter. *Bloomberg Businessweek.* Retrieved from http://www.businessweek.com/ap/financialnews/D9HE27P01.htm

de Villiers, J. J. R., & Books, S. (2009). Recruiting teachers online: Marketing practices and information dissemination practices of UK-based agencies. *Educational Review 61*(3), 315–325.

Diaz, R. (producer/director) (2011). *The learning* [motion picture]. U.S.: CineDiaz.

Dillon, S. (2009, April 7). Report envisions shortage of teachers as retirements escalate. *The New York Times,* p. A16.

Dillon, S. (2011, April 1). An annual rite, school layoff notices seem more dire. *The New York Times,* p. A13.

Eaton, S. E. (2006). *The children in room E4: American education on trial.* New York, NY: Algonquin Books.

Gabriel, T. (2011, March 2). Teachers wonder, why the scorn? *The New York Times,* p. A1.

Giroux, H. (2004). *The terror of neoliberalism: authoritarianism and the eclipse of democracy.* Boulder, CO: Paradigm.

Global Campaign for Education. (2009). *Education on the brink: Will the IMF's new lease on life ease or block progress towards education goals?* April [Online]. Retrieved from http://www.campaignforeducation.org/docs/reports/IMF%20 paper2_low%20res.pdf

Global Teachers Research and Resources. (2011). *Global Teachers Research and Resources.* Retrieved from http://gtrr.net/career.php

Green, E. L. (2011, March 4). City school buyout aims to reduce 'surplus' teachers. *The Baltimore Sun.* Retrieved from http://articles.baltimoresun.com/2011-03-04/news/bs-md-ci-teacher-surplus-costs-20110304_1_surplus-teachers-baltimore-teachers-union-marietta-english

Green, E. L. (2012a, April 11). City schools will have to shed more than 100 international teachers. *The Baltimore Sun.* Retrieved from http://articles.baltimoresun.com/2012-04-11/news/bal-job-market-test-finds-limited-positions-in-city-schools-for-international-teachers-20120411_1_foreign-teachers-surplus-teachers-work-visas

Green, E. L. (2012b, May 7). For children of Filipino teachers, an uncertain future. *The Baltimore Sun.* Retrieved from http://articles.baltimoresun.com/2012-05-07/news/bs-md-ci-filipino-teacher-students-20120430_1_filipino-teachers-immigrant-teachers-work-visas

Gutierrez, R. R. (2009). *Foreign teacher recruitment—A neoliberal response to the U.S. teacher shortage: A focus on teachers from the Philippines.* Unpublished Master's Thesis, DePaul University, Chicago, IL.

Hadley Dunn, A. (2011). Global village versus culture shock: the recruitment and preparation of foreign teachers for U.S. urban schools. *Urban Education, 46*(6), 1379–1410.

Harvey, D. (2007). *A brief history of neoliberalism.* London, UK: Oxford University Press.

H-1B visas: Designing a program to meet the needs of the U.S. economy and U.S. workers: A hearing before the Subcommittee on Immigration Policy and Enforcement Committee on the Judiciary, U.S. House of Representatives, 112th Cong. (2011) (Testimony of Ronil Hira).

Hoag, C. (2012, May 5). Calif.'s 4th year of teacher layoffs spur concerns", *The Seattle Times.* Retrieved from http://seattletimes.nwsource.com/html/nationworld/2018147042_apusteacherpinkslips.html

Imig, D. G., & Imig, S. R. (2008). From traditional certification to competitive certification: A twenty-five year retrospective. In M. Cochran-Smith, S. Feiman-Nemser, D. J. McIntyre & K. E. Demers (Eds.), *Handbook of research on teacher education: enduring questions in changing contexts* (3rd ed., pp. 886–907). New York, NY: Routledge.

Interagency Working Group on U.S. Government-Sponsored International Exchanges and Training. (2009). *FY 2009 annual report.* Retrieved from http://www.iawg.gov/rawmedia_repository/a0605aeb_18f6_4848_8795_b4cba6d01f11

Interagency Working Group on U.S. Government-Sponsored International Exchanges and Training. (2010). *FY 2010 annual report.* Retrieved from http://www.iawg.gov/rawmedia_repository/44c4ac01_4486_4a6c_8f03_f6bcb696eda5

Interagency Working Group on U.S. Government-Sponsored International Exchanges and Training. (2011). *FY 2011 annual report.* Retrieved from http://www.iawg.gov/rawmedia_repository/3a617beb_864e_4211_8175_5cbf0bba8330

Jaleco, R. (2012, June 17). US, PH vow to uphold migrant workers' rights. *ABS-CBN News*. Retrieved from http://www.abs-cbnnews.com/print/222268

John D., & Catherine T. MacArthur Foundation. (2011). *Global migration and human mobility: recent grants*. Retrieved from http://www.macfound.org/site/c.lkLXJ8MQKrH/b.1494541/k.EF0C/Migration.htm

Johnson, K. A. (2005, October 5). How immigration reform could help to alleviate the teacher shortage. *Backgrounder # 1884*, pp. 1–6.

Kozol, J. (2005). *Shame of the nation: The restoration of apartheid schooling in America*. New York, NY: Crown.

Kumashiro, K. K. (2010). Seeing the bigger picture: Troubling movements to end teacher education. *Journal of Teacher Education 61*(1-2), 56–65.

National Commission on Teaching and America's Future. (2008). *Learning teams: Creating what's next*. Retrieved from http://nctaf.org/wp-content/uploads/2012/01/NCTAFLearningTeams408REG2.pdf

Noah, T. (2011, October 20). F for effort: The migrant teacher fiasco. *The New Republic: A Journal of Politics and the Arts, 242*, p. 2.

Noblitt, G. (2011, November). *Teachers and class warfare*. Paper presented at the American Educational Studies Association Annual Conference, St. Louis, MO.

Oliff, P., & Leachman, M. (2011). *New school year brings steep cuts in state funding for schools*. Retrieved from http://www.cbpp.org/files/9-1-11sfp.pdf

Preston, J. (2011, April 1). Outsourcers are criticized on visa use. *The New York Times*, p. A20.

Professional and Intellectual Resources. (2011). *Professional and Intellectual Resources*. Retrieved from http://www.philippineteachers.com/company_aboutus.html

Reston, M. (2012, June 9). "No excuse for inaction"; Obama presses jobs plan in weekly address. *Los Angeles Times*. Retrieved from http://articles.latimes.com/2012/jun/09/news/la-pn-obama-weekly-address-20120608

Rice, A. (2011, March 20). Miss Grundy was fired today. *New York Magazine* [Online]. Retrieved from http://nymag.com/news/features/michelle-rhee-2011-3/index2.html

Robertson, S. L. (2008). "Remaking the world": Neoliberalism and the transformation of education and teachers' labor. In M. Compton & L. Weiner (Eds.), *The global assault on teaching, teachers, and their unions: Stories for resistance* (pp. 11–27). New York, NY: Palgrave.

Spreen, C. A., & Edwards, D. (2011). The decentralization and privatization of teacher migration in the U.S. In S. Manik & A. Singh (Eds.), *Global mobility and migration of teachers: issues, identities and infringements* (pp. 31–42). Delhi, India: Kamla-Raj Enterprises.

Teachers International Placement. (2011). *Teachers International Placement*. Retrieved from http://www.teachersinternationalplacement.com/

Teachers Placement Group. (2011). *Teachers Placement Group*. Retrieved from http://www.teachersplacement.com/

U.S. Department of Education, Office of Postsecondary Education. (2012). *Teacher shortage areas nationwide listing, 1990–91 thru 2012–2012*, April. Retrieved from http://www2.ed.gov/about/offices/list/ope/pol/tsa.pdf

U.S. Department of Homeland Security, U.S. Citizenship and Immigration Services. (2010). *Characteristics of specialty occupation workers: Fiscal year 2009 annual report.* Retrieved from http://www.uscis.gov/USCIS/Resources/Reports%20 and%20Studies/H-1B/h1b-fy-09-characteristics.pdf

U.S. Department of Homeland Security, U.S. Citizenship and Immigration Services. (2012). *Characteristics of specialty occupation workers: fiscal year 2009 annual report.* Retrieved from http://www.uscis.gov/USCIS/Resources/Reports%20 and%20Studies/H-1B/h1b-fy-11-characteristics.pdf

U.S. Department of Labor, Bureau of Labor Statistics. (2012). *Occupational outlook handbook 2012–13.* Retrieved from http://www.bls.gov/ooh/most-new-jobs.htm

U.S. Department of Labor, Employment and Training Administration. (2011). *OFLC frequently asked questions and answers.* Retrieved from http://www.foreignlaborcert.doleta.gov/faqsanswers.cfm#h1b1

U.S. Department of State, Bureau of Social and Cultural Affairs. (2012). *Designated sponsors list.* Retrieved from http://eca.state.gov/jexchanges/index. cfm?fuseaction=record.list&mode=&state=&sort=prog_name&cat=13&sc=&u serMax=5&nextStart=1

Wolfe, F. (2007, September 27). Foreign teachers benefit U.S. schools, unions: districts look abroad for cultural exchange. *Education Daily.* Reprinted on the VIF International Education Web site. Retrieved from http://www.vifprogram.com/about/newsarticle.pl?id=457

Source: AFT (2009), U.S. Department of Homeland Security (2010, 2012), and the Interagency Working Group on U.S. Government-Sponsored International Exchanges and Training (2009, 2010, 2011). Data on J-1 visa issuances for 2011 was not yet available.

CHAPTER 14

THE CULT OF PERSONALITY V. EXPERTISE IN THE EDUCATION DEBATE[1]

P. L. Thomas
Furman University

In March of 2012, I spoke at the Council of Educational Facility Planners International (CEFPI) conference in Columbia. At one of the keynote talks, another speaker ended his presentation by highlighting what he feels is the next wave of educational innovation—Khan Academy. Just a couple days later, Sal Khan appeared on a segment of *60 Minutes* (Cetta, 2012). At this intersection of technology, education, and media, I have to note that Khan and his wave of video-based education have something important in common with Arne Duncan as Secretary of Education, Bill Gates as education entrepreneur, and Michelle Rhee as draconian education administrator. First, let's consider how Duncan, Gates, Rhee, and Khan attained their status as educators, educational leaders, and educational reformers.

Secretary of Education Duncan reaped the benefits of appointment as his avenue to an influential status in education—as Smagorinsky (2012) explains:

Left Behind in the Race to the Top, pages 209–225
Copyright © 2013 by Information Age Publishing
All rights of reproduction in any form reserved.

Let's trace [Duncan's] path to the presidential Cabinet. One of Duncan's childhood friends, John Rogers, appointed Duncan director of the Ariel Education Initiative in Chicago. Duncan's directorship led to Ariel's reincarnation as a charter school, following which Duncan was advanced in the Chicago Public School system from deputy chief of staff to chief executive officer. Note that he worked exclusively at the executive level, never stooping to teach classes or learn about schools except from an operational perspective. (n.p.)

How about Bill Gates? To become an education expert and education reformer, Gates amassed billions of dollars, which apparently equates with expertise in any field he chooses (Cody, 2011). And Michelle Rhee? She bypassed the education establishment by not receiving any degrees in education, became a leader by entering the classroom through Teach for America (TFA), taught three years, and then built her celebrity status by firing teachers and creating an education system built on fraudulent test data (Evans & Kane, 2011; Merrow, J., 2013).

This brings us back to Khan, whose Wikipedia page identifies him as an "American educator." Pretty impressive considering that he—like Rhee, Duncan, and Gates—has *no degrees in education,* and like Duncan and Gates, has *no experience teaching.* Khan grew tired of his day job, started tutoring his relatives, made some videos, and now is identified in the media as a credible educator. And, according to CBS, he may be the future of education—if education is merely transferring knowledge from the electronic gadget of the day to passive students.

Ironically, Khan and his academy do offer us a powerful lesson about education and education reform, a lesson embodied by Duncan, Gates, and Rhee: *The cult of personality can garner one public fame and accolades as an educator and reformer, but that notoriety is all glitz, ultimately causing more harm than good.*

Let me return to my recent talk at CEFPI. Throughout the day, I noticed that speakers and participants at this conference—primarily architects, technology experts, engineers, and administrators—argued for the use of technology to support individualized, student-centered instruction as well as project-based learning. The participants and speakers appeared to believe that those ideas (individualized, student-centered instruction and project-based learning) were *innovative,* personified by the new-wave ideas of Khan and the naïve faith (unsupported by evidence over this history of education) that some technological advancement by itself will revolutionize education. (I am always fascinated that people who have no background or experience in education believe that ideas generated outside of education have somehow *never been considered* by educators.) During the final panel presentation at the conference, I highlighted two points. First, I clarified that *teachers have never made policy decisions for education in the U.S.* If education has failed, as most people claim, that failure isn't the result of decisions made by classroom teachers. Second, I informed them that individualized, student-centered learning and project-based learning were championed by John Dewey a century ago and popularized by William Heard Kilpatrick in the 1930s (Kliebard, 1995).

Khan, I added, is not being innovative—even if his video-based learning is as effective as Khan and his proponents claim. But beyond that, Khan has no expertise as an educator. Khan has been a stellar student (if we can trust Wikipedia), but that doesn't make him an educator any more than being a stellar athlete assures that person can coach. Or that being a frequent flyer qualifies a person to pilot a plane.

Khan's plan for education also fails on many other levels. Prepackaging content ensures a static approach to knowledge and understanding. This is the essential failure of the "banking concept" of education denounced by Paulo Freire (1993); a "banking concept" of education accepts knowledge as a fixed body that is easily transferred from some authority (the teacher) to passive students. Focusing on content leaves the student out of any decision making concerning *what* should be learned and *why*. Teaching is reduced to a service industry (Thomas, 2010), and students are just passive and thoughtless customers. Video lectures are essentially textbooks in audio-visual format, and thus carry the same traditional limitations textbooks do. More and more, credible experts who are examining Khan's videos are exposing that the content is often low quality (Golden, 2012). Furthermore, anecdotal feedback suggests the videos may be engaging, but accuracy and teacher–student engagement are being ignored by the allure of technology.

The praise heaped on Khan reflects what is essentially wrong with U.S. public education and the perennial move to reform it: We are trapped in the cult of personality and ignoring the enormous wealth of expertise that exists in the classrooms of K–12 schools and universities across the U.S. The cult of personality (when the celebrity of a person such as Khan, Gates, or Rhee supersedes that person's expertise and drives an agenda) is a self-serving dynamic. In the current personality-based education reform movement, Duncan, Gates, Rhee, and Khan are all feeding their own aggrandizement at the expense of students, teachers, and the common good.

For celebrity education reformers, their agenda is not about democracy or student autonomy or teacher professionalism. In fact, the cult of personality erodes the foundations of universal public education. While that celebrity fuels the death of U.S. public education (Thomas, 2012b), the cult of personality also sacrifices expertise in the public sphere. Instead of celebrity education reformers, a democracy needs educators who are also public intellectuals. Teachers as professionals, teachers as experts are enduring. Expertise deserves the attention and appreciation of the public as well as the political leadership.

EDUCATION AS "POLITICALLY CONTESTED SPACES"[2]

Steve Strieker (2012) confronts the current cult of personality paradigm influencing education from the specific events of his home state: "In Gov. Scott Walker's Wisconsin, teaching has been relegated from professional status to political fodder." He then builds to this conclusion:

> In Walker's Wisconsin, education is not a profession. It is politics....With the current attack on public education, however, our next generation of professional educators will have to be seasoned young, impervious, and politically active. Otherwise, future educators will be doing more political initiatives in education, for less than professional pay, and with less professional liberties. (n.p.)

This commentary offers the opportunity for educators to examine closely traditional calls for teachers to be objective and *not* political as well as many educators' own arguments that education shouldn't be political—especially as the call for objectivity rests inside the popular and political attraction to celebrity over experience and expertise.

First, let me suggest how I believe the discussion of education as political (or not) often becomes distorted. We must begin this discussion with a clarification of terms, specifically between "political" and "partisan." I will concede and even argue that classrooms, teachers, and education in general should avoid being *partisan*, in that teachers and their classrooms should not be reduced to campaigning for a specific political party or candidate. This, in fact, is what I believe most people mean (especially teachers) when they argue for education not to be *political*.

In the current accountability era, however, we must stop conflating *partisan* and *political*, and come to terms with both the inherent political and oppressive call for teachers *not* to be political and the inevitable fact that being human and being a teacher are by their nature *political*. Kincheloe (2005) notes: "[P]roponents of critical pedagogy understand that every dimension of schooling and every form of educational practice are politically contested spaces" (p. 2). Every choice made by an administrator, a teacher, and a student is a political choice. Humans are always in a state of *being political*, a ceaseless negotiation of power. To deny this is to push our political nature beneath the surface (that which shall not be spoken) and to relinquish power to the status quo.

Ayers (2001) recognizes that education that denies the inherent politics of teaching and learning is reduced to silence and compliance: "In school, a high value is placed on quiet: 'Is everything quiet?' the superintendent asks the principal, and the principal the teacher, and the teacher the child. If everything is quiet, it is assumed that all is well" (p. 51). The focus on silence and obedience, then, creates students (and teachers) who are "passive, quiet, obedient, dull" (Ayers, p. 51).

There are three facts before us. First, people in positions of authority who mandate or coerce others to be politically neutral or objective are themselves being political and oppressive; thus, they are either purposefully or implicitly using their authority to act politically themselves to maintain the imbalance of power in their favor. Politicians do this, administrators do this to teachers, and teachers do this to students. To remove another person's political autonomy is the most corrosive act of politics; it is oppression and a negation of political voice for the individual and the ideals associated with democracy. Second, silence and inaction are political acts, often invoked as stances against being political. This irony is not without consequences. To remain silent, to remain passive—both are political acts of compliance, both are acts of endorsing those who are speaking and acting. Third, teachers have only two choices: *Act or be the tools of other people's actions.*

Teachers have long been prone to being the tool of other people's actions, prone to put up a hand and wave off being political, prone to shutting doors and pretending that silence and stasis are objective and professional behaviors. These tendencies were *always political behaviors,* as Kincheloe (2005) notes:

> Shaped by history and challenged by a wide range of interest groups, educational practice is a fuzzy concept as it takes place in numerous settings, is shaped by a plethora of often-invisible forces, and can operate even in the name of democracy and justice to be totalitarian and oppressive. (p. 2)

To strike an objective pose, to wave off or deny the politics of teaching and learning, to withhold our voices because we must do as we are told are all political concessions to the *inexpert* and *inexperienced* in power who are the ones using their politics to beg for educator silence and inaction. Silent and inactive teachers are molding silent and inactive students. These acts are conceding the world to the status quo, conceding our voices and our humanity. Another irony: That's not teaching, and that's not education. Indoctrination is the result of silent and inactive teachers committed to being compliant.

Strieker's (2012) commentary asserts that the current state of education is a shame. I agree, but for me the shame is that educators remain silent and inactive, willing to be the tools of other people's politics. This stance does not reflect the necessarily active role of educators in a democratic society. Embracing the politics of teaching and learning, Ayers (2001) explains: "Education will unfit anyone to be a slave.... Education tears down walls; training is all barbed wire" (p. 132). Calling for teachers not to be political is barbed wire. It is far past time for teachers to tear down walls.

THE TEACHING PROFESSION?:
OF LICENSE, COMPULSION, AND AUTONOMY[3]

At Anthony Cody's (2012b) Living in Dialogue blog (*Education Week*), Educators for Shared Accountability[4] issued a value-added methods (VAM) report on Secretary of Education Duncan in the context of the past nine Secretaries of Education. The results place each Secretary in one of four categories (superior, average, inferior, ineffective), and Duncan ranks "ineffective," 8th of 9.

This important step in expanding the education accountability movement, which started with holding students accountable throughout the 1980s and 1990s and then expanded to holding teachers accountable in the first and second decades of the 21st century, comes in the context of what appears to be an unrelated event in Major League Baseball—Ozzie Guillen's claim that he loves Fidel Castro (Beasley & Leon, 2012), published in *Time* magazine.

On the ESPN talk show Mike & Mike in the Morning, the topic of Guillen's controversy prompted an email to the talk show hosts asking, "What ever happened to free speech?" As a nearly three-decades educator, I was surprised and somewhat frustrated that Mike Greenberg offered one of the most lucid comments about accountability I have heard in some time, particularly in the context that "accountability" has been used as a weapon over the past 30 years to leverage corrosive education reform.

Greenberg noted that in many countries outside the U.S., offensive or abrupt language results in government actions such as legal action or even death. In the U.S., free speech means citizens can criticize our presidents, and even make insensitive or inflammatory comments with little fear of government action. But free speech, Greenberg noted, is not license: Freedom is inherently matched with consequences.

In the case of Guillen, his comments were offensive to Cuban-Americans, and he as well as the Miami Marlins suffered direct and indirect consequences for the comments. The free speech controversy involving Guillen and the mock posting at Living in Dialogue highlight the need to consider the baseless and corrosive nature of misunderstanding and misapplying concepts such as "accountability," "freedom," and even "profession."

Education historically and currently is driven by a *lack* of expertise. In my home state of South Carolina, the current superintendent, Mick Zais, shares with Secretary Duncan that exact lack of experience or expertise in education. When Zais (2012) published an op-ed in several papers across the state, he stated: "Today, the most important information about teachers does not include the type of degree they have or their years of seniority" (n.p.). When

I posted in the comments my challenge to Zais's lack of credibility (Thomas, 2012a), one reader posted this:

> just take the zais' view about which thomas is most hyperplexic: "the most important information about teachers isn't the degrees they have or their years of seniority. their effectiveness in the classroom matters much, much more."
> lord forbid we should actually hold teachers accountable for results. (original informal surface features retained, n.p.)

Here is a typical snapshot of the political and public embracing of the inexpert as well as holding a less sophisticated view of accountability than even a sports talk show addressing a current controversy in baseball.

The accountability movement, then, as it currently functions can accomplish only a few corrosive outcomes: reducing learning to following a script, reducing teaching to a service industry, and diluting the impact of public education as a mechanism for supporting democracy and individual freedom. If education accountability is to accomplish ideals associated with democracy and human agency, we must confront what the term "accountability" can mean, and then address what accountability we honor. Accountability is impacted by three broad contexts:

1. *License:* In my 28 years in education, I have noticed that children and adolescents confuse "freedom" with "license." Children and teens idealize freedom as "doing whatever they please" without considering that freedom includes consequences. In the U.S., those people with the greatest power have the least accountability; they function with near license and ironically call constantly for the accountability of others. Return to the mock VAM report above that holds Secretaries of Education accountable for conditions beyond their control, exactly as the current system of accountability does with teachers. *License is a type of accountability that is above accountability, and thus, license is cancerous to both democracy and human freedom—and often comes in the wake of privilege.*

2. *Compulsion:* Compulsion is the most common distortion of accountability, particularly in education. Compulsion is holding one *subordinate* accountable for implementing the mandates of some *authority.* Compulsion as a form of accountability is dehumanizing and a mechanism of maintaining a hierarchy, a structure of authority (Thomas, 2011). As a form of accountability, compulsion is now entrenched in student accountability built on imposed standards and tests as well as the rising accountability of teachers also built on prescribed standards and state tests. Compulsion produces compliance and, like license, ultimately erodes democracy, human agency, and political voice. Accountability as compulsion in educa-

tion produces compliant workers from our students and teaching as a service industry.

3. *Autonomy:* Autonomous accountability is the complex manifestation of freedom I have noted above. Freedom comes with consequences, just as autonomy, especially for professionals, comes with consequences. But those consequences are not as obvious as most people think. For example, when a medical doctor has a patient with cancer, if the doctor has professional autonomy in the diagnosis and treatment of that cancer, that doctor is accountable for that treatment, not the outcomes of that treatment, and that doctor is not accountable for the *fact* of the cancer (the condition that leads the patient to the doctor). That the patient has cancer may be within the domain of that person's behavior (smoking, for example), and thus the patient is accountable, or that cancer may be genetic and then completely outside the realm of accountability for either the patient or doctor. *Autonomy is the only context for accountability that contributes positively to democracy, human agency, and political voice.* Human dignity grows from human agency, and human agency/autonomy results in consequences—consequences connected to those outcomes over which that human in that moment of freedom has control. Anything outside that dynamic is dehumanizing (such as the coercive accountability common in education reform); it is tyranny (see below).

Political and public authorities calling for accountability are often themselves (due to their status and privilege) functioning under license or near-license and promoting compulsion, primarily to maintain their status and privilege. This is the dynamic currently destroying public education and functioning under the mask of education reform. This is the type of accountability that I and almost all educators reject. DiCarlo (2012b) highlights this pervasive misuse of "accountability":

> In the context of a high-stakes accountability system—e.g., a school/district rating system with severe consequences for poor grades—this might be a big problem. It represents the conflation of student and school performance, which means that you will be punishing schools—sometimes severely, as in closure—based on ratings that may be largely a function of factors, such as students' backgrounds, that are out of their control.
>
> This is the exact opposite of what an accountability system is supposed to do. (See also, Di Carlo, 2012a, n.p.)

Educators are essential to fulfilling the promise of universal public education as a commitment to democracy, but not the way corporate reformers claim and never as the result of compulsion.

Public education needs to honor student and teacher autonomy as the only context for accountability that can build democracy, human agency, and political voice. Otherwise, our schools will continue to perpetuate the inequity of license and compulsion that has created the Corporate States of America—the land of the 1% practicing their license on the backs the 99%'s compulsion.

THE BULLY POLITICS OF EDUCATION REFORM[5]

America has bred the bully tactic of vigilantism in the sanctified Petri dish of law (Stand Your Ground), and the result is the person with the gun is the law while the victim's innocence is extinguished along with the person's life (Giroux, 2012). To mask the bully culture of the United States, bullying is confronted as a school-based problem among children (note the distraction of the R rating in the documentary on bullying addressed by Nancy Flanagan, 2012, and Douglas Storm, 2012). Yet, the ruling class who denounces bullying among children are themselves bullies. Thus, there is no surprise that the current education reform movement is characterized by bully politics, used as a shield to hide the reformers' lack of credibility.

In the mid-1800s, public education was called a "'dragon ... devouring the hope of the country as well as religion. [It dispenses] 'Socialism, Red Republicanism, Universalism, Infidelity, Deism, Atheism, and Pantheism—anything, everything, except religion and patriotism,'" explains Jacoby (2004, pp. 257–258). Bullying public education has deep roots, at least reaching back to the threat of universal public schooling detracting from the Catholic church's control of education in the 19th century.

Throughout the first half of the 20th century, the bullying of public schools continued, including a pattern of judging the quality of our public schools based on drop-out rates that persists to this day ("Get adjusted," 1947). We must recognize that the demonizing of public schools and the condemnation of school quality are the way people view, talk about, and understand schools in the U.S. popular discourse, but this historical badgering of schools has evolved recently into a more direct and personal attack on teachers. While it appears we cringe when children bully each other, we have no qualms about inexpert, inexperienced, and self-proclaimed education reformers bullying an entire profession.

The bullying can be witnessed in the discourse coming from Secretary Duncan, former-chancellor Rhee, and billionaire-reformer Gates, yet one of the most corrosive and powerful dynamics embracing bully politics is the rise of self-appointed think-tank entities claiming to evaluate and rank teacher education programs. A key player in bully politics is the National Council on Teacher Quality (NCTQ).

Broadly, NCTQ represents the rise of think tanks (Welner, Hinchey, Molnar, & Weltzman, 2010) and the ability of those think tanks to mask their ideologies (Yettick, 2009) while receiving disproportionate and unchallenged support from the media (Molnar, 2001). Think tanks have adopted the format and pose of scholarship, producing well-crafted documents (often easily accessed PDFs) filled with citations and language that frame ideology as "fair and balanced" conclusions drawn from the evidence. Nothing could be farther from the truth for NCTQ (Cody, 2012a; Hassard, 2012; Ravitch, 2012).

NCTQ grew out of the Thomas B. Fordham Foundation and the Education Leaders Council (ELC), associated with the Center for Education Reform, securing in the process unsolicited federal funds (over $9 million under George W. Bush [People for the American Way, 2003]). In short, NCTQ is not an unbiased and scholarly enterprise to evaluate and reform teacher education. NCTQ is a neoliberal, agenda-driven think tank determined to marginalize and discredit teacher education in order to promote a wide range of market-based ideologies related specifically to public education. Further, and powerfully connected to the bully politics of NCTQ, is the association between NCTQ and *U.S. News & World Report.* In other words, NCTQ lacks educational and scholarly credentials and credibility, but gains its influence and power through direct and indirect endorsements from government, the media, and entrepreneurs (re: Gates Foundation and funding).

NCTQ issued one report on student teaching (Greenberg, Pomerance, & Walsh, 2011), and released a self-proclaimed national review of teacher preparation programs in the fall of 2012. How, then, is this bully politics?

In their report process, NCTQ contacts departments and colleges of education with a simple but blunt request: Cooperate with us or we'll evaluate you however we can and publish our report regardless: "As the debate raged, NCTQ told the dissenters that they would be rated whether they agreed or not, and if they didn't cooperate, they would get a zero" (Ravitch, 2012). These requests demand extensive data from the departments and colleges and then subject these programs to standards and expectations designed by NCTQ completely decontextualized from the departments and colleges being evaluated against those standards (Hassard, 2012). The basis for NCTQ's evaluations has not been vetted by educators for being credible or valid. A department or college could very well be rated high or low and that rating mean little since the department or college may or may not consider the criteria of any value.

In fact, the first report by NCTQ has been reviewed (most think tank reports receive tremendous and uncritical media coverage without review, and when reviewed, those reviews tend to receive almost no media coverage), confirming that NCTQ produces biased and careless work. Benner's (2012) review concludes, in part:

The NCTQ review of student teaching is based upon the assumption that it is not only possible, but also worthwhile and informative to isolate student teaching from the totality of a teacher preparation program. This notion is in direct conflict with the perspective that effective teacher education programs avoid the isolation of pedagogy and classroom management content, offering such knowledge and skills within a learning environment centered upon a clinical experience.

The sample of programs cannot be characterized as representative based on any statistical standard or recognized sampling technique. . . .

Limitations in the development and interpretation of the standards, sampling techniques, methodology, and data analysis unfortunately negate any guidance the work could have offered the field and policy makers. However, the fact that this particular review is ill-conceived and poorly executed does not mean that all is well in teacher education. (pp. 2–3)

NCTQ, especially in its relationship with the media, appears more concerned about creating an appearance of failure within teacher education (Ravitch, 2012) than with genuinely addressing in a scholarly way what works, what doesn't work, and how to reform teacher education. The bully depends on status—the weight of appointment, designation—and the threat of wielding that power regardless of credibility. The bully depends on repetition and the volume of claims over the confirmation of evidence or logic.

The current education reform movement is in the hands of bullies and in the vortex of bully politics. Left unchecked, bullying is incredibly effective for the benefit of the bullies and detrimental to everyone else. Calling out the bullies, however, is possible and even relatively simple since the bully has nothing genuine to stand on. In the long run, truth trumps bullying, but truth cannot win in the cloak of silence and inaction.

ACCOUNTABILITY WITHOUT AUTONOMY IS TYRANNY[6]

When educational research reaches the public through the corporate media, the consequences are often dire. Chetty, Friedman, and Rockoff (2011) released "The Long-Term Impacts of Teachers: Teacher Value-Added and Student Outcomes in Adulthood" and immediately *The New York Times* pronounced in "Big Study Links Good Teachers to Lasting Gains":

Elementary- and middle-school teachers who help raise their students' standardized-test scores seem to have a wide-ranging, lasting positive effect on those students' lives beyond academics, including lower teenage-pregnancy rates and greater college matriculation and adult earnings, according to a new study that tracked 2.5 million students over 20 years. (Lowrey, 2012, n.p.)

The simplistic and idealistic headline reflects the central failure of the media in the education reform debate, highlighted by careless reporting such as including this quote from one of the study's researchers: "'The message is to fire people sooner rather than later,' Professor Friedman said" (Lowrey, 2012, n.p.).

This newest attempt to justify value-added models for identifying, rewarding, and retaining high-quality teachers (as well as firing so-called weak teachers) was not yet peer-reviewed at the time of the article, but two close examinations of the study have praised the data while urging caution about conclusions drawn by the researchers and the media response:

> This appropriately cautious conclusion stands in stark contrast with the fact that most states have already decided to do so. It also indicates that those using the results of this paper to argue forcefully for specific policies are drawing unsupported conclusions from otherwise very important empirical findings. (Di Carlo, 2012c, n.p.)

And:

> These are interesting findings.... But these findings cannot be immediately translated into what the headlines have suggested—that immediate use of value-added metrics to reshape the teacher workforce can lift the economy, and increase wages across the board! The headlines and media spin have been dreadfully overstated and deceptive. Other headlines and editorial commentary have been simply ignorant and irresponsible. (Baker, 2012, n.p.)

Despite these strong and careful cautions, Goldstein (2012) followed the *NYT* article with a praising piece in *The Nation* that links to Di Carlo's work, but on balance accepts claims by Chetty et al. (2011), asking: "Why not use value-added to help identify the most effective teachers, but then require these professionals to mentor their peers in order to earn higher pay?" (n.p.). Journalists, politicians, bureaucrats, and researchers are nearly uniform in failing to confront the central flaw in pursuing data as the holy grail of identifying and rewarding high-quality teachers. The persistent positive response to Chetty, Friedman, and Rockoff's study doesn't prove VAM works, but does reveal that there is little hope we'll make any good decisions about teachers and schools any time soon.

Ten years into the federalized accountability era designated as NCLB, one fact of education is rarely mentioned (except by people who do spend and have spent their lives actually teaching children day in and day out): Since 1983's *A Nation at Risk*, and intensified under NCLB, teachers have systematically been deprofessionalized, forced by the weight of policy and bureaucracy to implement standards they did not create, to prepare students for tests they did not create (and cannot review, and likely do not support), and to be held accountable for policies and outcomes that are not within their control.

And this is the fact of the accountability era that has evolved from holding students accountable for test scores in the beginning to the more recent call to hold teachers accountable because, as media pundits claim, teachers and their protective unions are all that is wrong with the U.S., at least according to Mort Zuckerman on CNN (Heather, 2012):

> I think there are huge problems in this country and a lot of it, in my judgment, stems *not from capitalism* [emphasis added] but from the government. . . .
>
> Because the education is a government function. If there ever was a public function in this country from the days it started, it's public education and we've done a lousy job. Part of it is frankly because we have lousy teachers.
>
> Part of the reason we have lousy teachers is we have teachers union that say won't deal with those issues. So there are lots of reasons why education is not being properly handled in this country. (n.p.)

If U.S. public education is failing (and that is at least complicated, if not mostly inaccurate), and if teachers are the source of that failure (and that is demonstrably untrue since out-of-school factors represent at least two-thirds of the influence on measurable student outcomes), let's consider where the accountability should lie.

For the past ten years, teachers have been reduced to mere conduits of policy, curriculum, and tests that have nothing in common with what educators and researchers know to be best practice. Teachers have had little or no autonomy in these decisions and practices. *To hold people accountable for implementing behaviors they do not control or support is, simply put, tyranny—not accountability.*

The teacher quality debate is misguided and misleading among political leaders, corporate elites, and the media in essence because none of them are educators. As a consequence, those without expertise are controlling a debate about reform, and thus they do not allow the debate to focus as it should—not on how to measure teacher quality, but on creating teaching and learning environments that honor the autonomy of children and teachers as professionals within the context of democratic goals.

The ugly truth is that political and corporate elites do not truly respect children (especially children of color, children living in poverty, and children speaking home languages other than English), and they genuinely do not want professional teachers. If children were treated with dignity in our schools and provided the environment they deserve to look critically at the world and if teachers were allowed their professional autonomy and held accountable for only that over which they have control, those children and teachers would likely notice and confront the tremendous inequity being controlled and perpetuated by corporate leaders, corporate politicians, and corporate media—threatening the privilege that is being protected by calls for more testing, more data, and more accountability.

Hasty and misleading reactions to research that confirm the corporate narrative and even moderate pleas for compromise, such as Goldstein's, are equally inexcusable because they all fail to confront that *accountability without autonomy is tyranny*. We are a people tragically enamored with quantitative data to the exclusion of humanity, dignity, and the very ideals we claim to be at center of our country—individual autonomy. And we have sold our souls to capitalism, blind to the reality that the only thing free about the market is that our consumer culture is free of any ethics, free of any commitment to social justice.

Of course teacher quality matters; of course every child deserves a quality teacher. But these conditions cannot be measured and forced to happen as if students and teachers are cogs in a machine. Ultimately, every second spent crunching data about VAM is wasted time; every moment and penny spent on more standards and testing are also wasted. Teaching, learning, and human autonomy are complicated beyond metrics, but they must become the ideals we put into practice. All else is tyranny.

NOTES

1. Originally posted as: Thomas, P. L. (2012, March 14). The cult of personality v. expertise in the education debate. Daily Kos. Retrieved from http://www.dailykos.com/story/2012/03/14/1074277/-The-Cult-of-Personality-v-Expertise-in-the-Education-Debate
2. Originally posted as: Thomas, P. L. (2012, February 22). Education as "politically contested spaces." Daily Kos. Retrieved from http://www.dailykos.com/story/2012/02/22/1067226/-Education-as-Politically-Contested-Spaces-
3. Originally posted as: Thomas, P. L. (2012, April 10). The teaching profession?: Of license, compulsion, and autonomy. Daily Kos. Retrieved from http://www.dailykos.com/story/2012/04/10/1082119/-The-Teaching-Profession-Of-License-Compulsion-and-Autonomy
4. This entire blog post is satire and thus the organization is fictional.
5. Originally posted as: Thomas, P. L. (2012, April 19). The bully politics of education reform. Truthout. Retrieved from http://truth-out.org/news/item/8615-the-bully-politics-of-education-reform
6. Originally posted as: Thomas, P. L. (2012, January 15). Accountability without autonomy is tyranny. Daily Kos. Retrieved from http://www.dailykos.com/story/2012/01/15/1055120/-Accountability-without-Autonomy-Is-Tyranny

REFERENCES

Ayers, W. (2001). *To teach: The journey of a teacher* (2nd ed.) / New York, NY: Teachers College Press.

Baker, B. (2012). Fire first, ask questions later? Comments on recent teacher effectiveness studies. *School Finance 101* [Web log]. Retrieved from http://schoolfinance101.wordpress.com/2012/01/07/fire-first-ask-questions-later-comments-on-recent-teacher-effectiveness-studies/

Beasley, A. H., & Leon, A. (2012, April 11). Miami Marlins manager Ozzie Guillen suspended for 5 games over Fidel Castro comments. *The Miami Herald.* Retrieved from http://www.miamiherald.com/2012/04/11/2739843/miami-marlins-ozzie-guillen-in.html

Benner, S. M. (2012, January 10). *Quality in student teaching: Flawed research leads to unsound recommendations.* Boulder CO: National Education Policy Center. Retrieved from http://nepc.colorado.edu/thinktank/review-student-teaching

Cetta, D. S., producer. (2012, March 11). Khan Academy: The future of education? *60 Minutes.* Retrieved from http://www.cbsnews.com/8301-18560_162-57394905/khan-academy%20-the-future-of-education

Chetty, R., Friedman, J. N., & Rockoff, J. E. (2011, December). *The long-term impacts of teachers: Teacher value-added and student outcomes in adulthood.* Working Paper 17699. Cambridge MA: National Bureau of Economic Research. Retrieved from http://obs.rc.fas.harvard.edu/chetty/value_added.pdf

Cody, A. (2011, November 6). How Bill Gates throws his money around education. The Answer Sheet [Web log]. *The Washington Post.* Retrieved from http://www.washingtonpost.com/blogs/answer-sheet/post/how-bill-gates-throws-his-money-around-in-education/2011/11/06/gIQAXqrasM_blog.html

Cody, A. (2012a, May 25). Payola policy: NCTQ prepares its hit on schools of education. Living in Dialogue [Web log]. *Teacher/Education Week.* Retrieved from http://blogs.edweek.org/teachers/living-in-dialogue/2012/05/payola_policy_nctq_prepares_it.html

Cody, A. (2012b, April 10). Educators Issue VAM Report for Secretary Duncan. Living in Dialogue [Web log]. *Teacher/ Education Week.* Retrieved from http://blogs.edweek.org/teachers/living-in-dialogue/2012/04/educators_issue_vam_report_for.html

Di Carlo, M. (2012a, May 29). We should only hold schools accountable for outcomes they can control. Shanker Blog [Web log]. Retrieved from http://shankerblog.org/?p=5959

Di Carlo, M. (2012b, April 10). There's no one correct way to rate schools. Shanker Blog [Web log]. Retrieved from http://shankerblog.org/?p=5603

Di Carlo, M. (2012c, January 8). The persistence of both teacher effects And misinterpretations of research about them. Shanker Blog [Web log]. Retrieved from http://shankerblog.org/?p=4708

Evans, M. C., & Kane, A. (2011, January 21). Is Michelle Rhee good for students? *American Thinker.* Retrieved from http://www.americanthinker.com/2011/01/is_michelle_rhee_good_for_stud.html

Flanagan, N. (2012, March 31). To see or not to see: Kids, movies, and reality. Teacher in a Strange Land [Web log]. *Teacher/Education Week.* Retrieved from http://blogs.edweek.org/teachers/teacher_in_a_strange_land/2012/03/to_see_or_not_to_see_kids_movies_and_reality.html

Freire, P. (1993). *Pedagogy of the oppressed* (M. B. Ramos, Trans.). New York, NY: Continuum.

People for the American Way. (2003, November 18). *Funding a movement: Department of Education pours millions into groups advocating school vouchers and education privatization.* [Press release]. Washington DC: Author. Retrieved from http://www.pfaw.org/press-releases/2003/11/funding-movement

Get adjusted. (1947, December 15). *Time.* Retrieved from http://www.time.com/time/magazine/article/0,9171,934231,00.html

Giroux, H. (2012, April 2). Hoodie politics: Trayvon Martin and racist violence in post-racial America. *Truthout.* Retrieved from http://truth-out.org/news/item/8203-hoodie-politics-and-the-death-of-trayvon-martin

Golden, J. (2012, June 18). Mystery teacher theatre 2000. Math hombre [Web log]. Retrieved from http://mathhombre.blogspot.com/2012/06/mystery-teacher-theatre-2000.html

Goldsetin, D. (2012, January 15). Teachers matter. Now what? *The Nation.* Retrieved from http://www.thenation.com/blog/165666/teachers-matter-now-what

Greenberg, J., Pomerance, L., & Walsh, K. (2011, July). *Student teaching in the United states.* Washington DC: National Council on Teacher Quality. Retrieved from http://www.nctq.org/edschoolreports/studentteaching/docs/nctq_str_full_report_final.pdf

Jacoby, S. (2004). *Freethinkers: A history of American secularism.* New York, NY: Henry Holt and Company.

Hassard, J. (2012, May 30). NCTQ assessment study flawed. Living in Dialogue [Web log]. *Teacher/Education Week.* Retrieved from http://blogs.edweek.org/teachers/living-in-dialogue/2012/05/jack_hassard_nctq_assessment_s.html

Heather. (2012, January 14). Mort Zuckerman blames lack of upward mobility in America on teachers unions. Video Café [Web log]. Crooks and Liars. Retrieved from http://videocafe.crooksandliars.com/heather/mort-zuckerman-blames-lack-upward-mobility

Kincheloe, J. L. (2005). *Critical pedagogy primer.* New York, NY: Peter Lang.

Kliebard, H. M. (1995). *The struggle for the American curriculum: 1893–1958.* New York, NY: Routledge.

Lowrey, A. (2012, January 6). Big study links good teachers to lasting gains. *The New York Times.* Retrieved from http://www.nytimes.com/2012/01/06/education/big-study-links-good-teachers-to-lasting-gain.html

Merrow, J. (2013, April 11). Michelle Rhee's reign of error. *Taking Note* [Web log]. Retrieved from http://takingnote.learningmatters.tv/?p=6232

Molnar, A. (2001, April 11). *The media and educational research: What we know vs. what the public hears.* Milwaukee, WI: Center for Education Research, Analysis, and Innovation. Retrieved from http://epsl.asu.edu/epru/documents/cerai-01-14.htm

Ravitch, D. (2012, May 24). What is NCTQ (and why you should know). The Answer Sheet [Web log]. *The Washington Post.* Retrieved from http://www.washingtonpost.com/blogs/answer-sheet/post/ravitch-what-is-nctq-and-why-you-should-know/2012/05/23/gJQAg7CrlU_blog.html

Smagorinsky, P. (2012, March 11). Why the Ed Department should be reconceived—or abolished. The Answer Sheet [Web log]. *The Washington Post.* Retrieved from http://www.washingtonpost.com/blogs/answer-sheet/post/why-the-ed-department-should-be-reconceived—or-abolished/2012/03/09/gIQAHfdB5R_blog.html

Storm, D. (2012, March 28). The unexceptional, unsurprising success of America's bully class. The Common Errant [Web log]. Retrieved from http://btownerrant.com/2012/03/28/the-unexceptional-unsurprising-success-of-americas-bully-class/

Strieker, S. (2012, February 22). Teacher: 'Tis a shame (that education has become so political). The Answer Sheet [Web log]. *The Washington Post.* Retrieved from http://www.washingtonpost.com/blogs/answer-sheet/post/teacher-tis-a-shame-that-education-has-become-so-political/2012/02/20/gIQAV6PDSR_blog.html

Thomas, P. L. (2010, November 14). The teaching profession as a service industry. *The Daily Censored.* Retrieved from http://dailycensored.com/2010/11/14/the-teaching-profession-as-a-service-industry/

Thomas, P. L. (2011, March 12). "A question of power": Of accountability and teaching by numbers. *OpEdNews.com.* http://www.opednews.com/articles/A-Question-of-Power—Of-by-Paul-Thomas-110311-481.html

Thomas, P. L. (2012a, March 25). The tragedy of education transformation: Leadership without expertise. *Daily Kos.* Retrieved from http://www.dailykos.com/story/2012/03/25/1077657/-The-Tragedy-of-Education-Tranformation-Leadership-without-Expertise

Thomas, P. L. (2012b, January 23). Universal public education is dead. *Truthout.* Retrieved from http://truth-out.org/index.php?option=com_k2&view=item&id=6245:universal-public-education-is-dead

Welner, K. G., Hinchey, P. H., Molnar, A., & Weltzman, D. (Eds.). (2010). *Think tank research quality: Lessons for policy makers, the media, and the public.* Charlotte, NC: Information Age Publishing.

Yettick, H. (2009). *The research that reaches the public: Who produces the educational research mentioned in the news media?* Boulder, CO and Tempe, AZ: Education and the Public Interest Center & Education Policy Research Unit. Retrieved from http://epicpolicy.org/publication/research-that-reaches

Zais, M. (2012, March 29). Upgrade education accountability. *The Post and Courier.* Retrieved from http://www.postandcourier.com/article/20120329/PC1203/120329637

CHAPTER 15

THE GED AS A COVER FOR SCHOOL PUSHOUT

Eve Tuck
State University of New York–New Paltz

Federal mandates that make funding contingent on test scores (like No Child Left Behind and Race to the Top) put pressure on public schools, especially poor schools, to show improvements in student scores, no matter what it takes. Tests that are required for federal and state funding overshadow all other activities in schools, even though there is little evidence that the tests measure what they purport to measure, and practically no evidence that this kind of testing is pedagogically worthwhile (Elmore, 2006; Rebell & Wolff, 2008; Sunderman & Orfield, 2006).

The original promise for NCLB was not just increased accountability, but also to improve educational opportunities for low-income students and students of color, in order to close the achievement gap. However, the myriad political compromises needed to get the act passed resulted in a law that focuses on accountability, with no features or resources that will bring more educational opportunities to historically underresourced communities (Rebell & Wolff, 2008). Thus, schools that serve low income students and students of color are held accountable for meeting ambitious goals without the resources they need. Further, underresourced schools, for which

Left Behind in the Race to the Top, pages 227–239
Copyright © 2013 by Information Age Publishing
All rights of reproduction in any form reserved.

federal funds comprise a larger percent of their school budget, are more likely to streamline instruction and curriculum in ways that they hope will ensure their viability. Under this schema, poor schools are disproportionately impacted by NCLB (see also Tuck, 2012a, p. 32).

At the same time that NCLB has narrowed and contorted the activities of public schooling, there has been a steady increase in the number of U.S. states that now require students to pass standardized exams in major subjects in addition to passing courses in those subjects. New York State, where I have done my research, is one of 26 states that require what are called exit exams. Indeed, much of what a student does in school is shaped by what will be on her state exams and on her high school exit exams.

Race to the Top (RTTT) is a national educational funding competition that was announced in 2009 by President Barack Obama and Secretary of Education Arne Duncan as part of the American Recovery and Reinvestment Act of 2009. The program is designed to prompt states to adopt standards and assessments that get students ready for college and work, build data systems to trace student performance, recruit and retain effective teachers, and dramatically improve low-performing schools (U.S. Department of Education, 2010). Critics detest the market-based competition component of the program, but also vehemently disagree with other neoliberal assumptions of RTTT, especially the over-reliance on charter schools as a turn-around strategy for schools with persistently low test scores (Lawyers Committee for Civil Rights under Law et. al., 2010). To be eligible for the funding, states must agree to close low-performing schools by turning them into public or privately run charter schools, or turning them over to private management companies. Teachers must be evaluated and retained or released based on test scores, and schools with persistently low scores can see staff and administrators fired. The connection between low-test scores, school restructuring, and the solution of private management is strengthened by RTTP. States including New York had to make changes to state law to enable them to take steps outlined by the program to be eligible for the funds. RTTT represents an expansion of the influence of neoliberal logic on public schooling in the Unites States. The competition requires states to conform to criteria that have no evidentiary grounding, only the pulse of neoliberal common sense. RTTT extends and deepens reliance on test scores to evaluate teacher and principal performance, and ultimately the performance of teacher and principal education programs. It pressures states to adopt the Common Core State Standards, alongside standardized assessments. It advocates charter schools as the solutions to low-performing public schools, and the increased role of private sector companies in managing schools and providing technical assistance. Finally, RTTT requires states to compete against one another (hence, the race) to ensure the precise conditions that enable the expansion of corporate and private influence in public schools (see also Tuck 2012a, p. 33).

For the past several years, I have been looking at how the test-obsessed school climate, fueled by federal mandates and state-level exit exams, gives schools a reason to get rid of students who are disruptive and/or who are unlikely to pass state tests or exit exams (presumably bringing the school-level scores down). Specifically, I have been researching schools' use of the General Educational Development (GED) credential option as a cover for pushing out unwanted students. Much of my empirical research on this and other forms of school pushout has been conducted with youth in New York City, some of whom worked as my co-researchers on the Gateways and Get-aways Project (2006–2008).

This chapter brings together arguments in two of my recent articles on school pushout (Tuck, 2011) and the over-use of the GED (Tuck, 2012b). I bring them together in a way that is hopefully helpful and informative for teachers and soon-to-be teachers, so that you can take notice of how federal mandates and state-level policies can over-determine who is welcome in a classroom, and who isn't; who is thought to be deserving of attention, time, and resources, and who is thought to be just in the way of others; who is a good student, and who is a disruptive student. When the activities of schooling shrink, and everything is meant to lead up to the test, students who are resistant or who will not pass the test can be seen as "difficult," and though many teachers get into the careers wishing to work meaningfully with difficult students, the downward pressure on teachers to raise student scores means they must choose to see those students as distractions. This chapter is not to invite teachers to sidestep their responsibilities to all students, but to explain the terrain and how easy it is to see the very students who inspired many to get in to teaching as the problem. The emphasi in the findings from my research that I discuss in this chapter is not on students as the problem, or on teachers as the problem, but on the policies that strain and constrain the relationships between teachers and students and lead to school pushout.

THE GATEWAYS AND GET-AWAYS PROJECT

I conducted the Gateways and Get-aways Project with a collective of youth researchers between 2006 and 2008. Several of my youth co-researchers identified as having been pushed out of their New York City public schools, and most had felt unwelcome in their schools at some point. We called our group the Collective of Researchers on Educational Disappointment and Desire (CREDD). Together, we designed and implemented a mixed-method participatory action research project on the role of the General Educational Development (GED) credential in New York City public schools, and the use of the GED option by urban youth as both a gateway to higher education and full employment and as a get-away from inadequate high schools (see also Tuck et al., 2008; Tuck, 2009a, in which the process of forming this collective, designing our study, and collecting our data is described in detail). Our study also explored the ways that the GED option was used by students and school personnel as a way to legitimize school pushout. The Gateways and Get-aways Project involved semi-structured individual interviews (n=35), focus groups (n=9, with 95 youth), and a questionnaire (n=476) with New York City youth. To participate in our study, youth needed to be 14–22 years of age, be residents of New York City, and be current or former students in New York City public high schools. The larger study also involved cold calls to college admissions officers and employers (n=80), and a variety of other innovative secondary methods constructed to engage out-of-school youth (see Tuck, 2012a, for a discussion of the larger study). Data reported in this chapter are from our one-hour semistructured individual interviews (n=35) and focus groups (nine focus groups, n=95) with youth GED earners and seekers.

Youth Participatory Action Research

The Gateways and Get-aways Project was conducted as youth participatory action research (PAR) that positioned pushed-out youth and young GED earners as researchers and experts on their own lives. These youth were my co-researchers and co-designers in this study, not my research subjects. We developed the research questions, designed the study, collected the data, analyzed our data, and determined our findings collaboratively (see also Tuck et al., 2008, Tuck, 2009b).

Participatory action research has emerged from many diverse peoples and distinct places all over the globe. Rather than a set of methods, PAR is best described as an ethic—as a set of beliefs about knowledge, where it comes from, and how knowledge is validated and strengthened (Fine, 2008). PAR aims to "return to the people the legitimacy of the knowledge they are capable of producing through their own verification systems...as a guide to their own action" (Fals-Borda & Rahman, 1991, p. 15). Elsewhere, my co-researchers and I have discussed the design and implementation of our study (Tuck et al., 2008; Tuck, 2009a); this chapter focuses on our findings.

SCHOOL PUSHOUT

Students who have been pressured to leave by factors inside their schools describe their schools as places that no one wants to be.[1] My co-researchers and I have utilized the term pushout throughout our work to describe the experiences of youth who have been pressured to leave school by people or factors inside school, such as disrespectful treatment from teachers and other school personnel, violence among students, arbitrary school rules, and the institutional pressures of high-stakes testing. Study participant Pilar, a youth GED earner in her thirties at the time of her interview, asserted this caveat to our definition of pushout:

> Sometimes we don't make the best choices in life. It's not just school that pushed me out. The structure of my school was chaotic. It was like, no. I couldn't get help and I sought help. You just get no support. Yes, ultimately, you are pushed out. If by pushed out you mean pushed out by more than just the school.

As I have indicated, our collective's use of the term pushout describes those components inside schools that detain and derail students' secondary school completion. However, as Pilar argues, outside forces compound students' needs, and in those times of crisis the lack of support afforded by school policies and practices is glaring. In a focus group, Gabriel told us,

> High school is fine for kids who are fine in their lives, but if there is anything hard going on in someone's life, school becomes very difficult. When things are hard in your life and you're not excelling academically, it's easy to be like, "This is stupid, I don't need to be here." And for adults in the school to feel the same way.

Interview participant Sophia told us, "I had this teacher who always told me 'Quit wasting my time, quit wasting my time.' One day, it came to me: This was a waste of *all* of our time."

In our interviews, in our focus groups, young people again and again taught us the following three things: (1) Some schools implicitly teach students they are not cut out for school; (2) students struggle to sustain their schooling in spaces that no one seems to want to be; and (3) poor students, students of color, and undocumented students are especially unwelcome in some schools. Miguel told us, "They didn't want *anybody* there. My high school was the *worst.*"

Hsaio, a GED instructor, told us about the experiences of undocumented youth who ended up at the doors of her GED program.

> Some of the students [when they come to the U.S.] they are turning 19 or 20. Sometimes 18. The schools, they refuse to take them. It's not just one case, it's like 10 different cases every month. They've been deferred. They've been pushed out of school and told go to [a] GED [program]. They don't even provide them a place they could contact. So, sometimes [the schools] use [the immigrant students'] English skills as an excuse. They say go and take the GED because they require less of this language than demanded in a school.

Many youth told us that their schools made them question if they were really cut out for learning, some telling us that they felt pushed out of school as early as 5th and 7th grade. Benji told us, "I walked [in the building] and I thought, 'No way, not me.' I mean, I knew right away that that place was not for me in the first place." Amaris observed, "I felt like there was no need for me to be there. They already had their minds set up that I was just going to continue doing what I had been doing. They weren't going to waste their time with me." Tyrone, however, insisted, "It's not that we aren't cut out for school, we don't want to be in school because we don't like it. If they [pushed-out youth] were in a different school, they would stay. If they were in a different environment, they would stay. That's not the case, so they leave."

Youth in our study described to us the ways in which they were acutely aware of the ironies of schooling—often gaps between expressed aims and values of the school and the realities of schooling encounters—and this awareness, compounded by their widely held connections between success in schooling and intelligence and worthiness, made each ongoing irony more and more humiliating. Unresolved ironies of schooling stab at students' experiences of themselves as intelligent enough or worthy enough to do well in school. These experiences accumulate into complete and pervasive, highly personalized feelings of being unwelcome. We asked interview participant Arimme, "Was there a specific time that you felt unwelcome?" She told us:

> It was so many times. It is hard to just pinpoint one of them. Most of the times what I would do is just get a pass to the bathroom and leave. The first exit I see, I'm out the door. They don't want me to be here. Here I am and you're acting like I'm invisible, and you're only paying attention to certain individuals in the class. Well, I'm going to get out of here, I'm getting the hell out of here. I'm not going to waste my time.

The feeling of unwelcoming in schools has been described to us by our participants as imprecise yet omnipresent. Youth describe it as all-encompassing but, as in Arimme's words above, hard to pinpoint. *Un*welcome, *un*wanted, *in*hospitable—youth in our study experienced schooling in ways that were largely marked by what was missing—yet these words barely hint at the aggression that youth reported. These are not mere inadvertent slights, but what amounts to systematic unwelcoming and contempt, way-paved by acute inflexibility and indifference.

Students expressed frustration about the many hypocrisies they observed in their schools. One frequently cited hypocrisy concerned what our participants observed as teachers' reluctance to educate all students. Miguel told us, "When I asked for help, they sucked their teeth. That's their job. Even if you are to ask a bunch of times, that's their job."

Almost half of our interview participants indicated that they believed that some school personnel were "only there to get paid." Every single one of the participants who made this assessment was careful to emphasize that this attitude was not held by all, but only some school personnel. However, the impact of these sentiments was invasive, serving to undermine compelling reasons for students to continue to attend school. The hypocrisy of being required to attend (and punished for not attending) when school personnel also don't seem to want to be there insulted youth and made their attempts toward school completion seem futile.

Another hypocrisy identified by our youth participants was the persistent narrative of meritocracy, despite the obvious falseness of this narrative. Almost all of our participants expressed frustration in the largely unspoken, grotesquely imbalanced playing field between well-funded and underfunded schools. In one focus group, Sandra passionately explained, "It's not fair that poor students go to poor schools."

In an interview, Wilson told us, "If you know the deck is stacked against you a lot of times you just stop playing the game." Several youth in our interviews described this stacked deck by citing funding per student in wealthy school districts such as nearby Nassau, Suffolk, and Westchester counties, compared to funding per student in New York City. Youth observed the absurdity of the prospect of schooling as the great equalizer in such unequal circumstances. Youth participants in one focus group called this the "Anybody can get into Harvard denial," and cited it as one of the persistent roots of school pushout.

Many of the youth participants in our study theorized the role of testing and their former schools' over-reliance on testing as influential in their pushout experiences. They framed the problem of testing in two ways. The first had to do with the pressure to pass the New York Regents exit exams and the fallout when students don't pass the exams. For example, many youth reported that teachers, guidance counselors, deans, and other administrators explicitly told them, "You're not going to pass this test, why bother [taking it again/staying in school]?" The second way youth framed the problem of testing dealt with the ways in which testing has narrowed and over-determined curricula. These two elements work in combination with the steep consequences and merit-based rewards of testing for schools creating a perfect storm-like climate for school pushout (see also Rebell & Wolfe, 2008).

A final humiliating irony has to do with youths' awareness of the number of their classmates exiting school before graduation while at the same time being squeezed into over-crowded classrooms. In a focus group, Jessica posed the phenomenon in this way: "I know it wasn't all honors kids dropping out, so why do they got no one in their classes and I got everyone in mine [sic]?" There are several betrayals at work here. First, youth see mass numbers of students exiting their schools; yet their schools continue as if nothing has occurred, as if those students had merely fallen through the cracks. Then, the courses in which they are supposed to get the help they need to move through their schooling are over-crowded and chaotic. Finally, though those who do not complete school are in the numeric majority of New York City youth, young people who have this experience are left feeling isolated, and like they are the aberrant ones.

MISUSE OF THE GED OPTION BY PUBLIC SCHOOLS

More than half of states in the U.S. use exit exams to determine eligibility for public secondary school graduation.[2] In states that have adopted exit exams of advanced skills, schools share the following characteristics:

- Higher numbers of low-performing students being retained in grade before key testing years
- Higher numbers of low-performing students being suspended before testing days, expelled from school before tests, or reclassified in ways that make students exempt from tests
- Higher numbers of students who have limited access to untested academic subjects, such as art, music, science, social studies, and physical education
- Higher numbers of students whose teachers limit instruction to material most likely to appear on the tests, with more hours spent memorizing and drilling
- Higher numbers of teachers who leave public school teaching
- Higher incidences of cheating by teachers and school personnel to increase test scores (Amrein & Berliner, 2003, p. 32)

Sipple, Killeen, and Monk (2004) conducted a qualitative study that sought to understand the impacts of state-level mandatory exit exam policy and the "alternative outcomes that may serve as a pressure release on the system," (p. 144) in a diverse sample of school districts in New York State. The study found that school districts frequently aligned curriculum to Regents exams, and that some districts used the generation of individualized education plans (IEPs—the documents that designate students as requiring special education) as a strategy for differentiating Regents testing modifications. Most important for this discussion,

> Four of the five superintendents and an array of high school principals shared a 'strategy' of shifting students on the verge of dropping out to GED programs. This practice allows districts to report that the student did not drop

out. The end result is that the state dropout data does not capture transfers to GED or alternative schools. To be counted as a dropout, districts need to completely lose track of a student. This was commonly discussed as students "disappearing"... While no respondent admitted to pushing students toward this path, several administrators across the districts made certain the students understood their options and that earning a GED was one. Several administrators stated, earning the GED "is better than nothing." One Deputy Superintendent noted that it was common "to put a student in a car and drive him downtown" to the GED center. (Sipple et al., 2004, p. 159)

All of the districts in the study used the GED option to balance the pressures of keeping dropout rates down, increasing graduation rates, keeping school tax burdens low, and increasing rates of students securing a Regents diploma. The GED option was the only option for districts trying to meet competing demands with limited resources. The GED provided a way for some students to disappear. Administrators and school personnel literally delivered students to GED centers, and one opened an in-house GED program when nearby GED centers were too full. The study yields windows to the practices that push students out of high school toward the GED from the perspectives of school personnel. These accounts confirm what youth told us in our study.

The youth we interviewed compared the value of the GED to the value of a high school diploma with complexity; their comparisons were full of nuance and context. Most felt that the GED is indeed not equivalent to a high school diploma, but that seemed less important when a high school diploma was structurally out of reach. Asia confessed that prior to being pushed out of school, she had a disparaging view on GED earners. "I laughed [at GED earners and seekers], 'You dummy. You can't go through high school,' and once I was sitting in a classroom getting my GED I was like, 'How could you say that to somebody? How could you make them feel bad like that?'"

Sophia told us that the GED is seen as "less than a diploma. You're a little—not dumb—but you're not as smart as the average. Even though they say that the GED test is harder." To this point Jovanne observed, "I think they're sending the wrong message because they say is the GED is fast, easy, get out of school, go to college. But that's not what it's about. They should let you know that... the GED is not for everybody just like high school is not for everybody."

Even in the stigmatized context of the GED, youth reported that they were explicitly advised by school personnel to get the GED because it would serve, as in Tyrone's telling, as "an alternative; no, they said an equivalency to high school. I [would have] an equivalency so I could be just as good as a high school diploma [earner]. But it is not true."

Most of our interview participants first learned about the GED from a dean, principal, teacher, or guidance counselor. In these cases, school personnel assured youth that GED is an alternative to a high school diploma that would afford them the same options as a diploma. Note that the title of the GED certificate awarded in New York State is the "New York State High School Equivalency Diploma."

In our interviews with youth GED earners and seekers, we learned that some school advisors also underplayed the difficulty of the exam procedures and the exam itself. At the time that they left school to pursue a GED, many young people were unaware that youth fifteen and younger are not eligible to take the exams in New York State. Sixteen-year-old youth can only take the exams if they are joining the military, or if they have completed a GED preparation program *and* have reached the compulsory school attendance age (seventeen in New York City.) Seventeen- and eighteen-year-old youth also need to show documentation demonstrating that they are in State institutions like hospitals or prisons, are a member of a graduating class that has already graduated, or it has been more than one year since officially leaving school, among other scenarios. Jordan told us,

> Not for nothing, taking your GED is not that easy. [It's not] like taking your [driver's] license; all you got to do is go to the DMV, stand on line for a million hours, take a primary, six months later come back, take the road test, and you got your license. But to get your GED, it's a whole big spectacle, and . . . it's not like they give it every week. It's only specific days of the year that they give it in specific locations throughout the five boroughs.

Pilar confirmed other youths' experiences of the content on the battery of tests as difficult:

> A lot of it is very technical. Things that you learn in high school, I guess, that I clearly didn't remember. . . . I remember the math being totally hard. Other things, I hustled a lot of it. It was a lot of logic and . . . trick questions. A lot of things about people, necessarily, quote unquote leaders of America. . . . Social studies, things like that. Science, biology of the body.

In interviews, we asked GED instructors (n=10) if they think the GED is an equivalent alternative to the high school diploma. All of the GED instructors told us that in their views, the GED is not an equivalent credential to a high school diploma. Yet, in a textured response, Kersha observed that not all high school diplomas are equivalent either:

> But do I think all high school diplomas are equal to one another? No. I think it depends on the quality of the education received at any place. Obviously, the GED is going to suffer a little bit, because like I said before there isn't a deep exploration. That could be challenging depending on how long the student goes to the preparation classes and how much the instructor is invested in moving beyond the actual test. Maybe that class and the preparation they

get there could mirror the information that they would receive in a low-performing school where the principal and teachers don't care but the students do. The kids are just in class doing worksheets all day. Which happens. No, I don't equate them, but I do not equate all high school diplomas either.

CONCLUSION

From my research, I have identified a number of school conditions that work together to produce school pushout (Tuck, 2012a).

The key conditions of school pushout:

- Passing the tests has replaced prior, more compelling motivations for high-quality curriculum and instruction.
- Zero-tolerance policies have replaced prior, more tailored and responsive school discipline practices.
- Teachers, administrators, and other school personnel are under so much pressure to raise scores that they are tempted to cheat on high-stakes tests.
- Rather than being seen as central to goals of improving learning, underperforming students are seen as in the way and as a drag on the potential success of other students.
- It is generally believed by most teachers, administrators, other school personnel, and students that the school would benefit by getting rid of students who don't attend classes regularly, don't get good grades, or don't pass state exams.
- Graduating class sizes shrink over the course of secondary schooling, but the numbers of missing students seem to go unrecognized.
- Students are explicitly advised to seek a GED, told that it is equivalent to a high school diploma but that is easier and more immediate to attain.[3]

It is important to note that schools that push out students push out teachers, too. At the same time that federal, state, and local policies work in concert to push students out before graduation, we face a national crisis in teacher attrition. Schools with high turnover rely more on short and long-term substitutes and unprepared educators, and they frequently need to spend moneys that could have gone to school improvement on replacing teachers. It is important, conceptually and strategically, to tie teacher well-being to student well-being. The proliferation of test-based accountability policies has resulted in many scenarios in which teachers and communities find themselves at odds with one another. Once it becomes evident that it is the very same conditions that produce school pushout that produce high teacher attrition, it also becomes evident that teachers, students, and communities must work together to challenge the dominant neoliberal narratives of test supremacy. For such a coalition to work, educators must also stop the blame game of putting the responsibility of low-school performance on parents. Teachers frequently explain low test scores by way of observing an overall change in "quality of families" (Dodson, 2009, p. 93), without recognizing how erosions of wages and working conditions for low-wage workers in recent decades can impact parents' participation in their children's schooling. Communities and teachers must be aware of the ways in which the current preoccupation with test scores pits them against each other and gets in the way of securing the quality of schooling that both parties desire (Tuck, 2012a).

As many lessons as we learned about the policies and practices inside schools that push youth out, my co-researchers and I also learned about the power of relationships. As teachers, we have a responsibility to all of our students, and we must interrogate the ways in which policy contexts cast some students as difficult, or the problem. It is these policies, not the students, that we must push out.

NOTES

1. Some of the discussions in this section have been published in Tuck (2011).
2. Some discussions in this section have been published in Tuck, E. (2012b).
3. In 2011, the American Council of Education, administrator of the GED from its inception, announced that it has formed a for-profit company with Pearson to administer the GED, starting in 2014. As a result, several states including New York have begun to pursue alternative certification models because the increased costs of the new GED will be exclusionary to many people seeking the credential.

REFERENCES

Amrein, A. L., & Berliner, D. C. (2003). The testing divide: New research on the intended and unintended impact of high stakes testing. Peer Review, 6(2), 31–32.

Dodson, L. (2009). The moral underground: How ordinary Americans subvert an unfair economy. New York: The New Press.

Fals-Borda, O., & Rahman, A. (1991). Action and knowledge: Breaking the monopoly with participatory action research. New York, NY: The Apex Press

Fine, M. (2008). An epilogue, of sorts. In J. Cammarota & M. Fine (Eds.), Revolutionizing education: Youth participatory action research in motion (pp. 213–234). New York, NY: Routledge.

Elmore, R. (2006, November). The problem of capacity in the (re)design of educational accountability systems. Paper presented at the Equity Symposium, Examining America's Commitment to Closing Achievement Gaps—NCLB and Its Alternatives, Teachers College, New York, NY.

Lawyers Committee for Civil Rights Under Law, et al. (2010). Framework for providing all students an opportunity to learn through reauthorization of the Elementary and Secondary Education Act. [Self-published policy brief]. Retrieved from https://docs.google.com/fileview?id=0B36JWPh1Vfr7OTc3ZWI 0NDctODVlMC00N2I2LWExNmItZmIyZGEzY2E5Yzlm&hl=en&authkey=CN G2pP4E&pli=1

Rebell. M. A., & Wolff, J. R. (2008). Moving every child ahead: From NCLB hype to meaningful educational opportunity. New York, NY: Teachers College Press.

Sipple, J. W., Killeen, K., & Monk, D. H. (2004). Adoption and adaptation: School district responses to state imposed learning and graduation requirements. Educational Evaluation and Policy Analysis, 26(2), 143–168.

Sunderman, G. L., & Orfield, G. (2006, September). Domesticating a revolution: No Child Left Behind reforms and state administrative response. [Policy report]. Cambridge, MA: The Civil Rights Project.

Tuck, E. (2009a). Theorizing back: An approach to participatory policy analysis. In J. Anyon, M. Dumas, D. Linville, K. Nolan, M. Perez, E. Tuck, & J. Weiss (Eds.), Theory and educational research: Toward critical social explanation (pp. 111–130). New York, NY: Routledge.

Tuck, E. (2009b). Re-visioning action: Participatory action research and Indigenous theories of change. Urban Review, 41(1), 47–65.

Tuck, E. (2011). Humiliating ironies and dangerous dignities: A dialectic of school pushout. International Journal of Qualitative Studies in Education, 25(7), 817–827.

Tuck, E. (2012a). Urban youth and school pushout: Gateways, get-aways, and the GED. New York, NY: Routledge.

Tuck, E. (2012b). Repatriating the GED: Urban youth and the alternative to a high school diploma. The High School Journal, 95(4), 4–18.

Tuck, E., Allen, J., Bacha, M., Morales, A., Quinter, S., Thompson, J. & Tuck, M. (2008). PAR praxes for now and future change: The collective of researchers on educational disappointment and desire. In J. Cammarota & M. Fine (Eds.), Revolutionizing education: Youth participatory action research in motion (pp. 49–83). New York, NY: Routledge.

United States Department of Education. (2010, August 24). Nine states and the District of Columbia win second round of Race to the Top grants. [U.S. Department of Education press release]. Retrieved from http://www.ed.gov/news/press-releases/nine-states-and-district-columbia-win-second-round-race-top-grants

PART IV

RESISTANCE:
OPTING OUT AND HOPE FOR CHANGE

CHAPTER 16

SEE SOMETHING, SAY SOMETHING

Collective Resistance to Teacher Education Reform

Barbara Madeloni
University of Massachusetts—Amherst

When I consider all that has been left behind in the race of corporate education reform, I see devastation at all levels. At the macro level, I see the loss of the very idea of the public good and democratic education, as neoliberal reformers tout the market as the "cure" for what they have successfully labeled a crisis in education (Lipman, 2004, 2011; Saltman, 2007; Watkins, 2011). At the micro level, I see the dull eyes of students who have been subject to high-control, high-stakes testing environments, and the tears of panic and anxiety from teachers trying to meet data-driven objectives. For these students and teachers, the possibilities for creative, meaningful teaching and learning are being left behind with each test-preparation lesson. As a teacher educator in a university-based teacher education program, I am

Left Behind in the Race to the Top, pages 243–256

witness to and participant in high-surveillance, standardized accountability regimes being imposed on our practice.

As mandates for accountability mount, I ask myself questions about compliance, complicity, and collaboration in the face of the undoing of teacher education and the public university. Daily, I make choices that either confirm or deny my values and beliefs. I face these choices within two competing fears. One is that I will lose my job. The other is that I will lose my soul. This is the story of my struggle to choose between those fears, a struggle all educators of conscience face under the profit-driven, privatizing, dehumanizing neoliberal regime that is the current socioeconomic and political reality.

THE CHOICE

I am a teacher educator in the secondary teacher education program at a public university in the northeast. I work with undergraduate and graduate students who are preparing to become teachers of English language arts, history, mathematics, and the sciences. Before entering higher education, I taught English in high school. As an educator, I am committed to social justice and critical pedagogy. By this, I mean that I design courses that invite knowledge and critique of the social contexts of teaching and learning. Education, for me, is about creating spaces for dialogue, for understanding and critiquing power, and for finding and using our voices as members of a community to create a more just and democratic world.

On September 17, 2011, Occupy Wall Street took up residence in Zucotti Park. I visited Liberty Plaza, marched, stood at the barricades face to face with policemen in riot gear, and brought these experiences and the challenges they presented back into my classroom. We discussed the growing inequality in the United States, the encroachment of private profiteers into public education, and the implications these had for us as educators and citizens. Many of the students were observing or teaching in districts with high rates of poverty and foreclosures, where K–12 students were subject to scripted curriculum and test preparation. We discussed how the political-economic world entered the classroom, what we could do within the context of our classrooms to make spaces for change, what were our broader obligations to speak out, and what were the risks and possibilities attendant to speaking out.

Also in the fall of 2011, I learned that Stanford University had contracted with Pearson Inc., a for-profit company and the largest assessment corporation in North America, to deliver and score the Teacher Performance Assessment (TPA), and that the University of Massachusetts Amherst, where I worked at the time, had agreed that student teachers would participate in the Stanford-Pearson field test of this assessment. The TPA, an outgrowth of the California Performance Assessment for Teaching and, before that, the assessment for the National Board Certification for Teachers (American Association of Colleges of Teacher Education, 2012), was being developed as a potential national assessment of student teachers. Depending upon individual state decisions, it would be used as the final high-stakes assessment of program completion or as a measure of the effectiveness of teacher education programs. In the 2011–2012 academic year it was being piloted in 20 states; by the spring, six of those states had signed on for accelerated implementation and would soon be requiring the TPA as part of the student teaching assessment (Baker, 2012).

I was aware of and concerned about the limitations of the TPA prior to learning of Pearson's involvement. I had worked with the TPA two years before, when three students agreed to be part of a mini-pilot being run within the context of a course offered by a colleague. The next year, lecturers at the university were scheduled to attend two-day sessions in order to be "calibrated" to score the TPA's numerous rubrics. (Most of us were waylaid by an ice storm and never made it. We were subsequently calibrated by webinar.) Though I had voiced concerns about its rigidity, its narrowing of the discourse about teaching and learning, and its dangerous pretense of objectivity, I had been able to avoid letting the TPA dominate the student teaching seminar in the spring of 2010, when we scored it locally with calibrated doctoral candidate supervisors. In the student teaching seminar, I told the student teachers: "The scores do not matter, it is your thinking that matters." But now, since assessments would be outsourced to a publicly traded for-profit company where student work would be viewed and scored by anonymous scorers hired on a piecework basis ($75 per scored TPA, which Pearson (2012) suggests takes two hours to score), I had to make a much more difficult decision. To comply was to participate directly in the privatization of teacher education and the narrowing of its curriculum. I found myself articulating an activist practice within my courses, excited about the revolutionary potential of Occupy Wall Street, while being told to participate in the privatization of teacher education. To resist meant risking my job. To be compliant meant abandoning what mattered most to me about teaching: its humanity. I chose to support student teachers is demanding the opportunity to opt in or out of the field test and publicized their hard-won victory by contacting the *New York Times*. This is the story of how and why I made that choice, and its ramifications.

TROUBLED BY THE TPA AND PEARSON

The TPA was a juggernaut. The Teacher Performance Assessment Consortium, which was leading the field test, announced each new "accelerated" state as a celebration. When I posted questions about the advisability of the TPA and informed consent from students on the Teacher Performance Assessment Consortium blog, they were taken down within minutes. Comments were only reposted when other commentators objected. Locally, we were denied meetings with administration to discuss our concerns. The experience was not of an assessment system under careful study, but of a product and systems test for Pearson and Stanford. After the students' opting out was publicized by Education Radio (2012) and in *The New York Times* (Winerip, 2012), we heard from faculty and students nationally who objected to the TPA but were afraid to speak out. These writers, both faculty and student teachers, spoke of the shared experience that this instrument had been foisted upon them with no opportunity to participate in decision making. Some of the local concerns were as follows:

Faculty Concerns

Faculty members in the secondary teacher education program were never asked if they wanted to participate in the field test. Because our program has lecturers doing the bulk of the practicum oversight, tenure line faculty had little knowledge or experience with the TPA. In the two years leading up to the Pearson field test, lecturers were told to be calibrated, to calibrate supervisors, and to be certain the student work was scored, but tenure line faculty were not calibrated, nor did they score TPAs. That lecturers, contract faculty, were responsible for carrying out the implementation of the TPA is critical. Due to our employment vulnerability, the expectation was that we would do as we were told. As well, in a system as hierarchal as ours, there was an assumption that our academic freedom was not as free, that we would or should be more willing than tenure line faculty to accept the imposition of this assessment on our course syllabi. However, though most tenure line faculty were not themselves familiar with the TPA, they were alert to concerns about any externally imposed assessment, uncomfortable with the involvement of Pearson, and troubled about issues of informed consent for the field test. We were determined to find out how the assessment data collected during the field test were to be used and expressed our concerns to the school administration that students be given informed consent and the opportunity to opt in or out of the field test.

Student Concerns

Student teachers expressed their concerns that they were supposed to produce work about the personal experience of learning to teach to send to an anonymous scorer working as contract labor for a private corporation. The involvement of Pearson was critical. Many of the students were alert to the increasing corporatization of public education. Many were astonished at the expectation to participate in what they experienced as a significant breech of their privacy and that of the students in their classrooms. They were troubled by how the TPA impacted their development and by the potential high stakes aspect of the assessment. As they came to work with the TPA itself, their concerns extended to it as an assessment.

The Teacher Performance Assessment, in the iteration we were given, consists of four tasks. For each task, planning, instruction, assessment, and analyzing teaching, student teachers are instructed to answer a series of questions. For the instruction task, students are told to videotape themselves teaching and submit two continuous 8–10 minutes clips that would show evidence of them having met criteria as delineated in rubrics. The five scale rubrics are explicit in their performance expectations. The TPA came emblazoned with the Pearson logo. Instructors were given specific guidelines about how we are to use the TPA in our courses and what constituted appropriate support of student work (Teacher Performance Field Test, 2012). Student instructions included the font style and size and the maximum number of pages for each response. As the students began to complete the assessment, they reported finding themselves constricted in their writing. The secondary teacher education program has a longstanding commitment to the development of reflective practitioners. Throughout their course of study, students write papers, engage in discussions, and produce work in various media in order to develop the habit of reflecting, questioning, and examining themselves and their experiences. These reflections are conversations with themselves, with their colleagues, with the faculty at the university, and with the teachers with whom they are working. The students were confused by the demand to write to a rubric for an anonymous scorer. How, they wondered, were they supposed to explore what they did not know when the rubric demands that they show what they know? Who were they writing to, and why would they reveal the vulnerability of their growth to an unknown stranger? How can you measure their growth within the numerical value of these rubrics?

My Concerns

My trouble with the TPA began before Pearson's involvement. Early on, I was afraid that it was being developed to go to scale, bringing in corporate ownership. Initially, however, my greatest concern was with the standardization of teacher assessment. Those of us who are engaged in nurturing and challenging pre-service teachers understand the personal nature of this work. Teachers understand that what happens in the classroom is deeply personal and complicatedly social. In *Teaching to Transgress*, hooks (1994) writes about the embodiment of teaching, of love and conflict, of openness to the uncertainty and possibility of the experience. Teaching involves vulnerability. Learning to teach is about learning to be both vulnerable and confident, to lead and follow, to enter with knowledge and embrace the unknown. There is no standard measure of a person's readiness to engage the core of this work. Standardization emerges from a different idea of teaching. It emerges from teaching and learning as content and skills based, as technocratic, and observable. Standardization excludes the soul of teaching, which is the development of relationships in which young people are free to explore their world and use their voices in it.

SOME CONTEXT: NATIONAL AND LOCAL

The Big Picture

That Stanford signed a contract with Pearson, Inc. to deliver and score the TPA on a national level is just another step in a decades-long journey by corporate interests to purchase and privatize all of the commons. The demands of the market, according to neoliberal ideology, require that every thing, person, idea, and creation is available to commodification. We, and our work, become subject to the rigors of the market: competition, standardization, accounting, efficiency (Hursh, 2009). The material reality of this corporatization is that public institutions are starved for resources, labor becomes contingent, and our rights as workers are first attacked and then taken away. Individuals are pressured to produce more for less compensation, and we lose control over not only our work life, but most areas of our lives, as spaces and services are owned and controlled by private interests. That financiers, corporate businessmen and the politicians and policy makers who serve them are driven by greed is not entirely surprising. That Stanford University signed this agreement, subjecting student teachers to increased fees, aiding the outsourcing of the work of teacher education, and opening the door for corporate interest to enter teacher education is evidence of the shift toward a more corporate model within higher education. As well, the American Association of Colleges of Teacher Education (AACTE, 2012), the professional organization for teacher education, joined hands with Pearson and Stanford to marginalize the knowledge and experience of the people who educate new teachers and support their development. At the same time, local universities, such as the one where I was working, signed on to support these efforts and silence those of us who raise objections. How did we come to these alliances, and why are the voices of resistance so rare?

Apple (2005) discusses the role of the middle-manager technocrats, whose ability to advance within accountability regimes is contingent upon their willingness to enforce the system. As the discourse of accountability took over teacher education, more middle managers were rewarded for their efforts to assure compliance with data management systems, rubrics, standards, data reports, and other measures demanded by states and professional organizations, including the National Council for the Accreditation of Teacher Education (NCATE). Varenne (2007) argues that faculty are "caught" in the hegemonic speech of NCATE and other accountability systems. He writes that efforts to free ourselves are confounded by the deeper trap of humanistic philosophy in which we are caught. Humanistic constructions of the individual keep us from seeing how the community and social systems of which we are a part shape our understandings and choices. The technocrats are doing their job. We are caught in a trap that our worldview keeps us from seeing. We may thrash, but without knowledge of the net, we cannot escape.

In his speech at Teachers College, Secretary of Education Arne Duncan (2010) was blithe in the ease with which he named colleges of teacher education as failing. When department faculty and students gathered to listen to his talk, I was the only person to question his characterization of teacher education. My comments were dismissed. I imagine that silencing occurring in departments across the country. Instead of mounting a counter to the Secretary's claims that included the devastating impact of budget cuts on universities, the attack on and devaluing of teachers, the crisis of poverty and increasing inequities, or the degree to which the Department of Education's policies were stifling the strengths of the best teachers, we nodded and worked diligently to produce more and better standards and rubrics. What are the sociocultural conditions that account for the readiness of teacher educators to accept the narrative of their own deficiencies? Public universities are in the midst of being dramatically unfunded (Newfield, 2008), and teacher educators, like others in higher education (Tuchman, 2009), are subject to deprofessionalization and accountability regimes. Duncan's verbal assault is designed to induce shock and fear (Klein, 2007). The impact of any assault on the group as a whole—in this case teacher educators—and the echoes within individual lives, is profound. At these moments we begin to talk ourselves into the reasonableness of compliance and the wisdom of silence. With this willingness to sacrifice our beliefs and value comes humiliation. This shame breeds more compliance and the slip into complicity, as we work to tell a narrative that shields us from our shared knowledge of not having been who we hoped to be. It becomes necessary to isolate those who challenge the narratives that we have adopted, for they remind us of the places in our hearts that we let go. Thus, we participate in isolating and marginalizing those who speak out. Such is the trap in which we are caught. Varenne (n.d.), citing others, suggests that we are never fully "caught." That there are places for disruption if we stop looking to explain or blame the individual and start looking to interrogate and name the larger systems of which we are a part. In the case of the TPA, the larger system to be named includes Pearson, Inc., which stands to make millions of dollars with the implementation of the TPA, and the state and professional organizations that have accepted and promulgate the hegemonic discourses of accountability.

When the earlier iteration of the TPA—the Performance Assessment for California Teachers (PACT)—was introduced, there were objections from teacher educators, including Berlak (2010), who saw that social justice education was excluded from the assessment, exposed the façade of the performance element, and named the absurdity of standardizing something as personal as a teacher's development. When Berlak's article was published in *Rethinking Schools*, letters in response were severely critical (Luna, 2010; Peck, 2010), an example of how tightly we come to police ourselves and silence outliers. Kornfeld, Grady, Marker, and Rudell (2007) studied themselves as they responded to state requirements to align their program with new standards. They found that no matter how forthright faculty were in disputing the standards and asserting their ability to maintain their values and ideals in spite of the standards, everyone's language became more technocratic and compliant. The Kornfeld et al. study challenges us to think carefully about assertions that we are never fully caught and to ask how we escape the traps of accountability discourse and practice.

Local Context

Over the three years that our department was working with the TPA, the administration did not sponsor any opportunities to discuss it. During the year when lecturers were being calibrated and calibrating others, our requests to meet with the associate dean, who was leading the TPA process, were denied. The only opportunities to discuss the instrument and its impact were during a graduate course that was examining the TPA as part of its study. The university participated in one conference on academic language with other University of Massachusetts system schools of education and Boston College in which the focus was on the TPA. Lecturers, who were the only people at the University of Massachusetts Amherst who were working with students and the TPA formally, were not invited to address this conference. Still, I found my place and voiced my concerns.

We were initially told that the TPA would be used locally for conversations about student development and that the scores would not measure individuals but would be aggregated to measure the effectiveness of teacher education programs. I cautioned that the demand for quantitative measures of program effectiveness came from political advocacy groups whose motivations were not democratic education, but the undoing of public education, including teacher education. At a meeting sponsored by the graduate class, I questioned the inclusion of and emphasis on academic language in the rubrics. Although Janks (2010) helps us to understand that learning the language of power is essential to social justice education, the codification of academic language in the rubrics of the TPA removes it from its disruptive potential and opens the door for reproductive practices. There is no similar demand in the rubric for exploring hierarchies, power, and inequities of wealth and access. Nor is there a demand for making space for students to speak from their experience in their language. In one community discussion of the TPA to which I was invited to speak, again sponsored by the graduate students course, I discussed the dangers of losing language of teaching that included words like love, conflict, relationship, social justice, critical pedagogy. I cautioned that words could disappear from our shared discourse, and that "the common good" was one example of a phrase that was once an essential consideration in decision making but that we no longer heard.

In the academy, we operate as if we are subject only to the considerations of merit and an unstated claim on objectivity—as if, even though everyone we study is subject to the exegeses of their social conditions and their impact, we somehow escape these. While Pearson, Inc. is a company, and AACTE and Stanford are institutions, these companies and institutions are maintained by human beings, and by the micropolitics and individual choices those individuals make. It is my contention that the success of neoliberalism in robbing us of our souls, of our memories and language for broader and deeper reasons to teach and teach teachers, its ability to give power to technocrats and silence those whose commitment is to a more complex and messy humanity, is precisely because it captures our minds and manipulates fear in our hearts at the most intimate places that we know ourselves and each other. This is how we got here, and this is where we need to look as we mount our struggle to reclaim teaching, learning, and democracy.

MY DECISION

Hedges (2010) suggests that when we defend the possibility to know and live as fully human, the act of resisting is what matters, because in resistance we assert our humanness. This is where I found myself in the fall of 2011.

Within the energy of the resistance as embodied in Occupy Wall Street and my activism as part of the Education Radio collective, I discovered spaces for imaginative possibilities that open up when we reject the discourses of the market. My practice was alive, conflicted, energetic, uncertain, and critical. At the same time, as Pearson and Stanford bore down with their TPA, I saw the marked contrast between what they were imposing and what could be. Colleagues engaged in the discourse of inevitability, suggesting that we could not stop the juggernaut that is the accountability regime. They suggested that we needed objective measures of teacher performance, or that the addition of a measure of student learning of academic language was a sign that the developers of this instrument understood teaching and learning, or that it was easier to have someone else score the student work, or that it was our job to take something that seemed onerous and get the students excited about the learning possibilities in it. Or they shrugged their shoulders and did what they were told. These colleagues did not understand what I saw and felt from my side of the resistance. I said: There is another way. It is human, complicated, beautiful, rich, frightening, and strong. It is alive in relationships, which is where teaching and learning reside, from which they grow. I said: Standardization, rubrics, accountability, surveillance, corporatization, outsourcing, and technical rationality are soul crushing and dehumanizing. So it came to be that I chose to respond not to mandates but to the student teachers in the seminar and the program, to their supervisors and cooperating teachers and the students in the classrooms where they taught. I chose to defend a place for all of the messy humanity that is teaching and learning.

THE RESISTANCE

The power of Stanford, the American Association of Colleges of Teacher Education, Pearson, Inc. and the School of Education of the University of Massachusetts Amherst is formidable, especially for a faculty of lecturers and individuals who are pre-tenure. Nationally we were up against a 20-state juggernaut, established names in teacher education, and the funding that accompanies professional organizations and grants. As well, with Pearson's involvement, we were up against the largest assessment company in North America. How could we Davids address this Goliath? It was with the issue of informed consent that we determined we could put a stick in the wheel of the machinery of this particular education reform.

Research that involves human subjects requires approval by a human subjects review board, which evaluates the protocol for confidentiality and security of identifying information, protection of participants' health and safety, and appropriate informed consent. A person may not be forced to participate in a research study. In December, I, as the coordinator of the secondary teacher education program, began requesting information from our licensure office about how the students' work would be scored, what would happen with the scores, what the scores represented in terms of students passing student teaching, and how we would address the issue of informed consent. The answers and obfuscation were nothing short of astounding. For example, no one from our licensure office would state that student scores would not be used to determine if students had passed or not. They did not say they would matter, but neither did they say individual scores would not matter. Email responses to my queries included that students were required to complete the TPA as part of their coursework, students were required to upload coursework to our data management system, and uploading to the data management system constituted consent. Further, while parents and school officials were themselves raising concerns about where the video would be sent and who would have access to it, we were informed that general media release forms signed by parents at the beginning of the school year would be sufficient consent to send videos to Pearson for scoring. There are two very troubling points of note in these email exchanges: first, the element of coercion in the statement that completing required tasks constituted consent, and second, the incredible disregard for the privacy of children in dismissing the need for specific consent for the Pearson-Stanford field test.

I was confused and fascinated that the question of informed consent was not treated as reasonable and appropriate. I heard through the grapevine that individuals in other University of Massachusetts teacher education programs shared our concerns, but our administration never communicated this to the secondary teacher education program. We received no information or validation about the question of informed consent until Stanford and Pearson released a security and confidentiality agreement, I saw it online, and I sent it out to department faculty. It was at that point, when the statement itself said that Pearson and Stanford reserved the right to use the data collected for research, that administrators relented and agreed to give students the opportunity to opt in or out of participation. The notification that students would be given informed consent came with an email encouraging faculty to pick up "prizes" to be awarded students who signed on to participate in the field test. From threatened coercion to trinkets, the pressure was there to conform.

Sixty-seven of 68 student teachers in the secondary program opted out of the Pearson-Stanford field test. Shortly after, Education Radio interviewed two of the students and me about the resistance. Within 24 hours of the release of that program through podcast, Pearson, Inc. was googling my name. Following the broadcast, Education Radio heard from student teachers and faculty who felt similarly silenced and coerced. It was then that I understood that my experience was not a local phenomenon, but a national silencing. That is why I contacted the *New York Times*, to give a national voice to the possibility of resistance and to expose attempts to silence dissent.

Three days after the *New York Times* published the article about the student resistance (Winerip, 2012), a meeting was scheduled with the department chair and associate dean. There I was told to be scrupulous (their word) about the power I held over students; to never speak for the university; and that I was assigned additional work that had previously been assigned to others. Seventeen days after the article appeared in the *New York Times*, I received a letter of non-renewal informing me that my contract would not be renewed at the end of its term in August of 2013.

THE ONGOING STRUGGLE

Although I write this article alone, and it was my contract that was not renewed, the resistance to Pearson and the TPA emerged from a shared struggle and solidarity. Throughout the semester, as the 34 students in the student teaching seminar that I facilitated took their patient stand and refused to agree to participate without the choice to opt in or out of the field test, we learned from and leaned on each other. We trusted each other. The moment when students were asked to sign the informed consent forms and say yes or no to Pearson, Inc., was silent, serious, and deeply moving. Though they made their choices as individuals, they had come to have that choice because of their collective action. The attempts by the department chair and associate dean to suggest that I had a special power over the students speak to the trap of seeing only the individual. The resistance to Pearson was a collective action, not because individuals were somehow coerced, but because we knew our strength in the collective, because we supported each other. But the strength within that seminar was itself built on other sources of support. These supporters emerged formally as we began organizing to fight the non-renewal, but they had been there all along as a micro network, unknown even to each other: a teacher from a local middle school who leads one section of the student teaching seminar; a cross-campus faculty member with whom I have sat in meetings discussing engaged pedagogy; doctoral candidates who have shared texts, argued and discussed the dilemmas of neo-liberalism in coursework; a community organizer with whom I have worked on peace and justice activism; department colleagues with whom I shared many conversations about our own position being caught in the neoliberal regime; and members of the Education Radio collective.

The student refusal to participate in the field test was one action, but going public was another. In going public, we named what was happening. We disrupted the narrative of the rightness of the juggernaut of the Pearson-Stanford

TPA. We reintroduced words into the national vocabulary of teacher education: social justice, resistance, relationships. In naming, we not only began to transform our world, but we invited others into the conversation. As language is used to infiltrate our minds and hearts, we must use language as action to banish neoliberalism. In their action, the students asserted their discourse about their development as teachers. In speaking publicly, they gave voice and courage to the many others out there who did not yet know that they were part of a community of resistance. But now we know, recognize each other, and are drawing strength and organizing for more actions.

In the neoliberal narrative, we are alone in a struggle for survival and success. This story gets its potency from the fear and uncertainty engendered by market competition and heightened surveillance. As I have come to know myself within this struggle, I have travelled from fear to courage not by some individual act of will, but by allowing myself to see and draw from the strength, wisdom, and support of others. Through classroom practice, speaking out in meetings, community organizations, and over martinis, I have been part of a weaving together of people who share worries and a perspective on what we should be worried about. As we join together and name the net in which we are caught, we can strategize on how to free ourselves. The student resistance to the Pearson-Stanford TPA was taking a knife to one string of the net and clipping it. As more of us do the same, the net will no longer be able to hold us.

REFERENCES

American Association of Colleges of Teacher Education. (2012). AACTE and Scale celebrate successful progress for national teacher performance assessment. Retrieved from http://aacte.org/News-Room/Press-Releases-and-Statements/aacte-and-scale-celebrate-successful-progress-for-national-teacher-performance-assessment.html

Apple, M. (2005). Education, markets and an audit culture. *Critical Quarterly, 47*(1–2), 11–29.

Baker, A. (2012, July 30). To earn classroom certification, more teaching and less testing. *The New York Times.* Retrieved from http://www.nytimes.com/2012/07/30/nyregion/with-new-standards-going-beyond-paper-and-pencil-to-license-teachers.html?ref=education

Berlak, A. (2010). Coming soon to a credentialing program near you. *Rethinking Schools. 24* (4), 41–45.

Duncan, A. (2010). *Teacher education: reforming an uncertain profession.* Remarks at Teachers College, Columbia University. Retrieved from http://www2.ed.gov/news/speeches/2009/10/10222009.html

Education Radio. (2012, March, 25). Teacher Performance Assessment: a money grab for Pearson. Retrieved from http://education-radio.blogspot.com/2012/03/teacher-performance-assessment-money.html

Hedges, C. (2010). *Death of the liberal class*. New York, NY: Nation Books.

hooks, b. (1994). *Teaching to transgress: Education as the practice of freedom*. New York, NY: Routledge.

Hursh, D. (2009). *High stakes testing and the decline of teaching and learning*. Lanham, MD: Rowman & Littlefield.

Janks, H. (2010). *Literacy and power*. New York, NY: Routledge.

Klein, N. (2007). *The shock doctrine: The rise of disaster capitalism*. New York, NY: Picador.

Kornfeld, J., Grady, K., Marker, P., & Rapp Ruddell, M. (2007). Caught in the current: A self-study of state-mandated compliance in a teacher education program. *Teachers College Record, 109*(8), 1902–1930.

Lipmann, P. (2011). Neoliberal urbanism, race and urban school reform. In W. Watkins (Ed.), *The assault on public education: Confronting the politics of corporate school reform*. New York, NY: Teachers College Press.

Luna, D. (2010). Parsing PACT. (Letter to the editor.) *Rethinking Schools, 25*(1).

Newfield, C. (2008). *The Un-making of the public university*. Cambridge: Harvard University Press.

Pearson, Inc. (2012). Pearson application for employment. Retrieved from https://vovici.com/wsb.dll/s/6bf3g4d59e

Peck, C. (2010). PACT: Intrusion or opportunity to learn? (Letter to the Editor.) *Rethinking Schools, 25*(1).

Saltman, K. (2007). Schooling in disaster capitalism: how the political right is using disaster to privatize public education. *Teacher Education Quarterly, 34* (2) 131–156.

Teacher Performance Field Test. (2012). Field test guidelines and policies for faculty. Retrieved from http://tpafieldtest.nesinc.com/PageView.aspx?f=GEN_Faculty Policies. html

Tuchman, G. (2007). *Wannabe U: Inside the Corporate University*. Chicago, IL: University of Chicago Press.

Varenne, H. (2007). On NCATE standards and the culture at work: Conversations, hegemony and (dis)-abling consequences. *Anthropology and Education Quarterly, 38*(10), 16–23.

Varenne, H. (n.d.) Blog discussion of his paper on NCATE in Teachers Education Quarterly, 2007. Retrieved from http://varenne.tc.columbia.edu/hv/edu/ncate/ncate-main.html

Watkins, W. (Ed.). (2011). *The assault on public education: Confronting the politics of corporate school reform*. New York, NY: Teachers College Press.

Winerip, M. (2012, May 7). New procedure for teacher licensing draws protest. *The New York Times*. Retrieved from http://www.nytimes.com/2012/05/07/education/new-procedure-for-teaching-license-draws-protest.html?ref=michaelwinerip

CHAPTER 17

STUDENTS AGAINST MILITARISM

Youth Organizing in the Counter-Recruitment Movement

Scott Harding
University of Connecticut

Seth Kershner
Massachusetts College of Liberal Arts

INTRODUCTION:
THE COUNTER-RECRUITMENT MOVEMENT

Since ending conscription in 1973, the United States has relied entirely on volunteers to staff its vast armed forces. With the United States in a permanent state of war preparation, and with the wars in Iraq and Afghanistan generating significant opposition, it has proven difficult to recruit sufficient volunteers to the military. Lack of viable economic prospects for many youth makes for an excellent recruiter's aid, drawing in a steady stream of enlistees who sign up for the promises of job training, help with

Left Behind in the Race to the Top, pages 257–273

paying for college, or cash bonuses and healthcare benefits. Nonetheless, in predicting that "at some point the economy will turn around," Major General David Mann, the U.S. Army's top recruiting officer, recently suggested that recruiters will need to make expanding "school presence" one of their "key focus areas" (Mann, 2011, p. 3). Such an emphasis fits into the post-conscription history of the U.S. military: Over the past 30 years, schools have increasingly become key sites for military recruitment. For example, due to federal legislation enacted in 2002, public schools must accept military recruiters on campus or else face loss of federal funding. As a result, recruiters now have a widespread—if not increasingly challenged—presence in school classrooms and hallways across the country. Recruiters' presence in schools goes beyond providing information to students who express an interest in the armed forces. In the Army's School Recruiting Handbook, recruiters are urged to fully immerse themselves in high school activities—by volunteering to chaperone dances, proctoring tests, coaching sports, and through other means—in order to achieve "school ownership" (United States Army, 2004, p. 2).

In an effort to counteract the growing presence of the military in U.S. public schools, military counter-recruitment (CR) has emerged as an effective grassroots movement. Counter-recruiters believe that unrestricted military access to schools is harmful to youth and detrimental to democracy, undermining the ideals of free thought and critical inquiry by exposing impressionable students to one-sided military propaganda. Operating on a small scale at individual schools in local communities, counter-recruitment applies community organizing methods to confront the structures supporting the socialization of youth to a culture of militarism. This is a considerable task, as youth confront daily examples embedded within popular culture that reinforce a narrowly constructed ideology and set of beliefs. Soldiers are depicted as modern-day "heroes" representing an ideal of American society, while the U.S. military is portrayed as an essential institution, especially in a "dangerous" world. Such representations are normalized and rarely challenged.

Counter-recruitment thus has several dimensions:

- It represents an effort to oppose the militarization of U.S. public schools that occurs via military recruitment and the proliferation of Junior Reserve Officer Training Corps (JROTC) units on campus.
- It provides alternative information to students about career options beyond the military, especially important for students in under-resourced areas with low school achievement.
- It allows activists in low-income neighborhoods and communities of color to address broader issues of economic (in)justice linked to American militarism.

- It offers an opportunity to confront U.S. foreign policy and the broader phenomenon of militarism in U.S. culture.

For many groups engaged in this work, "truth in recruitment" (the effort to address military recruiters' dis-information) is a more accurate description of their work than "counter-recruitment." Such framing allows activists to emphasize their attempt to provide students with adequate information to make "informed choices" about whether to join the military. Thus counter-recruiters often view their work as empowering youth to make informed decisions about military enlistment, making this approach similar to consumer advocacy.

The counter-recruitment movement is demographically diverse. The only comprehensive database of CR organizations, available at the National Network Opposing Militarization of Youth (NNOMY) website, lists approximately 150 groups engaged in CR organizing across the United States, mostly at the local level (NNOMY, 2012). However, it appears that many of these groups are no longer active. For example, we judged some groups to be inactive if their publicly available information turned out to consist of invalid email addresses or disconnected phones. In other cases, we were told by existing contacts that a certain group or individual had ceased being active. That some CR organizations are short-lived makes sense, given that counter-recruitment is generally done by small, mostly volunteer organizations with few paid staff. NNOMY provides some national coordination and information sharing to facilitate counter-recruitment efforts. Often, counter-recruitment is one of several issues addressed by a local peace and justice organization or a chapter of the American Friends Service Committee.

The counter-recruitment effort faces immense obstacles. It is challenged by a lack of resources, by a relative anonymity within the broader peace movement, and by its inherent opposition to cultural norms about the role of the military in American society. Nonetheless, in recent decades counter-recruitment has secured significant policy and legal changes that contest military recruitment in public schools while seeking to undermine the dominant social narrative about military service. While many local organizations engaged in counter-recruitment utilize diverse participants—veterans, teachers, and parents—we focus here on the role of youth. Though inconsistent, in recent years youth participation in counter-recruitment has emerged as a vital aspect of this activism.

THE DIMENSIONS OF MILITARISM IN THE UNITED STATES

Military counter-recruitment is a direct response to the growing presence of the military in public schools; it represents a key tactic used by activists to confront American militarism. As a *movement,* counter-recruitment has a 40-year history that stems directly from opposition to the Viet Nam war and related organizing against the military draft. Yet the *practice* of CR dates to the WWII era (Goossen, 1997). During the 1950s, the American Friends Service Committee maintained an active presence in public schools in an effort to promote peace education. While the Vietnam War was raging in the late 1960s and early 1970s, veterans of that conflict regularly spoke in high schools about opposing the draft. Thus while counter-recruitment draws on the energy and spirit of the anti-draft/anti-Vietnam War effort, the tactics deployed since the early days of CR—distributing pamphlets, public education, and supplying information on *alternatives* to the military—have deeper roots. However, the existence of the all-volunteer military force is what distinguishes the contemporary counter-recruitment movement from these earlier efforts. Before the draft ended in 1973, counter-recruitment efforts were secondary to the need for education and activism around conscription. Without a draft, contemporary counter-recruiters can often afford the luxury of focusing on specific aspects of this work, like outreach to immigrant communities or—the focus of this chapter—youth-empowerment work.

This chapter, part of a larger study of counter-recruitment organizing in the United States, is based on more than 40 interviews with activists in 22 cities. In three cases (Chicago, New York, and Oakland, CA), we assess the role of youth in counter-recruitment and evaluate efforts to integrate youth directly into the work of CR groups. We highlight several successful examples to illustrate what is working in terms of youth organizing in the counter-recruitment movement and also discuss some challenges of utilizing youth activists in future counter-recruitment efforts.

According to activists interviewed for this study, the conflict over the presence of military recruiters in schools signifies a struggle over control of educational space. The American military uses public schools both for direct recruitment and as a venue for socialization about the value and benefits provided by the military—a means to promote a singularly positive image of the armed forces. While school-based military recruitment has fluctuated in the past, the 2002 federal No Child Left Behind (NCLB) educational reform gave the Pentagon the right to access all public schools and most student data. It is now common in public high schools for military recruiters to have some type of regular presence, thus providing a direct means of communicating with future recruits. Because of this access to students, many activists view military recruitment as a form of "sales" targeting a captive and vulnerable audience, especially given the heavy presence of recruiters in low-income communities.

Indeed, researcher Tyler Jeffrey Wall finds that schools "are of extreme importance in the practices of U.S. war preparation in that they geographically corral youthful bodies for military recruiters to easily locate, communicate with, and eventually enlist" (Wall, 2009, p. 139). High school recruiting is also important because most people who enlist in the armed forces do so through the Delayed Enlistment Program (DEP). The DEP allows enlistees to delay—for up to a year—the date on which they begin active-duty training. Thus, the DEP is "pushed hard by recruiters to high school seniors who are unsure what to do after graduation" (NNOMY, 2012). The seventeen-year-olds who enlist under the DEP are often referred to as "future soldiers" in official armed forces publications and sometimes used by recruiters as a tool to gain further access to high schools (Pesature, 2012).

There are other ways for the Pentagon to access private student data, including the Joint Advertising Market Research and Studies (JAMRS) database. The archive took years to assemble and "includes names, birth dates, ASVAB test data, email addresses, grade-point averages, ethnicity, and the subjects that students are studying" (NNOMY, 2011, n.p.). In 2007, the Pentagon settled a lawsuit with the New York Civil Liberties Union by agreeing both to stop collecting data on children younger than 17 in the New York city school district and to provide a means for students to "opt out" of the database (Goodman, 2009; NNOMY, 2011). The latter represents a key (national) victory for the counter-recruitment movement, though military access to student information remains the norm.

One additional focus of counter-recruitment efforts, the school-based, military-sponsored Junior Reserve Officer Training Corps (JROTC), represents the educational-military nexus in its purest form. Approximately 3,000 JROTC units operate in U.S. schools, enrolling more than 400,000 students or "cadets." While offering coursework in history, communication, and citizenship studies, the program also contains a military drill component. JROTC students often travel to local military bases for tours, drill competitions, and the chance to "test" military hardware. The military denies that it views JROTC as a recruiting tool, yet nearly half of graduating cadets eventually enlist in a branch of the armed forces. Reflecting broader trends within the American military, a disproportionate number of minority students are enrolled in the JROTC: 54% of JROTC cadets are students of color (National Network Opposing the Militarization of Youth, 2010). That figure is as high as 96% in Chicago, the city with the nation's largest JROTC presence (Chicago JROTC, 2012; Christianakis & Mora, 2011).

COUNTER-RECRUITMENT IN TRANSITION

In key respects, contemporary counter-recruitment is operating in a transition period—much as this movement did in the aftermath of the 1991 Gulf War. Then, as now, peace activists displayed declining interest in counter-recruitment as U.S. involvement in a war with Iraq ended. While counter-recruitment organizing continued to percolate in local school districts across the country for another dozen years, it took the 2003 U.S. invasion of Iraq to serve as a catalyst for a revival of significant CR activism. As a result, counter-recruitment experienced a "renaissance" from 2004–2007 as peace activists engaged in diverse efforts to oppose the U.S. war in Iraq (Travieso, 2008). Hard-to-organize constituencies like students and parents became key allies during this period. In May 2005, national media attention focused on Seattle after the Parent–Teacher Association of Garfield High School passed a motion opposing military recruitment in public schools (Hagopian & Barker, 2011). The Iraq War even allowed CR activism to flourish outside the liberal West Coast. Between 2006 and 2010, activists in the conservative, pro-military community of Hilo, Hawaii used foundation funding to invite young veterans and conscientious objectors to speak in local schools (author interview, September 9, 2012). The involvement of veterans, as well as resisters and conscientious objectors to both wars was also notable. A key difference between these two periods, however, is the emergence of efforts to increase involvement of youth in direct counter-recruitment organizing activities.

During and after the Gulf War, attempts were made to recruit youth into CR work, in part reflecting older activists' concerns about the lack of involvement from young people. But successes in this area were mainly limited to urban areas on the West Coast, such as Oakland and San Diego. By the time of U.S. involvement in wars in Iraq and Afghanistan in the 2000s, student-initiated counter-recruiting work had begun to thrive. In some cases youth started their own CR groups, and in others they played a critical role at stimulating counter-recruitment organizing, only later inviting adult allies to join them. This is the inverse of the 1980s–1990s, when youth participation in counter-recruitment typically came after some form of adult appeal.

Two examples from the 2000s are instructive. In one, students from several area high schools organized the group Youth Activists of Austin, Texas (YAA). After gaining the support of adult allies affiliated with peace and anti-war groups, YAA led a successful lobbying campaign (in 2005–2006) that resulted in a new policy limiting access by military recruiters to local schools (author interview, May 17, 2012). In the second case, Zoe Pardee, a college student who experienced aggressive military recruitment at her high school, worked with adult allies in Ft. Worth to convince them of the need for counter-recruitment efforts. These adults had not viewed military recruiting as a "problem" until Pardee's activism. As a result, the group Peaceful Vocations was created (author interview, May 15, 2012).

The recent emergence of youth involvement in counter-recruitment is significant, as it provides an innovative response to the sustainability problem facing many organizations. Moreover, for some groups it also allows counter-recruitment to expand beyond a focus on military recruitment to make connections with other social issues like immigration and school funding. Such a perspective provides an opportunity for youth to understand how militarism and military recruitment are directly related to other concerns in their local communities.

Yet despite notable successes, especially at the local level, as a "movement" counter-recruitment faces significant challenges. Though effective at gaining entry to local schools and limiting recruiter access to students (and private student information), the overall impact of counter-recruitment remains uneven. We find a general lack of new initiatives and activities is occurring among most CR groups, with a relatively low level of counter-recruitment organizing the norm (with notable exceptions). There is also unevenness in terms of how many groups evaluate their counter-recruitment work; that is, no shared definition of "success" exists, and there is no common measurement or evaluative criteria of this organizing. Much like the larger U.S. peace movement, there is a lack of consistency among counter-recruitment organizations in working with groups outside the peace movement (labor, civil rights, religious, etc.).

Aside from limited coordination among CR groups, most organizations are understaffed and lack adequate resources for sustained counter-recruitment work and/or an expansion of their activities. Despite this reality, fundraising and development appears to be a low priority for many of the groups involved in this work. Many interviewees indicated that their fundraising work consisted of "doing what we've always done"—usually mass mailings and a special event or two per year. The climate for foundation giving within the broader peace movement is not particularly favorable: Groups across the country must compete for the largesse of a few foundations that support CR work and peace activism. Even then, grant monies awarded to a counter-recruitment group are typically less than $5,000—just enough to cover the considerable printing/copying expenses that a group can accrue throughout the course of a school year. While activists' busy schedules may not permit much creativity in the fund-raising realm, some strategies that are not especially time-intensive (e.g., major donor cultivation) appear to have been neglected by almost every CR group we assessed. Given their limited resources, most CR groups are reliant on the efforts of one or two key activists/paid staff, while volunteers play a crucial role in carrying out important activities. Of note, many organizations are reliant on an aging cohort of activists and face a loss of support and interest in counter-recruitment with waning U.S. military involvement in Iraq and Afghanistan. As a result, *sustainability*—linked to funding, staffing, and maintaining a baseline level of activity—is a key issue confronting many local counter-recruitment groups.

In providing examples of how youth have played key roles in CR organizing, we highlight the unique contributions young people can make in this movement. For example, with counter-recruitment focused largely on high school students, activists need to determine who is most effective at organizing youth to maximize their effectiveness. While military veterans have been essential to the success of many local CR groups, activists note their belief that youth often respond best to other youth. Thus, integrating youth into counter-recruitment organizing allows young adults to serve as peers and mentors to other youth. Greater involvement of youth is also *de facto* a response to issues of sustainability among local counter-recruitment groups. We find that some groups are making a strategic effort to create and nurture new leadership, and that youth-led counter-recruitment may be more sustainable than other efforts to broaden the base of CR supporters. Of course, maintaining youth involvement—in counter-recruitment and other forms of activism—is itself a challenge. However, the examples presented here illustrate the benefits of building stronger and more inclusive organizations that can help maximize innovative peace activism.

CHICAGO

Chicago, Illinois is the third-largest city in the United States and birthplace of progressive education. John Dewey first started testing his educational philosophy at the University of Chicago Laboratory School in 1896. His theories became the backbone of American educational thought in the decades that followed. Dewey was also a prominent social reformer in his day, and in the years following World War I—when many American colleges and universities began to make participation in ROTC compulsory for their students—Dewey declared that teaching military drill to youngsters was "undemocratic, barbaric, and scholastically wholly unwise" (quoted in Howlett, 1976, p. 51).

How ironic, then, that for the past 15 years Chicago has held the distinction of having the most militarized public school system in the nation: nearly 10,000 students from 53 middle and high schools are enrolled in JROTC. And just as military recruiters often target a specific demographic, JROTC enrollment reflects distinct tendencies. In a city with a history of racial (and class) segregation, JROTC has operated "primarily in less affluent urban school districts" (Christianakis & Mora, 2011, p. 103). Thus, 96% of Chicago's JROTC cadets are students of color (Chicago JROTC, 2013). Chicago also has the most military-sponsored public high schools (six) in the nation. At these schools, students wear uniforms and staff follows a military model of instruction: strict discipline, marching drills, and compulsory JROTC. At a 1999 ribbon-cutting ceremony of one such school, former Army Secretary

Louis Caldera claimed "the military academy stands as a national model for how inner-city schools can address discipline in the classroom and lay the groundwork for academic improvement" (Quintanilla, 1999, p. 2). Casting serious doubt on such claims is the fact that in the 2011–2012 school year all six of Chicago's military academies failed to show "adequate yearly progress," a set of performance criteria mandated by the terms of the NCLB; and some of the military academies have gone more than eight years without making the grade (Illinois Interactive Report Card, 2012). However, these schools are quite successful at sending a higher percentage of their graduating seniors on to the armed forces than regular high schools; nearly one in five graduates of these academies enroll in the military.

In 2008, U.S. Secretary of Education Arne Duncan—who was then CEO of the Chicago Public Schools—faced stiff community opposition to the building of new military academies. According to a teacher who was at a meeting of over 300 such activists, "Duncan responded, I come from a Quaker family, and I've always been against war. But I'm going to put the Naval Academy in there [at Senn High School], because it will give people in the community more choices" (Sharkey, 2008, n.p.). Of course, this choice-driven devotion to military academies runs counter to traditional educational values. When asked about military-sponsored public schools, author/scholar Henry Giroux suggested that John Dewey would "roll over in his grave."

> Dewey thought that education laid the foundation for students to become critical and social agents so that they could learn how to both govern and be governed. What military public schools suggest is that the ultimate aim of education is to be a kind of disciplinary apparatus that in its worst moments educates students to take part in the war machine and a society dedicated to the production of organized violence. (Kershner, 2011, p. 40)

Fortunately for those who care about progressive education, an effective counter-recruitment presence also exists in Chicago: the local chapter of the American Friends Service Committee (AFSC). During the Vietnam War when the AFSC was a key opponent of U.S. military intervention, AFSC staff trained draft counselors and eventually attracted the scrutiny of the city's feared "red squad." Much has changed since then. Chicago has become more diverse, lawsuits have forced the police to scale back intelligence-gathering operations, and the end of military conscription has made recruiting a key task in today's military.

In the early 1980s Chicago counter-recruiters affiliated with Clergy and Laity Concerned (CALC) struggled to gain access to the city's high schools to contest the growing military presence. A group of parents, students, and CALC activists eventually sued the city school board and in 1984 won their right to "equal access" in an historic federal district court decision.

Buoyed by greater school access, Chicago CALC continued organizing in city schools throughout the 1980s until its national parent organization dissolved. The 1990s were a relatively dormant period in Chicago counter-recruitment, as most organizing moved to the suburbs of Arlington Heights and Elgin (where activists engaged in their own equal access struggles). Since 2005, the Chicago AFSC chapter has resumed organizing against a military presence in the city's schools. These efforts have taken on various forms, including traditional tabling events at schools, opt-out campaigns, and outreach to engage social justice educators. However, a notable facet of Chicago organizing is their innovative youth outreach campaigns.

Recognizing that the most effective means of engaging young people around issues of militarism and military recruitment would be to empower them to educate their peers, project coordinator Darlene Gramigna designed special activities to attract youth participation. One project is the Social Justice Spring Break, a four-year effort to bring adult mentors and youth together for an intensive period of classroom instruction and interactive activities. A key goal is to develop leadership skills so that young people may become better organizers and advocates for social justice causes. In 2009, Gramigna brought members of Iraq Veterans Against the War (IVAW) to students at a Social Justice Spring Break on Chicago's North Side. As she explained in an interview, "There was a high school in that area that had suffered cuts to its arts programs so that there would be enough money for JROTC to come in. We gave them (students) some tools to become better educators for their peers around the JROTC issue and even helped them set up a career fair" (author interview, March 29, 2012).

As is typical with counter-recruitment work, success is hard to measure. While the AFSC views the Spring Break program to be a success, Gramigna noted "there was never enough time . . . the goal during the Spring Break is to try and make connections between street violence in Chicago and military violence in Iraq" (author interview, March 29, 2012). Youth are afforded more time to make those connections during the Peace Here, There, and Everywhere Summer Institute, which started as a three-week program in 2008. By 2012, the institute was only running for one week, and the authors were present on the day devoted to training on the topic of militarism, military recruitment, and counter-recruitment. The day's events included an informal survey to assess students' exposure to militarism in their lives, a brief video presentation about military enlistment (the AFSC-produced "Before You Enlist"), and facilitator-led interactive activities. Most of the latter were drawn from an AFSC organizing booklet and included a role-playing game in which youth were asked to alternate between the roles of student and military recruiter.

Despite having just one day devoted to the topic, seven of the ten students from the 2012 summer cohort cited "learning the reality of military recruitment" as something they gained in their evaluation of the program (author interview, July 21, 2012). To date, more than 80 students have graduated from the Summer Institute and an equal number have cycled through the Social Justice Spring Break. While tangible measures of success may be lacking, Gramigna has heard anecdotal reports from teachers in local schools that some AFSC Spring Break alums return to school eager to implement their ideas for projects. One was even selected as a student delegate in 2012 when new Nobel Laureates met in Chicago (author interview, March 29, 2012). While the AFSC's loss of some foundation funding may threaten the future of such efforts, these reports suggest the importance of youth outreach programs.

NEW YORK CITY

As the most populous American city with a reputation for offering immigrants a better life, New York has long been seen by the Pentagon as a key market for military recruiters. Top Army brass often appear at induction ceremonies of new recruits, helping attract media attention. Chief of Staff Gen. George Casey was present at the swearing-in of sixteen new soldiers at a Times Square ceremony in 2009; a reporter for the *New York Times* was careful to note that all the newly enlisted soldiers were first-generation immigrants and thus qualified to take advantage of a new "streamlined citizenship process" offered by the Army in return for military service (Semple, 2009).

As is true of school-based military recruiting in general, very little is known about techniques recruiters use to generate leads among high school students. However, in the case of New York, evidence compiled by the New York Civil Liberties Union (NYCLU) and the Office of the Manhattan Borough President, along with the grassroots Students not Soldiers Coalition, sheds considerable light on school-based recruitment practices. "In a survey of nearly 1,000 ninth-, tenth-, eleventh- and twelfth-graders at 45 New York City high schools," the NYCLU report (2008) found that

> more than one in five respondents (21 percent) at selected schools reported the use of class time by military recruiters.... Survey results also showed that 13 percent of respondents reported seeing military recruiters in their schools at least once a week, and 35 percent of respondents indicated that military recruiters have access to multiple locations within their schools, such as hallways and classrooms. (p. 11)

This damning evidence of a normalized military presence in New York city public schools may have gone largely unnoticed had it not been for the organizing of the Youth Allies/Youth Activists (Ya-Ya) Network. Using the data compiled in the report the group eventually won a six-year effort to restrict military recruiter access within New York City schools.

Since founding the organization in 1999, Amy Wagner—a former school social worker—has coordinated the Ya-Ya Network out of a small office in Manhattan. The group is composed mostly of young people (aged 15–19), who are enrolled, trained, and paid to engage in community organizing among their peers. Although the Ya-Ya Network is no longer a single-issue organization, for years various cohorts of youth activists have—under Wagner's direction—worked in counter-recruitment, an area where students gain valuable practical experience in community organizing. Part of their training involves a class in critical thinking; upon completing this course, students are expected to identify connections between counter-recruitment and other social justice issues. Thus, Wagner anticipates youth will understand why military recruiters often have a larger presence at schools whose students come from low-income communities. The Ya-Ya Network's innovative organizing strategy was put on display during their campaign to control military recruiter access in local schools.

In 2009, the New York Department of Education passed Chancellor's Regulation A825, which mandated that schools make it easier for students and their parents to opt out of releasing information to military recruiters; that military recruiters not be given unfettered access to school property; and that each school designate someone from the staff to serve as a "point person" on issues related to military recruiting on campus. This regulation represented an important victory for the entire counter-recruitment movement: one million students in all five boroughs of New York stand to benefit from the change in policy, while counter-recruiters elsewhere have a model to replicate in their own communities. Ya-Ya youth were involved in building the "strong coalition" that Wagner notes was key to victory. Putting their community organizing training to work, student activists organized community forums and gained valuable public speaking experience as they fanned out across the city to give presentations to groups of teachers, guidance counselors, and fellow students. These presentations often took the form of "Counter-Recruiting 101," a standard workshop format that focused on introducing audiences to the other side of the military recruiting message through videos, discussion, and hands-on activities. Youth activists also lobbied school stakeholders in their bid to pass the Chancellor's Regulation. They met privately with public officials, and one persistent youth secured an interview with officials at the Department of Education, an exchange that proved to be a crucial step in the path to victory.

But getting the regulation passed was the easy part. In an effort to monitor compliance with Regulation A825, in 2011 the Ya-Ya Network mailed out more than 400 surveys to every New York City public high school. However, the fact that only sixty schools responded caused Wagner to reconsider using the survey method to assess compliance with the terms of the policy. The Ya-Ya Network will again partner with the NYCLU as they seek access to relevant data (e.g., the number of schools with a designated point person for military recruitment issues, or the number of high school students who opt out of releasing their information to military recruiters.) Their strategy will—if necessary—include filing Freedom of Information Act requests to gain access to the data, a gambit increasingly being used by counter-recruiters who must deal with uncooperative school districts.

OAKLAND

More than one-third of public high school students in Oakland, California drop out before graduation. According to a recent report by the Oakland Unified School District (OUSD), 37% of dropouts eventually get in trouble with the law. Oakland schools, in the words of one OUSD official, are "resource poor and operating in crisis mode" (Grady, 2012, p.2). The state has reacted to a historic funding crisis by forcing crippling cuts to public schools: $7 billion lost since 2008 alone, 32,000 teaching positions eliminated, and up to 20% of all guidance counselors laid off. California's per student education expenditure is the third-lowest in the country ($8,818 annually per child). Given the amount the state spends each year to incarcerate a child in the juvenile justice system—$179,400—a picture of what is meant by the "school-to-prison pipeline" emerges (Grady, 2012).

Compared to other large U.S. cities, however, Oakland lacks a significant military presence in its public schools. One reason a *school-to-military pipeline* does not exist in Oakland is due to the efforts of activist groups like Better Alternatives for Youth (BAY-Peace). Operating on a shoestring budget, with no paid staff members, the core of BAY-Peace are its youth action teams. Coordinator Susan Quinlan recruits, mentors and provides either a small stipend or academic credit to youth action team members (Oakland high school students). Among other issues, youth spend a year addressing militarism and military recruitment in public schools and the local community. BAY-Peace activists frequently use art—videos, poetry, and short plays—to convey their message to diverse audiences. A former educator and experienced social justice advocate, Quinlan knows that listening to or giving a lecture has a "different energy" for young people. Youth activists with BAY-Peace appear to be "more engaged" when their work takes the form of art, and audiences tend to respond better to poetry than to preaching, Quinlan notes (author interview, April 25, 2012). The role of BAY-Peace activists in a district-wide policy battle illustrates the strength of this youth-led, art-oriented approach to counter-recruitment.

In 2008, BAY-Peace marked a new stage in its development as a social justice organization. Prior work emphasized training youth to give in-school presentations on alternatives to the military. However in 2008 the group shifted from public education toward organizing a long-term campaign for a change in school district policy regarding military recruiters' access to schools and private student information. A key part in this process was the youth action team's drafting of a "poetic petition," the BAY-Peace Youth Manifesto. Youth action team members were at that time leading a 10-week workshop on "arts and social studies" at the Emiliano Zapata Street Academy, an alternative public school in Oakland; Street Academy students were just as much a part of the creation of the Youth Manifesto as were the youth action team members (author interview, April 25, 2012).

Consisting of 300 words, the Youth Manifesto became a rallying cry for military-free schools. Underlying students' belief that "it is unfair that recruiters target the poor and communities of color," and that "military recruiters should not be given access to students' personal information without the students' and parents' permission," was the desire that military recruiters get "out of my school and community." The Manifesto's set of demands included that military recruiters "have no greater access to high school students than any other potential employer" and—for the first time among counter-recruiters—that a form be included in every student's registration packet allowing students to opt out of the JAMRS databse of private student information. The petition drive, which occurred during the 2008–2009 school year, resulted in more than 1,000 signatures supporting the students' demands. Efforts to publicize the Manifesto included the creation of a video and led to its endorsement by the American Friends Service Committee, Women of Color Resource Center, the San Francisco chapter of Veterans for Peace, and other community organizations (BAY-Peace, n.d.).

At the same time, youth activists were preparing to turn their poetic petition into a more formal resolution to the Oakland School Board. Besides meeting with local school board members to press their demands for change, in February 2010 BAY-Peace youth activists organized a Resource Fair and Youth Manifesto Rally where they created origami cranes out of signed petitions and strung together hundreds of cranes to create a banner that was brought to the school board offices. This creative organizing paid off in May 2010, when the Oakland School Board approved the student-crafted resolution. While certain parts of that resolution simply reflected policies practiced elsewhere in the country—the suggestion that military recruiters enjoy only as much access to schools as other types of recruiters—some sections had more far-reaching implications. For example, the victory made Oakland the first school district in the country to provide students a means of opting out of the JAMRS database. Counter-recruiters in several other cities have since replicated the successful campaign of

BAY-Peace: JAMRS opt-out policies have been passed by school boards in Honolulu, San Francisco, Berkeley, and the Chicago suburbs (author interview, May 27, 2012).

As a largely youth-led effort, the impact of BAY-Peace—both locally and on the national level—is significant. While Quinlan provided mentoring and support during the Manifesto campaign, the youth themselves were making decisions "every step of the way," she notes. "They were involved in every single aspect of that campaign, from writing the petition to contacting school board members and attending meetings." Though youth activists showed potential as leaders and organizers during this campaign, Quinlan's support and mentoring was crucial. "They were new to the intricacies of a drawn-out organizing campaign," she noted.

> Many of the youth on our teams are struggling with everyday life issues—they may have other jobs in addition to school, and some have learning disabilities. Some of them are even homeless. It's very easy to become frustrated in a community organizing experience. So I would help them compensate for what they lacked, which was the persistence that you need to win in a campaign like this. (author interview, April 25, 2012)

Moreover, Quinlan sees her role at BAY-Peace as supplementing the free education her young activists receive at school, with community organizing a key part of their broader educational process. Training youth activists is thus critical, as they represent the future of any movement for social change, whether focused on military recruitment, immigration, or community anti-violence work. "Community organizing," Quinlan concluded, "is a critical part of the process of developing youth as shapers of society, as critical thinkers who feel like they have a voice in how the world should be" (author interview, April 25, 2012).

CONCLUSION

We noted earlier that greater involvement of youth was, in part, a response to issues of sustainability among counter-recruitment groups. Today's young activists are, as Susan Quinlan said, the future of the movement. Although U.S. wars in Iraq and Afghanistan are winding down, the need for counter-recruiting remains. As movement veteran Rick Jahnkow (2009) stated at a national conference, "This work is part of a long-term, strategic vision, not merely a tactic for ending a particular war or an effort to educate individuals about recruiter deception." Thus a challenge arises in thinking of counter-recruitment's long-term perspective: There are too few young activists today who will be able to carry the struggle forward in the future. Many of the counter-recruiters we interviewed are in their fifties and sixties and have been active in peace and justice work for decades; many said that they would "retire" from activism if given the opportunity.

The "graying" of the counter-recruitment movement could be addressed if more organizations follow the models offered by activists in Chicago, New York, and Oakland who have successfully involved youth in various campaigns. However, grassroots groups that wish to increase their level of youth organizing activity face a serious obstacle: garnering adequate funding to support this work. Of the three cases profiled, two—New York and Chicago—involved adult mentors who work as full-time paid staff. Given the difficulty involved in organizing youth, it is essential to pay someone to do it. Unfortunately, the salaried organizer in the counter-recruitment movement has become a rarity in recent years. In the past counter-recruiters learned about strategies and tactics from traveling field organizers paid by organizations like the Central Committee for Conscientious Objectors and the American Friends Service Committee. But the former no longer exists and the latter sharply reduced its Youth and Militarism Program in 2009. The disappearance of national organizations that supported counter-recruitment organizing has led to a fracturing of the movement. A twenty-year veteran of counter-recruitment in the Southwest sums up the effect: "We kind of feel like we're out here in our own little world" (author interview, August 7, 2012). While it is unlikely to expect a revival of the work done in the past by national organizations, progressive funders should consider supporting counter-recruitment groups that focus on youth organizing. Rick Jahnkow, the outspoken movement veteran, has criticized some major foundations for ignoring counter-recruitment while "funding nuclear weapons work as though we're still in the 1980s with the Reagan-era arms race" (author interview, May 27, 2010). These foundations, historically generous donors to peace and progressive causes, should reassess their priorities and support innovative, youth-led counter-recruitment efforts like those described in this chapter. The future of the counter-recruitment movement depends on it.

REFERENCES

BAY-Peace. (n.d.). Curriculum & organizing: The Youth Manifesto campaign and JAMRS opt-out. Retrieved from http://www.baypeace.org/curriculum-organizing.

Chicago JROTC. (2013, March 5). Chicago Public Schools, Department of JROTC Fact Sheet. Retrieved from http://www.chicagojrotc.com

Christianakis, M., & Mora, R. (2011). Charting a new course for public education through charter schools: Where is Obama taking us? In P. Carr & B. Porfilio (Eds.), *The phenomenon of Obama and the agenda for education: Can hope audaciously trump neoliberalism?* (pp. 97–120). Charlotte, NC: Information Age Publishing.

Goodman, D. (2009, September–October). A few good kids? *Mother Jones*. Retrieved from http://www.motherjones.com/politics/2009/09/few-good-kids

Goossen, R. (1997). *Women against the good war: Conscientious objection and gender on the American home front, 1941–1947*. Chapel Hill, NC: University of North Carolina Press.

Grady, B. (2012, July 13). Beating the school-to-prison pipeline. *Oakland Local*. Retrieved from http://oaklandlocal.com/article/beating-school-prison-pipeline

Hagopian, A., & Barker, K. (2011). Should we end military recruiting in high schools as a matter of child protection and public health? *American Journal of Public Health, 101*(1), 19–23.

Howlett, C. (1976). A dissenting voice: John Dewey against militarism in education. *Peace & Change, 3*(4), 49–60.

Illinois Interactive Report Card. (2012, August 14). Retrieved from http://iirc.niu.edu/

Jahnkow, R. (2009, July). *NNOMY national conference plenary presentation*. Unpublished paper presented at the National Conference of the National Network Opposing the Militarization of Youth, Chicago, IL.

Kershner, S. (2011). Youth in a suspect society: Seth Kershner interviews Henry Giroux. *Z Magazine, 24*(7/8), 39–40.

Mann, D. (2011, October). FY 12 Focus. *Recruiter Journal, 63*(9), 3.

National Network Opposing the Militarization of Youth. (2012, January 3). Delayed Entry Program/ DEP. Retrieved from http://nnomy.org

National Network Opposing the Militarization of Youth. (2011, September 7). JAMRS. Retrieved from http://nnomy.org

New York Civil Liberties Union. (2008). *Soldiers of misfortune: Abusive U.S. military recruitment and failure to protect child soldiers*. New York, NY: Author.

Pesature, D. (2012). Creative strategies for engaging difficult high schools. *Recruiter Journal, 64*(6), 9.

Quintanilla, R. (1999, November 12.) Two more city schools to go military. *Chicago Tribune*. Retrieved from http://articles.chicagotribune.com/1999-11-12/news/9911120183_1_student-cadets-public-schools-increase-student-achievement

Semple, K. (2009, April 1). One oath leads to another. *New York Times*. Retrieved from http://www.nytimes.com/2009/04/02/nyregion/02recruits.html?_r=1

Sharkey, J. (2008, December 18). No school left unsold: Arne Duncan's privatization agenda. *Counterpunch*. Retrieved from http://www.counterpunch.org/2008/12/18/arne-duncan-s-privatization-agenda/

Travieso, E. (2008). The U.S. peace movement during the Iraq War. *Peace Review, 20*(1), 121–128.

U.S. Army Recruiting Command. (2004). *School Recruiting Program Handbook*. Retrieved April 19, 2013 from www.usarec.army.mil/im/formpub/rec_pubs/p350_13.pdf.

Wall, T. (2009). *War-nation: Military and moral geographies of the Hoosier homefront*. (Doctoral dissertation). Retrieved from ProQuest Dissertations & Theses. UMI: 3353886

CHAPTER 18

TAKE THIS TEST AND . . .

Doing Unto Policy-Makers
What They Do Unto Students

Doug Selwyn
State University of New York–Plattsburgh

Bob Howard
University of Washington—Tacoma

In response to the nationwide wave of educational reforms during the 1980s and 1990s, the State of Washington passed legislation, House Bill 1209, to create new curriculum standards and a new assessment system. HB 1209 required that the state test all students at the end of fourth, seventh, and tenth grades, with the tenth grade test serving as an absolute gatekeeper to graduation. Students had to pass all sections of what came to be called the Washington Assessment of Student Learning (WASL) in tenth grade or they could not graduate, no matter their grade point average, teacher recommendations, involvement in service projects or school activities, other school achievements, or test scores on other exams (e.g., SAT). This was true for all students, including those in special

Left Behind in the Race to the Top, pages 275–286
Copyright © 2013 by Information Age Publishing
All rights of reproduction in any form reserved.

education, English Language Learner programs, students whose families moved often, and students who were homeless.

THE WASHINGTON ASSESSMENT OF STUDENT LEARNING (WASL)

The Commission on Student Learning brought teachers together to develop learning standards for students in the different disciplines and then hired a private contractor, Riverside Publishing, to develop the Washington Assessment of Student Learning based on the work the teams of teachers had done. Riverside Publishing included this caveat to the use of the test they had created:

> While school and district scores may be useful in curriculum and instructional planning, it is important to exercise extreme caution when interpreting individual report. . . . *Scores from one test given on a single occasion should never be used to make important decisions about students' placement, the type of instruction they receive, or retention in a given grade level in school.* It is important to corroborate individual scores on WASL tests with classroom-based and other local evidence of student learning (e.g., scores from district testing programs). *When making decisions about individuals, multiple sources of information should be used. Multiple individuals who are familiar with the student's progress and achievement—including parents, teachers, school counselors, school psychologists, specialist teachers, and perhaps the students themselves—should be brought together to collaboratively make such decisions.* (Pearson, 2008, p. 16, emphasis added)

The state clearly did not follow the warnings issued by the makers of the test: The WASL was used as a high-stakes instrument.

Chapter author Doug Selwyn tells his experience with the WASL:

> I taught a fourth/fifth grade class at an elementary school in Seattle. Close to two thirds of the students at the school were on free and reduced lunch, and nearly that same number of students were from families who did not speak English at home as a first language. The students were bright, curious, creative, cooperative, and willing to work hard. They produced academic work throughout the year that made it clear they were learning the skills and content required of them, and more. The students demonstrated what they had learned through a wide array of assignments, discussions, and projects, working alone, in small groups, and as members of our larger learning community. We teachers expected that the test would be a challenge for many of our students, because (a) most of them were language minority and would be taking it in a second (or third) language, and (b) because we did not organize our classrooms to match the testing regime, but we could not imagine how bad it would turn out to be. It was a disaster. Our students took more than two

weeks (working a part of every day) to complete the WASL. For most of the WASL sections, we would test in the mornings and recover in the afternoons. However, on the writing portions of the test, many of our nine- and ten-year-old students worked from nine until three to finish the complete writing cycle in one sitting, as required by the test. By the last days of testing, students were in tears, humiliated and defeated, and they returned to their classrooms stunned by the experience. We teachers were beside ourselves with anger, concern, and curiosity. Since the law forbade teachers to see the WASL's content, we could not really imagine what was happening to devastate our students, who we knew to be so capable and excited as learners.

In response to our questions and concerns, I decided to share the tests with the entire staff at my school (in violation of the WASL secrecy policy). The students had completed the tests, but we had not yet mailed them back. I wanted our colleagues to understand what was happening, and why, so that we could be more useful to our students. As my colleagues looked through the tests and became aware of what our students were facing, they grew angrier and more concerned. They saw page after page after page of readings that wore down our students, who clearly at a certain point simply started to turn pages. They saw writing sections that required our students (as previously mentioned) to complete the entire writing process in one sitting. This violates the essence of the writing process, which honors and provides structure for writers to take time, to consider and reflect as they work their way through the process. It was, in addition, absolutely inappropriate for so many in our population, taking this test in a second or third language. We saw math problems that were (in many cases) inappropriate in their complexity and subject matter (more suitable for higher grades), that didn't necessarily correspond to what we were asked to teach. In spite of our knowledge, anger, and concern, there was nothing we could do to respond, since we were not supposed to have seen the tests, and since the state did not seem to care what we teachers had to say about what we were seeing.

I was, subsequently, brought up on charges of insubordination for having shared the tests with my colleagues, and was investigated by the school district on orders from the state after someone from the state "overheard" a conversation I had with another teacher on an Internet discussion board dealing with assessment. I was interviewed by an administrator with the school district, who told me that the investigation had been ordered by OSPI. I never heard a thing after the interview and investigation. I know that my colleagues at the school were questioned, as was the principal, but then the matter seemed to just disappear. No resolution, no finding, no apology, nothing. I still have heard nothing, ten years later.

I refused to administer the tests the following year, and it was handled quietly within the school; another teacher administered the tests to my students and I worked with students who were not being tested. The results that following year were the same: children in tears, teachers outraged and helpless, and the state still seemingly indifferent to our concerns and questions. I left the district at the end of that school year to join the faculty at Antioch University, in the teacher education program.

LAUNCHING INITIATIVE 780

Bob, Doug, and David Marshak, professor emeritus of education at Seattle University, appeared on a panel, and following the panel had a conversation about the WASL and the impact it was having on our university students and programs, and on the students and schools in the Pacific Northwest. We decided to file a citizen's initiative, a means by which citizens of Washington State can place issues on the statewide November ballot by gathering approximately 200,000 signatures over a six-month period, from January to July. We chose the initiative route because we thought it might be unusual enough to garner attention; it would be a vehicle for stimulating conversation about the testing policies within the state; and it would allow us to help to communicate the concerns and frustrations of educators across the state, who could seemingly find no effective way to be heard.

We launched I-780, in January 2002. The press release announcing the initiative read as follows:

> A group of Washington State educators has filed an initiative, I-780, that requires any candidate running for any local or statewide office in Washington to take the same high stakes test required of all tenth grade students, and to post their scores in the Voter's Pamphlet and on the Secretary of State's web site. The details of the I-780 are:
>
>> Anyone running for any local or statewide office in the state will take all sections of the tenth grade WASL, (the Washington Assessment of Student Learning) at their own expense. The tests will be offered in proctored sites around the state and will be scored by the office of the Superintendent of Public Instruction. Scores will be posted in Voter's Pamphlet provided before elections and on the Secretary of State's web site.
>
> There are no requirements that candidates must pass all or any sections of the test, but they must complete the WASL and post their scores. (See Appendix for full text of the press release.)

Gathering Signatures

When we decided to file the initiative, the three of us had neither adequate time nor money sufficient to support our campaign. We hoped that educators, students and their family members, and other concerned citizens across the state would gather the signatures necessary to place the initiative on the ballot in November. More importantly, we hoped that I-780 would stimulate conversations about the WASL and the harm it was doing.

What we failed to predict was the degree of fear that was rampant within the education community. As Doug went out to gather signatures he quickly became aware of the pressures educators were feeling on this issue, and the chilling effect that pressure was having on them speaking up in their districts, and in their willingness to gather signatures. When he was on the street gathering signatures, teachers would race over to sign, thanking us for our work. Here is the way reporter Rebekah Denn (2002) described the scene in her article in the *Seattle Post Intelligencer* when he went out on the streets for the first time:

> Minutes after Doug Selwyn started gathering signatures for Initiative 780 at Safeco Field, the teachers emerged from the crowd with their pens in hand.
>
> "I'm a fourth-grade teacher. Let me sign that thing," one demanded.
>
> In just a few weeks, fourth-, seventh-, and 10th-grade teachers around the state will administer the Washington Assessment of Student Learning, the standardized test that will be required for high school graduation by 2008.
>
> And Selwyn, a former Seattle Public Schools teacher and an education professor at Antioch University, has banded with two other education professors to sponsor I-780, which would require anyone running for state or local office to take the 10th-grade version of the test—and to have their scores published in the voters' elections guide.
>
> It's an idea that triggered more than a few snickers from baseball fans as Selwyn gathered signatures at Safeco yesterday and last week. But it drew plenty of signatures along with the laughs, particularly from people who either taught in the schools or had connections to those who did.
>
> "I think people don't realize how difficult the WASL is, and how time-consuming it is to teach to the WASL," Ashley Mullin, who seeks a master's degree in education from the University of Washington, said as she paused to sign the I-780 petition yesterday.
>
> The sponsors say they're using an eye-catching theme in an attempt to raise a real point: Politicians should show the same level of educational achievement they say is necessary for today's high school students to succeed, and if politicians are willing to make a standardized test a sole barometer of student quality, they should make it a measure of their own as well.
>
> "There is a bit of theater in it. There is a sense of humor in it. But we are really trying to raise a serious question," said co-sponsor Bob Howard, an assistant professor at the University of Washington-Tacoma.
>
> "We're certainly not opposed to finding out what students know," he said. "But to have such high stakes on a single test doesn't seem to be educationally valid."

The three co-sponsors, including Seattle University professor David Marshak, are heading an all-volunteer drive to gather nearly 200,000 signatures and put the initiative on the November ballot...

"The politicians are asking the children to do something the politicians know nothing about," said teacher Dawn McGhan, as she took a handful of blank petitions to circulate in her southeastern Washington town. "The parents would sign it, too," she said.

Seattle parent Mary Lantz was one who did. "You have to take (the WASL) next year," she told her son Michael, a sixth-grader at Eckstein Middle School. "Wouldn't you like to know the politicians can pass it, too?"

Susan Dodds, a Northshore School District parent, said she hated seeing teachers tailor their lessons to the WASL for weeks before the test and having students getting "scared about it and nervous."

And the line of signers kept growing: two teachers from Franklin High; one from Bainbridge Island; two from University Place. Then came a woman whose best friend is a teacher, a naturalist who works in the schools, a retired fourth-grade Renton teacher and a teacher's son.

A teacher at Fairmount Park Elementary in Seattle said his students have made tremendous progress this year, but were starting from such a deficit that they still won't pass the only test that is being used to judge their success.

For others, the petition tapped frustration with lawmakers.

"I'm so tired of those clowns," said Peter Guerrero of Seattle, who approached Selwyn to sign a petition after spotting him on a Metro bus. "They need a damn 10th-grade test for those knuckleheads."

State Superintendent of Public Instruction Terry Bergeson—who would also have to take the test if the initiative passed—has defended the test in the past, saying that education reforms have already led to significant improvements in state schools.

Reaction from elected officials has ranged from humor to disgust, with some saying they would have no problem taking the exam and others saying it's an unnecessary distraction.

Howard said 200,000 signatures may be unrealistic for a volunteer effort.

"If we don't get 200,000 signatures, I hope we create 200,000 conversations, or 200,000 reflective moments."

Doug reflects on this experience:

What was surprising was the response I got when I encouraged teachers and others to take blank petitions so they could gather signatures back in their communities. The great majority said they would love to but they could not because they would be placing themselves at great risk by doing so. Many of them replied that their administrations would punish them, no matter whether it was legal or not. I got the same response from principals and other administrators, including an assistant superintendent of a small district outside of Seattle. Fear was rampant in districts across the state, from top to bottom. Teachers would complain to each other behind closed doors but were too scared to talk publicly, much less to gather signatures for the initiative. We came to call what we were seeing educational McCarthyism.

Not all of the articles in the media were as appreciative or supportive as Rebekah Denn's article had been. The state's largest newspapers editorialized against I-780. A columnist in one Tacoma newspaper, the *News-Tribune*, wrote against I-780 (Callaghan, 2002) "Initiative 780 is meant to humiliate, not educate." He continued:

> The initiative process is important. It should be respected. It should be reserved for serious legislation. It shouldn't be used for cheap shots or for games of political gotcha. . . .
>
> It is sponsored by three education professors and is certain to draw chuckles as well as signatures in school staff rooms across the state.
>
> But it's wrong in so many ways. . . . (p. A-1)

Callaghan then went on to list his twelve ways. Bob Howard (2002) chose to respond—point by point, making clear that our intent was not to humiliate, or attack the system, as Mr. Callaghan's column asserted, nor to avoid accountability. He said, "Including the WASL as one measure is fine with me. None of the sponsors of I-780 opposes assessment of students' knowledge and skills. None of us oppose accountability for educators—teachers, administrators, *and* university professors. It is simply a question of how best and most fairly to do it."

Doug Selwyn's (2002) response to Callaghan's column took the form of an op ed, published by the *Tacoma News Tribune*:

> Peter Callaghan's column of April 14 takes issue with Initiative 780, saying that it is meant to humiliate rather than to educate, and that it is an attack on the educational reform effort taking place in Washington State.
>
> We have grave concerns about what has happened in schools around the state as a consequence of this high-stakes policy, and we are concerned that there is an absence of real dialogue about the very serious damage being done to our students in the name of education reform.
>
> Our purposes for filing Initiative 780 are relatively simple.
>
> * We want an end to high-stakes testing . . . There is no one test or measure that can accurately reflect who someone is or what he or she knows or

can do. No one mandatory measure should determine a person's future opportunities.

- We want educators to make use of an array of assessments (for example, grade-point average, classroom evidence, tests, projects, group experiences, community work, service to the school, etc.) to make decisions about who will graduate.
- We want those who make this crucial decision to consider as much information as possible about each student so that they can make the best possible decision.
- The educational resources of the state should be focused on serving the educational needs of our students and educators rather than lining the pockets of testing companies and consultants. The state has spent around $100 million in pursuit of the development and scoring of the WASL, even as funding per student has gone down when adjusted for inflation....

We all know many people who are highly intelligent, highly skilled and highly functional even though they do not score well on paper-and-pencil tests, especially in high-pressure situations. This likely includes many of those who would be running for office, or who currently hold office in our state, and it's also true for our students. If we are so worried about humiliating or embarrassing adults, why aren't we concerned in those same ways about how we treat our own children?

Assessment should guide instruction and help both students and teachers to recognize the learning that is happening (or that is still required). WASL does neither. The WASL was never intended to be used to assess individual students, and it was most certainly not designed to be used as a graduation requirement, but that's exactly how it is being used.

NCLB

Provisions of the federal No Child Left Behind (NCLB) legislation also had an impact. The WASL was not initially designed as a test for all grades; the 1209 legislation required an assessment at the elementary level, the middle school/junior high level, and the high school level. To comply with NCLB's requirement for an annual test for students in grades three through eight, and once in high school, the State of Washington chose to expand the use of the expensive WASL, developing additional tests for each grade.

After the graduation requirement took effect, in 2008, Superintendent Bergeson trumpeted in a press release, "More than 90 percent of seniors meet key graduation requirement: Success rates for all ethnic groups exceed 80 percent" (Office of the Superintendent of Public Instruction, 2008, n.p.). Others looked at the numbers and were less celebratory:

In calculating the statewide WASL passing rate for this year's seniors, officials didn't count the thousands of members of the class of 2008 who had dropped out or were reclassified into other grades. . . . Bergeson's office estimates that as many as 14,500 students in the class of 2008 in Washington have dropped out since they started ninth grade and 9,500 have been reclassified in other grades. (Blanchard, 2008, n.p.)

As a state-specific test, the WASL does not allow easy comparisons with other exams or other states. Even if policymakers wanted to make conclusions based on WASL data, it is not clear that the data reveal more about student achievement or the test itself.

As we write this, more than ten years after filing the initiative, former Superintendent Bergeson is out of office, defeated by a candidate whose main election promise was to do away with the WASL. Although Ms. Bergeson was strongly supported by the business community, she was strongly opposed by the WEA, the largest teachers' union in the state, largely because of her continued support of the WASL. The current superintendent, Randy Dorn, has in fact done away with the WASL, replacing it with a number of smaller, less onerous tests. This was an important step, but far from enough.

Washington State still requires students to pass all sections of their tenth grade testing regime in order to graduate. The state (along with most other states) is also moving inexorably towards a national curriculum and national tests, which violate everything we know about assessment, about child development, and about how people learn. Our efforts at bringing a significant educational issue to the public, to stimulate significant and meaningful conversation about the WASL, and about the nature of our schools clearly played a role in the subsequent defeat of Ms. Bergeson and the ending of the WASL, but the fundamental attack on public schools continues, and we can only hope that a determined, creative, and effective resistance to those attacks continues as well. Our children and our democracy depend on it.

APPENDIX

Contacts:
Robert Howard 206.374.2414
Doug Selwyn 206.268.4616
David Marshak 206 329-1282

Press Release
February 12, 2002

I-780—CANDIDATES FOR PUBLIC OFFICE TAKE THE WASL (WASHINGTON ASSESSMENT OF STUDENT LEARNING)

A group of Washington State educators has filed an initiative, I-780, that requires any candidate running for any local or statewide office in Washington to take the same high stakes test required of all tenth grade students, and to post their scores in the Voter's Pamphlet and on the Secretary of State's web site. The details of the I-780 (full text of I-780 at: www.democracy.org) are:

Anyone running for any local or statewide office in the state will take all sections of the tenth grade WASL, (the Washington Assessment of Student Learning) at their own expense. The tests will be offered in proctored sites around the state and will be scored by the office of the Superintendent of Public Instruction.

Scores will be posted in Voter's Pamphlet provided before elections and on the Secretary of State's web site.

There are no requirements that candidates must pass all or any sections of the test, but they must complete the WASL and post their scores.

The educators filing the initiative—Bob Howard, David Marshak, and Doug Selwyn—are taking this step for several reasons:

(1) The legislature has defined the WASL as basic education. Passing the WASL is what it means to be well educated and ready to move into the adult world, and it is the only measure of that status. This is true for all students, no matter what their backgrounds, interests, skills, language bases, or any other factors are.

We are asking anyone running for office to be measured alongside the yardstick defined by our state legislature, to see how they measure up against those standards set for basic education, for high school students, for 10th graders, for 16 year olds. If the WASL has validity for the students, it should certainly have validity for the candidates and voters. If the 10th grade WASL is a measure of what adults need to know and be able to do to be successful in our world, then would this not be the case for elected officials, too?

(2) A single test cannot be an accurate, defining measurement of any student's knowledge and skills. There is no single test that can accurately and fairly measure what someone knows and can do. All it can reflect is what the student knew on a particular day, through the limited and inevitably biased medium of a particular test.

We agree that students should have some common knowledge base and some common skills to graduate from high school. However, we believe that given the diverse nature of human beings and the diverse resources that students gain from their families and communities, we need to provide students with a variety of ways through which they can demonstrate that knowledge and these skills.

(3) We know that there are many people in our society who are bright, capable, and gifted people who do not perform well on standardized, paper and pencil tests. We know that there are people with gifts who do not perform well under the kind of pressure created by high stakes tests.

The WASL privileges people who are good test takers and harms those who are not good test takers. But the activity of taking tests has very little value in and of itself in our society. Who makes a living or contributes to society or helps other people simply by being good at taking tests?

What remedy do we propose? No single high stakes test. No one measure should determine a person's future opportunities.

An array of assessments that really communicates who a student is and what he or she knows and can do. The assessments should help students, teachers, and parents to know what the student's strengths and weaknesses are, and they should lead to more effective teaching and learning.

Adequate resources and support to meet the needs of each student. Putting educational dollars into the pockets of test makers does not serve the best interests of the students or society. More than a hundred million dollars has gone into the development and implementation of the WASL; this is money that could have been used to better educate our students. Now even more money will be spent on the WASL if we have to give it every year from grades 3–8, as required by new federal legislation just passed by Congress and signed by the President.

The proponents of this initiative are committed to gathering the required 200,000 signatures to put the measure before the voters in November. This is an entirely volunteer effort; volunteers can download petitions for I-780 at www.democracy.org and they can also contact the initiative authors at that site.

REFERENCES

Blanchard, J. (2008, June 4). 90% of seniors pass WASL, but critics say results skewed. *Seattle Post-Intelligencer.* Retrieved from http://seattlepi.nwsource.com/local/365595_graduation04.html

Callaghan, P. (2002). Initiative 780 is meant to humiliate, not educate. *The News Tribune.* Retrieved from http://search.tribnet.com/archive/archive30/0414b13.html

Denn, R. (2002, April 8). Subjecting politicians to WASL test gains support. *Seattle Post-Intelligencer.* Retrieved from http://seattlepi.nwsource.com/local/65657_wasl08.asp

Howard, R. W. (2002). Math ratings fail apples-oranges test. *The News Tribune.* Retrieved from http://www.thenewstribune.com/opinion/insight/story/89267.html

Office of the Superintendent of Public Instruction. (2008, June 3). *More than 90 percent of seniors meet key graduation requirement.* Office of the Superintendent of Public Instruction. Retrieved from http://www.k12.wa.us/communications/pressreleases2008/Class2008Update.aspx?printable=true

Pearson Publishing. (2008). *Washington Assessment of Student Learning, Grade 10, 2007 Technical Report.* Olympia, WA, Office of the Superintendent of Public Instruction.

Selwyn, D. (2002, April 21). Is too much weight placed on students' WASL scores? YES: High-stakes testing will backfire. *The News Tribune.* Retrieved from http://search.tribnet.com/archive/archive30/0421b112.html2

CHAPTER 19

HIGH-STAKES TESTING

A Parent's Perspective

Dora Taylor
Parents Across America

An excerpt from *An Open Letter to Arne Duncan* by Herb Kohl:

> ...I discovered then, in my early teaching career, that learning is best driven
> by ideas, challenges, experiences, and activities that engage students. My ex-
> perience over the past 45 years has confirmed this.
>
> We have come far from that time in the '60s. Now the mantra is high expecta-
> tions and high standards. Yet, with all that zeal to produce measurable learning
> outcomes we have lost sight of the essential motivations to learn that moved my
> students. Recently I asked a number of elementary school students what they
> were learning about and the reactions were consistently, "We are learning how
> to do good on the tests." They did not say they were learning to read.
>
> It is hard for me to understand how educators can claim that they are creating
> high standards when the substance and content of learning is reduced to the
> mechanical task of getting a correct answer on a manufactured test. (Kohl, 2009)

As this quote by Herb Kohl denotes, the emphasis on testing has created a culture of test takers and test givers in our public schools. This focus
on testing leads to unnecessary pressure on students to perform well on a

Left Behind in the Race to the Top, pages 287–296
Copyright © 2013 by Information Age Publishing
All rights of reproduction in any form reserved.

standardized test. It causes a teacher to emphasize a narrow scope of material. It leaves little opportunity for students to develop their creative and critical thinking skills, and it is used incorrectly as a tool in the evaluation of a teacher, a principal, and a school with serious consequences to the students and their community.

MY VIEWPOINT AS A PARENT AND A TEACHER

The results of high-stakes testing did not become apparent to me until my daughter and I moved to another state and a new school.

From pre-school through 7th grade, my daughter attended a small private school. The emphasis at the school was on understanding that there were different paths to solving a problem. This approach included math.

My daughter excelled in math. She found it to be fun and challenging and had accelerated to discussing areas of physics and astronomy with her teachers. The staff appreciated her interest and enjoyed spending time talking to her on related subjects.

Then we moved. I selected a public school based on state test scores. My reasoning was that if the overall test scores were excellent, the teaching staff and school must be excellent as well.

My daughter started school, ready to take on all subjects with confidence and a joy of learning that she had developed over the years at her previous school.

Then she started to have trouble with math. She found it boring and seemed to be struggling with it. She would come home and tell me that the other students knew how to take a test but she didn't. Her joy of exploring math began to diminish. She had learned that there were different ways to solve a problem, but at her new school, there was only one way. Instead of discussing String Theory she was learning baseball scores. Apparently the teacher thought that the class could better relate to how Ichiro was doing with the Mariners than other concepts related to math. My daughter, having no interest in baseball, also had no interest in the information that the teacher was providing. The material was no longer interesting or challenging. It had been distilled down to discreet pieces of information with little understanding of the relationship of one math function to another. These smaller pieces of information were easy for some students to memorize and retain at least long enough to provide the "correct" answer on a multiple choice exam. In other words the information had been dumbed down in preparation for a standardized test.

Fortunately, we discovered a progressive alternative school in Seattle that made her comfortable with her own intellect and methods of exploration. There she thrived. The emphasis at Nova High School was not on test scores but on project-based learning, which includes creativity and critical thinking when developing a project.

My other experience has been as a teacher introducing architecture to students in grades 3 through high school.

What I discovered over the last 12 years is that students who are inculcated in test taking expect me to provide answers for them to solve a design challenge. They think that there is one way to approach a design problem. During my time with these students, my goal has been to help them understand that there are as many ways to approach a problem as there are people in this world.

In general, I can guess correctly what type of school a student has been a part of, whether it is test oriented, alternative, private, or even British. When a child is raised understanding that problems can be solved in more than one way and that, many times, more than one answer is correct, there is also a joy in creating, building, and problem solving.

PUSH BACK: OPTING OUT

Parents, teachers, principals, school board members, and education administrators are beginning to understand that this focus on testing has damaging effects on their schools and their students.

In Seattle, for example, the MAP test is administered twice each school year with the choice for the student to be tested a third time. During the school year, there is also the statewide measurement of student progress (MSP) that is administered to students in Seattle. That is three if not four standardized tests that a student in public school is required to take unless the parents opt their student out of the testing.

Because of that, parents, communities, and even states are either signing resolutions to opt out of standardized testing, and students are being pulled out of the testing regimen by their parents. There are parent groups in Washington State, Florida, New York, Pennsylvania, and Texas that have formed to say "No" to the standardized testing. As of this writing, the list of parents opting their students out of standardized testing continues to grow.

The New York State Parent Teacher Association created a resolution on ending high-stakes testing in 2012. The introductory paragraphs are as follows:

> There is now more than two decades of scientific research demonstrating that high-stakes testing regimes yield unreliable measures of student learning. Such tests cannot serve as a basis for determining teacher effectiveness. In fact, scientific research shows that high-stakes testing lowers the quality of education. Some of the documented harmful outcomes of high-stakes testing are: "teaching to the test"; narrowed curriculum opportunities; increased emotional dis-

tress among children and increased "drop outs"; corruption; the marginalization of both very high performing students and students with special needs; an overall lowering of standards and disregard for individual difference, critical thinking and human creativity. Thus, high-stakes testing has been proven to be an ineffective tool for preparing students for the 21st century.

The intent of this resolution is to ask the State Education Department to suspend its testing program until such time as it can create a new one that reliably measures educational progress without harming children and lowering the quality of education. We need a testing program that helps students and schools, not harms them. (Taylor, 2012)

And one of the resolutions:

RESOLVED, that the New York State Parent Teacher Association calls on Andrew Cuomo, Governor of the State of New York, the Board of Regents of the State University of New York, and Dr. John B. King, Jr., Commissioner of the State Education Department to enact a moratorium on policies that force New York State public schools to rely on high-stakes testing due to the fact that there is no convincing evidence that the pressure associated with high-stakes testing leads to any important benefits to student achievement. (Taylor, 2012)

School #12 in Rochester, New York urged parents to have their students opt out of the state test. According to one of the members of the PTA:

"We're asking parents to boycott the test, still send their children to school," said Vicki Robertson, the PTA vice-president. "We've asked the principal to have an alternative activity for the children to do and she's assured us that there will be, so they can get some usefulness out of their day." (Taylor, 2012)

In Snohomish, Washington, parents organized to opt their students out of standardized tests and established a group called We Support Schools Snohomish.

Initially, the group had lobbied against budget cuts to education in Washington State and then continued by establishing a successful opt-out campaign in their school district. They started a Facebook page that grew quickly and began to catch the attention of the local press.

Newspapers in the state picked up the news, and word spread quickly. Some of the newspapers were the *Herald Net*, "Some Snohomish parents opt out of standard tests" (Dominguez, 2012), the *News Tribune*, "Parents of 550 Snohomish students refuse to let kids take MSPs" (Associated Press, 2012a), and the *Seattle Post Intelligencer*, "WA parents refuse to let their 550 kids take MAPS" (Associated Press, 2012b).

State Representative Mike Hope met with representatives of We Support Schools Snohomish, and after the meeting made this entry on his website:

> "Parents in my community are concerned because they see teachers being laid off while money is used for tests that don't benefit their kids," said Hope. "Parents are having to pay for additional tutoring outside of school, because kids aren't getting enough time with their teachers and class sizes are increasing. Meanwhile, the state spends millions of dollars on the MSP." ("Rep. Mike Hope," 2012)

Hope has supported changes to assessments and test funding in the past. In 2011, he sponsored House Bill 1519, which gave schools flexibility in how they test students with cognitive disabilities. Until the bill became law in July, the practice was for students to take a complicated assessment.

This year, Hope sponsored legislation (House Bill 2633) that would give parents information about required assessments and the cost for administering them. Hope plans to propose legislation that would allow parents and school districts to opt out of state-mandated tests. The legislation is necessary in order to avoid repercussions for students whose parents have opted out: "We need legislation that makes opting out a legal alternative for parents and an accepted option for students" ("Rep. Mike Hope," 2012). In the end, 550 students in the Snohomish School District opted out of the state test.

The state education commissioner in Texas, Robert Scott, said that standardized testing is the "end-all, be-all" and is a "perversion" of what a quality education should be (Burka, 2012). He called "the assessment and accountability regime" not only "a cottage industry but a military-industrial complex," and he attacked the Common Core Standards Initiative as being motivated by business concerns (Burka, 2012). He agreed to postpone the requirement that end-of-the-year test results should account for 15% of a student's final grade:

> I believe that testing is good for some things, but the system that we have created has become a perversion of its original intent, the intent to improve teaching and learning. The intent to improve teaching and learning has gone too far afield, and I look forward to reeling it back in. (Burka, 2012)

Kelli Moulton, the superintendent of Hereford Independent School District in Texas, was quoted as saying that she was considering not turning in to the state Education Department her students' end of the school year STAAR exam results (Smith, 2012a).

Tom Pauken, the Texas Workforce Commissioner, stated in a speech to students at Texas State Technical College that before he vacates his seat, he plans to focus on working with legislative leaders to do away with standardized testing. He stated that the focus has become "teaching to the test" and little else (Pauken, 2012). In an interview, Pauken was quoted as saying, "I'm really concerned we're choking off the pipeline of skilled workers that our employers need," he said. "We're spending too much time and effort teaching to the test instead of focusing on real learning" (Pauken, 2012).

In Florida, U.S. Representative Kathy Castor has called on Education Secretary Arne Duncan to investigate Florida's school accountability system and the state FCAT tests (Fitzpatrick, 2012). She stated during a press conference that "We need some accountability for Florida's accountability system" (Fitzpatrick, 2012). This is in reaction to variations in test scores and the state deciding to lower the bar on test scores. FCAT test results in Florida are tied to student promotion, graduation, and teachers' pay (Fitzpatrick, 2012).

Representative Castor has called for an outside audit of the testing system as called for in a resolution created by the Florida School Board Association.

In 2011, 1,400 principals in the state of New York formed an organization called The New York Principals and signed an open letter protesting the use of students' test scores to evaluate teachers' and principals' performance (Feeney & Burris, 2012).

A "National Resolution of High-Stakes Testing" was written by a group of organizations including the Advancement Project; Asian-American Legal Defense and Education Fund; Fair Test; Forum for Education and Democracy; Mecklenburg ACTS; Deborah Meier; NAACP Legal Defense and Educational Fund, Inc.; National Education Association; New York Performance Standards Consortium; Tracy Novick; Parents Across America; Parents United for Responsible Education–Chicago; Diane Ravitch; Race to Nowhere; Time Out From Testing; and United Church of Christ Justice and Witness Ministries and posted by Fair Test (National Resolution, 2012).

Within two weeks, 240 organizations and 6,000 individuals concerned about the damaging effects of high-stakes testing endorsed the resolution.

In Seattle, teachers, parents and students have boycotted the MAP test at several schools. According to the letter that was written to the superintendent from the teachers at Garfield High School:

December 21, 2012

To Whom It May Concern:

We, the Garfield teachers, respectfully decline to give the MAP test to any of our students. We have had different levels of experiences with MAP in our varied careers, have read about it, and discussed it with our colleagues. After this thorough review, we have all come to the conclusion that we cannot in good conscience subject our students to this test again. This letter is an objection to the MAP test specifically and particularly to its negative impact on our students. Here are our reasons:

- Seattle Public School staff has notified us that the test is not a valid test at the high school level. For these students, the margin of error is greater than the expected gain. We object to spending time, money, and staffing on an assessment even SPS agrees is not valid.
- We are not allowed to see the contents of the test, but an analysis of the alignment between the Common Core and MAP shows little overlap. We object to our students being tested on content we are not expected to teach.
- Ninth graders and students receiving extra support (ELL, SPED, and students in math support) are targets of the MAP test. These students are in desperate need of MORE instructional time. Instead, the MAP test subtracts many hours of class time from students' schedules each year. If we were to participate this year, we would take 805 students out of class during 112 class periods. The amount of lost instructional time is astounding. On average students would EACH lose 320 minutes of instructional time. This is over 5 hours of CORE class time (language arts and math) that students are losing. We object to participating in stealing instructional time from the neediest students.
- In an appeal of the Board's 2010 decision to renew the MAP contract, a parent group raised concerns about the negative impact of this test "on non-English speakers, Special Education students, and minority and low income children." These concerns were never addressed nor were the claims refuted. Imagine a native Somali student with limited English skills, sitting in front of a computer taking an evaluative reading test that will no doubt be confusing and overwhelming to the student. The test is supposed to determine the student's reading level, but without taking into account the student's language challenge or the student's limited time in the United States, which makes it almost impossible to understand the context of some passages. For these students and our students with IEPs, the test does actual harm. The students feel stupid yet are being forced to take a test that has NO benefit to them or their educational goals. We object to a test that may violate the rights of groups of students for whom schooling already constitutes an uphill battle.
- In addition to students losing class time to take the test, our computer labs are clogged for weeks with test taking and cannot be used for other educational purposes. For example, students who have a research project no longer have access to the computers they need to further their exploration into their research topic. This especially hurts students without computers at home. We object to our educational resources being monopolized by a test we cannot support.
- We see that our students do not take the test seriously as they know that it will not directly impact their class grade or graduation status. They approach it less and less seriously the more times they take it. Therefore, we see achievement scores go down after instruction. We object to spending scarce resources on a test that is peripheral to our students' education.

- The MAP test was originally introduced by then superintendent Maria Goodloe-Johnson while she was a board member of the Northwest Evaluation Association, the company that sells the MAP. When Dr. Goodloe-Johnson was fired, the MAP somehow survived the housecleaning. We object to having to give a test whose existence in our district is the result of scandal.
- Even the NWEA itself, the parent company to MAP, has advised districts to carefully restrict the use of the test and its results. NWEA also cautions to ensure 100% random selection of students enrolled in any course if the test is used for evaluation and to take into consideration statistical error in designing evaluation policies. NWEA says that problems become "particularly profound at the high school level." None of these or other criteria urged by NWEA has been met. We object to being evaluated by a test whose author suggests extreme caution in its use and warns against valid legal action if the test is used in personnel decisions.
- The Seattle Education Association passed a resolution condemning the MAP test that reads, "Whereas testing is not the primary purpose of education... Whereas the MAP was brought into Seattle Schools under suspicious circumstances and conflicts of interest... Whereas the SEA has always had the position of calling for funding to go to classroom and student needs first... Be it Resolved that... the MAP test should be scrapped and/or phased out and the resources saved be returned to the classroom." We object to having to give it after such an opinion from our collective voice has been registered.

We are not troublemakers nor do we want to impede the high functioning of our school. We are professionals who care deeply about our students and cannot continue to participate in a practice that harms our school and our students. We want to be able to identify student growth and determine if our practice supports student learning. We wish to be evaluated in a way that helps us continue to improve our practice, and we wish for our colleagues who are struggling to be identified and either be supported or removed. The MAP test is not the way to do any of these things. We feel strongly that we must decline to give the MAP test even one more time.

Sincerely,

The Teachers of Garfield High School

In Texas, a resolution on high-stakes testing passed by more than 360 school boards. Two websites have been created in response to this emphasis on testing. Fair Test (www.fairtest.org) provides information on testing and test assessments and updates on what is happening around the country in terms of testing and parents opting their students out of high-stakes testing. The other website, United Opt Out National (unitedoptout.com), provides useful information on how parents can legally opt their students out of standardized tests.

CONCLUSION

A University of Texas at Austin professor, Walter Stroup, developed a math pilot program in 2011 for middle school students in Dallas. The students' understanding of math had improved over the months as students took part in this pilot program, but at the end of the year, students' scores increased only slightly on a state standardized test, the Texas Assessment of Knowledge and Skills assessment (TAKS). TAKS had been administered since 2003 and was used as an indicator to what students should be promoted or allowed to graduate from high school.

Mr. Stroup and two other researchers studied the test and believe they found the reason for this and other discrepancies. According to Stroup, there is "a glitch embedded in the DNA of the state exams that, as a result of a statistical method used to assemble them, suggests they are basically useless at measuring the effects of classroom instruction" (Smith, 2012b).

Since then, the state of Texas has replaced the TAKS test with another standardized test referred to as STARR to be rolled out in 2013.

Will this new test be any better? Should it be used to decide who is promoted to the next grade and who can graduate from high school? Should it be used to determine the fate of a teacher's career or that of a community public school?

Until we know without any doubt that there is a fair and reliable way to measure student performance and growth, these tests should not be used to control the fate of our public schools.

There has been so much focus placed on test scores that our students are losing the joy of learning. One of my most memorable times in high school was when my English teacher took two weeks to read *A Tale of Two Cites* to us. His dramatic flair and probing questions left a permanent impression on my mind. I will never forget those days or that book. My concern is for those lost hours of exploration, wonder, and surprise that bring about the exciting sparks of learning and creativity.

Let's not allow that sense of excitement to be lost amidst the hours of memorization of facts that will become lost over time when not set into a meaningful context.

REFERENCES

Associated Press. (2012a). Parents of 550 Snohomish students refuse to let kids take MSPs. *The News Tribune*. Retrieved from http://www.thenewstribune. com/2012/05/13/2143215/parents-of-550-snohomish-students.html

Associated Press. (2012b). WA parents refuse to let their 550 kids take MAPS. *Kitsap Sun*. Retrieved from http://www.kitsapsun.com/news/2012/may/12/wa-parents-refuse-to-let-their-550-kids-take/#axzz2MhDrmRtG

Burka, P. (2012). The Big Test. *Texas Monthly, 40*. Retrieved from http://www.texas-monthly.com/story/big-test

Dominguez, A. (2012). Some Snohomish parents opt out of standard tests. *Herald Net*. Retrieved from http://www.heraldnet.com/article/20120326/NEWS01/703269935

Feeney, S. C., & Burris, C. C. (2012). An open letter of concern regarding New York State's APPR legislation for the evaluation of teachers and principals. *New York Principals*. Retrieved from http://www.newyorkprincipals.org/system/app/pages/search?scope=search-site&q=Open+Letter+of+Concern+Regardi ng+New+York+State%27s+APPR+Legislation+for+the+Evaluation+of+Teache rs+and+Principals+

Fitzpatrick, C. (2012). U.S. Rep Kathy Castor calls for federal review of FCAT. *Tampa Bay Times*. Retrieved from http://www.tampabay.com/blogs/gradebook/content/us-rep-kathy-castor-calls-federal-review-fcat/2069475

Kohl, H. (2009). Secretary of Education: Arne Duncan. *Seattle Education*. Retrieved from http://seattleducation2010.wordpress.com/race-to-the-top/arne-duncan/

"National Resolution on High Stakes Testing." (2012). *Time out from testing*. Retrieved from http://timeoutfromtesting.org/nationalresolution/

Pauken, P. (2012). Tom Pauken's speech at Texas State Technical College in Waco. *Texas GOP Vote*. Retrieved from http://www.texasgopvote.com/reclaim-education/tom-pauken-s-speech-texas-state-technical-college-waco-may-3-2012-004204

"Rep. Mike Hope supports Snohomish parent's stance on testing." (2012). *Washington House Republicans*. Retrieved from http://houserepublicans.wa.gov/tag/assessments/

Smith, M. (2012a). In Texas, a backlash against student testing. *The Texas Tribune, 29*(5). Retrieved from http://www.texastribune.org/2012/02/06/in-texas-a-backlash-against-student-testing/

Smith, M. (2012b). A serious design flaw is suspected in state tests. *The Texas Tribune, 29*(28). Retrieved from http://www.texastribune.org/2012/07/30/design-flaw-suspected-texas-standardized-tests/

Taylor, D. (2012). High stakes testing and opting out: The push back. *Seattle Education*. Retrieved from http://seattleducation2010.wordpress.com/2013/01/14/part-5-high-stakes-testing-and-opting-out-the-push-back/

CHAPTER 20

TEACHING YOUNG CHILDREN SOCIAL JUSTICE BASICS

The Public, Equality, and the Common Good

Ann C. Berlak
San Franciso State University (Retired)

INTRODUCTION

We live in a society of metastasizing inequality, where the degree of wealth owned by the One Percent is well beyond the comprehension of most of us. Conceptions of equity and the common good are peripheral to or absent from the school curricula that shape students' visions of possible and desirable futures; what is taught in schools, for the most part, insures that injustices will be reproduced in the next generations.

In the Spring of 2012, I, a recently retired teacher educator whose life work had been advocating that children be taught to think about social justice beginning in elementary schools, was wondering how to contribute to the burgeoning social movements that were springing up across the globe under the banner of "Occupy." Following Myles Horton's dictum "Dig

Left Behind in the Race to the Top, pages 297–313
Copyright © 2013 by Information Age Publishing
297

where you stand" (Adams, 1975), I arranged to teach what I now call "social justice basics" to first, fourth, and fifth grade students at Lakeview, a public elementary school in Oakland, California. I taught in each classroom one hour a week from the end of April until the close of the school year. This chapter presents several sketches of my adventures in those classes. I hope each sketch will demonstrate the possibility and value of making critical thinking, social justice, and empowerment "basic" in elementary schools. Such "basics" are essential for the survival of democracy and of the planet.

HISTORICAL AND LOCAL CONTEXTS: WISCONSIN, OCCUPY, AND THE OAKLAND UNIFIED SCHOOL DISTRICT

Wisconsin

The spring of 2012 was a time of hope for those who wanted to participate in the creation of a more just society. Progressives across the U.S. had our eyes on Wisconsin, where a wide range of groups—union members, retirees, farmers, public school teachers, firefighters, students, and many others—had initiated the recall of Wisconsin's Governor Walker (Nichols, 2012). The recall had been sparked by Walker's assault on Wisconsin's unions and public services. It had become a national symbol of hope for empowering poor and working/middle-class people and reversing the anti-union and austerity agenda of the One Percent. Opposition to the recall had been bank-rolled by corporate privatizers and billionaire political donors across the U.S.

In June, 2012, as I began to write, we learned that the attempt to unseat Governor Walker and all he represented had failed. The election's outcome indicated that, despite the energetic and historic solidarity of recall supporters across the country, the Wisconsin electorate was not ready to stitch up the disintegrating safety net nor put an end to the abrogation of workers' rights, foreclosures, and the explosion of homelessness, food insecurity, and child poverty (Knafo, 2012; Pugh, 2012).

The hopefulness of the recall moment and its ultimate demise provides one context for this chapter. It confirmed the principle that had guided me throughout my career: Teaching social justice basics to young children must be an essential part of any project that intends to challenge inequality and promote a more humane and sustainable world. Each lesson I taught at Lakeview provided additional evidence, some of which is presented below, that elementary-school-age children have already begun to take for granted some of the basics of *in*justice, including competition, individualism, hierarchy, obedience to authority, consumerism, and the primacy of private property—all of which the majority of the Wisconsin electorate endorsed when they voted against the recall.

The textbooks, prescribed curriculum, and "high-stakes" standardized testing continue to reproduce, reinforce, and normalize the basic elements of a worldview that sustains inequity and injustice. As the twig is bent, the tree grows. Teaching social justice basics is one way to interrupt this process. What are social justice basics? They include learning to value equality in all its complexity, social, political and economic; thinking about the social world in terms of the common, the public good, to recognize varieties of injustice and their underlying structures; and learning how people can act together to create a more just world (Berlak & Moyenda, 2001).

Oakland Unified School District: The Local Context

The magnificent Lakeview School building where I taught, the oldest public school building in Oakland, was located in a working/middle-class neighborhood. More than half its students commuted from poorer neighborhoods, many parents having chosen this school because it was a safe haven in a safe neighborhood. Sixty-eight percent of the children were African American, ten percent Latino, one percent Caucasian, and the others of Asian heritage or multiracial.

The school was one of the five elementary schools, all attended primarily by low-income black and brown students, that the Oakland Unified School Board had decided to close at the end of the school year. The closing of the five schools was part of a decades-long history of closing schools attended primarily by lower-income families. Lakeview was to be transformed into district administrative offices.

Each of the five schools had been a healthy stable school community. By the time I found my way to Lakeview, most parents, teachers, community members, and children, after a winter of significant organized protest, considered the school closings a done deal. However, Occupy Oakland Education, a small group of activists closely connected to Oakland schools as parents, community members, and staff still had not given up.

The Occupy Context

In the eight months before I began teaching at Lakeview, the notion that people acting together can change the conditions of their lives was in the air. The Occupy Wall Street Movement had initiated a shift in the national conversation from a fixation on austerity and balancing the budget to a discussion of income inequality, corporate greed, and the centralization of wealth by the richest One Percent. The concept of social class, previously absent from public discourse, had entered mainstream dialogue (Knefel, 2012). Then, as Occupy slowed down for the winter, partly in response to coordinated nationwide politically driven evictions of Occupy camps, media references to "Occupy Wall Street," "The Occupy movement," "income inequality," and, to an even greater extent, "corporate greed" waned. However, Occupy's most prominent slogan—"We are the ninety-nine Percent" and the other side of the equation, "the One Percent"—survived as new ways of talking about unequal wealth (Knefel, 2012).

In April, a parent activist at Lakeview introduced me to two experienced and talented African American teachers, Ms. Martin and Ms. Teagroves, who invited me to teach "social justice" to their fourth and fifth graders. I taught my first class two weeks before May Day.[1] Occupy Oakland Education and the Lakeview School community had planned to participate in the May Day citywide demonstrations by protesting against the school closings. The anti-school-closing demonstrations most children had attended during the past year, parents', teachers' and children's presentations to the school board, and the firsthand experience many students had had with the Occupy Oakland tent city located near some children's homes provided funds of knowledge that I thought would give Lakeview students an experiential "head start." I soon discovered that the most important thing they learned from their experience opposing the school closings was that organized protest is entirely ineffectual.

TEACHING FOURTH GRADE

On the first hot morning of the year, I walk across the concrete playground, ten minutes early for my visit to Ms. Martin's classroom. It will be my third visit, and I recognize many familiar faces. As I approach, I am surrounded by fourth graders who pause their jump rope and four-square to ask if I'm coming to their class today. I nod; they respond with their equivalent of a "thumbs up."

In the prior two classes, I've introduced the Occupy movement by reading from *Octopi*, a children's zine for understanding the Occupy movement, written by credential students I had taught during my last semester to convey some social justice basics, including unemployment, foreclosure, and solidarity. The children have shared personal experiences with unemployment: "My sister graduated from college and can't find a job;" "My uncle has been out of work for a year. He won't take a job at McDonald's, and my auntie is mad about it." We've role-played the banks doing foreclosures and acted out why bosses fire people and ship jobs overseas. The children have considerable firsthand understanding of these issues, though, given the specifications of the curriculum standards and the "policing" function of standardized tests, they previously hadn't had an opportunity to share it in their classrooms.

They've drawn pictures of their ideal communities; we've defined and begun to use the word *public* as a way of naming community features available for everyone, rich or poor, and they've made a preliminary list of public services and activities they want in their communities. I've told them that at one time there were many more public jobs than there are now—building roads or parks, for example, or writing plays, painting murals, or collecting songs. They were impressed to learn that not so long ago, after-school programs were absolutely free.

I had posed the big question: How will the public activities you want be paid for? The responses: "Obama," "the Mayor," "the Governor."

"Where would *they* get the money?" I asked. Several children had eventually suggested that people could pool their money to pay for public activities, and I had labeled this "taxes."

I had organized a simple simulation in which I paid each child $60 as wages for their work week—the amount determined by my limited supply of monopoly money—telling the children, "This is your pay for working at an automobile factory." Then I'd told them I make the laws and have decided that everyone must contribute twenty dollars of their pay for the creation and maintenance of public services they want most in their ideal community. I had listed their "public service" proposals horizontally on the whiteboard above the eraser shelf and asked the students to place twenty of their sixty dollars on the eraser shelf under the proposals they wanted most. I knew they were seriously weighing the alternatives when they asked for change for their twenty dollar bills, in order to spend their money on a broader array of choices. I had left them facing the reality that there really wasn't enough money to pay for everything we wanted.

I did not anticipate that someone (I was unable to identify exactly who) had taken it upon him or herself to reallocate other children's money to saving Lakeview. Next time we will have to discuss what to do when we disagree with others' priorities.

Vignette #1: Meritocracy, Equal Opportunity and Horatio Alger

May 7. I had been eagerly awaiting the third class. This time I tell all but two of the children they earn $60 a week on the assembly line. The classroom teacher and I pay the "employees" and send them "home" for the weekend. I then give a designated "boss" all the $500 bills I have—hanging a sign around his neck to label him the One Percent. I pay the "assistant boss" all the $100 bills, referring to her as a member of the upper ten percent.

Next, I asked students to talk in pairs to decide how much the boss, the assistant boss, and the workers should pay in taxes. What is fair? I tell them this is what President Obama is arguing with the Republicans about right now. I ask my One Percenter whether he thinks he should pay the same amount in taxes as the workers who earn sixty dollars a week. "Definitely," he says. I challenge him: "Don't you think you should pay more than the others? You have way more than you need!" "No way. If I did that I might not still be the One Percent." Some boos from his classmates. He assures them, "I'm just playing the role."

Most of the students are now debating what would be a fair taxing program, no longer using "classroom voices." They want to talk about this with the whole class, not only with one desk partner. (The archetypal teacher fear of "losing control" of the class floats at the edge of my consciousness.)

Thinking that perhaps after we have a whole-class discussion they will agree to talk in pairs, I ask if there are any questions. Without skipping a single beat, Angela blurts out "How did the rich get so rich in the first place?"

"Why do you want to know that right now?" I ask.

"I need to know in order to decide how much tax the One Percent should pay."

I respond, "How do *you* think the rich get rich?"

Again, many voices at once. "They went to college." "They worked hard in school." "They are on time to work and so the boss likes them." Horatio Alger is alive and well. "They won the lottery." This is followed by lively discussion in response to one child's claim that people who win the lottery spend all their money in one year.

I enter the conversation about who gets rich by introducing the idea that everyone inherits an economic status. Since neither the concept nor the term *inheritance* has as yet been mentioned by any child, I infer that it is not central in any student's consciousness.

* * *

In modern U.S. society, fairness is associated with equal opportunity: Everyone should have a fair shot at the American Dream. From their earliest years in school, children hear teachers telling them in countless ways, both explicitly and implicitly, that they live in a meritocracy and if they are honest, follow directions, and do all their work, they will be able to go to college and then to find a job that sustains at least a middle-class family life.

However, in spite of omnipresent homilies about working hard in school in order to get rich, schooling is not a magic key to wealth for most people in the U.S. In the U.S., the chances of someone making it to the top, or even to the middle, from a place near the bottom are lower than any other advanced industrial country, and those at the top can take comfort from knowing that their chances of becoming downwardly mobile are lower in the U.S. than elsewhere (Stiglitz, 2012).

Even if schools were to provide equal opportunity, according to the Bureau of Labor Statistics, by 2020 the overwhelming majority of jobs will still require only a high school diploma or less, and nearly three-fourths of job openings over the next ten years will pay a median yearly wage of less than $35,000. In other words, millions of Americans are and will remain over-educated and underpaid (Cockburn, 2012). Though, as we have seen, even young children may have firsthand knowledge about class mobility and economic opportunity that casts doubt upon the myth of meritocracy, most of the official school knowledge presented to them through the hidden and explicit curriculum eventually contradicts the personal knowledge they bring into the classroom. As adults they may recognize at some level of consciousness that meritocracy is a myth, but many will likely live their daily lives as if it were true, reflexively judging their and others' fortunes in terms of individual inadequacies rather than rigged elevators.

Why bother to disabuse young children of the myth of meritocracy? Won't doing so erode their motivation to learn in school? Young children must early on reconsider their unexamined beliefs in meritocracy and the pay-off of schooling because, if they do not do so, by the time they are adults the worldviews through which they apprehend social and political experience will already be substantially formed and these views will exclude accurate information about who does and does not get ahead. If such myths are not contested, most children will as adults find it difficult to recognize the omnipresent machinations of privilege and power that surround them and limit or facilitate their opportunities; those on the lower rungs will be unable to fully understand what they are up against as they try to climb the social ladder or earn a living wage.

Furthermore, for poor and black and brown children, the assumption of meritocracy is a recipe for internalized racism as well as internalized classism. If an alternative explanation is not available, these students are likely to accept the false idea that people are poor because they or their parents lack intelligence, honesty, or drive. On the other hand, if a child is able to see through the mist of myths that teachers unconsciously recycle regarding the rewards and value of consuming school knowledge, he or she is likely to come to believe what is taught in school is patently untrue. Neither of these outcomes contributes to the development of critical consciousness through schooling.

The children in Ms. Martin's fourth grade were beginning to envision the possibility of a community that assures a high quality of life for rich and poor. Yet a recent survey comparing ten industrialized countries found that

U.S. citizens rank eighth in the belief that government taxing the rich and subsidizing the poor is an essential characteristic of a democracy (Porter, 2012). Unless the belief that we all deserve and are able to have basic human needs satisfied is promoted in school, societal commitment to the well-being of all community members will atrophy further. What U.S. schools now teach and fail to teach about justice, economic inequality, and social mobility reproduces tacit acceptance of the suffering in the midst of plenty that surrounds us.

* * *

Late in the conversation, Tina offers another reason why working hard in school might not lead to prosperity. Recalling our role-play about the boss firing everyone and sending his factory to another country, she suggests there might not be enough well-paying jobs for U.S. workers. I infer from this that the notion that the employment scene is a game of musical chairs where there aren't enough chairs for everyone has to this point become integrated into at least one student's consciousness.

Class ends with this exchange:

> **Lamar:** I think the rich should just give lots of money to the 99 percent.
> **Ann:** If they don't want to do it should we pass a law to make them do it?

This is a topic for another day. After class I jot down, "Next steps: elections, lobbying, direct and representative democracy, consensus, media influence, minority rights, unions, minimum wage, profit."

Vignette #2: Hunger, Taxes, Human Rights, and the Public Good

May 18. I begin by asking who pays for public schools? Who pays the teachers? Who owns the library? The park? First responses: "The government," "the president," "the mayor." Evidently, the notions of public and its relationship to taxes and to individuals have not yet become a part of these children's worldviews. This is not surprising; the society has imprinted on us all that all property belongs to someone and the government is "they" not "we." I wonder if it is already too late for the concept of the commons, common property, and the common good to become basic elements of consciousness. Then I hear a barely audible whisper, "*We* pay taxes so *we* pay for public things." I begin a call and response, "Who owns the schools?"

"We do." "Who owns the police department?" "We do." The fact that only one single hesitant individual recalled the connection between taxes and public institutions such as schools that we discussed previously indicates that the concept of shared community ownership is not an easy one.

The notions of the public, the commons, taxes as a way to share community responsibility for one another, and the government (represented in many children's minds as the president or the mayor) as the servant of the people should certainly be considered "basic" in any curriculum intended to promote democracy. These notions are, however, almost entirely absent from the standardized tests and the common core standards that shape the curriculum and the textbooks.

Next, I ask the children if they know anyone who goes to bed hungry. One child offers, "My mother always says you shouldn't waste food. Think of the starving children in China." "My mother says the same thing, only it's Africa," adds a classmate. The classroom teacher and I share a complicit moment, and the teacher says, "We don't need to only think of people so far away. Many children in Oakland don't have enough to eat." Denise, a bright-eyed pale-faced White girl (who had earlier suggested that in her ideal community Child Protective Services would be well supported) tells us, "I am one of those people." Then a lean brown boy with an easy smile chimes in, "I am too." I am grateful that these children share their experiences. I tell the class that we are teaching one another some very important things that will not be tested by the tests they have been taking every day this week.

In an attempt to expand upon their notions of what could be "public," I show them a clipping and photo from yesterday's newspaper about a program in Oakland that provides healthy family community dinners for families that don't get nutritious meals every night at home. They add to their list of elements in their ideal community "food for everyone." I show them an *Oakland Tribune* headline: "Child Care System Threatened," and ask what it might mean. We discuss whether every parent of preschool children should get free high-quality child care. Many are well aware that childcare is indispensable for working parents.

The list of public services the children want in their communities has expanded to forty items. It now includes Lakeview School, parks, a fire station, free college, free day care, homes for the homeless, jobs, and hospitals. I pass out copies of the forty item list and ask the children to rank order their top twenty. I refer to these items as "rights" all people, rich and poor, are entitled to, that will be paid for by taxes. When the children rank their top choices, schools, colleges, healthy and nutritious food, child- and healthcare are near-unanimous choices. The swimming pool I had suggested—evidently a luxury for these children—is not high on most lists.

At the end of today's lesson, I find myself telling the children that there have been times and places where families have access to childcare, housing, and medical (including dental care) paid for by taxes (Sejersted, 2011), and that in the past in this country there was much more public housing than there is today, and many more public jobs. I make a mental note to find visual images to convey this to children. I add that the government is presently laying off teachers, childcare workers and social workers, and we talk a bit about "austerity."

This time Steven asks the question of the hour. "Why don't we have so many public things any more?" The class falls silent. Evidently the question has touched a nerve. Denise comes to the rescue. "Wasn't there a president who didn't want rich people to pay so many taxes?"

Vignette #3: How Rich Are the Very Rich? How Much Inequality Is Fair? How Can We Get More Equality?

May 22. Today I intend to get the children thinking more about inequalities in wealth. To set the stage, I first must convey how rich the really rich are. I doubt that I can even begin to comprehend this myself. Can *anyone* really comprehend that the yearly income of the top hedge fund operator—twelve billion six hundred million—is 13,000 times what each of the top five military leaders earns each year ("The new inequality," 2008)?

Though the activity hardly represents the outrageous levels of inequality in the U.S., I begin with the well-established "Chair" activity (United for a Fair Economy, 2012). I ask each of 10 children to sit in a chair at the front of the room. "Each chair," I say, "represents ten percent of all the wealth of the country and each of you has one chair. This is how wealth would be shared if everyone had equal amounts of money." I choose the tallest child and hang the One Percent sign around his neck. Then I say that in the U.S. Mr. One Percent would have at least eight chairs and I ask him to stretch out and take possession of his property. I show the children a *New York Times* chart of photos of the one hundred richest people in Northern California, almost all of whom are white men, to provide them with images of the One Percent. I tell the other nine children to share the two remaining empty chairs. Each empty chair can support only two children; the others sit on the floor nearby. "You are homeless," one of those who snagged a seat on an empty chair says derisively to those sitting on the floor. We eventually debrief: How did they feel in the different roles? What did they learn?

The chair activity is the prelude to a final tax activity, one I have done many times with credential candidates. I put the name "Kenneth Griffin" on the board, and under it write "$800 million." That's his take-home salary, I tell them, for one year. Next to that I write "Ms. Gonzales," and her yearly salary of $30,000. She cleans Mr. Griffin's offices at night, I tell them, and has two children.

Next, I write three tax plans on the board.

Plan #1 Tax Mr. Griffin $2000. Tax Ms. Gonzales $2000.
Plan #2 Tax Mr. Griffin $1 million. Tax Ms. Gonzales $2000
Plan #3 Tax Mr. Griffin $400 million. Tax Ms. Gonzales $2000

Then, on impulse I write a fourth plan: tax Griffin $795 million. As I do so, I mutter aloud, "That's an awful lot to tax him; he'll only have five million left." As I had hoped, Anita overhears me. She exclaims, "What do you mean 'only'? That's plenty for any human being." After discussing the virtues of a secret ballot we vote on which tax plan we prefer.

As we count the votes the classroom is pin-drop silent; the students eagerly anticipate the outcome of the vote, as if something of great importance is being settled. The results: No votes for Plan 1; three people vote for Plan 2. Tax Plans 3 and 4 are tied. Those who have voted for Plan 3 or Plan 4 cheer loudly. In closing, I tell the students that in some countries tax plans have looked a lot like Plans 3 and 4, and that at some times in U.S. history, the tax plans resulted in more equality between the rich and poor. I ask which plan they think their parents or guardians would choose.

As I gather up my papers for departure, I remember to ask if there are any questions. Many hands shoot up. The first question is one that has been asked before: How do the rich get rich? This time no student suggests winning the lottery. A boy who I was nearly certain had not been following the conversation responds, "Their people were probably rich. They probably got it when their father or grandfather died." This an authentic assessment of one child's learning. Next time we will discuss whether inheriting property is fair.

In this session our focus was on inequalities of wealth. Though children are daily drenched in images of the lifestyles of the rich and famous, the topic is rarely considered in classrooms. A major reason is that the views of venture philanthropists like Eli Broad and Bill Gates and other members of the One Percent about what students should learn shape the curriculum and the criteria for evaluating students' knowledge (Kumashiro, 2012). They want schools to prepare students with marketable skills, not to provoke them to think about how much inequality is fair. Their inordinate influence over what students learn is largely invisible to parents and community members and even to the teachers who ultimately teach the curriculum they dictate.

Challenging young children's tacit acceptance of vast inequalities of wealth will, in my view, prepare children to participate in the construction of a society that will make life healthier, happier, and less stressful for members of the corporatocracy as well as for the Ninety-nine Percent (Pickett & Wilkinson, 2010). Widely unequal societies do not function efficiently, and their economies are neither safe, stable, nor sustainable. The evidence is unequivocal: There comes a point when inequality spirals into economic dysfunction for the whole society, and when it does, even the rich pay a steep price (Steiglitz, 2012).

As I write, I reconsider what I hoped to teach about equality, and remind myself that the American Dream of equal opportunity is itself suspect, based as it is on the assumption that the possibilities for economic expansion are without limit. However, the planet cannot support the American Dream extended to every American, let alone every person on the planet. (It has been calculated that for everyone on the planet to have a "modest" middle-class American life, we would need the resources of six earths.) The real shift required is not to (for example) a Scandanavian-style economy, but to a steady-state economy that is neither growth nor profit oriented (Berman, 2012).

At the close of the lesson, the children pose other questions, suggesting new directions: "Why doesn't Obama or the mayor choose tax plans 3 or 4? If the tax money is ours, why doesn't the government use it for things people need like healthcare? Why do government officials spend money on war and drone weapons when people are hungry and homeless?"

Vignette #4: Teaching for Empathy and Outrage

May 29. After focusing so much attention on the injustices created by inequalities of opportunity and wealth, I decide to shift my focus to how to make the world more just. Learning to think critically about social justice is disempowering unless accompanied by investigations of solidarity and activism. The final days of the school year and of Lakeview School itself are rapidly approaching. I decide to teach a lesson on Unions. First I must teach about injustice at the workplace. I survey my resources and select Sherley Ann Williams' *Picking Cotton* (1997), a story about migrant workers in California. *Picking Cotton* evokes images of fourteen-hour workdays, below subsistence pay, repetitive and onerous physical labor, freezing in the pre-dawn dark and blazing in the high sun of noon, child labor, loneliness, and family solidarity. After one read-through, I ask the children to choose a character from *Picking Cotton* and listen to a rereading, paying particular attention to their chosen character. They then write *I Am* poems (Cummings, 2002/2006) from the perspective of the character they have chosen. To do this, they must call upon experiences they have had that can illuminate their character's experience. My intention is to evoke children's empathy and compassion for difficulties they and their own families have lived through, as well as for the difficulties of others. Recognizing and acknowledging our own suffering is the foundation for feeling compassion for the suffering of others and prepares the way for feeling outraged at injustice (Miller, 1983), and joining in solidarity with others against injustices they encounter or observe.

Chynah writes:

I am daddy.
I am fast and tired
I wonder how I do it.
I hear the wind blow
I want to rest and sleep
I pretend that this is just a dream.
I understand my life is hard.
I dream of sleeping all day
I hope my children have a better life.

The following day we read *Si Se Puede* and discuss the janitors' strike it depicts, worker solidarity, and unions.

TEACHING THE FIFTH GRADERS

I had first met with the fifth grade students a few weeks before the May 1 demonstrations. The following week was devoted to standardized testing, and I returned two weeks later. To provide a review of our first class I used the "exit cards" upon which the children had written one thing they'd learned during our first encounter: "I learned that occupy means people are getting together to stop the banks from taking people's homes." "I learned that people care about the community more than I thought." "I learned that occupy means getting together to fight for their jobs." "I learned a lot of stuff that was cool." "Today I learned that justice and injustice is (sic) really important." "Today I learned that solidarity means to stand together."

Vignette # 5: Questioning Deficit Theory; Understanding "Root Causes"

May 17. We return again to the question of why so many people they know are unemployed that we'd discussed two weeks earlier. The initial responses include: "People don't want to work." "They buy drugs instead of working." "They didn't try hard in school." "They didn't go to college." I am not surprised to find that one explanation I had offered two weeks ago—that the One Percent are firing workers and shipping jobs to countries where they can pay the workers less, and make more money for themselves—has not found a permanent niche in their understanding. After all, "We are a nation of fundamentalists about personal agency" (Williams, 2012, p. 10). I know it will require many more lessons before most of them will understand poverty and joblessness not in terms of the deficits, laziness, or school failure of the unemployed themselves, but will instead habitually use a lens that brings into focus root causes of unemployment, ending ultimately with the One Percent's quest for profits that is basic to capitalism. Then, a surprise—a single raised hand: "The jobs are being shipped overseas—like you said last time."

Ms. Groves, the classroom teacher, looks up from her papers to suggest we all look at the labels on our shirts, our hoodies, and our shoes to see where they were made. The children raucously call out more than a dozen countries, the Dominican Republic, Honduras, and Haiti. "Your mom or dad might have a job making these clothes if they were still made in the USA," I tell them. We trace the chain of reasons why a boss might want to move the factories out of the country back to the root cause—the desire to make a profit.

Vignette #6: The Limits of Curriculum and Schooling

May 21. We begin to draw our ideal communities, answering the question: What do you want in it that belongs to all of us, is paid for by taxes, is public, and is near enough to walk or ride your bike to? The question is met with a general buzz of enthusiasm. Responses include, "Day care, playgrounds, homes for the homeless, libraries with music studios in them, free colleges and universities, a lake, free art lessons." There is a scramble for art supplies as they set to work. The imagined communities begin to materialize before our eyes. I am hoping that the "take-home" will be that things do not have to be the way they are.

Two Black boys are sitting next to one another draw only video games. I can see the whole discussion has passed them by. One of the two, his teacher tells me, is homeless. I make suggestions to both. Neither wants free art lessons, or a library. One thinks an aquarium would be nice. One tells me he doesn't want a lake because it is dangerous to swim in lakes—there are alligators. Anyway, he doesn't know how to swim. I suggest that in their ideal community they might like every child to go to camp. The two agree they don't like camps, although one tells me he has no idea what camp is. I reflect upon the limits to how much schools can do in this society of limited opportunities for children.

I look up from talking with the two boys to notice an adult visitor who, after conferring with the classroom teacher, tells the children to stop what they are doing and put their drawings away. She gives directions for bubbling in forms to accompany the standardized tests that must be sent to Sacramento before the day's end. There is a murmur of conversation, primarily about which of the various "race" categories the children should claim as their own. The construction of ideal communities is set aside, perhaps forever. (As I lament the dissolution of my final lesson, I begin to imagine lessons flowing from their quandaries about race.)

That evening I attend a school board meeting. A major order of business is a new report by a district administrator citing the desperate prognosis for school success for Black boys in Oakland. The report suggests more research on this (already over-researched and well-understood) issue and leaves unsaid the need for schools to recognize the contributions that poverty and racism make to the vitality, experiences and attention of poor children and black and brown children, and the need for teachers to teach curricula that respect, recognize, and build upon the interests and funds of knowledge children of all backgrounds bring into classrooms. Apparently, neither the administrator nor any member of the school board thinks it is worth considering that schools alone can't solve the problems of an inequitable and uncaring social order, nor recognizes that the curriculum emanating from the highest rungs of power are designed—not necessarily intentionally—to reproduce these inequalities in generations to come.

WHAT NEXT?

My sojourn at Lakeview made it clear that there are more than a few teachers who, even in this neoliberal climate of great hostility to the creation of a truly democratic community and society, want to participate in the promotion of critical thinking, social justice, and empowerment in elementary classrooms. My experience also suggests that there are many more who are at the brink of understanding that if we, as a society and as educators, continue to turn a blind eye to the dangers and injustices that confront us, catastrophe is assured (Hedges, 2012a, 2012b).

If so many teachers are willing why is teaching social justice not a "basic" for young children is of value? The answer is in the complex of neoliberal schooling and extra-schooling policies that have been the focus of other chapters of this book (Au, Saltman, Garrison, and Tuck, for example). These policies emanate from the center of power of the plutocracy and circulate in the capillaries of all social processes, including schooling, invisible to most, to reproduce an electorate that is for the most part compliant, individualistic, disempowered, discouraged, and mystified, unable to identify and challenge the power of the One Percent.

What is needed at this time in history is awareness that alternative societies and schooling processes are possible. Schooling professionals and other members of society must also understand that schooling can only encourage the development of thoughtful, active, justice-oriented adults if the curriculum is conceived and executed in the political and social contexts of the present moment by justice oriented teachers.

NOTES

1. A celebration of the international labor movement.

REFERENCES

Adams, J., with Horton, M. (1975). *Unearthing seeds of fire. The idea of Highlander.* Winston-Salem, NC: John F. Blair.

Berlak, A., & Moyenda, S. (2001). *Taking it personally. Racism in the classroom from kindergarten to college.* Philadelphia, PA: Temple University Press.

Berman, M. (2012, July 26). Sociopaths rule. Review of the book *Heist: Who stole the American dream?* by F. Causey & D. Goldmacher. *Tikkun.* Retrieved from http://www.tikkun.org/nextgen/sociopaths-rule

Brady, M. (2012, August 18). Eight problems with Common Core Standards. *Washington Post.* Retrieved from http://www.washingtonpost.com/blogs/answer-sheet/post/eight-problems-with-common-core-standards/2012/08/21/821b300a-c4e7-11e1-8f62-58260e3940a0_blog.html

Cockburn, A. (2012, Mar 23). The myth of the knowledge economy. *Nation of Change.* Retrieved from http://www.nationofchange.org/myth-knowledge-economy-1332512349

Cummings, A. (2002, rev 2006). The "I Am" poem. *Support 4 change.com,* from http://www.support4change.com/index.php?option=com_content&view=article&id=175&Itemid=207

Hedges, C. (2012a, July 9). How to think. *TruthDig.* Retrieved from http://www.truthdig.com/report/item/how_to_think_20120709/

Hedges, C. (2012b, Jun 18). Occupy will be back. *TruthDig.* Retrieved from http://www.truthdig.com/report/item/occupy_will_be_back_20120618/

Hoffman, R., Shelby, J., Simpson, M., & Towner, R. (2011). Octopi: A children's zine for understanding the occupy movement. *Octopi.* Retrieved from http://octopizine.blogspot.com/

Knafo, S. (2012, May 31). U.S. Child poverty second highest among developed nations: Report. *Global Motherhood.* Retrieved from http://www.huffingtonpost.com/2012/05/30/us-child-poverty-report-unicef_n_1555533.html

Knefel, J. (2012). Bored with Occupy and inequality: Class issues fade along with protest coverage. *FAIR: Fairness & Accuracy in Reporting.* Retrieved from http://www.fair.org/index.php?page=4533

Kumashiro, K. (2012, May-June). When billionaires become educational experts: "Venture philanthropists" push for the privatization of public education.

Academe On-Line. Retrieved from http://www.aaup.org/AAUP/pubsres/academe/2012/MJ/Feat/Kuma.htm

Miller, A. (1983). *For your own good: Hidden cruelty in child rearing and the roots of violence* New York, NY: Farrar, Straus & Giroux.

The New Inequality. (2008, Jun 30). *The Nation.* Retrieved from http://www.thenation.com/issue/june-30-2008#

Nichols, J. (2012). *Uprising: How Wisconsin renewed the politics of protest from Madison to Wall Street.* New York, NY: Nation Books.

Pickett, K., & Wilkinson, R. (2010). *The spirit level: Why greater equality makes society stronger.* New York, NY: Bloomsbury Press.

Porter, E. (2012, September 19). The great American tax debate. *New York Times.* Retrieved from http://www.nytimes.com/2012/09/19/business/the-great-american-tax-debate.html?_r=0

Pugh, T. (2012, September 6). Record number in U.S. struggle to feed families. *San Jose Mercury News.* Retrieved from http://www.pressdisplay.com/pressdisplay/viewer.aspx

Sejersted, F. (2011). *The age of social democracy. Norway and Sweden in the twentieth century.* Princeton, NJ: Princeton University Press.

Steiglitz, J. E. (2012, May 31). The 1 percent's problem. *Vanity Fair.* Retrieved from http://www.vanityfair.com/politics/2012/05/joseph-stiglitz-the-price-on-inequality

United for a Fair Economy. (2012). TeachingEconomics.org–The ten chairs. *Teaching Economics as if People Mattered.* Retrieved from http://www.teachingeconomics.org/content/index.php?topic=tenchairs#3

Williams, S. (1997). *Working cotton.* New York, NY: Houghton-Mifflin.

Williams, Pat (2012) Guns and mental illness: Tragedies in waiting. *The Nation.* Retrieved from http://www.thenation.com/article/169294/guns-and-mental-illness-tragedies-waiting

CPSIA information can be obtained at www.ICGtesting.com
Printed in the USA
LVOW10s0911271213

367050LV00001B/27/P